Little One-YARD WONDERS

Irresistible Clothes, Toys, and Accessories You Can Make for BABIES and KIDS

Rebecca Yaker & Patricia Hoskins

Storey Publishing

personal independence in harmony with the environment.

Edited by Pam Thompson, Melinda A. Sheehan, and Nancy D. Wood
Art direction and book design by Jessica Armstrong
Text production by Jennifer Jepson Smith

Cover and interior photography by © Julie Toy, except © Gene Pittman, authors' photograph (inside back cover); Greg Nesbit, fabric borders 70, 204, 207, 208, 305, 306; Mars Vilaubi, 27, 29, 60, 201, 233 (bottom left), 240, 246 (right), 259, 265, 271 (right), 279, 283, and fabric borders 33, 34, 46, 59, 60, 74, 135, 136, 143, 193, 194, 225, 226, 276, 279
Illustrations by Missy Shepler

Indexed by Nancy D. Wood

Storey Publishing
210 MASS MoCA Way
North Adams, MA 01247
www.storey.com

Storey Publishing is committed to making environmentally responsible manufacturing decisions. This book was printed on paper made from sustainably harvested fiber.

Printed in China by R.R. Donnelley
10 9 8 7 6 5 4 3 2 1

Library of Congress Cataloging-in-Publication Data on file

CONTENTS

CHAPTER 1

SEW, WHY SEW?

IT IS THE RARE SEWIST WHO DOESN'T HAVE CHILDREN TO SEW FOR, whether they are your own children, nieces, nephews, grand-children, or those of good friends. In this book you will find 101 fabulous ways to use up a yard of your favorite fabric and create a unique keepsake for a special child in your life. From clothing to toys to accessories to home items and so many fun projects in between — let's start sewing!

The Backstory

When we started our respective families, we quickly realized just how all-encompassing parenthood can be. The majority of our craft projects were no longer for us, but rather for our children, some of our favorite projects being clothing, plush toys, and soft books. And if it wasn't something specifically for our kids, then it was an item to help us manage our day-to-day parenting lives, such as a diaper bag or booster seat.

We also learned just how meaningful it is when our friends and family lovingly hand-make something for our little ones. These are the items that we will treasure year after year, long after they have been outgrown or have outlasted their usefulness.

In our search for craft inspiration, we discovered that so many kids' sewing books focus on items for babies or girls. Few and far between are books with ideas for boys, or older children, or projects that aren't clothing at all — toys and play props, for instance. And what about projects for parents? We wanted to use our sewing skills to make our daily lives more convenient.

Little One-Yard Wonders addresses all these issues, and more. You'll find many boys' *and* girls' clothing projects, as well as designs specifically geared toward, or sized up to, tween ages. Of course, there's still a delightful array of cute girly dresses and tops as well.

The projects in this book also go far beyond clothing. Dolls, plush toys, props for imaginative play, tactile objects, and accessories for moms, dads, and children on the go — all of these can be found in the pages of *Little One-Yard Wonders*. You'll find something for just about every stage of your family's journey through childhood.

Time Well Spent

Life is a bit harried these days, parent or not, and you may wonder whether you can fit a children's sewing project into your busy schedule. Of course you can!

Children's projects fit very well into a tight schedule and budget. You can get much more immediate gratification due to the smaller dimensions of a dress or pair of shorts. The smaller scale also means fewer supplies, making it easy on the pocketbook — a win-win situation.

Meanwhile, sewing for the children in your life is greatly satisfying, for many reasons. If you are an accomplished sewist, you are likely already aware of how much individuality you can give your home and your wardrobe with your sewing. Enjoying your work, and seeing others enjoy it, instills great pride in yourself and your abilities. Watching the children you love cherish, wear, and play with your handiwork is even more motivation to get stitching!

Much can also be said in favor of setting an example for your kids. As you craft by hand, you are demonstrating self-reliance, creativity, and problem solving, all great values to pass on to your little ones. Since children learn so much by watching and modeling how you live, you will be leading by example with your sewing. Having instilled the joy of sewing in your child, you'll be creating projects together before you know it! As an added bonus, she or he will be much more agreeable on fabric-shopping excursions!

We believe that the inspiration you find in this book will spark your entire family's curiosity and creativity. The next time the child in your life says, "I want *x*," you'll be able to confidently exclaim, "Let's make it ourselves!"

Sewing for Children

When you're taking the time to sew for children, you'll want to consider a number of factors. For example, you want to be able to construct a well-fitting, easy-to-wear, durable garment with plenty of longevity. Read on to discover a slew of tips and tricks that will help ensure your projects are a success!

Sizing

Children's clothing sizes often correspond to age. This means that a typical two-year-old usually wears a size 2, although this is not always the case, especially if you have a short, husky kid or a tall string bean. In sewing, as in shopping, it is best practice to select a size according to your child's actual body measurements, not age.

If, when measuring the waist and inseam for bottoms, you come up with two different sizes, go with the inseam measurement. You can always adjust the elastic at the waist as needed. Remember that when you are making clothes for your child, you can always alter the pattern based on your child's own measurements to ensure a perfect fit.

Taking Measurements

Head Circumference: Measure across the forehead and around the head just above the ears. Keep the measuring tape snug for accurate results.

Chest Circumference: Measure under the arms, around the fullest part of the chest, and across the shoulder blades.

Waist Circumference: Measure the waist around the smallest circumference at the natural waistline, usually just above the navel.

Hip Circumference: Measure around the fullest part of the rump.

Inseam: Measure from the bottom of the crotch, along the inside leg, to the bottom of the ankle bone.

Height: Have your child stand barefoot with a flat back against the wall. Mark the wall at the top of the head, and measure from the mark to the floor.

The measurement chart in this book has two components. The first section illustrates standard measurements for clothing sizes from infant's size

head circumference

chest circumference

waist circumference

hip circumference

inseam

3 months up to children's size 12. The second section allows you to input your child's own measurements at all ages, corresponding to the sizes in the first section. This section also includes some new measurements in addition to those listed in the first section.

While we don't reference all of these measurements in the sizing for the projects in this book, they may come in handy for other sewing projects you tackle. We even included a few extra lines for additional, specialized measurements you may need for specific projects. You can use this chart to keep track of your child's sizing and how it may differ from the sizing standards; then you can adapt your favorite patterns, no matter what their source. Have more than one child? Simply photocopy the blank chart to make enough copies for all your little ones.

STANDARD BODY MEASUREMENTS

	3 mo.	6 mo.	12 mo.	18 mo.	24 mo.	2T	3T	4T	5	6	7	8	9	10	12
Head circumference (standard by age)	16"	17"	18"	18½"	19"	19"	19½"	20"	20¼"	20½"	20¾"	21"	21¼"	21½"	21¾"
Chest circumference	16"	17"	18"	19"	20"	21"	22"	23"	24"	25"	25¾"	26½"	27¼"	28"	30"
Waist circumference	18"	19"	20"	20½"	21"	21"	21¼"	21½"	22"	22½"	23"	23½"	24"	24½"	25"
Hip circumference	19"	20"	20"	21"	22"	22"	23"	24"	25"	26"	27"	28"	29"	30"	32"
Inseam	6¾"	7½"	8¾"	11"	12"	12½"	14¼"	16"	18½"	19½"	21"	22½"	23¼"	24¼"	26½"
Height	24"	26½"	31"	33"	36"	38½"	41"	43"	45½"	48"	50"	52"	54"	56"	58½"

YOUR CHILD'S MEASUREMENTS

Use this chart to keep track of your child's measurements to help you adapt your favorite patterns, no matter what their source.

	3 mo.	6 mo.	12 mo.	18 mo.	24 mo.	2 yrs	3 yrs	4 yrs	5 yrs	6 yrs	7 yrs	8 yrs	9 yrs	10 yrs	12 yrs
Head circumference															
Neck circumference															
Chest circumference															
Waist circumference															
Hip circumference															
Height															
Sleeve length															
Rise															
Inseam															
Foot length															
Other measurement															

Longevity

One consideration when sewing clothing for your child is how long the item will fit. Certainly, all children grow at different rates, and one thing to notice is that from about 18 months on, your child will grow much more in height than in width. This means that a size 2 garment (skirt, dress, pants) may even fit a four-year-old; the primary problem will be length (whether it is sleeve, skirt, or pant length). There are a couple of ways you can extend the longevity of a beloved handmade garment, and ensure wearability for two or even three years!

Waistbands

Elastic is great for growth! As we mentioned above, kids usually grow *up* much more than they grow *out*, so there may be little need to adjust an elastic waistband for a year or two, particularly if it was originally made ever-so-slightly loose-fitting. When there is finally a need to allow for increasing girth, you can usually replace the waistband elastic with a slightly longer length. Simply use a seam ripper to open the stitching on the waistband casing by a couple of inches, cut and slip out the elastic, insert a new, longer piece of elastic, and stitch the waistband closed as before.

An alternative to this would be to use buttonhole elastic, which is literally elastic with a series of buttonhole slots. Typically, a button is stitched on the inside of the garment at each side seam; you cinch the elastic as necessary, using a different buttonhole as needed to secure it. This type of elastic is most commonly used in the back of waistbands, allowing you to take in and let out the elastic without having to replace the garment as a child grows, or when you hand an item down to a younger child.

Hems

When cutting your fabric for bottoms, dresses, or sleeves, you may wish to add an inch or two to the bottom hem. When it comes time to hem the garment, make a deeper hem than called for in the pattern. As your child gets taller, let out the length and re-hem the garment with a narrower hem. If this isn't an option, there's no reason why this year's pants can't transition to next year's capris. Or, go ahead and pair last year's dress with leggings to create this year's tunic!

While you review the instructions and cutting layouts for the projects in this book, keep in mind that, if you want to add deeper hems, you'll need to add the appropriate length to the pattern pieces before cutting. Use the standard sizing chart and compare it against your own child's current measurements to determine how much extra allowance you think you'll need for another year's growth. Then adjust your cutting layout as necessary.

Choosing Materials

We all know that easy wash and easy wear are must-have characteristics for children's items. Comfort is also certainly an important consideration! When selecting textiles and trims for children's items, we encourage you to stick with high-quality, all-natural fibers (such as 100 percent cottons) whenever possible, especially for items that will be in close contact with your little one's skin. The higher cost will translate into greater wearability and durability, and you'll be so much more pleased with the finished product.

You may even choose to go organic, which is easier to do now than ever, with so many delightful prints available in both wovens and knits. Look for GOTS certification when selecting organic textiles. This means that the fabric has met a number of the rigorous criteria of Global Organic Textile Standards.

Speaking of knits, we know they can be somewhat intimidating, but what better way to get acquainted than trying them out on small-scale kids' projects? You don't need a serger or any special equipment; the zigzag stitch or other stretch stitches on your machine will work just fine. Why knits? Well, the natural stretch allows more ease and freedom of movement, which adds up to greater comfort for the active child.

It's also worth considering print scale. You may want to match the scale of the print to your child's size. That said, don't shy away from larger statement prints, especially for dresses and skirts.

Ease in Dressing

All kids love to exert their independence. One way to allow your little ones to be independent is to let them dress themselves. To support this, you'll want to choose garments that are easy to put on and take off, such as those with elasticized waistbands.

When you are selecting closures, Velcro may be a great option, so that your little one can "do it himself!" Otherwise, consider your own preferences in choosing closures. Anything goes, be it zippers, snaps, or buttons. But do remember, buttons are not advisable for infants and babies as they present a choking hazard. Instead, use snaps as an alternative. In all cases, make sure that closures and trims (on clothing as well as toys and home dec items) are securely attached. In general, you will have different considerations for different ages.

Constructing Projects

When you are working on any project for the child in your life, you'll want to take a number of construction details into consideration, such as seam finishing, pocket details, and using safe trims.

Fabric Types

You will find that different projects throughout this book are made from different fabrics, including knits, quilting cottons, home dec fabrics, and coated cottons to name a few. Depending on the type of fabric you use for each individual project, you will need to adjust your sewing machine needle, seam stitch length, and sometimes even sewing machine foot accordingly. To help you with this, we have included a handy Fabric/Stitch Cheat Sheet on the facing page that you will likely refer to again and again.

Stitching Seams

The most common seam-allowance width for projects in this book is ½". That said, pay attention to the individual project instructions, as you'll commonly see ¼" seam allowances used on children's toys and some accessory items. Not only do narrower seam allowances allow you to get maximum use out of your fabric, they also reduce bulk in the finished work. For clothing items, you may wish to trim some seam allowances to reduce bulk, making the garments more comfortable for kids.

Kids move around — a lot! You'll want to make sure that your handmade garments can withstand all the running, jumping, stretching, twisting, turning, and other forms of rough-and-tumble play. Sturdy seams rate very high as an important construction

FABRIC / STITCH TYPE CHEAT SHEET

Fabric	Needle Size/Type	Seam Stitch Length	Sewing Machine Feet/Other
Lightweight Cotton	universal 60/8-70/10	1.25-2mm	roller foot, straight stitch foot, or offset needle (move to left or right of center)
Quilting-weight Cotton	universal 70/10-80/12	2-2.5mm	standard foot
Home Dec	universal 90/14-110/18	3mm	walking foot, roller foot
Flannel	universal 80/12	2-2.5mm	standard foot
Woven Pile	universal 70/10-80/12	2.5-3mm	standard foot, walking foot, roller foot
Coated	universal sharp 70/10-100/16	3-3.5mm	Teflon foot, roller foot
PUL (Polyurethane Laminate)	ballpoint 70/10-80/12	straight 3-3.5mm or serger	walking foot, Teflon foot, serger
Knit	ballpoint 70/10-80/12	stretch stitch or small zigzag	walking foot, serger
Fleece	universal sharp or ballpoint 70/10-90/14	2.5-3mm	walking foot, satin stitch foot
Wool	universal 80/12-90/14	2-3mm	standard foot, walking foot

feature of kids' clothing. In particular, you'll want to stitch areas of strain (such as armholes, inseams, and crotch seams) twice: once at the designated seam allowance, and a second time within the seam allowance, ⅛" to ¼" away from the first stitching line. Using a slightly smaller stitch length can also provide additional durability. If you have a serger, go for it!

Finishing Seams

You will see more unlined pieces in children's projects in general, so seam finishing may be of greater consideration in construction. To completely hide raw edges in unlined pieces, you can explore the use of French seams. Otherwise, binding, edgestitching, or serging are common ways to finish seam allowances. We've provided a thorough glossary in the back of the book, beginning on page 339, that defines these, as well as additional useful techniques and terminology used throughout the book.

Pinking seam allowances is also a great finish alternative. You may find it particularly handy to pink around the tighter curved seams in children's clothing and accessories, to both notch the seam allowance and prevent fraying.

Childproofing

As previously mentioned, buttons are a no-no for very young children (under age two or three, depending on the child). Regardless of your choice, make sure all trims, closures, loops, handles, toy limbs, and such are stitched (or otherwise attached) very securely. This is particularly true for toys, which are meant to be handled frequently. Safety eyes and noses are a fantastic, secure way to add features to a doll or plushie. Although they are very rarely used in the projects in this book, we would be remiss not to mention that the use of drawstrings and ties also present a safety hazard. The Consumer Product Safety Commission (CPSC) advises against using them at neck and hood edges for ages 2-12. If you are planning to add drawstrings to a waist of a garment (be it a top, bottom, or dress) the CPSC advises that the total length of the drawstring be limited to 3" extending outside the drawstring casing when the garment is expanded to its fullest width. One way to help prevent safety risks would be to securely bar-tack the center of the drawstring in place, thereby preventing its removal from the casing. Please also be aware when adding ties to other, non-clothing children's projects.

Pockets

As a general rule, children love places to store their small, cherished possessions. Many of the projects in this book feature pockets. Don't skimp and skip the pockets! If anything, you may choose to add additional pockets (fabric permitting).

Making and Using Bias Binding

A great way to finish raw edges is to use bias tape, also called binding. Bias tape is made from a strip of fabric that has been cut along the bias grain. You can buy it packaged with a single or double fold. Both types come in a variety of widths and colors.

To make your own bias binding, follow these steps. Use these instructions for making drawstrings, straps, and ties, too.

Cutting

To find the bias of your fabric, place it wrong side up and align the 45-degree angle line of your quilting ruler along the selvage edge of your fabric. Using your fabric marker, draw a straight line along the edge of your ruler to mark the bias. Draw a second parallel line that is four times the desired finished width of double-fold finished bias tape (2 times the desired width of single-fold); for example, your lines should be 2" apart to create ½" double-fold bias tape. Determine how many strips to cut based on the length of bias tape required.

Folding and Pressing

To make single-fold bias tape:

1. With right sides together, stitch two short ends together to make one long strip. Press the seam(s) open.

2. With wrong sides together, fold the bias strip in half lengthwise, aligning the raw edges, and press.

3. Open the strip and press the long raw edges on both sides in to the crease. If you want finished ends, also press under both short ends ½".

To make double-fold bias tape:

1. Follow the above steps to make single-fold bias tape.

2. Refold along the original fold line and press.

Use for binding the raw edges of a project, or topstitch it closed (on one or both long edges) to use as a belt, drawstring, strap, or tie.

How to Apply

One common way to apply double-fold bias tape:

① Unfold one edge of the bias tape and pin it in place along the raw edge of the piece to be bound, with right sides together. If applying it to a curved edge, such as a neckline, stretch the bias slightly so that it will lie smoothly when you turn it over the raw edge.

② Stitch along the pressed crease, using a ¼" seam allowance for ¼"-wide double-fold bias tape or a ½" seam allowance for ½"-wide double-fold bias tape.

③ Refold the bias tape along the original creased fold line, turning it over the raw edge, to the wrong side of the piece being bound, encasing the unfinished edge.

④ Press, pin, and stitch in place, close to the folded edge.

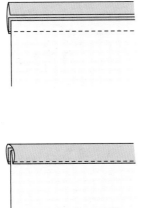

Applying Packaged Bias Tape

It is possible to apply packaged double-fold tape in one step. You will notice that it is folded with one edge narrower than the other. Simply slip the tape over the edge to be bound, placing the narrower edge on the right side of the fabric. Topstitch the binding in place from the right side of the project, close to the folded edge of the binding. Stitching on the narrower edge helps ensure that you will catch the wider edge on the wrong side in your stitching line.

Binding with Knit Fabric

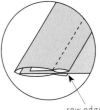

raw edge

Binding with knit fabric often differs from the way that woven double-fold binding is usually stitched; with knit fabrics, the inside binding edge may be left raw and unfinished. Knits do not unravel, or fray, which makes this technique possible. In addition, knits can be very bulky, especially when working with multiple layers. Eliminating the need to turn under the edge helps eliminate bulk.

Mitering Corners

Not sure how to miter outside corners with bias tape? Here's what you do:

① Stitch the bias tape in place until the needle is ¼" from the corner and backstitch. Remove the project from the machine and clip the threads.

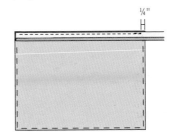

¼"

2 Fold the bias tape up and diagonally to form a 90-degree angle, and finger-press.

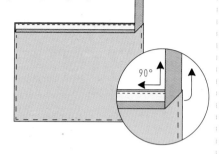

3 Fold the bias tape down so the raw edge of the tape aligns with the next raw edge of the fabric, and pin. Put the project back in the machine and resume sewing until the needle is ¼" from the next corner.

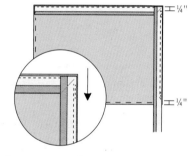

4 Backstitch and repeat at each corner.

5 Once you fold the bias tape over to bind the edges of the project, a diagonal miter will form on the stitched side. On the opposite side, fold the bias tape under the creased folds to form neat miters, which will be caught in the final stitching.

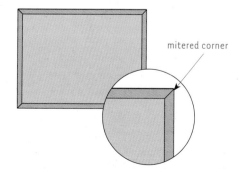

mitered corner

Making and Using Sewing Patterns

For each project in this book, the sewing pattern appears in one of the following ways:

* You'll be told to look for a full-size pattern in the attached pattern envelope.
* You'll be given instructions for drafting your own pattern from a set of measurements. You may do this directly on your fabric or play it safe and draft it first on sew-in interfacing, or on pattern-making or tissue paper. If it's a project you love, and you think you'll be making it again and again, draft it on paper, and save it for future uses. You'll save yourself time down the road! When drafting your pattern pieces, use a ruler for straight edges and a curved ruler (such as a French curve or curved dressmaker ruler) for curved and rounded edges. In general, take care that your lines are neat and tidy and that your measurements are exact. Your precision can help guarantee worry-free construction.
* You'll be given a page number for a pattern with instructions to enlarge it.

Please note that some projects in this book require a combination of pattern-piece types; you might need to find a pattern piece in the envelope, plus draft a piece based on the dimensions provided.

Pattern notations. Take note of any and all marks on the paper pattern pieces. Specifically, watch for notches, dots, darts, tucks, and other notations. All marks should be transferred to the wrong side of your cut fabric pieces before removing the paper pattern pieces.

Notches and dots help you put the project together smoothly and help eliminate any confusion. Always test your preferred marking tool on a fabric scrap or in a corner of the fabric to make sure the marks don't bleed through to the right side of the fabric.

To mark fabrics cut wrong side up in a single layer, simply place a piece of tracing paper, right side down, in between the paper pattern piece and fabric. For fabrics cut in a double layer with right sides together, use two pieces of tracing paper, placing one right side up under the fabric and the other right side down between the paper pattern and top layer of fabric. Some heavy fabrics may require you to mark one layer at a time. In all cases, gently use your tracing wheel to transfer markings.

We've got a sneaky trick to help you mark dots. Use a paper punch to punch out holes in your paper pattern pieces where the marked dots appear. You can then easily mark the fabric at the center of the punched out circle while the pattern template is still pinned on your fabric. For notches, you can cut around the notches or make a small clip into the seam allowances.

Your Sewing Pantry

Here's a list of the 42 essentials we think you'll want to have on hand, not just to complete your projects, but to ensure a frustration-free sewing experience every time! Just as you wouldn't attempt to cook a fabulous recipe without your essential cooking utensils, and just as you keep your kitchen stocked with a smattering of basic ingredients, so must you keep your sewing pantry stocked with some fundamental sewing necessities. Of course, you don't have to run out and buy everything for your first project, but build up your sewing pantry as you master the various projects and the techniques that go into making them.

16 Necessary Notions

1. Spools of thread in assorted colors
2. Elastic in various widths: ¼", ½", ¾", 1"
3. Zippers in assorted lengths: metal, polyester, invisible
4. Interfacing: sew-in and fusible, including double-sided fusible
5. Various closures: buttons, hooks and eyes, snaps, buckles, D-rings
6. Sew-in Velcro
7. Twill tape
8. Rickrack
9. Bias tape (homemade or store bought): single-fold and double-fold
10. Bias tape maker (available in five sizes: ¼", ½", ¾", 1", 2")
11. Ribbons and trims in assorted widths
12. Embroidery floss
13. Decorative buttons
14. Webbing
15. Liquid fabric sealant (such as Fray Check)
16. Fabric glue (such as Fabri-Tac)

26 Equipment Must-Haves

1 Sewing machine and assorted feet: zigzag, zipper, and walking feet are definitely at the top of the list. A magnetic seam guide and other machine accessories — especially long tweezers, a small screwdriver, a brush, and oil — are handy, too.

2 Sewing machine needles for various fabric weights

3 Seam ripper

4 60" tape measure

5 Point turner (knitting needle or chopstick can be used in a pinch)

6 Fabric shears (7" to 9" blade)

7 Pinking shears

8 Trimming scissors (4" blade)

9 Rotary cutter (go wild and get a pinking blade!)

10 Cutting mat

11 Clear quilter's ruler (3" × 18" is great, or 6" × 24")

12 Hand-sewing needles (assorted, including embroidery needles)

13 Tailor's chalk, disappearing and/or washable fabric marker, and/or soap slivers

14 Carbon tracing paper and tracing wheel for tracing patterns

15 Tissue, tracing paper, sew-in interfacing, or other pattern-making paper

16 Paper scissors

17 Straight pins (dressmaker's, quilter's, or similar)

18 Safety pins

19 Iron and ironing board

20 Pressing cloth

21 Curved ruler (French curve)

22 Bodkin (used to feed elastic and ribbon through casings; you can also use a large safety pin)

23 Lighter (used to prevent fraying on polyester webbing, grosgrain ribbon, and other man-made materials)

24 Pincushion (wrist-strap and magnetic versions make cleaning up spilled pins a cinch)

25 Thimble (metal, leather, plastic; experiment to find the most comfortable option for you)

26 Bobbins (always have a few prewound in your most-used thread colors)

CHAPTER 2

NURSERY

WELCOME BABY INTO YOUR HOME WITH LOVE AND STYLE.
Create projects from changing-pad covers to diaper
accessories, a unique, playful mobile, and many things
in between. Design your baby's new space just the
way you want it to be. Your options are endless!

safari sleep sack

Designed by Jamie Halleckson and Carmen Marti

Is there anything cozier than a snoozing baby in a sleep sack? We don't think so! This pattern works great with fleece for those cold winter nights, as well as in lighter-weight knits for the warmer months. The elastic bottom makes those middle-of-the-night diaper changes so quick and easy that you might even be able to get away without waking the baby! The sleep sack is long and roomy enough to keep those toes covered.

MATERIALS

* Pattern pieces (2), *see* sheet 1
* 1 yard of 58/60" lightweight knit fabric (such as jersey or interlock) or fleece
* 1 spool of coordinating thread
* 2½ yards of ½" double-fold bias tape (to make your own, see page 12)

* ⅔ yard of elastic cord or ¼"-wide elastic
* 2 size 16 or 20 snaps
* Scraps of fusible knit interfacing for snap reinforcement (optional, but recommended for lightweight knits)

Sizes – 0-3 months, 3-6 months, 6-9 months

Seam allowance – ½" unless otherwise specified

1 Measure, Mark, and Cut

Fold your fabric lengthwise so that the selvages meet in the middle, creating two folds on each side. Position the pattern pieces as shown in the layout and cut out the pieces. Transfer snap placements to the wrong side of the fabric.

* **Sleep sack front** (cut 1 on fold)
* **Sleep sack back** (cut 1 on fold)
* **Binding** If making your own binding, unfold the fabric and cut enough 1½" bias strips to make 2½ yards of binding.

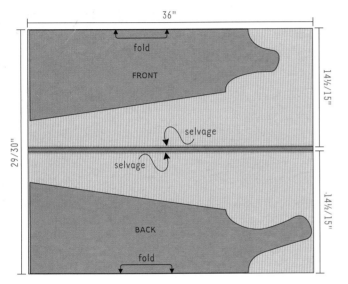

CUTTING LAYOUT

2 Stitch the Side Seams

Pin the front to the back, with the right sides together and side edges aligned. Stitch the side seams and turn the garment right side out.

3 Attach the Binding

* Fold under one short end of the bias tape. Starting with that end, pin the bias tape along the top raw edge of the sleep sack, with the right sides together, along the front and back neck edges, armholes and shoulders. When you get back to where you started, overlap the ends.

* Stitch with a ½" seam allowance. Press the binding up and over the edge of the sleep sack to the inside.

* Pin the binding in place and, from the outside of the sleep sack, stitch close to the folded edge. Because knits do not unravel, the inside raw edge doesn't need to be turned and pressed (see page 13).

4 Make the Casing

* Fold under the bottom edge ¼" to the wrong side and stitch. Turn under another 1" to form the casing, and stitch, leaving a 1" opening at one side seam for inserting the elastic.

* Thread the elastic through the casing; stitch the ends together. Tuck the elastic ends into the casing and stitch the opening closed.

5 Attach the Snaps

* Refer back to the pattern piece for snap placement. If using interfacing, fuse a patch to the wrong side of each shoulder tab at placement marks.

* Install the snaps according to manufacturer's directions, making sure the two snap halves line up.

NOTE: *Attach the male halves of the snaps to the right side of the front tabs so they don't dig into baby's shoulders. Attach the female halves to the wrong side of the back tabs.*

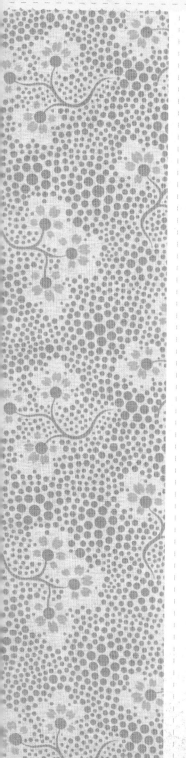

DiaPeR STaCKeR

Designed by Jamie Halleckson and Carmen Marti

Commercial diaper stackers can be so fussy, and the fabrics so blah. Yet they're so easy to make! Great for disposable or cloth diapers, this stacker can tie onto a crib, closet rod, or hanger placed anywhere in the nursery. This may just become your favorite go-to baby shower gift!

MATERIALS

* 1 yard of 44/45" quilting-weight cotton (not suitable for one-way prints)
* 1 spool of coordinating thread
* 1¼ yards of ½"-¾"-wide rickrack
* Serger (optional)
* 8" × 11" piece of heavy cardboard

Finished dimensions – 21½" high × 11½" wide × 8½" deep

Seam allowance – ¼" unless otherwise specified

① Measure, Mark, and Cut

Place your fabric in a single layer with the wrong side facing up. Measure and mark the following pieces directly on the wrong side of your fabric, and cut them out.

* **Side** 21½" tall × 9" base triangle (the angled sides should be 22") (cut 2)
* **Front/back** 22" × 12" (cut 2)
* **Bottom** 9" × 12" (cut 3)
* **Binding** 2" × 22" (cut 2)
* **Ties** 2" × 25" (cut 3)

NOTE: *In order to fit on a yard of fabric, some ties are rotated on the fabric 90 degrees.*

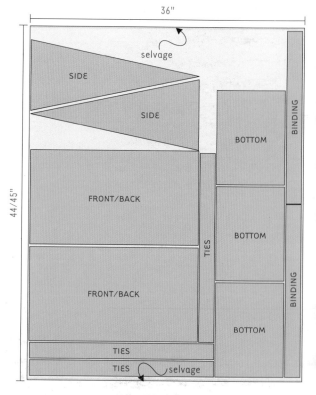

CUTTING LAYOUT

② Make and Bind the Front

* Cut one front/back piece in half length-wise to create two 22" × 6" front pieces.

* Fold and press the binding strips like double-fold bias tape (see page 12). Encase the 22" inside raw edge of each front piece in the folds of the binding; do not stitch yet.

* Cut the rickrack into two equal lengths. On each front piece, tuck the rickrack under the binding so that just half of the rickrack is visible. Pin in place, then edgestitch along the binding, making sure to catch the binding edge on the back side as you stitch.

③ Attach the Sides

* Pin a side triangle to a front piece, right sides together, with 22" raw edges aligned and the triangle base positioned at the bottom. Stitch, stopping ¼" from the bottom raw edge. Repeat for the other side triangle and front piece.

* Stitch the remaining long triangle edges to the back piece. Finish seam allowances with serger or zigzag stitch. Press seams toward the side.

④ Stitch the Top and Attach Ties

* Fold and press both short ends of each tie strip ½" to the wrong side. Fold and press each tie into double-fold bias tape. Stitch long edge to close. Fold each tie at the center (12" on each side).

* With the stacker wrong side out, pin the top edges of front and back together (the bound edges of the front pieces should meet in the center). Sandwich each folded tie between the fabric layers, aligning the fold with the fabric raw edges; position a tie at each end and one in the center. Stitch across the top edge, and then finish the seam allowance with a serger or zigzag stitch. Turn right side out and edgestitch along the top for reinforcement.

⑤ Attach the Bottom

Pin one bottom piece to the sides, right sides together and raw edges aligned. Stitch, starting and stopping ¼" from each corner. Pin the remaining sides of the bottom to the front and back in the same way, and stitch. Finish all seam allowances with serger or zigzag stitch. Press seams toward the bottom. Clip corners and turn right side out.

⑥ Make the Insert

* Test the fit of the cardboard insert at the bottom of the finished stacker. Trim to fit if necessary.
* Pin the remaining bottom pieces together, right sides facing and raw edges aligned. Stitch on three sides, leaving one short edge open. Turn right side out. Turn under the raw edges of the opening ¼" to the wrong side and press all around.
* Slip the cardboard into the insert and edgestitch the opening closed. Slide the insert into the bottom of the diaper stacker.

PLAYARD SHEET

Designed by Kymy Johnson

A perfect project for new parents, this removable and washable playard sheet is so quick and easy to make, you can have several on hand for those frequently needed changes. In fact, you can probably stitch one up during naptime, for the inevitable sheet change upon waking. This sheet will fit all standard playard mattresses.

MATERIALS

* 1 yard of 44/45" flannel, quilting-weight cotton, or knit fabric
* 1 spool of coordinating thread
* Serger (optional)
* 1 yard of ⅜"-wide elastic, cut into four 9" pieces

Finished dimensions – 26" × 36" × 3"

Seam allowance – ½" unless otherwise specified

① Measure, Mark, and Cut

Lay your fabric in a single layer with the wrong side facing up. Measure, mark, and cut a 34" × 44" rectangle from the fabric.

* **Playard sheet 34" × 44"**

2 Make the Box Sheet Corners and Hem

* Cut a 3½" square out of each of the four corners.
* Fold each corner diagonally, so the cut edges are right sides together, and the outer corners of each cutout meet. Stitch each corner with a ¼" seam (see Box Corners on page 339).
* Serge or zigzag stitch the raw edges all around the sheet, including the corner seam allowances, to finish and prevent fraying. Hem the raw edge with a single-fold ¼" hem.

3 Add the Elastic

* Fold one 9" length of elastic in half and mark the center. Then, on the wrong side of the playard sheet, mark 9" from each side of one corner seam. Pin the elastic to the wrong side of this corner, aligning the center of the elastic with the corner seam and each end of the elastic with a 9" mark.
* Repeat for remaining elastic and sheet corners. Zigzag stitch the elastic to the hemmed edge, stretching the elastic to fit as you go.

POUFY BALL MOBILE

Designed by Rebecca Yaker

This is the perfect eye-catching mobile to hang over your little one's crib or changing table. Use a bold fabric with fun colors to keep your little one goo-goo-ga-ga-ing as the mobile spins and moves.

MATERIALS

* 1 yard of 44/45" home dec-weight fabric (or other stiff fabric, such as corduroy)
* 1 spool of coordinating thread
* 4½ yards of clear fishing line
* 6" metal or plastic ring (such as an embroidery hoop)
* 2½ yards of ½"-wide ribbon to cover the ring
* Fabric glue (optional)
* 1" metal or plastic ring
* 4 yards of ½"-wide ribbon for streamers (1 yard each in four different colors)

Finished dimensions – Width of mobile ring is 6".

Seam allowance – None, as this project is sewn by hand.

① Measure, Mark, and Cut

Fold your fabric in half lengthwise, with right sides together, aligning the selvages. Measure and mark the following pieces directly on the wrong side of your fabric and cut them out.

* **Poufy circle 4¾" in diameter (cut 63)**

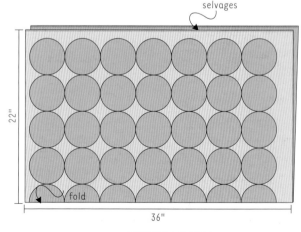

selvages

22"

fold

36"

CUTTING LAYOUT

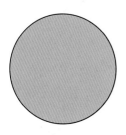

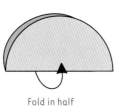

Fold in half

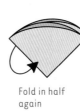

Fold in half again

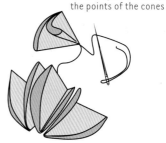

Stitch together through the points of the cones

STEP 2

② Make the Balls

Three balls will be made from 16 circles each, while the fourth will be made from 15 circles. Separate the circles into four stacks, one for each ball.

* Fold a circle piece in half with right sides together. Fold in half again, creating a conical shape. Using a hand-sewing needle and thread, stitch through the point of the cone to hold the circle in the folded shape. Do not cut thread.

* Fold a second circle in the same manner and, using the same needle and thread, stitch through the point of the second cone, attaching it to the first.

* Continue in the manner until all 16 circles have been stitched together. Knot and cut thread. Fluff the circles to make the ball poufy.

Repeat to create the remaining three balls. Cut four 20" pieces of fishing line and stitch a piece to the center of each poufy ball, knotting the fishing line in place. Set balls and fishing line aside for a later step.

③ Make the Mobile Ring

Tightly wrap the 6" ring with the 2½ yards of ribbon, sewing it or gluing it in place. Make the hanger for the ring by cutting four 20" pieces of fishing line. Tie one piece every 90 degrees around the ring. Tie all four threads together in a knot about 10" above the ring. (Note that the length of all four threads must be equal so that the mobile will hang level.) Tie all four threads to the 1" ring close to the knot.

④ Assemble the Mobile

* Hang the mobile ring, and then tie each ball every 90 degrees around the ring at varying heights, adjusting as necessary so the mobile hangs level. (For the mobile pictured, the center of the lowest ball hangs 17" from the ring, while the center of the highest ball hangs 8" from the ring.) Secure the fishing line to the ring with a knot, and trim excess line.

* With the mobile still hanging, cut varying lengths of streamer ribbon to hang from the ring between each poufy ball. (For the mobile pictured, the streamer length varies between 6" and 14".) Evenly space three pieces of ribbon in each gap between balls. Carefully hand-sew or glue the ribbon in place along the inside of the ring. Notch the ends of the ribbons to give them a playful look.

PRINCE(SS) CHARMING CHANGING STATION COVER

Designed by Lisa Powers

Commercial changing pad covers are functional but boring. Why not have the best of both worlds? You can make this cover out of PUL fabric (polyurethane laminated to a polyester knit) or laminated cotton for maximum waterproofing, but fabrics that are quilting weight, flannel, and home dec weight work great as well. Might as well enjoy one part of the diaper-changing experience, right?

MATERIALS

* 1 yard of 54/55" wide medium-weight woven, knit, or laminated cotton
* 1 spool of coordinating thread
* Serger (optional)
* 1⅛ yards ¼"-wide elastic

Finished dimensions – fits standard-size changing pad

Seam allowance – ¼" unless otherwise specified

FABRIC NOTE: *If using a 44/45"-wide fabric, you will need 1⅓ yards of fabric.*

❶ Measure, Mark, and Cut

* Fold your fabric in half in the cross-grain direction, right sides together, aligning the cut edges. Fold the fabric in half again in the other direction, aligning the selvages.

* Measure and mark a 16" × 24" rectangle directly on the wrong side of your fabric, positioned on the folds as shown. Cut out an 8" square (thus cutting out all four box corners at once).

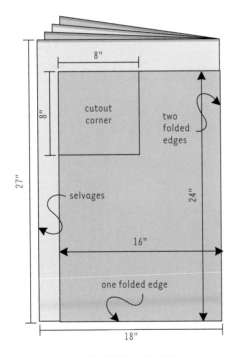

CUTTING LAYOUT

❷ Stitch the Box Corners

Fold each corner diagonally, so the cut edges are right sides together, and the outer corners of each cutout meet (see Box Corners on page 339). Stitch each corner. Finish the seam with a serger or zigzag stitch.

❸ Make the Casing and Thread the Elastic

* Beginning at the center of one short end, hem the raw edge with a ½" double-fold hem to form a casing for the elastic, leaving a 2" gap at the end of stitching to insert the elastic in the casing.

* Thread the elastic through the casing. Overlap the ends of the elastic by 1", making sure the elastic isn't twisted, and stitch the ends together with a box stitch (see the glossary). Tuck the stitched ends of the elastic into the casing and stitch the opening closed.

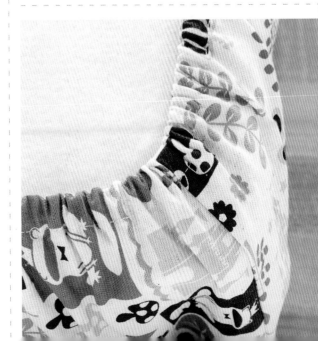

WOODLAND FUN CRIB RAIL GUARD

Designed by Tamera Gagne

This is the perfect project to help protect your baby from ingesting small bits of wood, varnish, or paint, all the while keeping your crib unmarred from their little, budding teeth. As an added bonus, these rail guards help liven up your otherwise plain crib, and you may even choose to keep them in place long after crib gnawing has ceased. The front rail guard is secured with Velcro trees, while the side guard rails are tied to the crib's corners.

MATERIALS

* Pattern template (1 in three sizes), *see* sheet 1
* 1 yard of 54" home dec-weight fabric
* ½ yard of 90"-wide cotton quilt batting, or ¼ yard of 124"-wide batting
* 1 green craft felt square (for leaves)
* 30" length of 1"-wide double-fold bias tape (for the "tree" fasteners)
* 1 spool of coordinating thread for main stitching (plus additional coordinating colors as needed)
* 15" of ¾"-wide Velcro, cut into five 3" pieces
* 2 yards of ¾"-wide ribbon in coordinating color (for the corner ties), cut into eight 9" pieces

Finished dimensions – front rail guard 52" × 8"; side rail guards 26" × 8" each

Seam allowance – ½" unless otherwise specified

1 Measure, Mark, and Cut

Lay your fabric in a single layer with the wrong side facing up. Measure and mark the following pieces directly onto the wrong side of your fabric and cut them out.

* **Front rail guard** 53" × 9" (cut 2)
* **Side rail guard** 27" × 9" (cut 4)

From cotton quilt batting, cut:

* **Front rail guard** 53" × 9" (cut 1)
* **Side rail guard** 27" × 9" (cut 2)

From green felt, cut:

* **Leaf templates** (or your own design) 15 leaves (5 of each size)

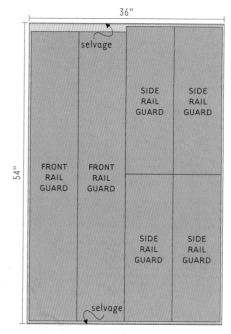

CUTTING LAYOUT

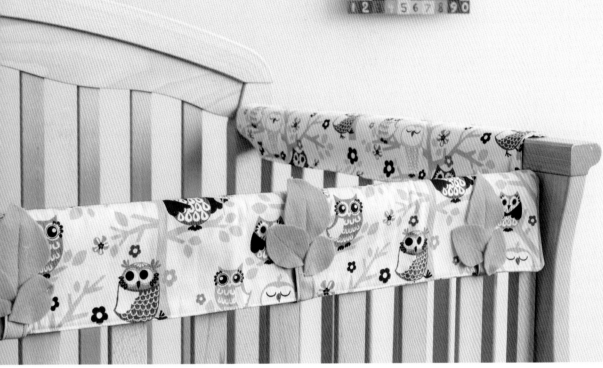

② Make the Tree Fasteners

* With the bias tape folded, edgestitch both long edges to stitch it closed, and then cut it into five 6" pieces. Position the loop side of Velcro at one end of each piece, and topstitch around all four sides of the Velcro.

* Arrange a grouping of three different felt leaves on the right side of each piece of bias tape, covering the stitching line from the loop Velcro. Stitch the leaves to the bias tape and continue stitching through the center of each leaf.

③ Mark the Placement of the Tree Fasteners

The placement and width of vertical crib slats varies from crib to crib. To determine the best placement for your tree fasteners, fold one front rail guard piece over the crib rail and use a fabric marker to mark five locations. Generally speaking, place one close to each end, with the remaining three equally placed in between. If you are using a fabric with a one-way design, make sure that the print will face the correct direction once the rail guard is finished.

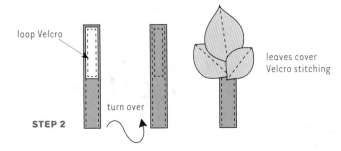

loop Velcro

leaves cover Velcro stitching

turn over

STEP 2

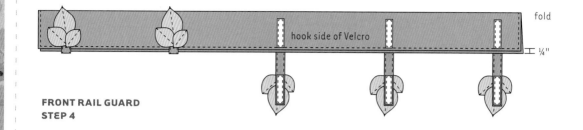

**FRONT RAIL GUARD
STEP 4**

④ Assemble the Front Rail Guard

Layer the front rail pieces as follows:

* Lay out the marked front rail guard piece right side up on a work surface.
* Pin the tree fasteners at the placement marks with the Velcro side facing up, aligning the bottom raw edge of each fastener with the raw edge of the guard rail piece.
* With right sides together, pin the remaining guard rail piece on top, aligning raw edges and sandwiching the tree fasteners between the layers.
* Pin the front rail guard batting piece on top of both fabric layers, again aligning the raw edges.

Stitch around all four sides, leaving a 4" opening along one edge for turning. Clip the corners, turn the front rail guard right side out, and press. Edgestitch around all four sides of the front rail guard, closing the opening used for turning.

Place the front rail guard on a surface with the Velcro on the tree fasteners facing up. Fold the rail guard in half lengthwise and fold the tree fasteners up to determine placement for the hook side of the Velcro. Mark the Velcro locations, ¼" up from the bottom edge, and pin Velcro in place. Unfold the rail guard and stitch the hook Velcro pieces in place. Use the Velcro to attach the front rail guard to the front edge of the crib.

⑤ Make the Side Rail Guards

Layer the side rail pieces as follows:

* Place one side rail guard on a surface with the right side facing up.
* Position a 9" piece of ribbon in each of the four corners at a 45-degree angle, aligning raw edges. Pin in place.
* With right sides together, align the raw edges of two side rail guard pieces, sandwiching the ribbon in between the layers.
* Pin the side rail guard batting piece on top of both fabric layers, again aligning the raw edges.

Stitch around all four sides, leaving a 4" opening along one edge for turning. Clip the corners, turn right side out, and press. Edgestitch around all four sides, closing the opening used for turning.

Repeat to assemble the second side rail guard. Tie the finished side rail guards to the side edge of the crib.

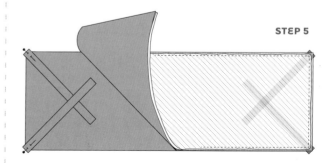

STEP 5

CHAPTER 3

Bath Time & Bedtime

BUBBLES AND SPLASHES AND SNUGGLES AND SNOOZES —

these are the things that beds and baths are made of.

Incorporate some more fun into your evening routine.

Dry off with a cozy retro cover-up, retrieve the jammies

from a pajama monster, and rest your child's head on

a pillowcase that houses secret treasures. Before you

know it, they'll be begging for bedtime to arrive!

pajama Monster & Little stuffie

Designed by Jennifer Rodriguez

Watch out for pajama-eating monsters! Aargh! This fun pajama bag is a great room accent and helps make morning chores more entertaining, with tabs that can be secured over a closet rod, bed rail, or chair back. The matching stuffie is a great bedtime friend – who better to keep nightmares away than a monster who can scare them off? Plus, the mini monster can keep an eye on the bigger one. You never know when the Pajama Monster will try to nab a spare sock as a treat.

MATERIALS

* Pattern pieces (2 for Pajama Monster, 2 for Little Stuffie), *see* sheet 1
* 1 yard of 44/45" quilting-weight cotton
* ⅔ yard of 44/45" fusible lightweight interfacing or 1⅓ yd of 21" interfacing
* 3 craft felt squares, 1 each in red, white, black (for eyes, tongue, teeth, and feet
* Various circle templates: ⅜", ⅝", 1¼", 1½", 1¾", 2½", 3¾"
* 1 spool of coordinating thread
* Serger (optional)
* One 20/22" invisible zipper
* Invisible zipper foot (optional)
* 2 buttons, 1½"–1¾" in diameter (for Pajama Monster eyes)
* Embroidery floss
* 6" of ¾"–1"-wide Velcro, cut into two 3" lengths
* 2 buttons, ¾"–1" in diameter (for Little Stuffie eyes)
* 10 ounces of fiberfill

Finished dimensions – Monster 22½" × 19"; Stuffie 11" × 9½"

Seam allowance – ¼" unless otherwise specified

① Measure, Mark, and Cut

Lay out your fabric in a single layer with the wrong side facing up. Measure and mark the following pieces directly on the wrong side of your fabric and cut them out.

* **Monster back** 23" × 20½" (cut 1)
* **Monster top front** 10" × 20½" (cut 1)
* **Monster bottom front** 15" × 20½" (cut 1)
* **Monster tabs** 4" × 22" (cut 2)
* **Stuffie** 12" × 10" (cut 2)

From interfacing, cut:

* **Monster back** 23" × 20½" (cut 1)
* **Monster top front** 10" × 20½" (cut 1)
* **Monster bottom front** 15" × 20½" (cut 1)

NOTE FOR FELT PIECES: *Since this is a monster, perfect circles, triangles, and exact measurements are not necessary. Use the patterns provided to cut the tongues and feet. Freehand if you like! Also, grainline is not important for the felt pattern pieces.*

From white felt, cut:

* **Monster small eye** 2½" circle (cut 1)
* **Monster large eye** 3¾" circle (cut 1)
* **Monster small tooth** 1¼" × ⅝" triangle (cut 2)
* **Monster large tooth** 1¾" × ¾" triangle (cut 2)
* **Stuffie small eye** 1¼" circle (cut 1)
* **Stuffie large eye** 1¾" circle (cut 1)
* **Stuffie small tooth** ¾" × ½" triangle (cut 2)
* **Stuffie large tooth** 1¼" × ⅝" triangle (cut 2)

From red felt, cut:

* **Monster tongue** (cut 1 from pattern)
* **Monster earlobe** ⅝" circle (cut 2)

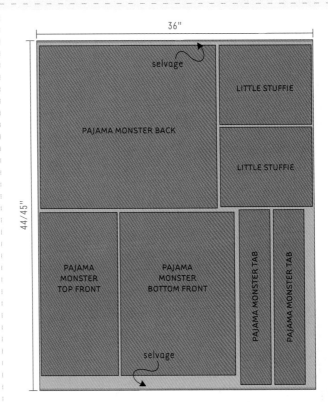

CUTTING LAYOUT

* **Stuffie tongue** (cut 1 from pattern)
* **Stuffie earlobe** ⅜" circle (cut 2)

From black felt, cut:

* **Monster foot** (cut 2, 1 reversed from pattern)
* **Monster ear/eyebrow** 3½" circle (cut 2)
* **Stuffie foot** (cut 2, 1 reversed from pattern)
* **Stuffie ear/eyebrow** 1¼" circle (cut 2)

② Interface the Pajama Monster

Fuse the interfacing to the Pajama Monster back, top front, and bottom front pieces following manufacturer's directions. Finish all raw edges of the interfaced fabric pieces with a serger or zigzag stitch.

③ Install the Zipper

Insert and install the invisible zipper between the Pajama Monster top front and bottom front pieces, along the 20½" abutting edges, following manufacturer's instructions.

④ Attach the Pajama Monster Face

* Clip each ear/eyebrow piece into two pieces, but a bit off center, so the eyebrow piece is about one-third of the circle and the ear piece is about two-thirds of the circle.

* Appliqué the felt eyes, eyebrows, and teeth to the right side of the assembled Pajama Monster front piece, where desired. Top-titch the tongue to the front bottom, just below the zipper and centered from side to side.

* Appliqué each Pajama Monster earlobe piece to a Pajama Monster ear piece. Pin each ear to an opposite side edge of the top front, right sides facing and raw edges aligned, even with the eyes. Baste with an edgestitch.

* Hand-sew the two larger buttons to the center of each of the eyes with embroidery floss.

⑤ Make and Attach Tabs

* Fold one tab piece in half across the width, right sides facing. Stitch both long sides with a ¼" seam allowance, leaving the short edge open for turning. Clip corners and turn right side out. Press. Pin one 3" length of hook Velcro ¼" from and parallel to the finished short edge. Stitch.

* Repeat to make remaining tab.

* Pin the unfinished edge of one tab to the right side of the Pajama Monster front along the top edge, 2" from the top left corner. The Velcro should be facing up. Repeat with the remaining tab on the opposite side of the top edge. Baste each in place.

⑥ Complete the Pajama Monster

* Place the back piece on a work surface, right side up, with one 20½" edge at top. Measure and mark 2" in and down from each top corner of the Pajama Monster back. Pin and stitch each 3" length of loop Velcro to the right side of the back piece, aligning the outer corner of the Velcro with the marks.

* Pin front and back pieces together, right sides facing and raw edges aligned. Open the zipper about halfway, and make sure the ears and tabs are sandwiched between the fabric layers. Sandwich the feet between fabric layers, about 3" in from each bottom corner, aligning straight and raw edges.

* Stitch on all sides. Trim corners, excess zipper tape, and turn right side out. Press.

⑦ Make the Little Stuffie

* Appliqué and attach face pieces and ears to the right side of one Little Stuffie piece as you did for the Pajama Monster, using the photo as a guide.

* Pin both Little Stuffie pieces together, right sides facing and raw edges aligned. Make sure the ears are sandwiched between the fabric layers. Sandwich the feet between fabric layers, about 2" in from each bottom corner, aligning straight and raw edges.

* Stitch on all sides, leaving a 3" opening on the bottom edge, between the feet. Clip corners and turn right side out. Press. Stuff with fiberfill to desired fullness and hand-sew the opening closed.

secret pocket pillowcase

Designed by Kathy Beymer

This standard-size pillowcase features a super-cute inset pocket for tucking in nighttime treasures. Kids can use the pocket to store a small flashlight or bedtime friends. As a bonus, French seams mean no fraying in the wash! That's sweet dreams for the whole family!

MATERIALS

* 1 yard of 44/45" quilting-weight cotton
* ¼" yard of contrasting fabric for pocket and optional trim
* Card stock for template
* 1 spool of coordinating thread

Finished dimensions – 20" × 29"

Seam allowance – ½" unless otherwise specified.

1 Measure, Mark, and Cut

Place your fabric in a single layer with the wrong side facing up. Measure and mark the following pieces directly on the wrong side of your fabric, side by side, with the long dimensions measured selvage to selvage. Cut out the pieces.

* **Pillowcase body** 26" × 42" (cut 1)
* **Pillowcase hem** 10" × 42" (cut 1)

From contrast fabric, cut:

* **Pillowcase accent piece** 1½" × 42" (cut 1)
* **Pocket** 5" × 11" (cut 2)

From card stock, cut:

* **Template** 3½" diameter circle (cut 1, then cut in half to form semicircle)

2 Make the Pocket

* Place the pillowcase hem piece on your work surface, right side up, with the 10" edge at the bottom. Place one pocket piece, right side down, on top, aligning one long and bottom edge as shown. Pin in place.
* Place the semicircle template on the left edge, 1" down from the top edge of pocket. Trace and cut from both layers.
* Stitch pieces right sides together along the curved edge. Clip along the curve within the seam allowance. Turn the pocket to the wrong side of the pillowcase hem and press. Edgestitch along the semicircle.

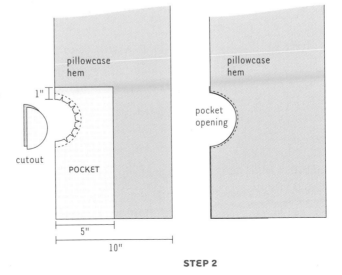

STEP 2

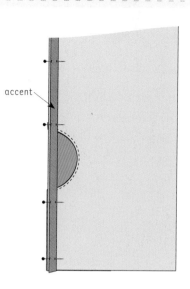

accent

1ST * OF STEP 3

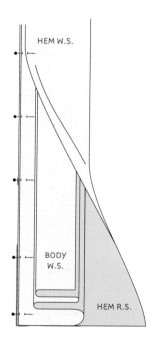

HEM W.S.

BODY W.S.

HEM R.S.

3RD * OF STEP 3

* Pin the pocket pieces with right sides together. Stitch along the long edge opposite the semicircle, and both short edges. Be sure not to catch the pillowcase hem in your stitching. Reinforce the pocket stitching with a zigzag stitch within the seam allowance. Baste all three layers together with an edgestitch at the long edge, on each side of the semicircle.

❸ Assemble the Pillowcase

* Fold the pillowcase accent along its length, wrong sides together, and press. With right sides facing, pin to the edge of the pillowcase hem with the semicircle cutout, aligning raw edges.

* Pin the pillowcase body on top of the hem/accent piece, right sides facing, aligning long raw edges. Fold or bunch up the bulk of the pillowcase body so that the free long edge of the pillowcase hem is completely visible.

* Make a burrito shape by bringing the free edge of the hem up and around the body as shown. Pin and stitch, making sure to catch all layers (pocket, accent, body, and hem) in your stitching. Take care that the folded-up bulk of the body isn't caught in your stitching.

* Turn the "burrito" right side out and press. Topstitch the hem ⅛" from the seam. At the pocket, you may wish to change your thread color to match.

❹ Finish with a French Seam

* Fold the pillowcase in half across the width, with *wrong* sides together. Carefully match the ends of the hem and accent pieces. Stitch with a French seam (see page 341), being sure to catch all the layers (including the pocket) in your stitching. Trim the bulk in the seam where the pocket meets the pillowcase hem after stitching the first seam. Turn pillowcase right side out and press after stitching the second seam.

* Stuff the pocket with nighttime treasures!

Frannie Fox HOT & COLD Pack

Designed by Lindsey Cooke

Frannie Fox is a serious multitasker! Heat up her flaxseed insert, place it in her tummy and wrap Frannie around your little wonder's neck for the ultimate soothing experience. Frannie will gladly warm up your wee one's crib, too, making for a cozy bedtime. You can also store the insert in the freezer for days when your little wonder needs a cold pack. Boo-boos be gone!

MATERIALS

* Pattern pieces (9), *see* sheet 1
* 1 yard of 44/45" cotton flannel
* Scrap of light-colored contrast cotton flannel
* 1 spool of coordinating thread
* Black embroidery floss
* 1⅔ cups of flaxseeds (for filler)

Finished dimensions – 28½" × 4"

Seam allowance – ¼" unless otherwise specified

❶ Measure, Mark, and Cut

Lay out your fabric in a single layer with the wrong side facing up. Position the patterns provided, and measure and mark the following pieces directly on the wrong side of your fabric and cut them out.

* **Back** (cut 1)
* **Tummy A** (cut 1)
* **Tummy B** (cut 1)
* **Face** (cut 2)
* **Tail** (cut 2)
* **Outer ear** (cut 2)
* **Insert** 17½" × 4" (cut 2)

From contrast fabric, use the patterns provided to cut:

* **Face detail** (cut 2, one reversed)
* **Tail detail** (cut 2)
* **Inner ear** (cut 2)

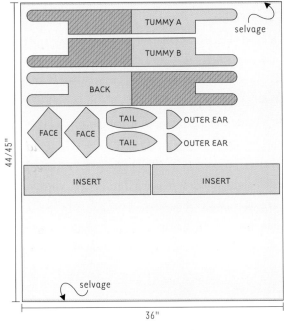

CUTTING LAYOUT

NOTE: *Mirror the pattern pieces along the lines indicated.*

❷ Assemble the Tail

Pin each contrast tail detail piece, right side up, to the right side of each tail. Appliqué the tail detail with a zigzag stitch on the jagged inner edge only. Pin the tail pieces together, right sides facing and raw edges aligned. Stitch along both curved edges, leaving the short straight edge open. Turn right side out and press.

❸ Assemble the Body

* Press a ¼" double-fold hem along the edges marked on the tummy A and tummy B pattern pieces. Edgestitch.
* Pin the tail on the right side of the fox back, centered between the legs. Align raw edges so that the tip of the tail points inward. Baste the tail in place along the raw edge.
* Pin both tummy A and B to the back, right sides facing and raw edges aligned. The hemmed edge of B should overlap the hemmed edge of A. Stitch around all sides. Notch curves and clip corners, turn right side out, and press.

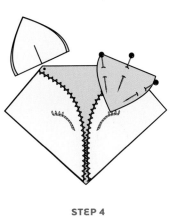

STEP 4

❹ Assemble the Face

* Fold each inner ear, right sides facing, along marked dart lines. Stitch darts starting at the raw edge. Press seam flat.
* Pin each inner ear to an outer ear, right sides facing and raw edges aligned. Stitch around curved edges, leaving the straight edge at the base of the ear open. Clip corners, turn right side out and press.
* Pin both face detail pieces, right side up, to the right side of one face piece. Appliqué the face detail with a zigzag stitch on the curved inner edge only. Embroider the eyes with black embroidery floss. This becomes the face front.
* Pin ears to the right side of the face front, aligning the dart of the inner ear with the placement dots on the face. The corners at the base of the ear will overhang the face slightly.

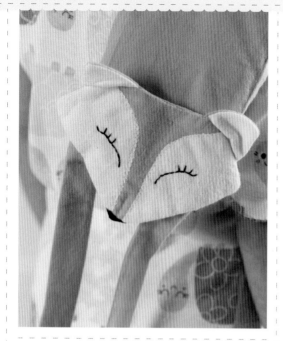

⑥ Make the Insert

* Pin the insert pieces together, right sides facing and raw edges aligned. Stitch, leaving one short end open. Clip corners and turn right side out. Turn wrong sides of opening ¼" to the wrong side and press all around.
* Starting at the finished short end, measure and mark the intervals shown down the width of the insert.
* Pour ⅓ cup of flaxseeds into the bottom of the insert. Pin and stitch along the first marked line. Pour ¼ cup of flaxseeds into the insert, and stitch at the next marked line. Continue filling the insert, stitching as you go, as shown. Finish by edgestitching along the opening to close.

	3½"	2½"	2½"	2½"	2½"	3½"
open end	⅓ cup	¼ cup	¼ cup	¼ cup	¼ cup	⅓ cup

⑦ Put Frannie to Work

Frannie is now complete! To use, microwave the insert for 30 seconds. Be sure not to overheat! Never leave your microwave unattended while heating. If necessary, heat further at 30-second intervals, checking for overheating or scorching. After heating, flaxseeds continue to retain some heat up to 1 hour. Once the insert reaches a comfortably warm temperature, slip it into Frannie's body through the tummy flap. Place around your little one's neck and shoulders, or place in a bed or crib to warm it up before bedtime. Always remove Frannie Fox before placing your baby in the crib, and don't let your child sleep with Frannie around his or her neck. For a boo-boo wrap, store the insert in a freezer or refrigerator instead.

⑤ Complete and Attach the Head

* Pin the face front to the remaining face piece, right sides together, ears sandwiched between and raw edges aligned. Stitch around, leaving an opening on the top of the head between the ears for turning.
* Trim the ear overhang and clip corners. Turn right side out and press, turning raw edges of the opening ¼" under to wrong side. Hand-sew the opening closed.
* Embroider the nose with embroidery floss, using a satin stitch (see glossary, page 342).
* Pin the head to the back so that nose is centered between the front legs, and overhangs the body by about 1½". Hand-sew in place by tacking the back of the head to the body. Our sample is hand-tacked just below both eyes and at the top center of the head.

Go Away Big Monster Towel

Designed by Rachael Theis

Bath time can be challenging when you have a child who does not want to get clean. This entertaining and functional towel looks like a monster costume and will help infuse a little fun into your bathing routine. The hood is complete with monster eyeballs and a big toothy grin. Pull the towel over the head like a poncho; the front pockets hold all the necessary bath-time accoutrements, such as bubble bath and rubber duckies.

MATERIALS

* Pattern pieces (4), *see* sheet 1
* 1 yard of 44/45" terry-cloth fabric (or a large bath towel)
* 1 square of white craft felt (for the teeth)
* 1 spool of coordinating thread
* Serger (optional)
* Red thread (for the eyes)
* 4 mismatched buttons, two ¾" and two ⅜" in diameter
* A couple handfuls of fiberfill (for the eyes)

Sizes – S (corresponds to 2T–4T) and M (5/6)

Seam allowance – ½" unless otherwise specified

① Determine Your Child's Size

The sizing of this towel is based on the child's height. The towel has been designed to fall at or just above the knee. Certainly it will work with both shorter and taller kids, but the finished monster towel length will then vary.

	S	M
Height of Child	34"–41"	43"–46"
Finished Length of Towel	19½"	22½"

② Measure, Mark, and Cut

Place your fabric in a single layer with the wrong side facing up. Measure and mark the following pieces directly onto your fabric and position the Eyeball pattern piece according to the layout. Cut out all pieces.

	S	M
Body (cut 2)	20" × 20½"	21½" × 23½"
Hood (cut 1)	18½" × 11"	19" × 12"
Pocket (cut 2)	7½" × 7½"	8" × 8"

* **Eyeball** (cut 6)   *From the white craft felt, cut:*
  * * **Eyeball iris** (cut 2)
  * * **Top teeth** (cut 2)
  * * **Bottom teeth** (cut 2)

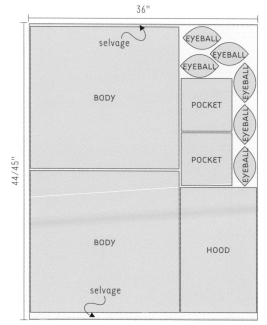

CUTTING LAYOUT

❸ Overlock the Edges (optional)

After cutting out your pieces, you may find it beneficial to overlock all the cut pieces separately before starting to sew. This will help minimize fabric shedding. If you don't have a serger, you can simply zigzag the cut edges.

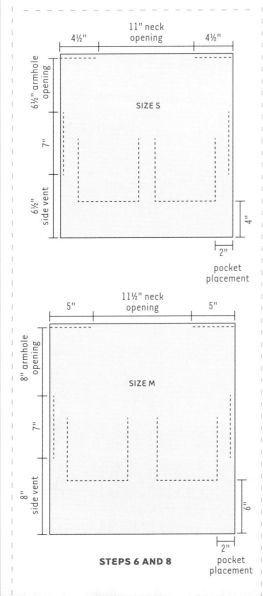

SIZE S

4½"   11" neck opening   4½"

6½" armhole opening

7"

6½" side vent

4"

2"
pocket placement

SIZE M

5"   11½" neck opening   5"

8" armhole opening

7"

8" side vent

6"

2"
pocket placement

STEPS 6 AND 8

❹ Make the Hood

* With right sides together, fold the hood piece in half across the width, aligning the short edges. Stitch along one side only, from the fold to the raw corner, to create the top seam of the hood. Press seam allowance open.
* Press the seamed edge of the hood ½" to the wrong side and topstitch in place. This finished edge is the hood opening.

❺ Make and Attach the Pockets

* Press the top edge of the pocket ½" to the wrong side and stitch. Press under the remaining three unfinished edges of the pocket ½". Repeat with second pocket.
* Pin the pockets on the front body piece as follows:
    Size S: 2" from each side edge and 4" up from bottom edge
    Size M: 2" from each side edge and 6" up from bottom edge
* Stitch the pockets in place along the three folded edges, leaving the top edge open.

❻ Stitch the Shoulder Seams

With right sides together, align the raw edges of the body pieces.
* *Size S:* Measure and mark two 4½" marks from each side seam along the top edge. Stitch along these lines to create the shoulder seams, leaving the center 11" open for neck.
* *Size M:* Measure and mark two 5" marks from the side seams along the top edge. Stitch along these lines to create the shoulder seams, leaving the center 11½" open for neck.

❼ Attach the Hood

* With right sides together, pin the bottom raw edge of the hood to the raw edge of the neckline. Align the center back of the hood with the center back of the neckline. (Note that the hood edges will not meet at center front. There will be approximately 4½" between the hood edges.) Stitch together and press seam allowance open.
* From the right side of the towel, topstitch seam allowance on both sides of the neck/hood seam.

8 Stitch the Side Seams

With right sides together, align the side seam raw edges of the body pieces, referring back to the illustration for step 6. *Size S:* On both side seams, measure down 6½" from the shoulder seam and make a mark. Measure up 6½" from the bottom edge and make a second mark. Stitch the 7" in between these marks for the side seams.

Size M: On both side seams, measure down 8" from the shoulder seam and make a mark. Measure up 8" from the bottom edge and make a second mark. Stitch the 7" in between these marks for the side seams.

* Press seam allowance open, turning the armhole and side vent openings ½" to the wrong side. From the right side of the towel, topstitch at a ⅜" seam allowance on both sides of the seam to hem the vents and the armhole opening.
* Press under the bottom edge of the towel ½" and stitch.

9 Make and Attach the Eyes

* With right sides facing up, center one felt eyeball iris on top of one terrycloth football-shaped eyeball. Stitch along the lines, as indicated on the pattern, using red thread. Hand-sew two buttons (small one layered on top of a larger one) to the center of the felt to create the pupil. Repeat to make a second iris/eyeball.
* With right sides together, pin and stitch two eyeball pieces (one with iris, one without) together along one curved edge. Stop and start the stitching within ½" of each end. Press seam allowance open. Add a third eyeball piece in the same way to make the back of the eyeball. Turn the stitched eyeball right side out (it should look like one half of a ball), and turn and press the bottom raw edge ½" to the inside. Repeat to make second eyeball.
* Stuff each eyeball with fiberfill and pin onto the hood at the desired location. Using a whipstitch, hand-sew the eyeballs in place.

10 Make and Attach the Teeth

* Stack the bottom teeth pieces together and edgestitch around all edges. Repeat with the top teeth pieces.
* Center the top teeth inside the top center front edge of the hood. Line up the dotted line on the pattern piece with the hemmed edge of the hood. Topstitch top teeth in place.
* Center the bottom teeth in the opening at the center front neck edge, again lining up on the dotted line. Topstitch in place.

RETRO-INSPIRED BATHING COVER-UP

Designed by Sharon Madsen

Your little one will splish-splash in style wearing this cover-up reminiscent of the popular 1960s versions. With only one seam, the sizing is forgiving, allowing for freedom of movement to build a sand castle, toss a beach ball, or simply dry off after a nice, cozy bubble bath. There's even a pocket in which to tuck a treasured seashell. The elastic waist and length can be adjusted to fit your child as needed. The pompom trim gives it an extra playful feel.

MATERIALS

* ✳ Pattern piece (1), *see* sheet 1
* ✳ 1 yard of 44/45" terry-cloth fabric (or substitute a large bath towel)
* ✳ 6" diameter circle of coordinating quilting-weight cotton (for pocket lining)
* ✳ 1 spool of coordinating thread
* ✳ Serger (optional)
* ✳ 4 yards of ½"-wide double-fold bias tape (to make your own see page 12). The sample shows double-fold bias tape made from pocket lining fabric.
* ✳ 5 buttons, ¾" in diameter
* ✳ 1½ yards of coordinating pompom trim
* ✳ 1 yard of ½"-wide single-fold bias tape
* ✳ ⅔ yard of ¼"-wide elastic

Sizes – 2T, 3T, 4T, 5, 6

Seam allowance – ½" unless otherwise specified

① Determine Your Child's Size

Measure your child's chest to find the right size.

	2T	3T	4T	5	6
Chest Size	21"	22"	23"	24"	25"

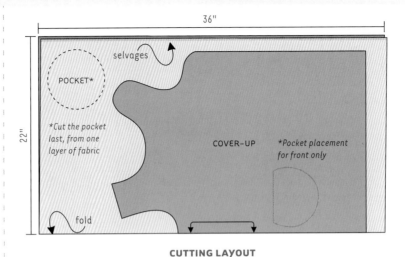

CUTTING LAYOUT

2 Measure, Mark, and Cut

Fold the fabric in half lengthwise along the grainline with right sides together, aligning selvages. Position the cover-up pattern and mark a round pocket piece according to the layout, then cut them out. Transfer the markings from the pattern piece to the wrong side of the fabric.

* **Cover-up** (cut 1 on fold)

Unfold your fabric and cut:
* **Pocket** 6"-diameter circle (cut 1)*
* **Lining** 6"-diameter circle (cut 1)*

3 Overlock the Edges (optional)

After cutting out your pieces, you may find it beneficial to overlock all the cut pieces separately before starting to sew. This will help minimize fabric shedding. If you don't have a serger, you can simply zigzag the cut edges.

4 Make the Pocket

* Place the exterior and lining pocket pieces with wrong sides together and baste with a ¼" seam allowance. Bind the entire edge of the pocket (both layers) with double-fold bias tape (see page 12). As you approach the end, cut the bias tape, turn the end to the wrong side and overlap the ends by ½".
* Fold the top edge of the pocket over 1½", exposing the lining fabric, and lightly press. Stitch a decorative button in place to secure the fold.
* With both right sides facing up, position the pocket along the placement lines as indicated on the front of the pattern piece. Sandwich a piece of pompom trim in between the pocket and cover-up along the curved edge of the pocket. Pin the pocket and trim in place. Stitch the pocket to the cover-up, catching the pompom trim in the stitching line.

⑤ Sew the Shoulder Seam

With right sides together, stitch the left shoulder seam. Press seam allowance toward the back.

⑥ Bind the Edges

* Starting at the bottom of the left armhole, bind the entire armhole edge with double-fold bias tape, as you did for the pocket.

* Starting at the center of the bottom edge of the cover-up, encase the remaining raw edges with double-fold bias tape. To miter the right-angle corners, follow instructions on page 13.

⑦ Add the Pompoms

Pin the pompom trim on the inside of the cover-up, along the bottom edge, making sure the pompoms hang freely. Topstitch in place through all layers.

⑧ Make the Buttonholes and Attach Buttons

Make three horizontal buttonholes along the right front edge at the placement lines as indicated on the pattern piece. In addition, make one buttonhole in the center of the right back shoulder strap, as indicated. Position and stitch the buttons on the right back edge as they correspond to the buttonhole placement.

⑨ Make the Waist Casing

* Pin the ½"-wide single-fold bias tape to the wrong side of the cover-up along the waistline marking, as indicated on the pattern piece. Turn both short ends of the bias tape ½" to the wrong side. Edgestitch along both long edges of the bias tape, leaving the ends of the casing open.

* To determine the length of elastic required, measure around your child/s waist and add 2". Cut elastic to this measurement. (Alternatively, you may choose to consult the waist measurement on the body measurement chart in the front of the book on page 8 to help determine the required elastic length, adding 2".) Thread the elastic through the bias tape casing with a bodkin or safety pin, being sure to pin the elastic at each end so it doesn't slip through the casing. Secure the elastic by stitching back and forth several times near each opening edge of the bias tape.

CHAPTER 4

Home & Kitchen

IN THIS CHAPTER YOU WILL FIND FUNCTION AND FUN.

Start with some tools to help teach table manners and contain messes. Next, your child might graduate to a desk chair cushion with pocket, or lounge on a groovy tween pouf. There's something for every stage of childhood here.

Hexie Pouf

Designed by Adrienne Lodico

Any tween or teen would love to have this accent in his or her room for reading books, playing games, or hanging out with friends. Comfortable for one but roomy enough for two to share, the Hexie Pouf is the perfect floor pillow for kids of all ages. Plus, the removable cover makes for easy washing and long-term use.

MATERIALS

* 1 yard of 54" corduroy, velveteen, or home dec-weight fabric
* 1 spool of coordinating thread
* 2½ yards of jumbo pompom or other trim
* 14" invisible zipper
* Invisible zipper foot (optional)
* 4"-thick upholstery foam, at least 24" × 28"
* two pieces of batting, at least 24" × 28"

Finished dimensions – 24" × 28" × 4"

Seam allowance – ½"
  unless otherwise specified

❶ Measure, Mark, and Cut

Lay out your fabric in a single layer with the wrong side facing up. Measure and mark the following pieces directly on the wrong side of your fabric and cut them out.

* **Side panel** 5" × 54" (cut 2)
* **Rhombus panel** 13" × 54" (cut 2)

Position the two rhombus panels with right sides together, aligning all raw edges. From each rhombus panel, you will mark 3 individual rhombus pieces, for a total of 6 cut rhombuses. Following the measurements as indicated on the cutting layout, measure, mark, and cut the 3 rhombus shapes. The shaded area on the cutting layout will be waste fabric, not needed for this project.

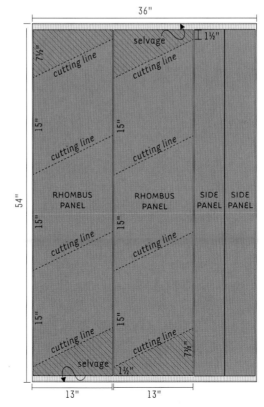

CUTTING LAYOUT

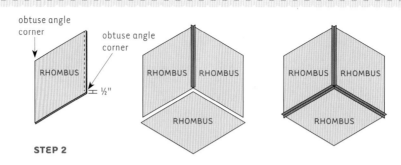

STEP 2

❷ Assemble the Rhombuses into Hexagons

* Pin two rhombus pieces together, right sides facing and aligning all raw edges. Stitch together along one side, stopping ½" from the edge at the obtuse angled corner. Open layers and press seam open.
* With right sides facing, attach a third piece to these two, stopping ½" from the raw edge where all three pieces meet. Press seams open. This makes the top hexagon.
* Repeat with remaining three rhombuses to form the bottom hexagon.

❸ Attach Pompom Trim and Side Panel

* With right sides facing and raw edges aligned, baste the pompom trim to one edge of the hexagon with an edgestitch.
* Pin the side panels together, right sides facing, and stitch along one short end. Press seam open.
* Measure the perimeter of the pieced hexagons; this should be approximately 87". Trim the pieced side panel to match the length of the hexagon perimeter, plus 1" for seam allowance.
* Pin the side panels together again, right sides facing, and stitch the open short end to form a ring. Press seam open.

* Pin the side panel to the top hexagon, right sides facing and raw edges aligned. Stitch on all sides, pivoting at the corners. Press seam down toward the side panel.
* Repeat to attach side panel to the bottom hexagon, leaving one 15" side open for zipper installation.

❹ Insert the Zipper

Install the zipper following manufacturer's instructions. Clip corners and turn the pouf right side out, pushing out corners.

❺ Cut and Add the Foam

Using the completed pouf as a template, cut upholstery foam and batting to fit. Insert foam into pouf, rolling or folding as needed to insert into opening. Insert each batting into pouf, on either side of the foam, taking care to flatten and smooth batting fully. Close the zipper to complete the pouf.

SET-THE-TABLE PLACEMAT SET

Designed by Jessica Roberts

Maybe you never liked setting the table as a kid because you couldn't remember where everything went. These appliquéd placemats help take the guesswork out of the task. Now your little helper can set the table all by her- or himself! Inspired by the concept that children learn best by doing, this placemat set is perfect to get your young apprentices involved in dinnertime activities.

MATERIALS

* ✳ Pattern piece (1), *see* sheet 1
* ✳ 1 yard of 44/45" double-sided quilting-weight cotton (see Fabric Note)
* ✳ ½ yard of double-sided fusible web
* ✳ 1 spool of coordinating thread

Finished dimensions – Makes 2 placemats (14½" × 12½"), and 2 napkins (10" × 10")

Seam allowance – ½" unless otherwise specified

① Measure, Mark, and Cut

Lay your fabric in a single layer with the wrong side facing up. Measure and mark the following pattern pieces onto your fabric and cut them out.

* ✳ **Placemat** 15½" × 13½" (cut 4)
* ✳ **Napkin** 11" × 11" (cut 2)
* ✳ **Appliqué template** 12¼" × 8½" (cut 2)

② Interface the Appliqué Pieces

* ✳ Because you will be using both sides of your fabric for this project, decide which side will be the right side of the placemats, and which will be the right side of the appliqué.
* ✳ Fuse the double-sided web to the back of the appliqué template rectangles, according to the manufacturer's instructions. Transfer markings from the template to the wrong side of the fabric, directly on the web.

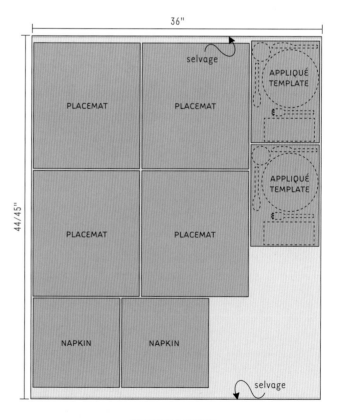

CUTTING LAYOUT

✳ Cut out the individual appliqué pieces; you will have two of each shape.

❸ Appliqué the Placemats

Refer to the photograph for recommended placement of the appliqué pieces. Fuse appliqués in place following manufacturer's instructions. Use a narrow zigzag stitch around all the pieces to help hold them in place.

❹ Make the Placemats

With right sides together, align the raw edges of an appliquéd and non-appliquéd placemat piece. Stitch around all four sides, leaving a 4" opening along one edge for turning. Clip the corners and turn right side out. Neatly turn the raw edges at the opening to the inside and press. Edgestitch around all four sides of the placemat, closing the opening used for turning as you go. Do the same for the second placemat.

❺ Make the Napkins

Again, decide which side you would like to use for the right side of the napkins. Press under and stitch a ¼" double-fold hem around all edges of both napkins.

FABRIC NOTE: *A print or woven dobby would work well, as long as there is a strong and attractive distinction between the front and back of the fabric.*

seat cushion and pocket

Designed by Jo Ebisujima

Is there ever enough room on your kid's desk for all those bits and pieces? Fear not, this customizable chair cover incorporates two handy pockets with a matching seat cushion. It will keep little bottoms comfortable as they are busy at work, while keeping supplies close at hand. These instructions show you how to make a cover to fit your own chair, from toddler to teen size!

MATERIALS

* ✳ 1 yard of 44/45" quilting-weight or home dec-weight cotton fabric
* ✳ ½ yard of 1"-wide elastic
* ✳ 1 spool of coordinating thread
* ✳ 3 yards of ½"-wide double-fold bias tape
* ✳ 3-4 ounces of fiberfill

Finished dimensions – varies depending on chair size

Seam allowance – ½" unless otherwise specified

❶ Make the Pattern Pieces

Measure the chair-back and chair-seat dimensions, as follows. To make matters less confusing, draft the patterns on paper, and then use them to cut out the fabric.

Chair Back

* ✳ *Chair back height:* Measure from the center of the top edge of the chair back down to the desired bottom hem. Add to that 1" for seam allowance.
* ✳ *Chair back width:* Starting at the widest point of the chair back, measure from the center of one side edge to the center of the opposite side edge. Add to that 1" for seam allowance.
* ✳ *Corner cutout:* Measure the side edge width of the chair back. Halve this number to determine the size of the corner cutout.

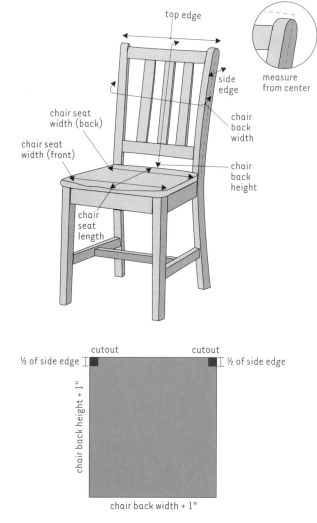

CHAIR BACK PATTERN

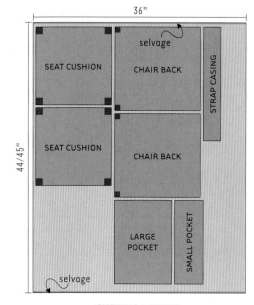

CUTTING LAYOUT

Chair Pockets

Using the same measurements, plot a small pocket that is one-third of the chair-back height, and a large pocket that is two-thirds the chair-back height. (Note that the corner cutouts will be eliminated from these pieces.)

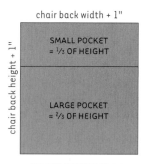

POCKET PATTERNS

Seat Cushion

* *Seat cushion length:* Measure from the inside back to the front edge of the seat. Add to that 1" for seam allowance plus 1" for cushion thickness. If you want a thicker cushion, adjust measurement accordingly.

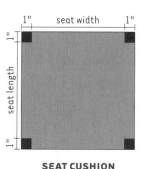

SEAT CUSHION PATTERN

* *Seat cushion width:* Measure the width of the seat at the front and the back. If they differ significantly, you may want to shape the cushion as a trapezoid accordingly. Add to each measurement 1" for seam allowance plus 1" for cushion thickness (again, if you want a thicker cushion, adjust measurement accordingly).
* *Corner cutout:* 1" square, for a 1" cushion thickness. If you want a thicker cushion, adjust measurement accordingly.

Strap Casing

A strap at the back of the cushion is slipped over the back of the chair to hold the cushion in place. Plan for it as follows:

* *Cushion strap casing:* The casing pattern piece height should be 2½". For the width, measure the width of the seat along the back edge, then multiply by 1.5.
* *Elastic:* Elastic length should be equal to the width of the seat, plus 1" for seam allowance.

❷ Cut Out the Pieces

Lay out your fabric in a single layer with the wrong side facing up. Use the patterns you drafted to cut out the following pieces. Be sure to cut out the corners where indicated.

* **Chair back** (cut 2)
* **Large pocket** (cut 1)
* **Small pocket** (cut 1)
* **Seat cushion** (cut 2)
* **Strap casing** (cut 1)

From elastic, cut:

* **Strap** (cut 1)

NOTE: *This layout is a guide; your chair's dimensions may vary. Take care to lay out and cut the pieces for your chair accordingly.*

❸ Prepare the Pockets

* Bind the top edge of the large pocket with bias tape (see page 12). Repeat for the small pocket.

* Place the small pocket on top of the big pocket, both with right sides facing up, aligning the bottom and side raw edges. Baste along the side and bottom raw edges. Topstitch a vertical line down the center of the small pocket to divide it into two.

❹ Make the Chair Back Cover

* Place the pockets on top of one chair back, both with right sides facing up, aligning the bottom and side edges. Place the remaining chair back on top, with right sides together, and pin in place, sandwiching the pockets in between the two layers. Stitch along two sides and the top, leaving the cutouts and bottom edge unsewn.

* Open up the sides at both cutouts and stitch boxed corners (see glossary, page 339). Turn the cover right side out, and bind the bottom edge with bias tape.

❺ Make the Cushion Strap

Fold the strap casing lengthwise, right sides together, and stitch the long raw edge. Turn right side out and press. Thread the elastic through the casing with a bodkin or safety pin and baste each end to the raw edge of the casing opening to secure.

❻ Make the Seat Cushion

* Pin the cushion pieces with right sides together, aligning raw edges. Stitch along the outer raw edges, skipping the cutout corners and leaving a 5" gap for turning along the back edge.

* Thread the strap between the cushion layers along the back edge, making sure it is not twisted, and aligning raw edges. Pin or baste in place.

* Stitch the boxed corners, as you did for the chair back cover, being sure to catch the ends of the strap in your stitching. Stitch reinforcement seams where the strap is attached.

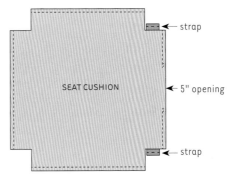

SEAT CUSHION — strap — 5" opening — strap

* Turn the cushion right side out. Stuff to desired firmness. Slipstitch or whipstitch opening closed.

* To install the seat cushion, slip the strap around and down the back of the chair. This holds the cushion in place. After the seat cushion is in place, slip the chair back cover over the back of the chair.

keep-it-clean kitchen set

Nonslip Messy Mat designed by Kathy Beymer
Pouch Bib designed by Stacey Whittington

This bib and "messy mat" work together to keep mealtime messes to a minimum! As an added bonus, the pouch bib has a handy pocket on the back side for stashing utensils and wipes on the go, plus elastic for keeping everything folded up tidily. The mat can easily double as a playmat for a toddler, perfect for play dough, painting, or coloring. The nonslip rubber fabric on the back makes the mat safe under a highchair and ensures art projects don't wind up on the carpet. If you want a larger mat for larger messes, simply increase the size of the cut pieces listed below (45" wide fabric allows for up to a 35" × 30" mat). Alternatively, cut smaller pieces to make a placemat or two instead.

MATERIALS

* Pattern piece (1), *see* sheet 1
* 1 yard of 44/45" laminated cotton, oil canvas, oilcloth, or similar coated fabric
* 1 spool of coordinating thread
* Binder clips

For the Messy Mat:

* ½ yard of rubberized shelf-liner or other non-skid material
* ½ yard of 30"-wide sew-in interfacing, or ⅞ yard of 20"-wide sew-in interfacing (optional)
* 2¾ yards of ½"-wide double-fold bias tape

For the Pouch Bib:

* 9" × 12½" square of cotton batting
* ¼ yard of ¼"-wide elastic
* 1" square of sew-in Velcro tape, or one set of size 16 or 20 plastic or metal snaps

Finished dimensions – The Messy Mat is 16" × 28", and the Pouch Bib is 9" × 11½".

Seam allowance – ½" unless otherwise specified

① Measure, Mark, and Cut

Lay out your fabric in a single layer with the wrong side facing up. Position the pattern piece according to the layout, and measure and mark the additional pieces. Cut out the pieces and transfer markings to the wrong side of the fabric.

* **Bib** (cut 2)
* **Bib pocket** 8" × 9" (cut 1)
* **Mat front** 18" × 30" (cut 1)

From the batting, cut:

* **Bib** (cut 1)

NOTE: *Mirror the pattern bib piece along the line indicated.*

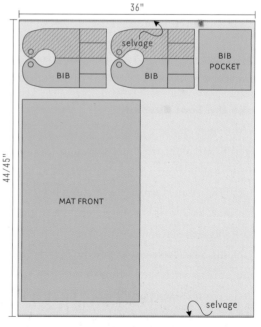

CUTTING LAYOUT

Messy Mat

① Cut the Backing

From the non-skid material, cut:
* **Mat back** 18" × 30" (cut 1)

From the sew-in interfacing (optional), cut:
* **Mat interfacing** 18" × 30" (cut 1)

② Assemble the Mat

* Place the mat backing on your work surface, right (rubber) side down. If using interfacing, place it on top of this layer, aligning all raw edges.
* Place the mat front on top, right side up, aligning all raw edges. Clip all layers together to hold in place.

③ Bind the Mat

* Clip double-fold bias tape around the mat, starting at the bottom edge, enclosing all layers in bias tape. Stitch it in place, making sure to catch back side of bias tape in stitching. (For how to miter the corners, see page 13.)
* When you reach the beginning again, overlap the tape a couple of inches and fold the raw edge to the wrong side before completing the stitching.

Pouch Bib

① Make and Attach the Pocket

Fold the pocket in half to make a 4" × 9" pocket piece with the fold at the top. Pin the pocket on the right side of a bib piece (this will become the back of the bib), aligning side and bottom raw edges. Topstitch the pocket sections, following placement marks on the bib pattern piece.

② Attach the Elastic

Place the elastic just below the top edge of the pocket, as indicated on the pattern piece, basting or clipping the ends to secure.

③ Assemble the Bib

* Place the bib front on the bib back, right sides facing, sandwiching the elastic between the layers. Place both layers on top of the batting, aligning all raw edges. Clip together to hold in place.
* Stitch around all sides, leaving an opening along one straight edge, above the pocket. Notch and clip curves and corners, and turn the bib right side out. Finger-press all around, then topstitch along all edges, closing the opening as you go.

④ Attach the Closure

Stitch Velcro or install snaps at placement marks as indicated on the pattern piece, following manufacturer's instructions. Double-check that your closures will overlap properly before securing.

⑤ Load up and Go!

If taking the pouch bib on the road, load up the center pocket with wipes or a placemat, and the side pockets with a utensil or two. Fold the top half of the bib down to cover the pocket, and tuck this under the elastic. Fold the sides of the bib in, twist the elastic, and loop it around the bib to keep it all together in a tidy little package.

STORAGE BIN REDUX

Designed by Rebecca Yaker

There's a good chance you are using ubiquitous storage boxes to hide anything and everything, from toys to books to mail – whatever works to help hide clutter. The only problem with these ever-so-useful boxes is that they visually leave a little something to be desired and never quite match your decor. With a yard of fabric you can redesign those blah storage boxes to create the perfect box slipcover, complementing any room in your home.

MATERIALS

* 1 yard of 44/45" home dec-weight fabric
* 1 spool of coordinating thread
* 1½ yards of ½"-wide double-fold bias tape (to make your own, see page 12)

* One storage box (for this project we are using the Dröna storage box from Ikea; if you are using something else, see Customizing, page 63)

* 1½ yards of home dec Velcro (one side sew-in, the other side with self-adhesive)

Finished dimensions – customizable, the project in the book measures 13" wide × 15" deep × 13" high

Seam allowance – ½" unless otherwise specified

① Measure, Mark, and Cut

Lay your fabric in a single layer with the wrong side facing up. Measure and mark the following pattern pieces onto your fabric and cut them out. (Remember to plug in your custom measurements if you are not using the Dröna box from Ikea.)

* **Front/back** 13¾" × 17½" (cut 2)
* **Side** 15¾" × 17½" (cut 2)
* **Bottom** 13¾" × 15¾" (cut 1)
* **Handle** 11" × 5" (cut 2)

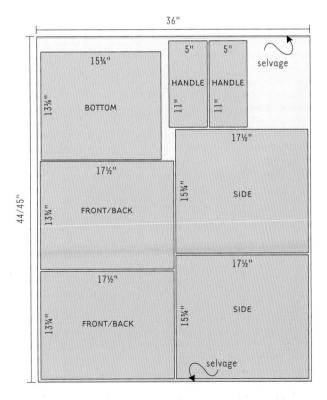

CUTTING LAYOUT

② Make and Attach the Handles

* Press under the short ends of the handle pieces ½" to the wrong side. Fold and press the handles in half along the length, with the wrong sides together. Unfold and then press under both long edges ½". Refold along the original fold line, and edgestitch around all four sides of the handle pieces.

* Position the handles on the right side of the front/back pieces, 8" down from the top edge and 2¾" in from both side edges. Pin in place. Note that the handles will not lie flat against the front/back pieces. (If you are using custom measurements, position your handle in the center of your storage-box front/back). Stitch the handles in place with a 2" box stitch (see glossary, page 340) at each end.

③ Attach the Front, Back, and Sides

* Position a front/back and side piece with right sides together, aligning top, side, and bottom raw edges. Stitch together along one side edge, stopping ½" from the bottom raw edge. Stitch the top 4" together again using a ¾" seam allowance.

* Repeat, stitching the remaining front/back and side pieces together, alternating front, side, back, and side pieces until all four have been stitched together. Press all seam allowances open.

④ Attach the Bottom

With right sides together, pin the bottom piece to the front/back pieces, lining up the corners and raw edges. Stitch together, leaving ½" unstitched at each end. Attach the bottom to the side pieces in the same fashion. All bottom seams should meet each other ½" from the corner raw edges. Turn right side out.

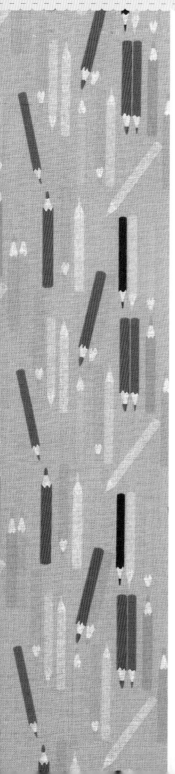

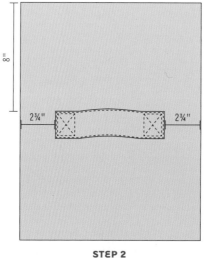

8"

2¾"   2¾"

STEP 2

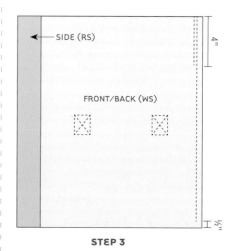

← SIDE (RS)

4"

FRONT/BACK (WS)

½"

STEP 3

⑤ Finish the Storage Box

* Fully encase the top edge of the storage-box slipcover using the double-fold bias tape.

* Cut the Velcro into two 12" pieces (for the front/back) and two 14" pieces (for the sides). (If using custom measurements, cut Velcro pieces 1" narrower than the width of each side of the storage box).

* On the wrong side of the slipcover, position the sew-in side of the Velcro just below and parallel to the bias tape (approximately ¾" from the finished edge), and centered side to side. Stitch it in place along all four sides. When complete, you will have sewn a strip of Velcro to the front, back, and both sides of the slipcover.

* Position and attach the adhesive strips of Velcro on their corresponding sewn-in sides, without removing the backing (the adhesive is still covered).

* Slide the slipcover over the storage box, carefully aligning the side seams of the slipcover with the side edges of the box. The slipcover will fit snugly and will extend 4" higher than the actual storage box.

* Fold the top 4" of the slipcover to the inside of the box, pulling it snugly. Carefully remove the adhesive backing from each strip and press the Velcro to the inside of the storage box to adhere.

CUSTOMIZING

Although this project uses the Dröna storage box from Ikea, it's possible to customize the measurements to meet the needs of your specific storage box. Here's what you need to do:

* Measure the front/back and sides of your storage box.
* Add ¾" to the width measurements (for seam allowance).
* Add 4½" to the height measurements (this allows ½" for seam allowance and 4" to wrap to the inside of the box).
* The bottom piece should be the width of the front/back piece by the width of the side piece.
* The handle piece is 5" wide by 80 percent of the front/back width.

BOOSTER CHAIR

Designed by Trish Hoskins

Too big for high chairs, too little for your standard dining set — such is the dilemma of a preschooler. The age-old booster chair receives an upgrade with this nicely streamlined seat that provides at least 4 inches of boost for your not-so-little one. Coated fabrics such as laminated cottons or oilcloth are ideal, as they provide a wipe-clean surface, but you can use a home dec-weight fabric instead if desired. Need more boost? It can be done! See below to customize the height of the booster.

MATERIALS

* Pattern pieces (4*), *see* sheet 1
* 1 yard of 44/45" laminated cotton, oilcloth, or home dec-weight fabric
* 2 yards of 1"-wide webbing
* ⅞ yard of 18"-wide, 2"-thick high-density foam or Nu-Foam (see facing page)
* 7" diameter circle template
* 1 spool of coordinating thread
* 2 sets of 1"-wide parachute buckles (also known as quick-release buckles)

Finished dimensions – 8" high × 14" wide × 11" deep

Seam allowance – ½" unless otherwise specified

① Measure, Mark, and Cut

Lay out your fabric in a single layer with the wrong side facing up. Position the pattern pieces according to the layout, and measure and mark the additional pieces. Cut out the pieces, and transfer markings from the pattern to the wrong side of the fabric.

* **Seat** (cut 1)
* **Bottom** (cut 1)
* **Arm/top** (cut 1)
* **Front** 5" × 11" (cut 1)
* **Inner back** 5" × 26" (cut 1)
* **Outer back** 9" × 33" (cut 1)

From webbing, cut:

* **3-point strap** 9" (cut 1)
* **Waist strap** 13½" (cut 2)
* **Chair strap** 18" (cut 2)

From foam, cut:

* **Seat foam** (cut 1 if using 4" thick foam; cut 2 if using 2" thick foam)
* **Back foam** 8" × 31½" (cut 1 from 2" thick foam)

NOTE: *If you want more boost, you'll need to add an additional 1" thickness of seat foam, and increase the height of the outer back; the front; and both ends of the arm/top piece by 1" for every 1 inch of additional boost.*

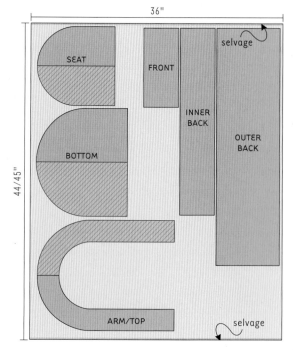

CUTTING LAYOUT

NOTE: *Mirror the pattern pieces, along the lines indicated.*

Seat patterns are layered together with outer and inner cutting lines.

REGARDING FOAM

This project requires an 8" × 31" piece of 2"-thick foam for the back and arms, plus one 10" piece of 4"-thick foam or two 10" pieces of 2"-thick foam for the base. For additional booster height, adjust base foam thickness accordingly. Our sample uses Nu-Foam, which may be easier for the home sewist to cut and work with, and it comes in 18"-wide rolls. Hi-density foam makes for a firmer seat, but it may be more difficult to cut into the rounded shapes used in this project.

② Round the Corners

Fold the inner-back and outer-back pieces across the width, aligning the short ends. Round the top corners of the inner-back and outer-back pieces using the 7" circle template. Mark each piece at the center fold of both the top and bottom edges. Round the top corners of the back foam using the same 7" circle template.

③ Attach the Straps

3-Point Strap

* On one end of the 3-point strap, make a ½" double-fold hem to the wrong side. Fold over another 2" and stitch the hemmed end to the strap to create a 2" loop. The waist strap will feed through this loop to secure the child in the booster chair.
* Place the 3-point strap on the right side of the seat at the placement mark, aligning raw edges. Baste in place.

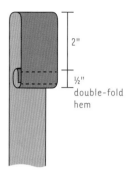

3-POINT STRAP

Waist Strap

* Thread one waist strap through the female half of one parachute buckle. On one end, make a ½" double-fold hem to the wrong side. Stitch the hemmed end to the strap, close to the parachute buckle, to secure.
* Thread the remaining waist strap through the male half of the parachute buckle. On one end, make a ½" double-fold hem to the wrong side and stitch, leaving the strap free. This allows the waist strap to be adjustable.
* Place each waist strap on the right side of the seat at the placement marks, as indicated on the pattern, aligning raw edges. Baste in place.

Chair Strap

* Thread one chair strap through the female half of the remaining parachute buckle. Hem one short end as before, then stitch that end to the strap, close to the parachute buckle, to secure.
* Thread the remaining chair strap through the male half of the parachute buckle. Hem and stitch as you did the waist strap, leaving the strap free.
* Place each chair strap on the right side of the bottom piece at placement marks, aligning raw edges, and baste.

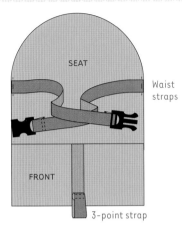

FRONT AND SEAT ATTACHED

❹ Attach the Front

Pin the top edge of the front piece to the straight edge of the seat, right sides facing and raw edges aligned. The 3-point strap should be sandwiched between the layers. Stitch, starting and stopping ½" from each edge. Stitch a reinforcement seam within the seam allowance at the strap for added safety.

❺ Attach the Inner Back

Pin the long edge of the inner back to the curved edge of the seat, right sides together, matching corners and center backs. Stitch, starting and stopping ½" from each corner, taking care not to catch the free ends of the waist straps in your stitching.

❻ Attach the Arm/Top to Front and Inner Back

* Clip into the Arm/Top piece seam allowance where indicated on the pattern.

* Pin the inside edge of each end of the arm/top piece to opposite short sides of the front piece, right sides together and bottom corners and raw edges aligned. Stitch along each side edge of the front piece, starting at the corner and stopping at the seat seam. Take care not to catch the inner back in your stitching.

* Adjust the fabric pieces so that the inner edge of the arm/top piece is now aligned with the front and top edges of the inner back, right sides together. Finger-press all seam allowances open at this join.

* Pin pieces together at center marks and stitch, easing the inner back into the curve of the arm/top piece (and vice versa) as needed. Start and stop at the seat seam.

❼ Attach Arm/Top to Outer Back

Pin the long edge of the outer back to the outer edge of the arm/top piece, right sides together, matching corners and center marks. Stitch, starting and stopping ½" from each corner, easing the outer back into the curve of the arm/top piece (and vice versa) as needed.

❽ Attach the Bottom

* Pin the remaining long edge of the outer back to the bottom, right sides together, matching front corners and center marks. Stitch the outer back to the bottom along the curved edge, starting and stopping ½" from the corners.

* Pin the bottom to the short ends of the arm/top piece and stitch, starting ½" from each corner and stopping at the seam between the arm/top and front pieces. This leaves a 10" opening at the front bottom seam of the chair cover for turning and stuffing.

❾ Complete the Assembly

Turn the chair cover right side out. Carefully insert the back foam, curving it to fit the curve of the arm/top piece. Once this foam is in place, insert the seat foam piece(s). Hand-sew the opening closed.

CHAPTER 5

TOPS

FROM CASUAL TEES TO GIRLY TUNICS and a classic Western shirt, this chapter has the best everyday, everywhere tops for both boys and girls. Sizes range from infant up to size 12, giving you a great assortment of fashionable tops to fit almost any child in your life.

Easy Dolman Top or Tunic

Designed by Angie Lusco

Long or short, this top is the perfect solution for the fashion-conscious tween in your life. Comfortable, stylish, and easy-to-sew, this style looks great paired with skinny jeans in the fall and skirts in the summer. Your tween is going to love it so much that we can pretty much bet you will make both lengths!

MATERIALS

* Pattern piece (1), *see* sheet 2
* 1 yard of 54/60" knit fabric, preferably jersey (not suitable for one-way prints)
* ¼ yard of coordinating 54/60" knit fabric (for bottom band)
* 1½ yards of ⅝"-wide fold-over elastic in coordinating color
* 1 spool of coordinating thread

Sizes – 6, 8, 10, 12

Seam allowance – ½" unless otherwise specified

1 Determine Your Child's Size/Length

Measure your child's chest to find the right size, and then check out the finished length to see if you want to adjust it.

	6	8	10	12
Chest Size	25"	26½"	28"	30"
Finished Top Length	19"	21½"	23½"	24¾"
Finished Tunic Length	21"	23½"	25½"	26¾"

② Measure, Mark, and Cut

Lay your fabric in a single layer with the right side facing up. Position the pattern pieces according to the layout and cut them out.

∗ **Front/back** (cut 2)

From the coordinating fabric, cut the following rectangular pieces.

	6	8	10	12
Bottom Band contrast (cut 2)	6" × 15½"	6" × 16½"	6" × 17¾"	6" × 19"

From the fold-over elastic, cut the following pieces.

	6	8	10	12
Neck Binding (cut 1)	15"	17"	20"	22"
Sleeve Binding (cut 2)	11"	13"	14"	15½"

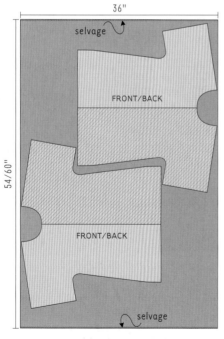

CUTTING LAYOUT

NOTE: *Mirror the pattern piece along the line indicated.*

③ Attach the Tunic Front and Back

Pin the front and back pieces with right sides together, aligning all raw edges. Stitch together along the shoulder, side seams, and underarm edges. Press all seam allowances toward the back piece.

④ Attach the Contrast Band

∗ With right sides together, stitch the short ends of the contrast bottom band to form a circle. Press the seams open. Fold the band in half lengthwise with wrong sides together and press. Mark the band into fourths.

∗ With right sides together, pin the bottom raw edge of the tunic to the raw edges of the contrast band, matching side seams and markings with center front and center back on the tunic. Stitch the contrast band to the tunic, gently stretching the band to fit as you sew. Press the seam allowance up toward the tunic.

⑤ Bind the Neck

Mark the neck binding elastic in fourths. Starting at a shoulder seam, pin neckline elastic to the neck edge of the tunic, sandwiching the raw edge of the tunic in between the fold of the elastic. Match the marks on the elastic with center front, center back, and the shoulder seams. Overlap ends of the elastic by ½" at the starting/finishing point. Stitch in place with a zigzag stitch, gently stretching the elastic as you sew.

⑥ Bind the Sleeve Openings

Bind the sleeve openings in the same way as the neck binding, starting at the underarm seam.

LONG BEACH TEE

Designed by Natalie Stone and Naomi Regan

There's nothing quite like hanging out at home in a comfy T-shirt. Now little ones can enjoy that feeling, too! This super comfortable tee was inspired by a vision of little ones running around at the seaside. Designed with extra length, you get the look of a big baggy T-shirt, but downsized to provide a proper fit. When you're done, head for the nearest beach, and be sure to bring your camera!

MATERIALS

* Pattern pieces (3), *see* sheet 1
* 1 yard of 54/60" knit fabric
* 1 spool of coordinating thread

Sizes – 12-18 months, 18-24 months, 2T/3T, 4/5

Seam allowance – ½" unless otherwise specified

FABRIC NOTE: *54/60"-wide fabric is listed because it's the most common width available for knits. This could easily be cut from a narrower fabric width, though, if you find something you like.*

1 Determine Your Child's Size

Measure your child's chest to find the right size.

	12-18 mo	18-24 mo	2T/3T	4/5
Chest Size	18"-19"	19"-20"	21"-22"	23"-24"

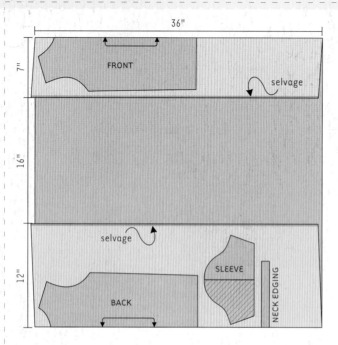

CUTTING LAYOUT

NOTE: *Mirror the pattern piece along the line indicated.*

② Measure, Mark, and Cut

Lay your fabric in a single layer with the right side facing up. Fold over the top edge 7" and the bottom edge 12", leaving 16" of a single layer of fabric in the middle. Position the pattern pieces according to the layout, measure and mark the neck edging directly on the fabric, and cut out the pieces.

- **Front** (cut 1 on fold)
- **Back** (cut 1 on fold)
- **Sleeve** (cut 2)
- **Neck edging** 1" × 16" (cut 1 on fold)

③ Attach the Neck Edging

Pin the front and back pieces with the right sides together. Stitch the *left* shoulder seam only with a ½" seam allowance.

Fold neck edging strip in half lengthwise with wrong sides together and press.

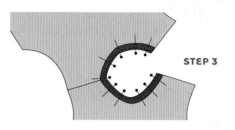

STEP 3

Pin the folded neck edging strip to front and ba[ck] neck edge of tee, right sides together, aligning raw edges. Take care not to stretch the fabric out of shape around the curve of the neck. If necessary, trim any excess neck edging so that i[t] ends at the open shoulder edges. Stitch in place[.]

Press neck edging and seam allowance up, away from tee. Position the front and back pieces wit[h] right sides together, aligning raw edges, and stitch the right shoulder seam. Press shoulder seam allowance toward the back of the tee.

④ Attach and Hem the Sleeves

Press under the bottom edge of a sleeve ¼" to the wrong side, then another ½". Stitch hem in place. Repeat with the second sleeve.

With right sides together, pin the top curved edge of a sleeve to each armhole opening, aligning the raw edges. Stitch the tee and sleeves together and press the seam allowances away from the sleeves, toward the tee.

⑤ Stitch the Side Seams

With right sides together, stitch the side seams and underarm edges in one continuous seam, taking care to align the armhole seams and sleeve hems.

⑥ Hem the Tee

Press under bottom edge of the tee ¼" to wrong side, then another ½". Stitch hem in place.

WESTERN SHIRT

Designed by Rebecca Yaker

The Western shirt shouldn't only be reserved for rodeo cowboys and rockabilly musicians — your little one needs this stylish piece of Americana in his or her wardrobe as well. This shirt features classic, stylized yokes, pockets, and pocket flaps cut on the bias, adding visual interest to this great American staple. Make it out of your favorite nontraditional fabric, and your little cowpoke will kick up his or her spurs in delight! As a fun alternative, you could also try adding a contrast yoke.

MATERIALS

* Pattern pieces (9), *see* sheet 2
* 1 yard of fabric (size 2-4: 44"/45"; size 6: 54"/60")
* ¼ yard of lightweight fusible interfacing
* 1 spool of coordinating thread
* 7 size-16 snaps or buttons ½" in diameter for sizes 2T and 4T; 8 for size 6

Sizes – 2T, 4T, 6

Seam allowance – ½" unless otherwise specified

1 Determine Your Child's Size

Measure your child's chest to find the right size.

	2T	4T	6
Chest Size	21"	23"	25"

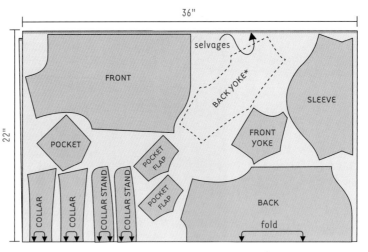

Cut the back yoke last, from one layer of fabric

CUTTING LAYOUT

2 Measure, Mark, and Cut

Fold your fabric in half lengthwise with the right sides together and the selvages aligned. Position the pattern pieces according to the layout and cut them out. Transfer the markings from the pattern pieces to the wrong side of the fabric.

* **Front** (cut 2)
* **Front yoke** (cut 2)
* **Back** (cut 1 on fold)
* **Sleeve** (cut 2)
* **Pocket** (cut 2)
* **Pocket flap** (cut 4)
* **Collar** (cut 2 on fold)
* **Collar stand** (cut 2 on fold)

Unfold your fabric and cut:

* **Back yoke** (cut 1)*

From interfacing, cut the following pieces:

* **Pocket flap** (cut 2)
* **Collar** (cut 1 on fold)
* **Collar stand** (cut 1 on fold)

From interfacing, cut the following to the measurements:

	2T	4T	6
Placket Facing (cut 2)	1¼" × 13¾"	1¼" × 15¼"	1¼" × 17"

3 Apply the Interfacing

* Fuse the interfacing to the wrong sides of the corresponding pieces, following the manufacturer's instructions. Fuse the placket interfacing pieces to the wrong side of the front pieces as indicated on the pattern piece.

* In addition, fuse a small scrap of interfacing to the wrong side of the pocket pieces at the snap placement mark. This will provide reinforcement when applying the snaps in a later step.

④ Make the Front Plackets

* On the right front piece, press the interfaced edge ¼" to the wrong side. Press under an additional 1" and topstitch close to the folded edge.
* On the left front piece, press under the interfaced edge 1¼" to the wrong side. Press under an additional 1¼", and then stitch along the folded edge using a ¼" seam allowance. Unfold the stitched placket and press. Topstitch along the opposite folded edge using a ¼" seam allowance.

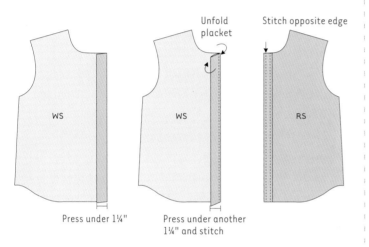

Unfold placket

Stitch opposite edge

WS

WS

RS

Press under 1¼"

Press under another 1¼" and stitch

LEFT PLACKET CONSTRUCTION

⑤ Make and Attach the Pockets

* Press under the top raw edge of the pocket ¼" to the wrong side, press under an additional ½", and stitch close to the folded edge. Press under the remaining raw edges ½" to the wrong side, starting with the bottom angled edges. Unfold the side edges and press the raw edges in to meet the crease, approximately ¼". Refold along the original fold lines and press to create a ¼" double-fold hem. Repeat with second pocket piece.
* Position a male snap piece on the right side of a pocket, as indicated on the pattern piece. Apply the snap according to manufacturer's instructions. Repeat with second pocket. (If you choose to use buttons, stitch a button at this location instead).

* With both right sides facing up, position a pocket on a front piece along the pattern placement lines. Edgestitch the pocket in place along the side and bottom edges. Repeat to attach the second pocket.

⑥ Make and Attach the Pocket Flaps

* With right sides together, align the raw edges of one interfaced pocket flap and one non-interfaced flap. Stitch together around all edges, leaving a 2" opening in the center of the top straight edge for turning. Clip corners and curves, turn right side out, and press. Press unstitched edges to the wrong side. Edgestitch along the side and bottom edges of the flap, leaving the top edge unstitched. Repeat to make second flap. (The female side of the snap, or buttonhole if using buttons, will be placed in step 13.)
* Position the top edge of a pocket flap ¾" above the top edge of a pocket. Edgestitch the flap in place along the top unstitched edge, closing the opening. Stitch again ¼" away from the top edge of the flap. Repeat to attach the second flap.

⑦ Stitch Shoulder Seams and Yokes

* With *wrong* sides together, pin and stitch the front to the back along the shoulder seams. Press seam allowance open. (The seam allowance will be concealed by the yoke).
* With *right* sides together, pin and stitch the front yokes to the back yoke along the shoulder seams. Press seam allowance open.

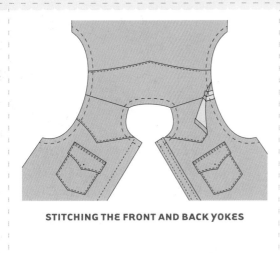

STITCHING THE FRONT AND BACK YOKES

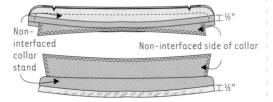

Non-interfaced collar stand

Non-interfaced side of collar

ASSEMBLING THE COLLAR AND COLLAR STAND

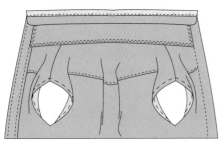

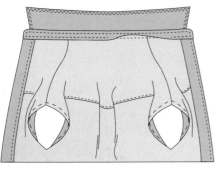

ATTACHING THE COLLAR

∗ Press under the outer angled edges of the front and back yokes ½" to the wrong side, leaving the neck and armhole edges unturned. With both right sides facing up, pin the yoke on top of the shirt, matching shoulder seams and aligning the raw edges at the neck and armholes. Edgestitch the yoke to the shirt along the folded edges. Baste together along the neckline and armholes with a ½" seam allowance. Press.

8 Make the Collar

∗ With right sides together, align the raw edges of the collar pieces. Stitch together along the top and side edges, leaving the notched edge unstitched. Clip corners, turn right side out, and press. Edgestitch along the finished edges of the collar, and then topstitch again ¼" away from the finished edge.

∗ Press the bottom unnotched edge of the *non-interfaced* collar stand ½" to the wrong side. Position the collar-stand pieces with right sides together, sandwiching the collar in between the layers as shown. The interfaced collar stand should be against the interfaced side of the collar. Align the raw edges, matching notches and centers, and pin together.

∗ Stitch along the raw edge through all layers. Notch curves, trim seam allowance, turn right side out, and press.

9 Attach the Collar

∗ With right sides together, align the raw edge of the interfaced collar stand with the neckline of the shirt, matching centers and marks on collar stand with shoulder seams of shirt. The ends of the collar stand should meet the front edges of the shirt. Stitch together, keeping the folded edge of the non-interfaced collar stand out of the stitching line.

NOTE: *It might be easier to stitch with the shirt on top so that you can adjust it as you sew. You may also find it necessary to clip into the seam allowance of the shirt neckline to help it lie flat when stitching.*

* Notch the seam allowance and trim. Press seam allowance upward, in between the layers of the collar stand.
* On the inside of the shirt, position the folded edge of the non-interfaced collar stand over the seam allowance and pin in place. From the right side of the shirt, edgestitch along the straight, bottom edge of the collar stand, catching the folded edge in your stitching line. From the right side of the shirt, edgestitch along outer curved edge of the collar stand.

⑩ Attach the Sleeves

With right sides together, pin the curved edge of the sleeve to the armhole opening of the shirt, matching the notches and the center of the sleeve cap to the shoulder seam. Stitch. Press the seam allowance toward the shirt and topstitch ¼" from the seam. Repeat to attach the second sleeve.

⑪ Stitch the Side Seams

With right sides together, stitch the front to the back along the side seams and underarm edges in one continuous seam. Press the seams toward the back of the shirt.

⑫ Hem the Sleeve and Bottom Edges

* Press the sleeve edges ¼" to the wrong side, then press under an additional ¾" and stitch close to the folded edge.
* Turn, press, and stitch a narrow ¼" double-fold hem along the bottom edge of the shirt. This may prove to be somewhat challenging due to the curved edge. To make this task a bit easier, before folding and pressing the raw edge, use a longer stitch length to stitch a guideline along the bottom edge of the shirt at a ¼" seam allowance. Turn and press the bottom edge along this stitching line, easing out fullness as necessary. Press another ¼" to the wrong side, carefully easing out fullness as necessary. Stitch the hem in place close to the folded edge. Carefully remove any guideline stitches visible on the right side of the shirt.

⑬ Attach the Snaps

* Position the male snap pieces along the edge of the right front and right side of the collar stand, following the pattern placement marks. Apply the snaps according to manufacturer's instructions.
* Repeat, attaching the female snap pieces along the left front edge and left side of the collar stand. In addition, attach a female snap on each pocket flap per the placement on the pattern piece.
* Alternatively, if you are using buttons, stitch vertical buttonholes along the left front placket, and a horizontal buttonhole on the left side of the collar stand. Stitch a vertical buttonhole in each pocket flap. Hand-sew the buttons along the right center front as they correspond to the buttonholes.

Yia-Yia's snuggle Hoodie

Designed by Susan Lirakis and Megan Nicolay

For little ones on the move, this hooded fleece pullover is cozy and durable for long days of adventuring with grandma, followed by champion rounds of snuggling at home. A perfectly placed pocket serves the dual purpose of warming cold hands and carting home treasures from the woods, beach, or garden. This hoodie slips easily over the head. There are no tricky buttons, zippers, or drawstrings to contend with while trying to dress a squirmy toddler!

MATERIALS

* ∗ Pattern pieces (5), *see* sheet 2
* ∗ 1 yard of 58/60" fleece
* ∗ 1 spool of coordinating thread

Sizes – 12-18 months, 2T, 3T, 4T

Seam allowance – ½" unless otherwise specified

① Determine Your Child's Size/Length

Measure your child's chest to find the right size.

	12-18 mo	2T	3T	4T
Chest Size	19"	21"	22"	23"

② Measure, Mark, and Cut

Place your fabric in a single layer with right side facing up. Position and pin the pattern pieces according to the layout and cut them out. Note that you must flip the hood pattern piece in order to cut both a right and a left. Transfer markings from the patterns to the wrong side of the fabric.

* ∗ **Front** (cut 1)
* ∗ **Back** (cut 1)
* ∗ **Pocket** (cut 1)
* ∗ **Sleeve** (cut 2)
* ∗ **Hood** (cut 2)

NOTE: *Mirror the pattern pieces along the lines indicated.*

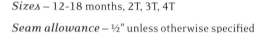

CUTTING LAYOUT

❸ Make and Attach the Front Pocket

* Fold and press the diagonal side edges of the pocket to the wrong side along the fold lines as indicated on the pattern piece. Topstitch in place with a 1" seam allowance.
* Press the top and two short side edges of the pocket ½" to the wrong side. Center the pocket on the front piece, aligning the bottom edge of the pocket with the bottom edge of the front piece, and pin in place. Edgestitch the pocket in place along the folded top and short side edges, leaving the diagonal edges open. Baste in place across the bottom edge.

❹ Attach the Front and Back

With right sides together, pin and stitch the front to the back along the shoulder seams. Press seam allowances open.

❺ Make and Attach the Hood

* With right sides together, stitch the hood pieces together along the center back seam. Press the seam allowance open. Press the front edge of the hood ½" to the wrong side and topstitch in place.
* With right sides together, position the hood along the neck edge, aligning the center-back seam of the hood with the center back of the hoodie. The front hemmed edges of the hood should meet at center front on the hoodie. Stitch together.

❻ Attach the Sleeves

With right sides together, pin the curved edge of the sleeve to the armhole opening of the hoodie, matching centers and aligning raw edges. Stitch. Press the seam allowance away from the sleeves, toward the hoodie. Repeat to attach the second sleeve.

❼ Stitch the Side Seams

With right sides together, stitch the front to the back along the side seams and underarm edges in one continuous seam. Press the seams toward the back of the hoodie.

❽ Hem the Edges

Press the sleeve openings ¼" to the wrong side, and then another 1". Topstitch in place close to the folded edge. Do the same on the bottom edge of the hoodie, with the bottom edge of the pocket folded and stitched into the bottom hem.

SPRiNgTiME TOP

Designed by Tanja Ivacic-Ramljak
and Suada Ivacic

*Pick out your favorite floral print
and say hello to springtime with
this easy-to-make top for the little
girl in your life. Dress it up or dress
it down; this top will be a staple
through all the seasons. Simply
throw on a cardigan in the cooler
months and think fondly of spring!*

MATERIALS

* ∗ Pattern pieces (4), *see* sheet 2
* ∗ 1 yard of 44/45" quilting-weight or
  other lightweight cotton fabric
* ∗ 1 spool of coordinating thread
* ∗ 1 button, ¾" in diameter
* ∗ 2 yards of ½"-wide rickrack (optional)

Sizes – 2T, 3T, 4T, 5

Seam allowance – ½" unless
  otherwise specified

1 Determine Your Child's Size

Measure your child's chest to find the
right size.

	2T	3T	4T	5
Chest Size	21"	22"	23"	24"

2 Measure, Mark, and Cut

Lay your fabric in a single layer with
the right side facing up. Fold over the
top edge 11½" and the bottom edge 8",
leaving 5" of a single layer of fabric in

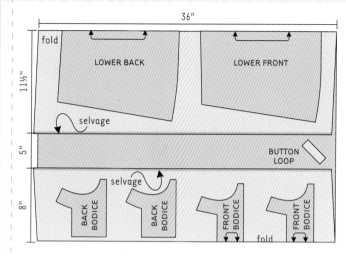

CUTTING LAYOUT

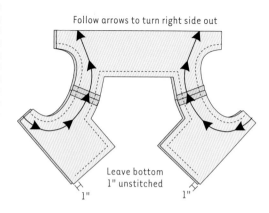

the middle. Position the pattern pieces according to the layout, measure and mark the button loop, and cut out the pieces. Transfer the markings from the pattern to the wrong side of the fabric.

* **Front bodice** (cut 2 on fold)
* **Back bodice** (cut 4)
* **Lower front** (cut 1 on fold)
* **Lower back** (cut 1 on fold)
* **Button loop** 3" × 1" (cut 1 on bias)

Make and Attach the Button Loop

* Fold and press the loop as you would to make double-fold bias tape (see page 12). Edgestitch the folded edges.
* Fold the loop in half crosswise and position it on the right side of the right-hand back-bodice piece along center back, 1" down from the top edge, with raw edges aligned. Baste in place. The loop will be secured in the next step.

Assemble the Bodice

* With right sides together and raw edges aligned, stitch a front bodice to a right-hand and left-hand back bodice at the shoulder seams. Press seams open. Repeat with the remaining front and back bodice pieces. The bodice with the button loop is the exterior; the second set is the lining.
* With right sides together, pin the bodice lining to the bodice exterior, matching side edges. Stitch around armholes. Clip the curved seam allowance to, but not through, the stitching line.
* Stitch around entire neckline and back opening, leaving the bottom 1" of the center back seam unstitched. Clip seam allowance on corners on front and back neckline. Turn right side out and press. Take care to press the seam allowance at bottom 1" at center back to the wrong side.
* Open out the exterior and lining at side seams to work the layers separately. Pin the front bodice exterior to back bodice exterior at side seams, right sides together, aligning raw edges and underarm seams. Stitch and press seam allowance open. In a similar manner, pin lining sections together, stitch, and press seams open.

⑤ Assemble the Lower Front and Backs

With right sides together, stitch the lower front and back pieces together at side seams. Press seam allowance open. (Now referred to as tunic.)

⑥ Attach the Lower Tunic and Bodice

✳ Use a basting stitch to gather the top raw edge of the lower tunic between the two stars as indicated on the pattern piece on both the front and the back.

✳ With right sides together and raw edges even, pin the lower edge of the exterior bodice to the top edge of the lower tunic, matching side seams, center front, center back, and adjusting gathers to fit. The center back edges of the bodice should abut at the center back of the lower tunic.

✳ Stitch in place, taking care not to catch the bodice lining in the seam. Press the seam allowance up toward the bodice.

✳ Press under the bottom raw edge of the bodice lining ½" to the wrong side and slipstitch in place, covering the seam allowance.

✳ Edgestitch the bodice along the bottom edge, around the neck, armholes, and center back.

⑦ Hem the Bottom Edge and Add Button

✳ Press under ¼", and then another ¾" along the bottom edge of the tunic. Topstitch in place.

✳ Hand-sew a button along the left edge of the back opening, opposite the loop.

⑧ Apply Rickrack (optional)

Topstitch rickrack trim along the armholes ½" from the edge. Topstitch rickrack along bottom of the tunic, 1¼" from the edge.

BoHeMian's DauGHTeR

Designed by Andrea Jones

Once a staple of the 1960s, this contemporary dolman-sleeve, caftan-style top is flowy, casual, and carefree. Your little girl will love this look, especially paired with her favorite leggings.

MATERIALS

* 1 yard of 44/45" quilting or other lightweight fabric (not suitable for one-way prints)
* 1 yard of ⅛"-wide elastic
* 6" diameter circle template or bowl for sizes 2T–4T; 7" diameter circle template or bowl for sizes 6–12 (to create the neck edge)
* 1 spool of coordinating thread
* 1 yard of ¼"-wide single-fold bias tape
* 4 yards of decorative lace trim (optional)

Sizes – 2T, 4T, 6, 8, 10, 12

Seam allowance – ½" unless otherwise specified

● Determine Your Child's Size

Measure your child's chest to find the right size.

	2T	4T	6	8	10	12
Chest Size	21"	23"	25"	26½"	28"	30"

● Measure, Mark, and Cut

Fold your fabric in half lengthwise with the right sides together and the selvages aligned. Measure and mark the following pieces onto the wrong side of the fabric, with the straight edges along the grainline, and cut them out.

	2T	4T	6	8	10	12
Front/Back (cut 2)	19" × 16"	20" × 18"	22" × 20"	23" × 21"	25" × 21½"	26" × 21½"
Sleeve (cut 2)	2" × 31"	2½" × 35"	3" × 39"	4" × 41"	4" × 42"	4" × 42"

From ⅛"-wide elastic, cut:

	2T	4T	6	8	10	12
Elastic (cut 2)	10"	11"	12"	13"	14"	14"

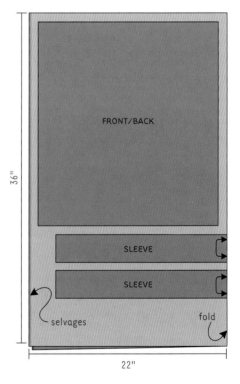

CUTTING LAYOUT

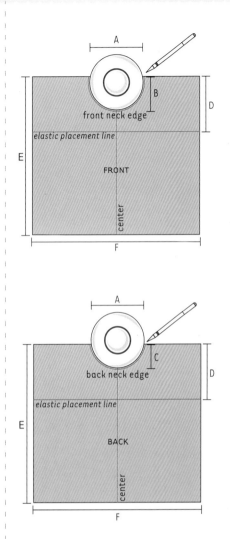

STEP 3
**All sizes, refer to chart
for measurements**

③ Prepare the Front and Back Pieces

* Fold both front and back pieces in half along the long edge to find the center. Press a light crease to mark the center, and then reopen the fabric.
* Lay out one front/back piece with the wrong side up and one long edge at the top. Measure down the crease from the top edge to determine the depth of the front neck by the distance shown for your size in the illustration and chart, and make a small mark (B).
* Center the circle template (A) over the center crease as shown, positioning the edge of the template at the mark in the center crease. Trace the curve onto the fabric to create the front neck shape. Cut along the line to create the front piece. Cut a neckline for the back in the same way, using the illustration and chart as guides (C).
* On the wrong side of both the front and back pieces, mark an elastic placement line parallel to the top edge, at the distance (D) shown from the top edge for your size.

	2T	4T	6	8	10	12
A (diameter of circle template)	6"	6"	7"	7"	7"	7"
B (depth of front neck from top edge)	2"	2½"	3"	3½"	4"	4"
C (depth of back neck from top edge)	1½"	1½"	2"	2"	2"	2"
D (elastic placement from top edge)	5"	6"	7"	8"	9"	10"
E (length of front and back)	16"	18"	20"	21"	21½"	21½"
F (width of front and back)	19"	20"	22"	23"	25"	26"

④ Stitch the Elastic

* Fold each elastic piece in half to mark the center point. Starting at one side edge on the wrong side of the front piece, pin a piece of elastic along the placement line, matching the center mark of the elastic with the center crease of the front. This will help distribute the elastic evenly across the front.
* Using a small zigzag stitch, stitch the elastic to the wrong side of the front, stretching the elastic to fit as you stitch. Repeat for the back.

⑤ Stitch the Front and Back

With the right sides together, stitch the front and back pieces together along the shoulders. Press the seam allowances open, and turn the top right side out.

⑥ Bind the Neck Edge

* Unfold the single-fold bias tape and fold the short end ½" to the wrong side. Starting at a shoulder seam with the folded short end, pin the bias tape along the entire neck edge with the right sides together and raw edges aligned. Continue pinning the bias tape until it overlaps the folded end slightly. Trim away the remaining bias tape.

* Stitch the bias tape to the top, in the crease closest to the raw edge.

* Press the bias tape up, away from the neck edge. Refold along remaining crease and then press to the inside of the top, and pin. From the inside of the top, stitch along the pinned folded edge of the bias tape to finish the neck edge.

⑦ Attach the Sleeves

Press a light crease across the width of each sleeve to mark the center. With the right sides together, align the long raw edge of one sleeve with the raw side edge of the front and back, matching the sleeve crease with the shoulder seam. Stitch the pieces together and press the seam allowance toward the body. Repeat with the second sleeve.

⑧ Stitch the Sides

* With the wrong sides together, fold the top in half along the shoulder seams, lining up the raw edges. Along the sleeve seams stitched in step 7, measure and mark down from the top edge by the distance shown for your size in the illustration below, and 2" up from the bottom edge.

* Stitch the front and back together between the marks directly over the previous stitching, through all layers. The top opening in the stitching creates the sleeve openings, and the bottom openings serve as side vents.

* Stitch the other side in the same way.

⑨ Hem the Edges

Stitch a narrow ¼" double-fold hem along the sleeve and bottom edges.

⑩ Apply Lace Trim (optional)

Topstitch lace trim along the sleeve openings and bottom hem edges.

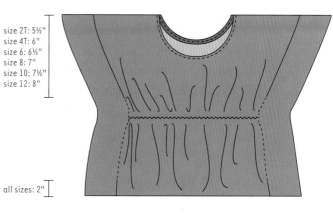

size 2T: 5½"
size 4T: 6"
size 6: 6½"
size 8: 7"
size 10: 7½"
size 12: 8"

all sizes: 2"

STEP 8

riviera Tee

Designed by Rebecca Yaker

Fabric designed by Bethany Berndt Shackelford

While you might not make it to the coastline hailed as one of the first modern resort areas of the world, there's nothing stopping you from dreaming. Imagine yourself getting comfortable on your yacht, surrounded by assorted celebrities and artist friends. This sea-themed tee is the perfect casual item for your little one to wear to such an event, inspired by sunshine, blue water, and warm, salty air.

MATERIALS

* Pattern pieces (3), *see* sheet 3
* 1 yard of 54/60" knit fabric (preferably jersey)
* 1 spool of coordinating thread
* 1 yard of ¼"-wide elastic
* ⅔ yard of ⅜"-wide contrast ribbon or bias tape for embellishment
* 1 button, ½" in diameter (for the flower's center)

Sizes – 2T, 3T, 4T, 5, 6, 7, 8

Seam allowance – ½" unless otherwise specified

1 Determine Your Child's Size

Measure your child's chest to find the right size.

	2T	3T	4T	5	6	7	8
Chest Size	21"	22"	23"	24"	25"	25¾"	26½"

2 Measure, Mark, and Cut

Lay your fabric in a single layer with the right side facing up. Position the pattern pieces according to the layout and cut them out. Note that you must flip the sleeve piece in order to cut both a right and left sleeve. Transfer the markings from the patterns to the wrong side of the fabric.

* **Front** (cut 1)
* **Back** (cut 1)
* **Sleeve** (cut 2, one reversed)

NOTE: *Mirror the pattern pieces along the lines indicated.*

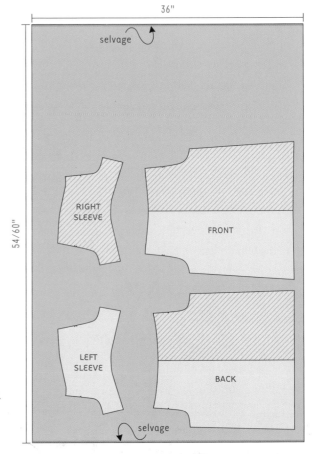

CUTTING LAYOUT

The fabric for the tee pictured here was the winner of a Spoonflower Weekly Design Challenge (Congrats, Bethany!). The printed knit fabric is available (for size 8 only) to order directly from Spoonflower at *www.spoonflower.com/fabric/1615912*.

❸ Attach the Front, Back, and Sleeves

With right sides together, pin the front edge of the sleeve to the front piece, matching notches along the armhole edge. Stitch and press the seam allowance toward the shirt. Repeat, stitching the back edge of the sleeve to the back piece, matching notches. Press the seam allowance toward the shirt. Repeat to attach the second sleeve.

❹ Stitch the Side Seams

With right sides together, stitch the front to the back along the side seams and underarm edges in one continuous seam. Press the seams toward the back of the shirt.

❺ Hem the Tee Edges

Press the sleeve openings ¾" to the wrong side and topstitch in place. Do the same for the bottom edge of the tee.

❻ Make the Neck Casing

* Make the neckline casing at the top edge of the tee by pressing under ¼", and then another ½". Edgestitch close to the folded edge of the casing, leaving a 1" opening at one of the back sleeve seams to thread the elastic through.
* Cut a length of elastic, following the sizing chart. Thread the elastic through the neckline casing. Overlap the ends of the elastic ½" and stitch them together securely, making sure the elastic is not twisted. Slide the ends of the elastic back into the casing. Stitch the casing opening closed.

	2T	3T	4T	5	6	7	8
¼"-wide elastic	17"	17½"	18"	18½"	19"	19½"	20"

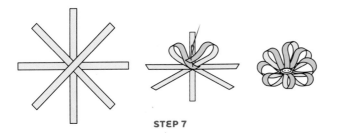

STEP 7

❼ Add Looped Flower Embellishment

* Cut the 24" length of ribbon into four 6" pieces. Lay the pieces wrong side up, crossing them at their center points to form a circle, spacing the ribbon pieces equal distances apart.
* Using a hand-sewing needle and thread, stitch through the center of the pieces to hold all four pieces together. Turn the ribbon pieces over and, one by one, starting with the bottom layer, fold each piece of ribbon up toward the center, forming a loop. Anchor each piece of ribbon with a stitch or two. Repeat until all the petals have been stitched.
* Position the flower along the neckline of the Riviera Tee, at the left raglan seam, and make several additional stitches through the center of the flower to secure it to the shirt. Stitch the button to the center of the flower to finish.

CHAPTER 6

Pants & Skirts

IN THIS CHAPTER, YOU WILL FIND FOUNDATION PIECES
for your little one's wardrobe — an assortment of
pants, skirts, shorts, and even a quirky, surprising
pair of overalls. Although the individual pieces may
be basic, there are plenty of features to give each and
every great-fitting garment a unique personality.

simple pants

Designed by Caroline Critchfield

Few clothing projects could be as simple as this cute pair of basic pants. There is only one pattern piece (plus the pocket), making the project a breeze. Don't be fooled by the name, however. Although these pants are easily constructed, they will soon become a very stylish staple in your child's wardrobe. Add optional pockets or other embellishments, as desired. The fit is loose and comfortable, perfect for wovens and knits.

MATERIALS

* Pattern pieces (2), *see* sheet 3
* 1 yard of 44/45" quilting-weight cotton (also great in knit, flannel, and fleece)
* 1 spool of coordinating thread
* Additional fabric scraps (or main fabric) for pockets (optional)
* 6" piece of 1"-wide grosgrain ribbon for pocket tab (optional)
* ⅔ yard of 1"-wide elastic

Sizes – 9 months, 12 months, 18 months, 2T/3T, 4/5, 6/7, 8/9, 10

Seam allowance – ½" unless otherwise specified

❶ Determine Your Child's Size

Measure your child's waist and inseam to find the right size. If you come up with two different sizes, go with the inseam measurement. You can always make the elastic at the waist shorter or longer as needed to fit.

	9 mo	12 mo	18 mo	2T/3T	4/5	6/7	8/9	10
Waist	19½"	20"	20½"	21¼"	22"	23"	24"	24½"
Finished Inseam	10½"	11½"	12½"	14½"	16½"	18½"	20½"	21½"

❷ Measure, Mark, and Cut

Fold your fabric in half lengthwise with the right sides together, aligning the selvages. Position the pattern piece according to the layout and cut it out. Transfer markings from the pattern to the wrong side of the fabric.

* **Pants** (cut 2)
* **Back pocket** (optional; cut 2 from main or contrast fabric; see Pocket Possibilities on facing page)

In addition to the paper pattern pieces, measure, mark, and cut the following optional pocket flap piece directly onto your fabric, or use contrast fabric if needed/desired:

	9mo	12mo	18mo	2T/3T	4/5	6/7	8/9	10
Back Pocket Flap (cut 2)	4¼" × 4¼"	4½" × 4½"	4¾" × 4¾"	5¼" × 5¼"	5¾" × 5¾"	6¼" × 6¼"	6¾" × 6¾"	7" × 7"

POCKET POSSIBILITIES

If you want pockets and flaps, you will be able to cut them from your yard of main fabric for sizes 4/5 and under. For sizes 6/7–10, you will either need to buy an extra ¼ yard of your main fabric, or use coordinating fabric you have on hand. Check out the Cargo Board Shorts (page 96) for additional front pocket shapes and placement options that also work with these pants.

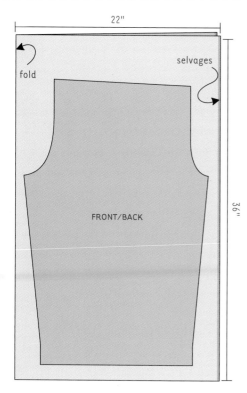

CUTTING LAYOUT

❸ Make and Attach the Back Pockets and Flaps (optional)

The following instructions are to make the Clean and Classic pockets shown. For the Gathered and Ruffled pocket option, see pages 98-99.

* Press the top, straight raw edge of the pockets ¼" to the wrong side. Press an additional 1" to the wrong side and stitch close to the folded edge.

* Fold and pin the pocket darts along the center of each dart with the right sides together. Stitch along the marked dart lines. Press each dart toward the center of the pocket. Press the side and bottom raw edges ½" to the wrong side. Set pockets aside.

* Fold the flap pieces in half with right sides together. Stitch around the three raw edges, leaving a 2" opening centered along the long edge for turning. Clip corners, turn flaps right side out, and press. Press the seam allowances of the opening to the inside.

* Cut the 6" piece of grosgrain ribbon into two 3" pieces. Fold the ribbon in half, aligning the short ends. Insert the raw ends of the folded ribbon tabs into the flap openings, centering the tabs along the edge of the flaps, and leaving 1" of the folded end exposed. Pin in place, and then edgestitch around the side and bottom edges of the flap, securing the tab. (You could also use fabric to make this tab, as pictured.)

With right sides facing up, position the pockets on the back of the pants at the following locations:

	9, 12, 18 mo	2T/3T, 4/5	6/7, 8/9, 10
Distance from Center Back Edge	1½"	1¾"	2"
Distance from Top Edge	3"	4"	5"

* Pin the pockets in place and stitch along the side and bottom edges.

* With right sides facing up, center the top edge of the flaps ½" above the top edge of the pockets (for all sizes). Stitch flaps in place along the top edge.

9 mo, 12 mo, 18 mo: 1½"
2T/3T, 4/5: 1¾"
6/7, 8/9, 10: 2"

9 mo, 12 mo, 18 mo: 3"
2T/3T, 4/5: 4"
6/7, 8/9, 10: 5"

back edge

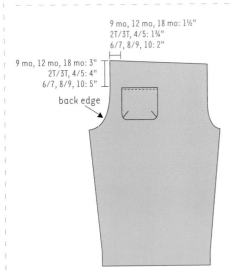

top edge of pocket flap ½" above top edge of pocket

½"

④ Stitch the Crotch Seam

Place your pants pieces with right sides together. Stitch along both the front and back curved crotch edges. Stitch again ¼" away within the seam allowance to reinforce the seam. Trim the seam allowance close to the second stitching line.

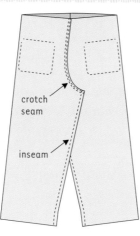

crotch seam

inseam

⑤ Stitch the Inseam

* With right sides together and raw edges aligned, line up the center front and center back seams.

* Stitch along the leg inseam in one continuous seam. Press the seam allowance toward the back of the pants.

⑥ Hem the Pants

Stitch a 1" double-fold hem at the bottom edge of each pant leg. (You may wish to lengthen or shorten the pants based upon the needs of your child.)

⑦ Make the Waistband Casing

* Make the waistband casing at the top edge of the pants by pressing under ¼", then another 1". Edgestitch close to the folded edge of the casing, leaving a 2" opening at the center back seam.

* Cut a length of elastic to snugly but comfortably fit around your little one's belly, adding an extra 1". (Alternatively, you may also follow the elastic size chart).

	9mo	12mo	18mo	2T/3T	4/5	6/7	8/9	10
Elastic	20½"	21"	21½"	22¼"	23"	24"	25"	25½"

* Thread the elastic through the waistband casing. Overlap the ends of the elastic ½" and stitch them together securely. Slide the elastic back in the casing. Stitch the casing opening closed.

CARGO BOARD SHORTS

Designed by Caroline Critchfield

Surf's up, so make your kiddo a pair of board shorts and say hello to summer! These casual-fitting shorts feature four cute pockets that are perfect for collecting seashells from the beach. In fact, there are two different pocket variations: one a bit ruffled for the little lady in your life, and the other more classic and clean. Pay close attention throughout the instructions to construct the pocket styling of your preference.

MATERIALS

* Pattern pieces (3), *see* sheet 3
* 1 yard quilting-weight cotton (size 9 month-6/7: 44/45"; size 8/9-10: 54")
* 1 yard of 1"-wide grosgrain ribbon
* 1 spool of coordinating thread
* ⅔ yard of 1"-wide elastic

FABRIC NOTES: *Sizes 8/9 and 10 require a fabric width wider than 45" to accommodate all four pockets and flaps. The shorts are also great in lightweight canvas and twill.*

Sizes – 9 months, 12 months, 18 months, 2T/3T, 4/5, 6/7, 8/9, 10

Seam allowance – ½" unless otherwise specified

① Determine Your Child's Size

Measure your child's waist to find the right size.

	9 mo	12 mo	18 mo	2T/3T	4/5	6/7	8/9	10
Waist	19½"	20"	20½"	21¼"	22"	23"	24"	24½"
Finished Inseam	2¾"	3¼"	3¾"	4¾"	6¼"	8¼"	10¼"	11¼"

② Measure, Mark, and Cut

Fold your fabric in half lengthwise with the right sides together, aligning the selvages. Position the pattern pieces according to the layout and cut them out. Transfer markings from the pattern to the wrong side of the fabric.

* **Front/Back** (cut 2)
* **Front pocket** (cut 2)
* **Cargo pocket** (cut 2)

NOTE: *The shorts pattern is the same as for the Simple Pants (page 92), but with different lengths marked for the shorts.*

In addition to the paper pattern pieces, measure, mark, and cut the pocket flap piece directly onto your fabric or contrast fabric, using the chart on page 92.

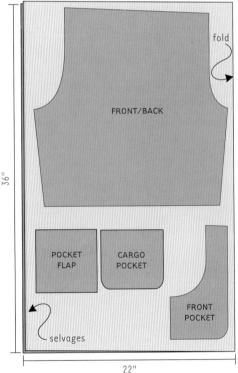

FRONT/BACK

fold

36"

POCKET FLAP

CARGO POCKET

FRONT POCKET

selvages

22"

CUTTING LAYOUT

❸ Mark the Side "Seams" of the Shorts

Although these shorts do not have side seams, it is necessary to mark the side seam location of the shorts to help determine the front and cargo pocket placement. Choose one of these methods:

* Use tailor's chalk or some other disappearing marker to draw the line on the wrong side of the shorts as indicated on the pattern piece.

* Alternatively, you may choose to make a small ⅛"–¼" notch in the shorts fabric piece at the top and bottom edge at the side seam location (as marked on the pattern). After removing the pattern, form a fold down the length of the shorts between the notches and lightly press a crease.

❹ Make the Pockets

Decide which pocket variation you prefer based on the illustrations on page 98 and follow that set of instructions:

Clean and Classic Front Pocket

* Cut two pieces of grosgrain ribbon 1" longer than the curved front pocket openings. Fold the grosgrain in half lengthwise and press. Bind the curved front pocket openings with this folded grosgrain.

* Fold and pin the pocket darts along the center of each dart with the right sides together. Stitch along the marked dart lines. Press each dart toward the side of the pocket.

* Press the curved raw edge and straight side edge ½" to the wrong side, leaving the top, short raw edge unturned.

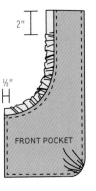

Clean and Classic Cargo Pocket and Flaps

* To make the clean and classic cargo pockets and flaps, follow the back pocket instructions from the Simple Pants project, step 3 on page 94.

Gathered and Ruffled Front Pocket

* Cut two pieces of grosgrain ribbon one and a half times longer than the curved front pocket openings. Run a gathering (basting) stitch along the center of each piece of ribbon.

* Adjust gathers so that the grosgrain fits along the pocket opening. Pin gathered ribbon on the right side of the front pocket along the pocket opening, aligning the edge of the ribbon with the raw edge of the pocket opening. The gathers in the ribbon should start ½" from the side seam and 2" from the top edge of the pocket, as shown in the illustration.

* Stitch the gathered ribbon in place along the gathering stitch (using a ½" seam allowance). Press the pocket opening and gathered grosgrain ribbon ½" to the wrong side. Topstitch the pocket opening edge using a ¼" seam allowance.

* Instead of making darts, baste around the side and bottom curved raw edge of the pocket using a ½" seam allowance. Pull the gathering thread only slightly, making the total raw edge of the pocket 1½"-2" shorter. Push the gathers toward the bottom corner of the pocket, positioning them within the dart lines as indicated on the pattern piece. Baste the gathers in place using a ¼" seam allowance.

* Press the curved, gathered raw edge and straight side edge ½" to the wrong side, leaving the top, short raw edge unturned.

Gathered and Ruffled Cargo Pocket and Flaps

* Press the top straight raw edge of the pockets ¼" to the wrong side, then press under an additional 1". Stitch close to the folded edge.

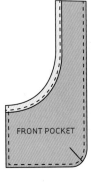

CLEAN AND CLASSIC

GATHERED AND RUFFLED

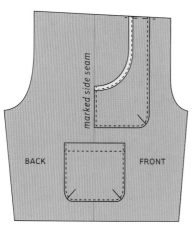

CLEAN AND CLASSIC

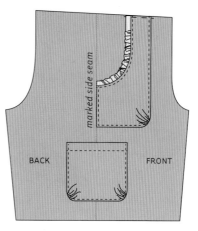

GATHERED AND RUFFLED

✳ Instead of making darts, baste around the side and bottom raw edges of the pocket. Pull the gathering thread only slightly, making the total raw edge of the pocket 2½"–3½" shorter. Push the gathers toward the bottom corners of the pocket, positioning them within the dart lines on the pattern piece. Baste the gathers.

✳ Press the side and bottom raw edges ½" to the wrong side, using the gathering basting stitch as a guide. Set pockets aside.

✳ To make the cargo pocket flaps, follow the Simple Pants pocket flap instructions in step 3 on page 94.

⑤ Attach the Pockets

These placement instructions apply to both pocket variations.

Front Pockets

With both right sides facing up, position the front pockets on the front sides of the shorts pieces, aligning the pressed side edge with the marked side "seam" of the shorts, and the top raw edge with the top raw edges of the shorts. The side edges of the front pockets should be parallel to the side seam. Pin the pockets in place, then edgestitch along the turned and pressed side edges. Baste the pockets in place across top raw edges.

Cargo Pockets

With right sides facing up, center the cargo pockets along the marked side "seam" between the bottom edge of the front pocket and the bottom raw edge. (For sizes 4 and smaller, the bottom edge of the cargo pocket must be placed at least 2¼" above the bottom raw edge of the shorts to allow enough room to hem the shorts in a later step.) The side edges of the cargo pocket should be parallel to the side seam. Pin the pockets in place and stitch along the side and bottom edges.

Flaps

With right sides facing up, center the top edge of the flaps ½" above the top edge of the cargo pockets. Stitch flaps in place along the top edge.

⑥ Finish the Shorts

To complete the shorts, follow steps 4–7 of the Simple Pants project on page 95.

secret monster overalls

Designed by Pam McFerrin

Shhhhhh and beware. There's something lurking beneath these seemingly traditional overalls. Surprise your friends or just keep it to yourself — simply turn back the cuffs, open the flap on the bib, and pull out the tail to reveal the secret monster! Cute and cozy, no one will ever suspect what awaits when your little one dons these surprise overalls!

MATERIALS

* Pattern pieces (12), *see* sheet 3
* 1 yard of 44/45" corduroy, twill, denim, or another heavyweight fabric
* Scrap of red patterned cotton fabric (for suspender tabs, cuffs, and mouth)
* Scrap of solid red cotton fabric (for throat and tongue)
* Scrap of solid white cotton fabric (for toes)
* Scrap of brown felt (for claws)
* 1 square white craft felt (for teeth)
* Scrap of faux fur (for the tail tip)
* 1 spool of coordinating thread
* 11" piece of ½"-wide elastic
* Two sets of white Velcro dots
* 2 decorative large buttons, 1⅜" in diameter (for the eyes)
* 4 coordinating buttons, ⅞" in diameter

Sizes – 2T with 12½" inseam; pattern can be altered to accommodate sizes 3T, 4T, and 5, which will require more than 1 yard of fabric; see step 1 for details.

Seam allowance – ½" unless otherwise specified

❶ Adjust the Pattern

As your child grows, his or her inseam will change much more dramatically than the waist measurement. These overalls are designed to fit a child with a standard waist measurement up to a size 5. However, you will need to lengthen the inseam of the overalls for larger sizes, and doing so will also require slightly more than 1 yard of fabric. To adjust the pattern piece, simply cut the front and back pattern pieces along the "lengthen pattern here" line, and spread the pattern the appropriate distance according to the chart below.

	3T	4T	5
Finished Inseam	14½"	16½"	18½"
Adjust the Pattern Length	Spread 2"	Spread 4"	Spread 6"
Fabric Requirements	1⅛ yard	1¼ yard	1¼ yard

❷ Measure, Mark, and Cut

Fold your fabric in half lengthwise with the right sides together, aligning the selvages. Position the pattern pieces according to the layout and cut them out. Transfer markings from the pattern to the wrong side of the fabric.

* **Front** (cut 2)
* **Back** (cut 2)
* **Bib** (cut 2)
* **Suspenders** (cut 2)
* **Pocket** (cut 2)
* **Side facing** 3" × 6½" (cut 2)
* **Tail** 12" × 2½" (cut 1)*

*Open up your fabric and cut the tail last, as it only needs to be cut from a single layer of fabric.

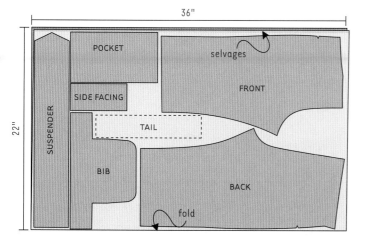

CUTTING LAYOUT

From the red patterned cotton fabric, cut:
* **Cuffs** (cut 2)
* **Mouth** (cut 1)
* **Suspender tabs** 4" × 3" (cut 2)

From the solid red cotton fabric, cut:
* **Throat** (cut 1)
* **Tongue** (cut 1)

From the solid white cotton fabric, cut:
* **Toes** (cut 2)

From the brown felt, cut:
* **Claws** (cut 6)

From the white felt, cut:
* **Teeth** (cut 2)

From the faux fur, cut:
* **Tail tip** 2½" × 4" (cut 1)

❸ Stitch the Back Pieces

* Pin the back pieces with right sides together. Stitch along the curved crotch edges. Stitch again ¼" away in the seam allowance to reinforce the seam. Trim the seam allowance close to the second stitching line and press it to one side.

* Make the waistband casing at the top edge of the back pieces by pressing under ¼", then another 1". Edgestitch close to the folded edge of the casing.

* Thread the elastic through the back waistband casing and stitch the ends securely in place.

* Fold the suspender tabs in half with right sides together, aligning the 3" edges. Stitch together along three sides, leaving a small opening on the long edge for turning. Clip corners, turn right side out, and press. Edgestitch around all four sides, close opening in stitching.

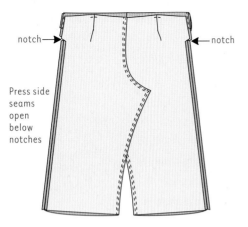

STEP 5

notch➤

◄notch

Press side
seams
open
below
notches

* Position suspender tabs on the wrong
  side of the back pieces as indicated on
  the pattern piece, with 1" extending above
  the top of the waistband casing. Securely
  stitch tabs in place along the casing
  stitch line and edgestitch in place along
  the top edge of the back waistband.

4 Stitch the Front Pieces

* Pin the front pieces with right sides
  together and stitch along the curved crotch
  edges. Stitch again ¼" away in the seam
  allowance to reinforce the seam. Trim
  the seam allowance close to the second
  stitching line and press it to one side.

* Make the pleats on the front pieces
  as indicated on the pattern piece: fold
  the fronts along the fold line and align
  the folded edge of the pleat with the
  placement line, matching dots, folding
  the pleats away from the center front
  of the pants. Pin pleats in place and
  baste the pleats along the top raw
  edge using a ¼" seam allowance.

5 Stitch the Front and Back Together

* With right sides together, align the raw edges of the front and
  back pieces. Stitch together along the inside leg, pivoting at
  the crotch seam. Stitch again ¼" away in the seam allowance to
  reinforce the seam. Trim the seam allowance close to the second
  stitching line and press toward the back.

* Stitch the side seams, starting at the notch as indicated on the
  pattern piece, and stitching down to the leg opening. Clip into
  the seam allowance at the notch, and press the seam below the
  notch open.

6 Attach the Side Facing

* Turn and press the short top raw edge of the side facing pieces
  ½" to the wrong side.

* On the side seam of the overalls, above the notch, pin the right
  side of the facing to the wrong side of the back pant, aligning top
  folded edges and raw side edges. Stitch from the top edge down
  to the notch. With the needle in the downward position, pivot
  the front pant so that the raw side edge of the front pant aligns
  with the remainder of the facing edge. Continue stitching the
  facing to the front side edge, from the notch to the top edge of
  the front pant.

* Press the seam allowance toward the facing. Turn the free, long
  edge of the facing ½" to the wrong side and press.

* Fold the facing to the right side of the overalls, covering the
  seam, and stitch close to the folded edge.

* Turn the side facing on the front pants to the inside, folding at
  the seam, and press. Edgestitch the facing to the front along the
  top edge.

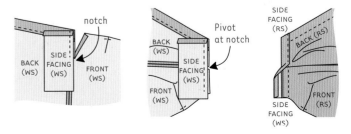

7 Appliqué the Monster Pocket

* With all right sides facing up, position the tongue and throat pieces along the top and bottom edges of the mouth. Stitch around the inside edges with a narrow, tight zigzag or satin stitch, leaving the outside edges unstitched.

* With right sides facing up, center the mouth on one pocket piece and use the same stitch around the outside edge of the mouth.

* Position the teeth pieces on the top and bottom edges of the mouth as shown in the photo and stitch in place. You may choose to use a straight edgestitch to hold the individual teeth in place.

* Stitch the corresponding Velcro dots in the bottom and top outside corners of the teeth.

8 Finish the Pocket

* Stitch the two decorative button eyes on the right side of the remaining pocket piece, as indicated on the pattern piece.

* Place the two pocket pieces with right sides together. The end with the button eyes should correspond to the end with the throat appliqué. Stitch around all four sides, leaving 2" open along the bottom edge for turning. Clip corners, turn right side out, and press.

* Position the pocket on the right side of one bib piece along the placement lines. The appliqué mouth should be facing up, with the tongue piece closest to the bottom pocket placement line. Edgestitch the pocket to the bib along the placement line as indicated on the pattern piece, leaving the top half of the pocket unstitched (it will extend beyond the bib). Fold the pocket in half, holding the mouth closed with the Velcro dots applied in the previous step. This is the bib exterior.

9 Make the Suspenders and Bib

* Fold one suspender piece in half lengthwise with right sides together. Stitch along the long straight edge and short slanted edge, leaving the short, straight end unstitched. Clip corners, turn right side out, and press. Repeat with the second suspender.

* With right sides together, pin suspenders to the remaining bib piece (without the pocket; this is now the bib facing) at placement marks, aligning raw edges. Stitch suspenders in place using a ¼" seam allowance. Turn bottom edge of bib facing ½" to the wrong side and press.

* With right sides together, center the top raw edge of the overalls front with the bottom raw edge of the bib exterior, aligning raw edges and matching dots. Stitch together and press the seam allowance up toward the bib.

* Position bib pieces right sides together, aligning all raw edges (the suspenders and monster pocket will be sandwiched in between the bib pieces), and pin together. Stitch around all raw edges of the bib. Clip corners and notch curves. Turn right side out and press.
* From the right side of the overalls, edgestitch along the bottom edge of the bib, catching the bib facing in the stitching line.

⑩ Make and Attach the Cuffs

* With both right sides facing up, position the toes pieces on a cuff piece along the placement lines indicated on the pattern. Stitch around the outside edges of the toes with a narrow, tight zigzag or satin stitch. Position the claw pieces on the toes as indicated and again stitch around the outside edges. Repeat for the second cuff.
* With right sides together, fold the cuff in half crosswise, aligning the short ends. Stitch the short ends together and press seam allowance open. Turn and press the top edge ½" to the wrong side. Repeat for the second cuff.
* With right sides together, align the leg opening of the overalls with the raw, unfolded edge of the cuff, matching side seams and making sure that the toes and claws are positioned on the front of the overalls. Stitch together.
* Turn the cuff to the inside of the pant leg and press. Edgestitch around the top edge of the cuff close to the folded edge and through all layers. Repeat for the second cuff.

⑪ Make and Attach the Tail

* Press all edges of the tail piece ½" to the wrong side. Fold the tail in half lengthwise with wrong sides together and edgestitch along three open, folded edges.
* Fold the faux fur piece in half lengthwise around the tail piece at one end. Invisibly stitch in place, attaching the fur to the tail.
* Position tail on the inside of the pants, aligning the short, non-fur end of the tail with the top edge of the pants at center back. Securely stitch tail in place along the casing stitching line and the top edge of the back piece.

⑫ Make Buttonholes and Attach Buttons

* Make two horizontal buttonholes on the bib as indicated on the pattern piece. Make two vertical buttonholes on each suspender following the placement lines indicated on the pattern.
* Position and stitch two buttons, one centered on each suspender tab. Position and stitch the remaining two buttons, one on each side facing to correspond to the bib buttonholes.

sierra Tiered skirt

Designed by Sue Kim

Make this bohemian-inspired three-tiered skirt out of lightweight cotton for the summer months, and from heavier twill for the fall and winter months. Although we are showing it in one fabric, you could certainly choose three coordinating fabrics, making each tier a different print. Have fun with the options and make this skirt colorful and unique!

MATERIALS

* ✳ 1 yard of 54/60" cotton fabric
* ✳ 1 spool of coordinating thread
* ✳ ⅔ yard of 1"-wide elastic

Sizes – 3T/4T, 5/6, 7/8

Seam allowance – ½" unless otherwise specified

① **Determine Your Child's Size**

Measure your child's waist to find the right size. For a tall child, you may choose to go with the longer skirt length. You can always make the elastic at the waist shorter or longer as needed to fit.

	3T/4T	5/6	7/8
Waist	21¼"–21½"	22"–22½"	23"–23½"
Finished Length	18½"	21½"	24½"

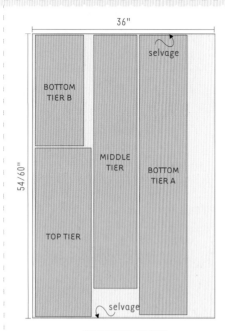

36"

54/60"

BOTTOM TIER B

MIDDLE TIER

BOTTOM TIER A

TOP TIER

selvage

selvage

CUTTING LAYOUT

❷ Measure, Mark, and Cut

Lay your fabric in a single layer with the wrong side facing up. Measure and mark the following pattern pieces onto the wrong side of your fabric and cut them out.

	3T/4T	5/6	7/8
Top tier (cut 1)	29" × 9"	31" × 10"	32" × 11"
Middle tier (cut 1)	43" × 6½"	46½" × 7½"	48" × 8½"
Bottom tier A (cut 1)	43" × 7½"	50" × 8½"	53" × 9½"
Bottom tier B (cut 1)	24" × 7½"	22" × 8½"	21" × 9½"

❸ Make the Tiers

* Fold the top tier piece in half with right sides together, aligning the short ends. Press a light crease in the fold to mark the "side seam." Stitch the short ends together, and press seam allowance open.
* Repeat for the middle tier.

* Position bottom tier A and bottom tier B with right sides together, aligning the short ends to make one continuous piece. Stitch together along both short ends and press seam allowances open. Find the center point opposite one of the seams and mark it on the top and bottom raw edges. These marks denote a "side seam."

❹ Attach the Tiers

* Gather the top raw edge of the middle tier using a basting stitch and a ¼" seam allowance. With right sides together, pin the top of the middle tier to the bottom of the top tier, aligning seams and pressed side seams. Adjust the gathers so that they are evenly distributed between the side seams (see Gathering in glossary, page 341). Stitch together and press the seam allowance up toward the top tier.
* Use a basting stitch to gather the top raw edge of the bottom tier. With right sides together, pin and stitch the top of the bottom tier to the bottom of the middle tier, as before.

❺ Hem the Skirt

Stitch a ½" double-fold hem at the bottom edge of the skirt and topstitch close to the folded edge.

❻ Make the Waistband Casing

* Make the waistband casing at the top edge of the skirt by pressing under ½", then another 1". Edgestitch close to the folded edge of the casing, leaving a 2" opening at a side seam.
* Cut a length of elastic to fit snugly but comfortably around your little one's belly, adding an extra 1". Alternatively, you may choose to follow the following size chart:

	3T/4T	5/6	7/8
Elastic	22½"	23½"	24½"

* Thread the elastic through the waistband casing. Overlap the ends of the elastic ½" and stitch them together securely. Slide the ends of the elastic back in the casing. Stitch the casing opening closed.

BALLOON SKIRT

Designed by Yasuko Solbes

This slightly voluminous skirt couldn't be more comfortable or adorable. Originally popular in the 1950s, this mod skirt continues to make comeback after comeback. The hem is gathered and tucked under to create a bubble effect along the bottom edge. Simple to make, with a very original look, this skirt is perfect paired with leggings, sandals, boots – you name it!

MATERIALS

* Pattern pieces (2), *see* sheet 4
* 1 yard of 44/45" quilting-weight cotton (not suitable for one-way prints)
* 1 spool of coordinating thread
* ⅔ yard of ½"-wide elastic

Sizes – 12 months, 2T, 3T, 4T

Seam allowance – ½" unless otherwise specified

① Determine Your Child's Size

Measure your child's waist to find the right size.

	12 mo	2T	3T	4T
Waist	20½"	21"	21¼"	21½"

② Measure, Mark, and Cut

Lay your fabric in a single layer with the wrong side facing up. Position the pattern pieces according to the layout, and measure and mark the additional pattern piece onto the wrong side of your fabric. Cut out all pieces and transfer markings from the pattern to the wrong side of the fabric.

* **Skirt exterior** (cut 2)
* **Skirt lining** (cut 2)

	12 mo	2T	3T	4T
Waistband (cut 1)	21" × 2½"	24" × 2½"	26 × 2½""	28¾" × 2½"

NOTE: *Mirror the pattern pieces along the lines indicated.*

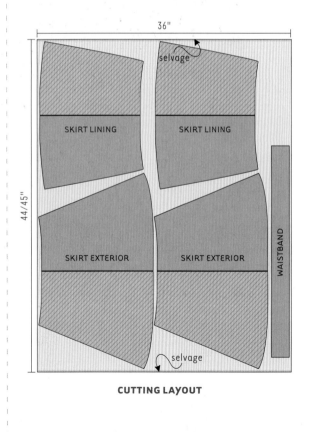

CUTTING LAYOUT

③ Stitch the Sides

With right sides together and raw edges aligned, pin and stitch the side seams of the skirt exterior pieces. Press seams open. Repeat to stitch the skirt lining pieces together.

④ Attach the Exterior and Lining

* Use a basting stitch to gather the bottom raw edge of the skirt exterior using a ¼" seam allowance.
* With right sides together, pin the exterior and lining pieces together, aligning the bottom edges. Match centers and dots as indicated on the pattern piece and side seams. Adjust gathers evenly on the skirt exterior to match the circumference of the lining.
* Stitch the exterior and lining together along bottom edges. Press the seam allowance toward the lining. Edgestitch along the seam on the lining side.

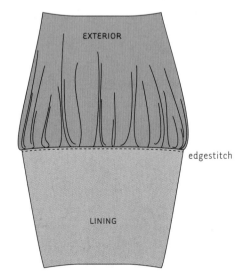

❺ Add the Waistband

* Flip the lining to the inside of the skirt so that wrong sides are together. Align the top raw edges and side seams of the exterior and lining pieces and baste together along the top edge using a ¼" seam allowance. (The lining is shorter than the exterior to create the balloon effect).

* With right sides facing, stitch the short ends of the waistband together to form a loop. Press seam allowance open. Turn under the top raw edge of the waistband ½" and press. With right sides together, pin the raw edges of the skirt and waistband together, matching up the side seams. Stitch and press the seam allowance up toward the waistband.

❻ Make the Waistband Casing

* Fold the waistband in half, toward the inside of the skirt, so that the folded edge overlaps and covers the seam.

* From the right side of the skirt exterior, topstitch the waistband close to the seam, catching the inside folded edge in your stitching. Leave a 2" opening at one side seam for inserting the elastic.

* Cut a length of elastic to fit snugly but comfortably around your little one's belly, adding an extra 1". Alternatively, you may choose to follow the following size chart:

	12 mo	2T	3T	4T
Elastic	21"	21½"	21¾"	22"

* Thread the elastic through the waistband casing. Overlap the ends of the elastic ½" and stitch them together securely. Slide the elastic back in the casing. Stitch the casing opening closed.

CHAPTER 7

DRESSES & ROMPERS

KNITS AND WOVENS ABOUND IN THIS CHAPTER of comfortable, fashion-friendly frocks. You will find dresses of varying lengths suitable for many occasions. Your little lady will also enjoy a comfy romper or two — the perfect playwear ensemble — light and loose fitting, ideal for movement.

SHiRRED Sunsuit

Designed by Bella van Doorn

This is the perfect little romper for your summertime beauty. The frills over the shoulder provide an extra bit of coverage to help keep the sun off your little one's skin. The feminine shirring combined with shorts keeps the sunsuit in place. The entire romper is constructed using French seams, giving this garment a very professional finish.

MATERIALS

* ✳ Pattern pieces (2), *see* sheet 4
* ✳ 1 yard of 44/45" quilting-weight cotton
* ✳ 1 spool of coordinating thread
* ✳ 1 spool of elastic thread
* ✳ ½ yard of ¾"-wide elastic

Sizes – 2T, 3T, 4T, 5

Seam allowance – ½" unless otherwise specified

● Determine Your Child's Size

Measure your child's chest to find the right size.

	2T	3T	4T	5
Chest Size	21"	22"	23"	24"

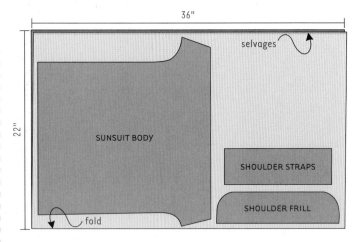

CUTTING LAYOUT

Labels within the layout: 36", 22", selvages, SUNSUIT BODY, SHOULDER STRAPS, SHOULDER FRILL, fold

② Measure, Mark, and Cut

Fold your fabric in half lengthwise with the right sides together and the selvages aligned. Position the pattern pieces according to the layout, and measure and mark the shoulder straps onto the wrong side of your fabric. Cut out all pieces.

* **Sunsuit body** (cut 2)
* **Shoulder frill** (cut 2)
* **Shoulder straps** 12¼" × 4" (cut 2)

③ Stitch the Inseams

Fold one sunsuit piece with wrong sides together, aligning the inseam raw edges. Stitch the inseam at a scant ¼" seam allowance. Turn wrong side out (with the right sides together) at the inseam and stitch another ¼" seam to enclose the raw edges. You have just created a French seam (see glossary, page 341). Press the seam allowance toward the back. Repeat with the second sunsuit piece.

④ Stitch the Center Seams

Turn one sunsuit piece right side out. Slip one inside the other so that wrong sides are together. As in the previous step, create a French seam along the center front, crotch, and center back seam. Press the seam allowance to one side.

⑤ Hem the Sunsuit

* Stitch a ¼" double-fold hem at the bottom edge of each leg opening.
* If possible, try the romper on your little one at this point to check the body length. The top edge should sit just below the underarms. If it is too long, simply trim the necessary amount off the top edge, leaving an additional ½" on the length to allow for a ¼" double-fold hem. Hem the top edge.

⑥ Prepare the Bobbin

Load your bobbin with elastic thread. To do this, manually wind the elastic thread onto your bobbin by hand, giving it a very slight stretch as you wind. Throughout the course of stitching the sunsuit, you will need to wind more than one bobbin to complete the project.

⑦ Mark and Stitch the Shirring Lines

* Lay the sunsuit, right side out, on a flat surface with the back facing up. Measure 7½" down from the top edge and use a disappearing fabric pen to mark a line at center back, perpendicular to the seam. This is where you will stop your shirring.
* Set your machine to the longest stitch length you have (ideally, something close to a basting stitch). Your elastic thread should be loaded in the bobbin, with the coordinating thread to match your fabric in the top of the machine.

With the sunsuit right side out, begin sewing at center back, ¾" below the top finished edge. Stitch your shirring lines as one continuous spiral line starting at this point and ending at the 7½" center-back mark. To help space your shirring line, simply use the edge of your pressure foot, making the distance between each row the width of your machine's foot. Sewing in a spiral simplifies the process, as you will not need to stop and start your stitching lines and cut and knot threads every row. Be sure to stretch your fabric flat in front of the needle as you sew.

Steam your shirring lines heavily to help shrink up the elastic and make the shirring more pronounced. Take care when doing this, as applying heat directly on the elastic will damage it; always press from the right side.

⑧ Make and Attach the Shoulder Frills and Straps

* Make a ¼" double-fold hem along the curved edges of the shoulder frill pieces, leaving the straight edge unstitched.
* Use a basting stitch to gather the straight raw edge of the shoulder frill pieces. Adjust the gathers so that the finished length of the shoulder frills is 10". Stitch gathers in place using a ¼" seam allowance.
* Fold and press the shoulder strap as you would to make double-fold bias tape (see page 12). Center the 10" gathered shoulder frill along the open folded edge of the shoulder strap, and sandwich ½" of the raw gathered edge of the frill in between the folded edges of the strap. Pin in place. Edgestitch along this edge, stitching the frill to the shoulder strap.
* Cut two 8" pieces of elastic and insert them into the shoulder straps, stitching both ends in place. The elastic will gather the shoulder straps, as well as add additional gathers to the frills.
* Finally, position the straps on the inside (wrong side) of the sunsuit, narrow ends approximately ¾" from the top finished edge. The front strap placement should be 3" from the center front seam, and back placement should be 2¼" from the center back seam. Stitch in place.

MERRY-GO-ROUND DRESS

Designed by Caroline Critchfield

This cute and comfortable dress features a clever loop of elastic concealed inside the halter. This wraps around the neck, back, and shoulders, creating a wonderful ruched detail. Paired with leggings, this comfortable, flowy dress is the perfect choice for any playground adventure!

MATERIALS
* Pattern piece (1), *see* sheet 4
* 1 yard of 44/45" quilting-weight cotton
* 1 spool of coordinating thread
* 1 yard of 1"-wide elastic

Sizes – 18 months/2T, 3T/4T, 5/6, 7/8

Seam allowance – ½" unless otherwise specified

❶ Determine Your Child's Size
Measure your child's chest to find the right size.

	18 mo/ 2T	3T/4T	5/6	7/8
Chest	19"–21"	22"–23"	24"–25"	25¾"–26½"

❷ Measure, Mark, and Cut
Fold your fabric in half lengthwise with the right sides together and the selvages aligned. Position the pattern piece according to the layout, and measure and mark the additional piece as listed. Cut out the pieces and transfer the markings from the pattern to the wrong side of the fabric.
* **Dress** (cut 1 on fold)
* **Halter strap** 42" × 3½" (cut 2)

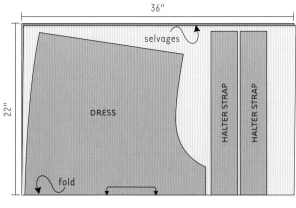

36"

selvages

22"

DRESS

HALTER STRAP

HALTER STRAP

fold

CUTTING LAYOUT

⓷ Prepare the Halter Strap Casing

* With right sides together, align the short raw ends of the halter strap pieces. Stitch these short ends together to create one long piece and press the seam allowance open.

* Fold the strip in half lengthwise with the right sides together. Measure 14" from the center seam in both directions, and make a ½" clip into the raw edges of the fabric with your scissors. Stitch together along the long edge in between the clip marks, leaving the 27½" lengths on the outside of the clip marks unstitched.

* Turn the strap right side out. With right sides together, align the unstitched short ends, and sew them together using a ½" seam allowance to form a circle. Press seam allowance open.

* Fold the entire halter strap casing in half lengthwise with wrong sides together and press lightly. Baste the raw edges together at a ½" seam allowance, leaving a 2" opening.

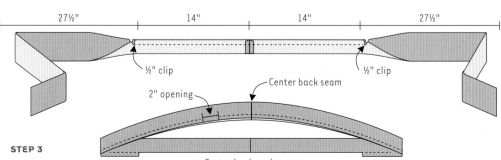

27½"   14"   14"   27½"

½" clip   ½" clip

2" opening   Center back seam

STEP 3

Center back neck seam

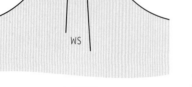

reverse pleat

RS

¼" double fold hem

WS

STEP 5

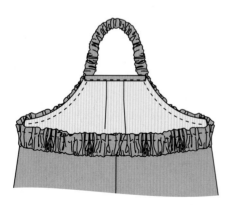

STEP 6

④ Cut and Insert Elastic

* Cut a length of elastic according to the following chart:

	18 mo/ 2T	3T/4T	5/6	7/8
Elastic	26"	28"	30"	32"

* Insert the elastic into the halter strap casing opening left in the previous step and thread all the way around. Join the two ends of the elastic by overlapping the ends ½" and stitching them together securely (make sure the elastic is not twisted). Slip the ends back into the casing and baste the opening closed.

⑤ Make the Front Pleat and Stitch the Back

* Fold the dress in half, right sides together, along the center front. Stitch through both layers along the 1" pleat line as indicated on the pattern piece and backstitch. Unfold the dress front and press to create a reverse pleat at the center front. Stitch a ¼" seam at the top edge to hold the pleat in place.
* Stitch a ¼" double-fold hem along the top straight edge of the dress, topstitching close to the folded edge.
* With right sides together, align the center back raw edges and stitch together. Press seam allowance open.

⑥ Attach the Halter Strap

* With right sides together, pin the raw edge of the elastic casing to the top raw edge of the dress, matching center back seams. The fully finished portion of the halter strap will not be attached to the dress; it becomes the neck strap. Evenly distribute the gathers as you pin the pieces together. Stitch the halter casing and dress together, pulling the dress taut so it does not gather (the only gathers should be in the halter strap).
* Trim the raw edges to ¼" and finish with a zigzag or overcast stitch. (Once the dress is on, it may be necessary to further adjust the elastic within the casing until the dress fits the child properly.)
* Gently press the gathered halter strap up, away from the dress.

⑦ Hem the Dress

Stitch a ¼" double-fold hem at the bottom edge of the dress.

RUFFLED ROMPER

Designed by Caroline Critchfield

You've likely encountered the fun stretch knit fabric featuring horizontal ruffles, but wondered what to make with it outside of flirty lingerie. Well look no further. Perfect for photo shoots, dressing up, or just play, this little romper is sure to capture everyone's attention and steal the show!

MATERIALS

* Pattern piece (1), *see* sheet 4
* 1 yard of ruffle-knit fabric (this is typically found in a standard 50" width)
* 1 spool of coordinating thread
* 1 yard of ½"-wide single-fold bias tape
* 1½–2 yards of 2"-wide ribbon for shoulder straps
* Fray Check (optional)

Sizes – 12 months, 18 months, 2T, 3T/4T, 5/6, 7/8

Seam allowance – ½" unless otherwise specified

❶ Determine Your Child's Size

Measure your child's chest to find the right size.

	12 mo	18 mo	2T	3T/4T	5/6	7/8
Chest	18"	19"	21"	22"–23"	24"–25"	25¾"–26½"

❷ Square Up the Ruffle Fabric

Four-way-stretch ruffle-knit fabric has characteristics different from other knits and requires special handling. Most importantly, do not press this fabric with an iron, as you run the risk of scorching and/or crushing your ruffles. Square up the cut edge of the fabric as follows:

* Shake out the fabric to determine which way the ruffles should lie. Smooth the ruffles in the appropriate direction. Notice that there is an opaque stripe and a much more transparent stripe directly under each row of ruffle.
* Square up the cut edge of your fabric by trimming along the width of the fabric just above an opaque stripe, so the cut edge of the fabric begins with an opaque stripe followed by the first ruffle (see page 118).

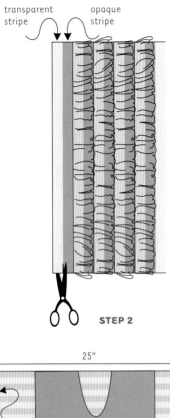

transparent stripe

opaque stripe

STEP 2

25"

fold

ROMPER

36"

selvages

CUTTING LAYOUT

③ Measure, Mark, and Cut

Fold your fabric in half lengthwise with the right sides together and the selvages aligned. Holding the selvages together, gently shake your fabric to align all the ruffles in the correct direction, then place the folded fabric on a cutting surface. Position the pattern piece according to the layout, with the top edge of the pattern piece along the squared edge of your ruffle fabric. Cut out the piece and transfer the markings from the pattern to the wrong side of the fabric.

  ✳ **Romper** (cut 2)

④ Prepare the Romper Pieces

To ensure that the ruffles will lie in the correct direction when you stitch the seams of the romper, it is necessary to secure them in place. To do so, simply machine- or hand-baste a ¼" seam allowance along the edges of the romper pieces in the direction of the ruffles.

⑤ Stitch the Front and Back Seams

  ✳ With rights sides together, align all raw edges of the romper pieces. Take extra care to ensure that the individual rows of ruffles align at the seams. Pin pieces together along center front, matching single notches, and along center back, matching double notches.

  ✳ Stitch the center front seam, taking time to double check that the ruffles align as you sew. Stitch again along the curve of the crotch seam at a ¼" seam allowance to reinforce the seam. Repeat to stitch the center back seam.

⑥ Stitch the Inseam and Finish the Leg Openings

  ✳ With right sides together and raw edges aligned, line up the center front and center back seams. Stitch along the leg inseam, again double-checking that the ruffles align as you sew.

  ✳ Turn the romper right side out to make sure that the bottom ruffles on both leg openings match. In the event that the ruffles do not line up or something else looks odd, simply trim off the lowest, unwanted ruffles. There is no need to hem the leg openings, as the cut edge will not fray. Simply trim away the striped fabric underneath the lowermost ruffles, taking care not to cut into the ruffles.

⑦ Finish the Armholes

* Unfold one edge of the single-fold bias tape and, with right sides together, align the raw edge of the bias tape with the raw edge of the armhole. Pin the bias tape in place along the entire armhole and trim off the extra bias tape.

* Stitch in the bias tape crease closest to the raw edges. Again, take your time to ensure that the ruffles are lying in the correct direction.

* Turn the bias trim to the inside of the romper, finger-press, pin in place, and stitch from the inside of the romper. Repeat for the second armhole.

⑧ Make the Shoulder Strap Casing

* Fold the top front edge of the romper 1½" to the wrong side to create a casing. Pin in place, lifting up the ruffle that would fall within the stitching line so it does not get pinned in place. You will need to do this separately on both sides of the center seam.

* From the right side of the romper, carefully stitch the casing in place, continuing to hold the ruffle out of the way so that it does not get caught in the stitching line. Stop and start the stitching on both sides of the center seam and as close as possible to the armhole stitching, backstitching to lock your stitches. Repeat for the back casing.

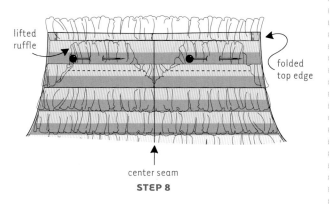

lifted ruffle

folded top edge

center seam

STEP 8

⑨ Cut and Insert the Ribbon

* Cut a length of ribbon according to the following chart:

	12 mo	18 mo	2T	3T/4T	5/6	7/8
Ribbon	45"	50"	55"	60"	65"	70"

* Insert the ribbon through the front and back casings, and tie over one shoulder. You may apply Fray Check to the ends of the ribbon, or melt the ends with the flame from a lighter to prevent fraying.

SWING DRESS

Designed by Georgia Solorzano

This dress is easy, fun, and carefree, especially because it is made out of a comfy knit fabric! It's kind of like your girl's favorite T-shirt, but lengthened into a dress. The subtle pintucks, button embellishment, and appliquéd flower are the perfect finishing touches to this soon-to-be fave.

MATERIALS

* Pattern pieces (3), *see* sheet 5
* 1 yard of 54/60" knit fabric
* 1 spool of coordinating thread
* 2 buttons, ½" in diameter*

Sizes – 12 months, 18 months, 2T/3T, 4/5, 6/7, 8/9, 10

Seam allowance – ½" unless otherwise specified

FABRIC NOTE: *Sizes 12 months to 6/7 will fit on 44/45" fabric, if you find a knit you like in that width.*

*Sample shows 4 buttons, two that are ½" in diameter and two that are ¾" in diameter, stacked together for depth.

❶ Determine Your Child's Size

Measure your child's chest to find the right size.

	12 mo	18 mo	2T/3T	4/5	6/7	8/9	10
Chest	18"	19"	21"-22"	23"-24"	25"-25¾"	26½"-27¼"	28"

❷ Measure, Mark, and Cut

Place your fabric in a single layer with the right side facing up. Fold over both selvage edges to meet in the center (11" for 44/45" fabric; 13½" for 54" fabric; 15" for 60" fabric). Position the pattern pieces according to the layout and measure and mark the additional binding pieces. Cut out the pieces and transfer the markings from the patterns onto the wrong side of the fabric.

* **Dress front** (cut 1 on fold)   * **Flower** (cut 1)*
* **Dress back** (cut 1 on fold)

	12 mo	18 mo	2T/3T	4/5	6/7	8/9	10
Neck Binding (cut 1)*	1½" × 13¼"	1½" × 13½"	1½" × 13¾"	1½" × 14"	1½" × 14"	1½" × 14¼"	1½" × 15¾"
Armhole Binding (cut 2)	1½" × 6¾"	1½" × 7¼"	1½" × 7¾"	1½" × 8"	1½" × 8"	1½" × 8½"	1½" × 9"

Open up your fabric and cut the neck binding and flower last, as they only need to be cut from a single layer of fabric.

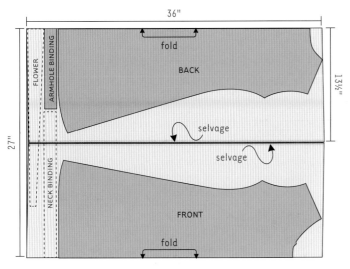

CUTTING LAYOUT

❸ Make the Front Pintucks

On the front piece, fold the fabric with the wrong sides together, aligning and pinning the first set of pintuck lines as marked on the pattern (four pintucks total). Stitch along the lines, then press away from center front. Repeat for 3 more pintucks. Stitch the pintucks in place using a ¼" seam allowance along the neck edge. Hand-sew two buttons at center front, centered between the pintucks.

❹ Attach the Front and Back

Pin the front and back dress pieces with right sides together. Stitch the shoulder seams and side seams. Reinforce all seams by stitching again at a ¼" seam allowance. Press all seams toward the back of the dress.

❺ Bind the Neck Edge

* With right sides together, stitch the short ends of the neck binding to form a circle. Press the seam open.
* Mark the binding strip in fourths. Pin the neck binding along the neck edge with right sides together, matching the marks on the binding with the shoulder seams, center front,

and center back. Stitch the binding to the neck edge.

* Press the binding up and over the seam allowance to the inside of the dress. Pin the binding in place so that the loose edge covers the seam allowance inside the dress.

* From the right side, edgestitch close to the seam, catching the loose binding edge in the stitching. Because knits do not unravel, the inside raw edge does not need to be clean-finished (see Binding with Knit Fabric on page 13).

6 Bind the Armholes

* With right sides together, stitch the short ends of each armhole binding to form a circle. Press the seams open.

* Mark the binding strip in halves. Position each binding along the armhole edges with the right sides together, matching the marks on the binding with the shoulder and side seam. Stitch the binding to the dress, following the instructions in the previous step.

7 Hem the Dress

Stitch a ½" double-fold hem at the bottom edge of the dress, pressing under ½" then another ½". Topstitch close to the folded edge.

8 Make the Fabric Flower

* Use a basting stitch to gather the long, straight, nonangled edge of the flower. Pull the threads to gather the flower.

* Make a spiral with the fabric flower, placing the wider 2" end on the bottom, while the shorter ¾" end will spiral into the center of the flower.

* Hand-sew along the basting line, through all thicknesses, to hold the shape of the flower. Leave 1½" of the center length unstitched. Carefully position the 1½" to conceal the stitching, and hand-tack in place.

* Hand-sew or machine-stitch the flower onto the dress at your desired location. Please note that for the smaller sizes (or for a child who is more likely to pull on the flower), take extra care to ensure that the flower is very securely attached to the dress.

LUCY-CATE SMOCKED BISHOP DRESS

Designed by Maggie Bunch

This future heirloom features neck and sleeve smocking, both signatures of bishop dress detailing. The subtle smocking changes color from top to bottom, making this piece very unique. This is an excellent simple smocking design, perfect for a beginner. By the time you have finished the dress, you will have mastered two basic smocking stitches and created a keepsake to treasure for years to come.

MATERIALS

* Armhole template pattern (1), *see* sheet 2
* 1 yard of 44/45" quilting-weight cotton
* Spool of coordinating thread
* Washable ink fabric pen with a fine point
* Spool of contrast quilting thread
* Embroidery floss in three shades (light, medium, and dark)
* 3 clear nylon snaps, ¼"-wide

Size – 2T/3T

Seam allowance – ½" unless otherwise specified

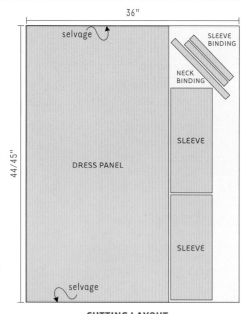

CUTTING LAYOUT

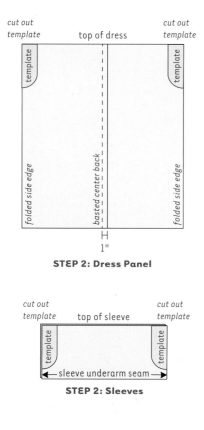

STEP 2: Dress Panel

STEP 2: Sleeves

❶ Measure, Mark, and Cut

Lay out your fabric in a single layer with the wrong side facing up. Measure, mark, and cut out the following pieces, squaring off your fabric as neatly and evenly as possible.

* **Dress panel** 24" × 44" (cut 1) (leave the selvage on the fabric)
* **Sleeves** 7" × 17" (cut 2)
* **Neck binding** 1" × 13" (cut 1 on bias)
* **Sleeve binding** 1" × 9½" (cut 2 on bias)

❷ Cut the Armhole Shapes

* With right sides together, align the short edges of the dress panel and baste with a 1" seam allowance; this seam marks the center back of the dress. Lay the dress panel down with the back seam centered on one layer. Lightly finger-press the folded sides.
* Position the folded armhole template on the dress panel, first on one side and then the other, as shown; trace the template and cut through both layers. Remove basting along center back.
* Position both sleeve pieces with right sides together, aligning all edges. Position the template as shown, trace, and cut through both pieces.

❸ Sew the Sleeves

* Use a basting gathering stitch along the bottom raw edges of the sleeves at a ¼" seam allowance, starting and stopping 1½" from each edge and secure tail ends of threads for a later step.
* To make a French seam (see glossary, page 341), fold one sleeve piece in half with wrong sides together, aligning raw edges. Stitch the underarm seam at a scant ¼" seam allowance. Turn pieces wrong side out (with the right sides together) at the underarm and stitch another ¼" seam to enclose the raw edges. Press the seam allowance to one side. Repeat with the second sleeve.
* With right sides together, pin a sleeve to the dress at the arm curve opening, matching top edges and the underarm seam of the sleeve with the side creased edge of the dress. Stitch together and trim the seam allowance slightly. Finish the raw edge of the seam allowance with a narrow zigzag stitch. Repeat to attach the second sleeve.

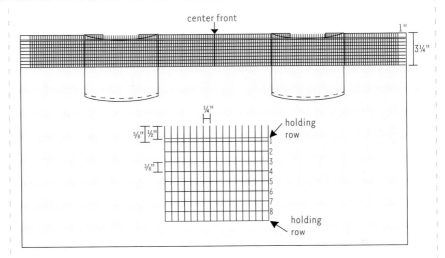

STEP 4: Mark the Pleat Lines

❹ Mark the Pleats

* Using a fine-tipped washable fabric pen and clear ruler, mark a 3¼"-long vertical line at the center front of the dress on the wrong side of the fabric.

* To mark the horizontal smocking rows, mark the first horizontal line ½" from the top edge (this is the holding row), perpendicular to the line previously marked. Mark a second horizontal line ⅝" from the top edge of the dress (this will be the first row of smocking). These continuous horizontal lines must be drawn across the dress front, back, and sleeves. Continue marking eight additional horizontal lines spaced ⅜" apart. (The last row will be a holding row).

* Mark vertical spacing lines ¼" apart on both sides of the center line previously drawn. These lines should be 3¼" long and perpendicular to the horizontal rows. Do not mark vertical lines 1" from the back selvage edges.

❺ Gather the Pleats

Thread a sharp hand-sewing needle with contrast quilting thread at least 105" long. Do not knot the thread.

* Working from the wrong side of the fabric, make very small, consistently sized stitches along the first marked horizontal line (the first holding row) at each intersection of a vertical and horizontal line.

* Repeat this technique using a new piece of thread for each of the 10 marked horizontal rows, leaving the ends of the thread unknotted. These threads will be used as guidelines for smocking, and will be removed in a later step.

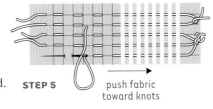

STEP 5 push fabric toward knots

* Along one side of the dress, knot the threads in pairs. On the opposite side, grasp the loose threads with one hand and push the fabric toward the knotted end, carefully pleating the fabric along these threads. Use your fingers to gently smooth the folds of the fabric until the pleats looks neat and uniform. When the pleated width of the fabric is 12" (not including the 1" non-pleated edges), knot the loose ends of the threads in pairs. Trim the threads.

⑥ Prepare the Embroidery Floss

Cut 40" lengths of floss from each of the three shades of embroidery floss and separate threads to create the following thread color combinations:

* Row 1 – 3 strands light floss
* Row 2 – 2 strands light floss, 1 strand medium floss
* Row 3 – 1 strand light floss, 2 strands medium floss
* Row 4 – 3 strands medium floss
* Row 5 – 2 strands medium floss, 1 strand dark floss
* Row 6 – 1 strand medium floss, 2 strands dark floss
* Row 7 – 3 strands dark floss

HINT: *If you have extra needles on hand, you may find it easier to thread seven needles with the different color combinations, keeping them in sequence. This will aid in the smocking process. While smocking, frequently untwist the floss so that the different colors will be most visible.*

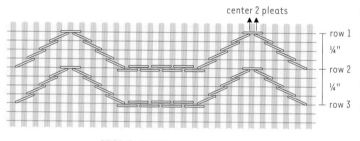

center 2 pleats

row 1

¼"

row 2

¼"

row 3

STEP 7: SMOCKING SCHEMATIC

⑦ Smock the Dress

For this dress, you will smock using the same motif repeat for all seven rows. To begin, using a needle with Row 1 threads, pull the needle to the right side of the dress at Row 1 center front (skip the holding row), and position the threads so that half of the floss is in use on the front of the dress, while the other half of the embroidery floss hangs unknotted on the wrong side of the dress. This will help keep your threads from knotting.

* Begin smocking on Row 1 at the center 2 pleats with a cable stitch (see Basic Smocking Tutorial on facing page).

Then begin the repeat pattern:

* Trellis for four stitches down to Row 2.
* Cable seven stitches along Row 2.
* Trellis for four stitches up to Row 1.
* Cable one stitch on Row 1.

Continue to follow this pattern until you reach the end of the pleated section, ending each smocked row with the same trellis portion of the pattern. Leave 1" unstitched at the center back of the dress, knotting the floss on the back of the dress.

Return to the center-front cable stitch. Unstitch this cable stitch, turn the work upside down, rework cable stitch and smock to the other edge in the same fashion, following the pattern above. Unstitching and re-stitching the center front cable will help keep a knot from forming behind the center front.

Continue to follow the schematic for the order and combination of stitches used on this dress, always beginning at the center front with cable stitch, smocking across the front, sleeve, and back, and ending each row with the same trellis portion of the pattern. Use the appropriate strands of embroidery floss as they correspond to each row, in sequence. Do not smock along the last pleating thread row, as this is a holding row intended to stabilize your smocking.

When you have completed the smocking pattern, baste ¼" from the top edge, across the entire width of the smocking; this helps hold the pleats in place when adding binding in a later step.

BASIC SMOCKING TUTORIAL

Cable stitch. This is a tight embroidery stitch worked in double rows that joins alternating columns of gathers, creating single pleats. It is a great foundation stitch to hold individual pleats in place.

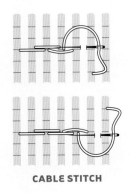

CABLE STITCH

Trellis stitch. This stitch pattern alternately employs loose diagonal stitches and holds sections of pleats together. In the case of this project, 4 stitches are worked diagonally to create each side of the trellis, connecting 2 rows of pleating lines. When working the up side, always keeping the thread below needle; when working the down side, always keep the thread above the needle.

TRELLIS STITCH

⑧ Make the Back Placket

* With right sides together, sew the center-back seam from the bottom edge of the dress with a 1" seam allowance, stopping 7" below the top edge.

* With the dress wrong side out, clip the right-hand side of the seam allowance at the 7" mark to, but not through, the stitching line. Press the bottom portion of the seam allowance open. Press the top right 7" to the wrong side by ½", then press both sides of the top 7" toward the left back. This will give you an overlap in the open area for attaching snaps in step 11.

* Fold the top of the right-back seam allowance at a 45-degree angle and machine-stitch through seam allowance to hold the fold in place. Stitch across the bottom folded edge of placket through all layers to secure.

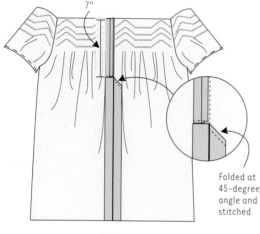

7"

Folded at
45-degree
angle and
stitched

STEP 8

⑨ Bind the Neck Edge

Press the short ends of the neck bias strip ¼" to the wrong side, then make double-fold binding and bind the neckline (see page 12).

⑩ Bind the Sleeve Openings

* With right sides together, stitch the short ends of each armhole binding strip to form a circle. Press the seams open. Make the strip into double-fold binding as above.

* Mark the binding strip in halves and position along the sleeve edges with the right sides together, matching the seam of the binding with the underarm seam. Pull the gathering threads at the bottom edge of the sleeve until its circumference matches that of the binding. Distribute gathers evenly and pin pieces together. Stitch the binding in place, to fully encase the raw edge at the sleeve opening.

⑪ Finish the Dress

* Press the bottom edge of the dress 2" to the wrong side, then fold and press an additional 2". Stitch along the bottom folded edge of the dress using a ½" seam allowance. Unfold the hem, press, and tuck downward.

* Hand-sew three nylon snaps, evenly spaced in the smocked portion of the center-back placket.

* Carefully remove the contrast quilting thread from pleating rows.

RUTHIE BORDER PRINT DRESS & TOTE

Designed by Laura Bednash

This is the perfect project to maximize the visual impact of your favorite border print fabric. The pattern pieces are cut in such a way to make it look as though multiple fabrics have been used. The dress itself has a sweet, feminine bodice without a complicated closure. In fact, there is even adjustable elastic at the waist, allowing the dress a longer life span. There is just enough fabric left over to make a coordinating tote to complete the look. And although we used a border-printed fabric, this dress would be just as beautiful using one fabric, or even three different fabrics for the bodice, empire waistband, and skirt. Have fun with it!

MATERIALS

* ✳ Pattern piece (1), *see* sheet 4
* ✳ 1 yard of 44/45" border print fabric (the border will run along the selvage); home dec weight was used for this project
* ✳ 1 spool of coordinating thread
* ✳ 1¼ yards of ¼"–½"-wide double-fold bias tape
* ✳ ½ yard of buttonhole elastic
* ✳ 4 buttons, ⅝" in diameter
* ✳ 2 yards of 1"-wide webbing (for tote)
* ✳ Safety pins

Sizes – 2T/3T, 4/5, 6/7, 8/9

Finished dimensions of tote –
   7" tall × 13" wide × 3" deep

Seam allowance – ½" unless otherwise specified

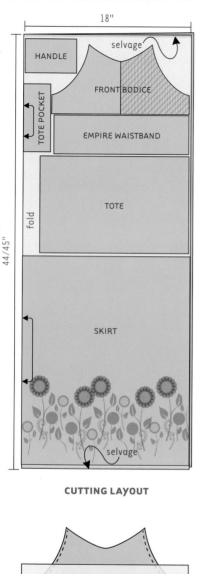

CUTTING LAYOUT

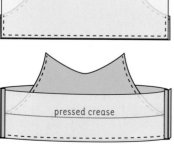

STEP 1

① Determine Your Child's Size

Measure your child's chest to find the right size.

	2T/3T	4/5	6/7	8/9
Chest	21"-22"	23"-24"	25"-25¾"	26½"-27¼"

② Measure, Mark, and Cut

Fold your fabric in half crosswise, with the right sides together and the raw edges aligned. Position the pattern piece according to the layout, and measure and mark the additional pieces as listed. Cut out the pieces and transfer markings from the pattern to the wrong side of the fabric. Separate the pieces by project.

For the Dress:

* **Front bodice** (cut 2)

NOTE: *Mirror the pattern piece along the line indicated on the pattern.*

	2T/3T	4/5	6/7	8/9
Empire waistband (cut 2)	4" × 12¾"	4" × 13½"	4" × 14"	4" × 14½"
Skirt (cut 1 on fold)	15½" × 36"	17½" × 36"	19½" × 36"	21½" × 36"

For the Tote:

* **Tote** 10" × 16" (cut 2)
* **Tote pocket** 7" × 6" (cut 1 on fold)
* **Tote handle** 3½" × 5½" (cut 2)

Dress

① Assemble the Front Bodice and Empire Waistband

* With right sides together, align the raw edges of the front bodice pieces. Stitch together along the three curved edges. Notch seam allowance, clip corners, turn right side out, and press. Edgestitch along finished armhole edges.
* With right sides together, center the bottom raw edge of the front bodice on a long raw edge of a waistband piece and stitch together along the bottom and side edges as shown.
* With right sides together, align the short ends of the waistband pieces, sandwiching the front bodice in between. Stitch the short ends together, forming a tube. Press these side seams open. Fold the waistband in half lengthwise with wrong sides together, aligning the bottom raw edges. Press a crease and unfold the waistband.

* Topstitch a 1" long × ¾" wide rectangle centered over both side seams, ⅝" up from the bottom edge. The stitches in the side seam within this rectangle will be picked open in a later step to insert the buttonhole elastic.

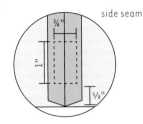

* Using a washable ink fabric marker, mark the halfway and quarter points along the top edge of the skirt. Use a basting stitch to gather the top raw edge of the skirt.
* With both wrong sides facing out, insert the skirt inside the bodice and waistband. Pin the top raw edge of the skirt to the bodice front and waistband, aligning center front, center back, and side seams with marks. Adjust the gathers so that they are evenly distributed between the four marks. Stitch together and press the seam allowance, bodice, and waistband up, away from the skirt.
* Fold the waistband in half with wrong sides together along the fold line pressed in the previous step. Fold the raw edge of the waistband ½" to the wrong side so that it covers the seam allowance. Pin in place and edgestitch from the right side of the waistband along both folded edges. Note that the front waistband will cover the bottom 1½" of the bodice, and will be stitched to the bodice.

② Make and Attach the Skirt

* Fold the skirt in half with the right sides together, aligning the shorter ends. Stitch together and press seam allowance open. This seam becomes the center back of the skirt.
* Stitch a double-fold hem at the bottom edge of the skirt, first pressing under ¼", then another 1". Topstitch close to the folded edge.

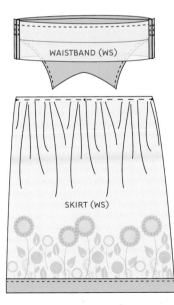

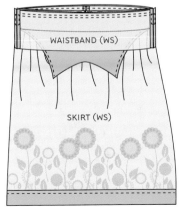

STEP 2

③ Attach the Bias Tape

Cut a 38" piece of bias tape. Open up the short ends and press ½" to the wrong side; refold. Find the halfway point of the bias tape and pin it in place at the center-front top edge of the bodice, encasing the raw edge. Continue pinning the bias tape in place along the top front edge, fully encasing the finished neck edge of the bodice between the folds of the bias tape. The ends will extend off the dress to form the neck ties. Edgestitch the bias tape to the dress, and continue sewing the entire length of the tape, stitching the edges closed.

④ Insert the Buttonhole Elastic

* Using a seam ripper, on the wrong side of the dress, carefully open the waistband side-seam stitches that fall within the 1" rectangles stitched in step 1.
* Thread the buttonhole elastic through these openings into the back waistband only. Secure the ends of the elastic with safety pins.
* Hand-sew two buttons on the inside of the front bodice next to the side-seam waistband openings. Take care that your stitches do not show on the front of the dress.
* Remove safety pins and secure buttonhole elastic to these buttons, adjusting the elastic as necessary for your little girl.

Tote

① Attach the Pocket

* Encase the top (6") edge of the pocket with the remaining double-fold bias tape. Trim the ends of bias tape even with the raw edges of the pocket, if necessary.
* With both right sides facing up, center the pocket on one tote piece, aligning the bottom raw edges. Baste in place using a ¼" seam allowance along the pocket's three unfinished edges. This is the tote front.

② Make and Attach the Straps

* Cut the webbing into two 36" pieces. Find the center points and mark them.
* Press the short ends of the tote handle pieces ½" to the wrong side. Fold the handle pieces in half, with wrong sides together and raw edges aligned, and press. Open the handles, and press the raw 5½" edges ½" to the wrong side. Refold on the original center fold lines.

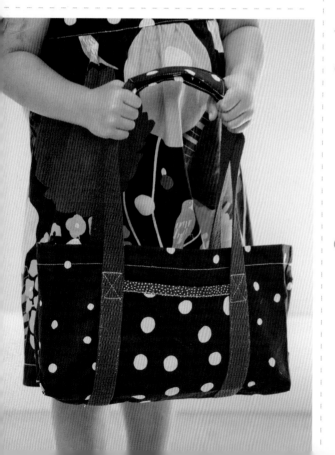

* Sandwich one 18" webbing between the folds of one handle, aligning the center of the webbing with the center of the handle. Pin the webbing and handle together and edgestitch around all four sides of the handle. Repeat with the second piece of webbing and handle.
* Place the tote front on a work surface with the right side facing up. Align the cut ends of the webbing with the bottom edge, 4½" from the sides of the tote (covering the raw pocket edges on the front piece), taking care not to twist the webbing. Edgestitch in place, stopping 2½" below the top edge of the tote and making a box stitch (see glossary, page 340).
* Repeat to attach the webbing to the tote back.

❸ Assemble the Tote with French Seams

Position the tote pieces with wrong sides together and stitch the side and bottom edges with a scant ¼" seam allowance. Turn the tote wrong side out, placing right sides together, and stitch the same edges with a ¼" seam allowance to create a French seam (see glossary, page 341). Press the side seams toward the back of the tote (the side without the pocket) and turn right side out.

❹ Make the Bottom Gusset

With wrong sides together, pinch the bottom corners of the tote, aligning the bottom and side seams. Stitch across the corner, 1½" from the end point of the fold. Fold up the two lower corners and invisibly hand-sew them in place. Sew a button over each gusset flap to finish.

❺ Hem the Tote

Stitch a double-fold hem at the top edge of the tote, first pressing under ¼", then another 1". Topstitch close to the folded edge, keeping the handles out of the stitching line. You may also choose to press creases along the side and bottom edges of the bag to create the illusion of more structure.

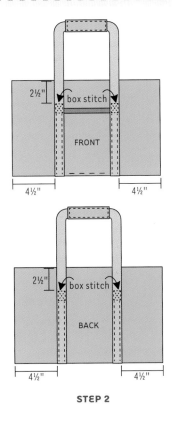

STEP 2

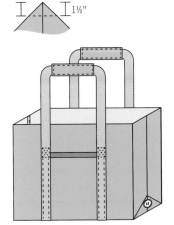

STEP 4

Fun in the sun(dress)

Designed by Katy Dill

This delightful, summer-inspired, shirred dress is quick and easy to make, not to mention incredibly comfortable. You may choose to keep your fabric simple and emphasize the elegant shirring by using a solid color or a dotted-swiss texture. Give the dress a pop of color by using trim for a little contrast in the shoulder straps and binding. Now go have some fun in the sun!

MATERIALS

* 1 yard of 44/45" (sizes 6 and under) or 54"/60" (sizes 7-12) quilting-weight cotton
* 1 spool of coordinating thread
* 1 spool of elastic thread
* ¼"-wide double-fold bias tape: 1¼ yards (sizes 2T-6) or 1½ yards (sizes 7-12)
* ¾ yard of 2"-4"-wide decorative trim for the shoulder straps or ¼ yard contrast fabric for shoulder straps, sizes 7-12 only (see Shoulder Strap Options)

Sizes – 2T, 3T, 4T, 5, 6, 7, 8, 9, 10, 12

Seam allowance – ½" unless otherwise specified

1 Determine Your Child's Size

Measure your child's chest to find the right size.

	2T	3T	4T	5	6	7	8	9	10	12
Chest	21"	22"	23"	24"	25"	25¾"	26½"	27¼"	28"	30"

2 Measure, Mark, and Cut

Fold your fabric in half lengthwise with the right sides together and the selvages aligned. Measure and mark the following pattern pieces directly onto the wrong side of your fabric and cut them out.

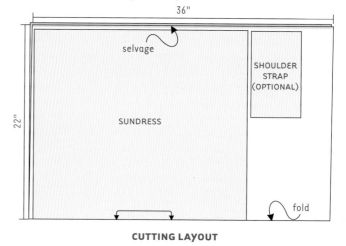

CUTTING LAYOUT

	2T	3T	4T	5	6	7	8	9	10	12
Sundress (cut 1 on fold)	37" × 17½"	39" × 19½"	40" × 21½"	42" × 23½"	44" × 25½"	45" × 27½"	46" × 29½"	48" × 31½"	49" × 33½"	52½" × 35½"
Shoulder Strap (cut 2)	5" × 8½"	5" × 9"	5½" × 9½"	5½" × 9¾"	6" × 10"	6" × 10½"	6" × 11"	6" × 11½"	6" × 12"	6" × 13"
Purchased trim length (cut 2)	8½"	9"	9½"	9¾"	10"	10½"	11"	11½"	12"	13"

Shoulder Strap Options

Purchased trim: If using a purchased trim (as listed in Materials), see the *length* listed in the chart on the facing page to cut your trim to size.

Make-your-own straps: For sizes 2T-6, cut and sew the pieces from your main fabric as listed in the chart. For sizes 7-12, you will need to either use purchased trim, a contrast fabric, or purchase approximately ¼ yard more fabric in order to get the shoulder straps out of your main fabric.

❸ Prepare the Bobbin

Load your bobbin with elastic thread. To do this, manually wind the elastic thread onto your bobbin by hand, giving it a very slight stretch as you wind. Throughout the course of stitching the sundress, you will need to wind more than one bobbin to finish the project.

❹ Mark and Stitch the Shirring Lines

✳ Lay your sundress, right side up, on a flat surface. Use a disappearing fabric pen to mark horizontal lines ½" apart across the width of the sundress. The first line should be marked ¾" below the top edge. Refer to the chart on page 136 to determine the total height of shirring lines from the top edge of the sundress according to size.

* Set your machine to the longest stitch length you have (ideally, something close to a basting stitch). Your elastic thread should be loaded in the bobbin, and the basic coordinating thread to match your fabric loaded in the top of the machine.
* Begin sewing along the marked lines, backstitching at the beginning and end of each stitch line. When you finish stitching (and backstitching) one line of shirring, lift your pressure foot and turn the fabric around to begin sewing in the opposite direction on the next marked line. This minimizes waste of the elastic thread, and also results in fewer threads to clip when you are completely done with the shirring. Be sure to stretch your fabric flat in front of the needle as you sew. Continue in this fashion until all the lines have been stitched.

	2T	3T	4T	5	6	7	8	9	10	12
Height of shirring from top edge of dress	4¼"	4½"	4¾"	5¼"	5¾"	6¼"	7¼"	7¾"	8¼"	8¾"

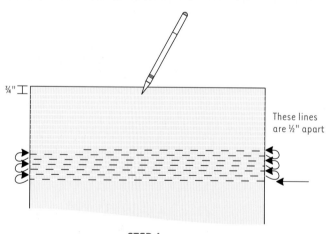

¾"

These lines are ½" apart

STEP 4

* Steam your shirring lines heavily to help shrink up the elastic and make the shirring more pronounced. Applying heat directly on the elastic will damage it, so take care and always press from the right side.

⑤ Stitch the Center Back Seam

Fold the sundress with right sides together, aligning the center back. Pin and stitch the seam. Finish this seam with a zigzag or overcast stitch if desired.

⑥ Finish the Top and Bottom Edges

* Pin the double-fold bias tape along the top edge of the sundress. Overtapping raw ends and folding ½" to the wrong side, stitch in place to fully encase the raw edge.
* Stitch a double-fold hem at the bottom edge of the dress, pressing under ½" then another 1". Topstitch close to the folded edge.

⑦ Make and Attach the Shoulder Straps

* *If making your own strap:* Fold the shoulder-strap pieces in half lengthwise with the right sides together and stitch along the long edge. Turn right side out and press. Edgestitch along both long edges.
* Fold raw edges of the straps or trim ½" to the right side, and press. Position the handmade straps or purchased trim on the wrong side of the sundress, placing the ends ½" below the first row of shirring. Both the front and back straps should be placed approximately 1" from the side edges of the dress. Stitch in place, along the first row of shirring.

Racerback sundress

Designed by Lorraine Teigland

This knit sundress is reminiscent of those you are likely to see in beach resorts — super comfortable and cool. You'll love that these shoulder straps will stay on your girl's shoulders and never slip off. This racerback dress will soon become a favorite, and you'll get requests to make a second and a third before the first one even wears out.

MATERIALS

* ✳ Pattern pieces (3), *see* sheet 4
* ✳ 1 yard of 44/45" knit fabric
* ✳ 1 spool of coordinating thread
* ✳ 2 yards of ½"-wide rickrack
* ✳ ¾ yard of ⅜"-wide clear elastic

Sizes – 3T/4T, 5/6, 7/8

Seam allowance – ½" unless otherwise specified

① Determine Your Child's Size

Measure your child's chest to find the right size.

	3T/4T	5/6	7/8
Chest	22"-23"	24"-25"	25¾"-26½"

② Measure, Mark, and Cut

Place your fabric in a single layer with the wrong side facing up. Position the pattern pieces according to the layout, and measure and mark the additional pieces as listed. Cut out the pieces and transfer the markings from the patterns to the wrong side of the fabric.

* ✳ **Front bodice** (cut 1)
* ✳ **Back bodice** (cut 1)
* ✳ **Pocket** (cut 2)
* ✳ **Pocket binding** 1½" × 10" (cut 2)
* ✳ **Neck and armhole binding** 1½" × 44"(cut 1)

	3T/4T	5/6	7/8
Shoulder Strap (cut 1)	4" × 13½"	4" × 15"	4" × 17"
Skirt (cut 1)	17" × 40"	18" × 42"	20" × 44"
Clear Elastic (cut 1)	23"	24"	26"

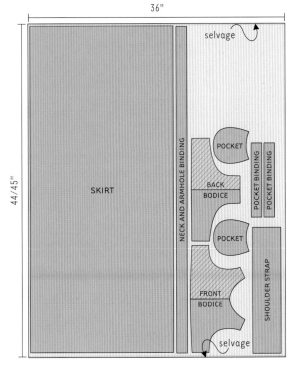

CUTTING LAYOUT

NOTE: *Mirror the pattern pieces along the line indicated on the pattern.*

❸ Bind the Neck and Armhole Edges

* Fold and press the neck and armhole binding as you would to make double-fold bias tape (see page 12). Open up the 44" piece of binding, and with the front bodice and binding, wrong sides facing up, pin the strip along the front neck edge, from shoulder to shoulder. Trim excess binding to save for the armholes. Stitch the binding strip to the neck edge using a ⅜" seam allowance. Press the binding up and over the edge of the front neckline to the right side of the front bodice.

* Before stitching the front neck binding in place, insert a piece of rickrack in between the binding and the dress, leaving half of the rickrack exposed. From the right side of the front bodice, stitch the binding and rickrack in place.

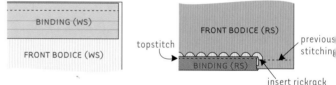

* Position the front and back bodice pieces with right sides together, aligning the side seam edges. Stitch the side seams and press seam allowance open.

* Use the remainder of the binding to bind the front and back armhole edges, following the same steps as above but omitting the rickrack.

* Fold the top edge of the back bodice ¼" to the wrong side, then another 1", and press. Topstitch close to the folded edge.

❹ Attach the Shoulder Strap

* Fold the shoulder strap in half lengthwise with right sides together, aligning raw edges. Stitch along the long edge. Turn right side out. Position the seam in the center of one side of the strap and press. Press the short ends ¼" to the right side (the side without the center seam).

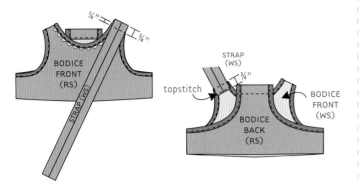

* Position one front bodice shoulder and one short end of the shoulder strap with right sides together. Stitch these together with a ¾" seam allowance on the strap and a ¼" seam allowance on the front bodice.

* Press the strap up, away from the bodice. On the wrong side, topstitch the ¾" strap seam allowance over the seam, close to the folded end.

* Slide the shoulder strap through the channel at the top center back of the back bodice. Attach the other end of the shoulder strap to the front bodice as above, making sure the strap is not twisted.

5 Make and Attach Skirt

* Fold the skirt in half with the right sides together, aligning the shorter ends. Stitch together and press seam allowance open. This becomes a side seam of the skirt.

* Stitch a double-fold hem at the bottom edge of the skirt, first pressing under ¼", then another 1". Topstitch close to the folded edge.

* Using a washable fabric marker, mark the halfway and quarter points along the top edge of the skirt and the bottom edge of the bodice. Use a basting stitch to gather the top edge of the skirt.

* With right sides together, pin the bottom edge of the bodice to the top edge of the skirt, matching the marks with the center front, center back, and side seams. Evenly distribute the gathers between the four points. Stitch together.

* Make quarter marks along your length of clear elastic. Pin the elastic to the waistline seam allowance, matching the quarter marks with center front, back, and both side seams. Stitch the elastic to the seam allowance (you should not see this from the right side of the dress) using a zigzag stitch, stretching the elastic to fit as needed. You should not stretch the fabric at all in this step, only the elastic. The elastic will help the dress maintain its shape at the waist.

6 Finish the Dress

* Bind the top edges of the pockets as described in step 3, inserting rickrack in between the binding and the pocket pieces. Press the side and bottom curved edges of the pockets ½" to the wrong side.

* Position pockets on the front of the skirt approximately 6½" below the waist seam and 4½" from center front. Edgestitch pockets in place, leaving the bound edge unstitched.

* On the right side of the skirt, pin rickrack trim along the hem stitching line and topstitch.

CHAPTER 8

accessories

- -

COMPLEMENT YOUR LITTLE ONE'S LOOK with a stylish fashion accessory. In this chapter, you'll find those that are carried (such as wallets and backpacks) as well as those that are worn (such as hats, shoes, and belts). Most are suitable both for smartly dressed girls and dapper boys.

simple sunbonnet & Anabelle Baby sandals

Simple Sunbonnet designed by Halee Schlangen
Anabelle Baby Sandals designed by Sue Kim

This simple sunbonnet and pretty little sandals are the perfect must-haves for your baby this summer. Whether in the stroller, on the beach, or at a picnic, the bonnet provides some shade from the summer sun, while the sandals allow circulating air to keep baby's feet cool. Have fun making these items. You'll find that using two fabrics creates a reversible bonnet, adding even more visual interest!

MATERIALS

* Pattern pieces (4 for bonnet, 2* for sandals), *see* sheet 4
* 1 yard of 44/45" home dec-weight fabric
* ¼ yard of medium-weight fusible interfacing
* 1 spool of coordinating thread
* 3 snaps (size 16), or Velcro (for bonnet)
* 2" piece of ½"-wide Velcro (for sandals)

Sizes – Bonnet is XS, S, M, L, and the sandals are 0-3 months, 3-6 months, 6-9 months, 9-12 months, 12-18 months, and 18-24 months

* Different sandal patterns for different sizes

Seam allowance – ½" for the bonnet and ¼" for the sandals, unless otherwise specified

① Determine Your Child's Size

Measure your child's head and foot length to find the right size. For the head measurement, start ½" below one ear and measure across the top of the head to ½" below the opposite ear.

For the Bonnet	XS	S	M	L
Head	14"	15"	16"	17"

For the Sandals	0-3 mo	3-6 mo	6-9 mo	9-12 mo	12-18 mo	18-24 mo
Foot length (heel to toe)	3¾"	4"	4¼"	4½"	4¾"	5"

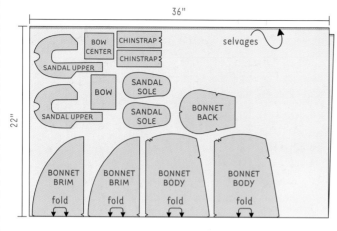

CUTTING LAYOUT

➋ Measure, Mark, and Cut

Fold your fabric in half lengthwise with right sides together, aligning the selvages. Position the pattern pieces according to the layout, measure and mark the additional pieces, and cut them out. Transfer the markings from the pattern pieces to the wrong side of fabric. Separate the pieces by project.

For the Bonnet:
* **Bonnet brim** (cut 2 on fold)
* **Bonnet body** (cut 2 on fold)
* **Bonnet back** (cut 2)
* **Chinstrap** (cut 4)

For the Sandals:
* **Sandal Sole** (cut 4)
* **Sandal Upper** (cut 4)

	0–3 & 3–6 mo	6–9 & 9–12 mo	12–18 & 18–24 mo
Sandal bow (cut 2)	3" × 2½"	3½" × 2¾"	4" × 3"
Sandal bow center (cut 2)	2" × 2½"	2½" × 3"	3" × 3½"

NOTE: *When you cut the sandal uppers on two layers of fabric, one set will automatically be reversed; this is correct for making one left shoe and one right shoe. To help avoid confusion, separate the right and left pieces of the upper when attaching the sole.*

➌ Cut and Apply the Interfacing

Use the pattern pieces to cut the following from fusible interfacing. Following manufacturer's instructions, fuse all the interfacing pieces to their corresponding fabric pieces. The interfaced pieces are the exterior pieces.
* **Bonnet brim** (cut 1 on fold)
* **Sandal sole** (cut 2)
* **Sandal upper** (cut 2; 1 needs to be reversed)

Bonnet

➊ Attach the Bonnet Brim and Body

With the right sides together, match the straight edge of interfaced brim with the front straight edge of one bonnet body piece, aligning center notches and end points. Stitch together. Press seam allowance toward the body and topstitch ⅛" from the seam on the body piece. This is the bonnet exterior. Repeat with the second set of brim and body pieces for lining.

➋ Attach the Bonnet Back

* Use a basting stitch to gather the back raw edge of the body piece between the two dots, as indicated on the pattern piece.
* With right sides together and raw edges even, pin the bonnet back to the gathered raw edge of the body piece, matching center back and notches. Adjust gathers evenly to fit. Stitch in place and press the seam allowance toward the back piece.
* Repeat with second set of brim/body and back pieces for the lining. Turn lining right side out.

❸ Make and Attach the Chinstraps

* Pin two chinstrap pieces with right sides together and stitch along the three unnotched edges. Clip corners, turn right side out, and press. Topstitch along the three finished edges. Repeat to create second chinstrap.

* With right sides together, position chin straps at placement marks on the bonnet exterior. Align raw edges and stitch in place using a ¼" seam allowance.

❹ Finish the Bonnet

* Pin sewn bonnet lining to bonnet exterior with right sides together. Align all raw edges and seams and pin in place. Stitch around the raw edges of the bonnet, leaving an opening as indicated on the bonnet back for turning. Notch the curved seam allowance, clipping to, but not through, your stitching line.

* Turn bonnet right side out through the opening. Press the edges of the bonnet, folding in the seam allowance at the opening. Topstitch around the edge of the bonnet, ⅛" from the seam, closing the opening used for turning as you sew.

* Add snaps to the chinstraps at the placement marks as indicated on the pattern piece (or use Velcro instead).

Sandals

❶ Make the Uppers

* With right sides together, align the raw edges of one interfaced (exterior) upper with the matching non-interfaced upper. Stitch together along edges as illustrated.

* Clip corners and notch the curved seam allowance, taking care not to clip through the stitching line. Turn right side out and press. Edgestitch along all finished edges.

* Repeat to create the second upper.

❷ Attach the Upper to the Sole

Position an upper with the exterior (interfaced) side up and place one non-interfaced sole piece underneath with right side up. Match the marks at the toe as indicated on the pattern piece, and pin in place. Stitch the upper to the sole piece, using a ⅛" seam allowance. Repeat for the second sandal.

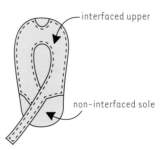

interfaced upper

non-interfaced sole

❸ Stitch the Bottom Sole

* With right sides together, position an exterior (interfaced) sole on a non-interfaced sole, sandwiching the upper in between the two layers. Pin the sole in place taking care to align the toe and heel.

* Stitch around the perimeter of the sole using a ¼" seam allowance and leaving a 2" opening along one side edge for turning. Take care not to catch the heel strap in your stitching line.

* Clip and trim the seam allowance and turn the sandal right side out. Turn the seam allowance at the opening to the inside and slipstitch the opening closed. Neatly edgestitch around the sole, through all layers.

* Repeat for the second sandal.

❹ Attach the Velcro

Cut the Velcro to the finished size shown on the pattern piece. Separate Velcro pieces and stitch the hook side to the strap, and the loop side to the sandal, following the placement marks.

❺ Make and Attach the Bow

* Fold the bow piece in half along the crossgrain with right sides together, aligning all raw edges. Stitch around three sides, leaving a small opening along the long side for turning. Clip corners, turn right side out, and press.

* Using a needle and thread, hand-sew a running stitch in the center of the bow, and slightly gather.

* Fold the bow center piece in half along the crossgrain with right sides together, aligning all raw edges. Stitch along the long edge. Turn right side out, and press.

* With right sides up, wrap the bow center around the bow piece. Hand-sew the short raw ends of the bow center together underneath the bow.

* Hand-tack the bow to the top of the sandal, taking care to secure both ends as well as the center of the bow.

opening for turning

running stitch to gather
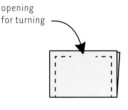

wrap bow center
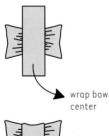

STEP 5

GiRLie unDies & Tank TOP

Girlie Undies designed by Misty Somers

Tank Top designed by Rebecca Yaker

Having a difficult time finding the perfect cute undies? Something with great coverage and quality material that doesn't ride up, chafe, or squeeze? This quest can be near impossible. Well, look no further, as these girlie undies are sure to fit the bill! And why stop with just the undies? Make her the perfect tank top for a day-in, day-out coordinating set!

MATERIALS

* Pattern pieces (3), *see* sheet 5
* 1 yard of 54/60" cotton/spandex knit fabric (preferably jersey)
* ¼ yard of coordinating 54/60" cotton/spandex knit fabric (preferably jersey) for waistband and trim
* 1 spool of coordinating thread

Sizes – 2T/3T, 4/5, 6/7, 8, 10, 12

Seam allowance – ½" unless otherwise specified

❶ Determine Your Child's Size

Measure your child's chest and hip to find the right size.

For the Undies	2T/3T	4/5	6/7	8	10	12
Hip	23"	25"	27"	29"	31"	33"

For the Tank	2T/3T	4/5	6/7	8	10	12
Chest	21"	23"	25"	26½"	28"	30"

❷ Measure, Mark, and Cut

Lay your fabric in a single layer with the right side facing up. Fold over one selvage 7", leaving the remaining 40" of fabric in a single layer. Position the pattern pieces according to the layout and cut them out. Transfer the markings from the pattern pieces to the wrong side of the fabric. Separate the pieces by project.

* **Undies** (cut 1 on fold)
* **Tank front** (cut 1)
* **Tank back** (cut 1)

NOTES: *Mirror the tank pattern pieces along the line indicated on the pattern. The cutting layout is illustrated with size 12. Smaller sizes can be placed more economically.*

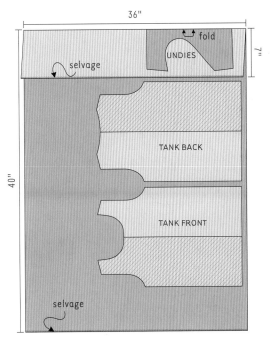

CUTTING LAYOUT

Girlie Undies

❶ Cut the Waistband Pieces

Cut the waistband from the ¼ yard of coordinating knit fabric; cutting crossgrain to maximize the stretch of the fabric.

	2T/3T	4/5	6/7	8	10	12
Waistband (cut 1)	15" × 4"	16" × 4"	17" × 4"	18" × 5"	19" × 5"	20" × 5"

❷ Finish the Leg Openings

Press the leg opening ½" to the wrong side. Topstitch in place using a zigzag or coverstitch.

❸ Stitch the Side Seams

With right sides together, stitch the side seam edges. Trim seam allowance at a 45-degree angle at the leg opening. Press seam allowance open.

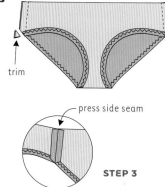

trim

press side seam

STEP 3

❹ Make and Attach the Waistband

* With right sides together, stitch the short ends of the waistband to create a circle. Press the seam open. Fold the waistband in half lengthwise with wrong sides together and press.

* Fold the waistband in half at the seam; this is center back, and the point opposite the seam is center front. Pin the waistband along the top raw edge of the undies with right sides together, matching the waistband seam with center back and the halfway mark with center front.

* Stitch the waistband to the undies, gently stretching the waistband to fit as you sew.

* Press the seam allowance down, toward the undies. From the right side, use a zigzag, stretch stitch, or coverstitch to topstitch along the seam on the undies piece, catching the seam allowance in the stitching.

Tank

❶ Cut the Binding Pieces

Cut the appropriate binding lengths (according to the chart) from the ¼ yard of coordinating knit fabric, cutting cross grain to maximize the stretch of the fabric. See chart on facing page.

❷ Attach the Tank Front and Back

With right sides together, pin the front and back tank pieces together, aligning all raw edges. Stitch together along the shoulder and side seams. Press all seam allowances toward the back piece.

❸ Attach the Armhole Binding

* With right sides together, stitch the short ends of one armhole binding piece together to create a circle. Press the seam open. Repeat with the second armhole binding.

* Mark the binding pieces in half. Pin one binding piece along the armhole edge with right sides together, matching the binding seam with the side seam and the halfway mark with the shoulder seam.

* Stitch the binding to the armhole using a ½" seam allowance, gently stretching the binding to fit the armhole opening as you sew. Press the binding over the edge of the seam allowance to the inside of the tank. Pin the binding to cover the seam allowance (see Binding with Knit Fabric on page 13). From the right side, use a zigzag or coverstitch to stitch close to the folded edge, catching the raw binding edge on the inside of the tank in the stitching.

* Repeat to bind the second armhole.

❹ Attach the Neck Binding

* With right sides together, stitch the short end of the neck binding piece together to create a circle. Press the seam open. Mark the binding piece in half. Pin the binding along the neck edge with right sides together, matching the binding seam with center back and the halfway mark with center front.

* Stitch the binding to the neck edge in the same way as the armhole binding.

❺ Hem the Tank

Press the bottom edge of the tank ¾" to the wrong side and topstitch in place.

CUTTING BINDING PIECES						
	2T/3T	4/5	6/7	8	10	12
Armhole binding (cut 2)	8½" × 1½"	10" × 1½"	11" × 1½"	12" × 1½"	13" × 1½"	14½" × 1½"
Neck binding (cut 1)	13½" × 1½"	14½" × 1½"	15½" × 1½"	16¼" × 1½"	17" × 1½"	18" × 1½"

TANK: STEP 1

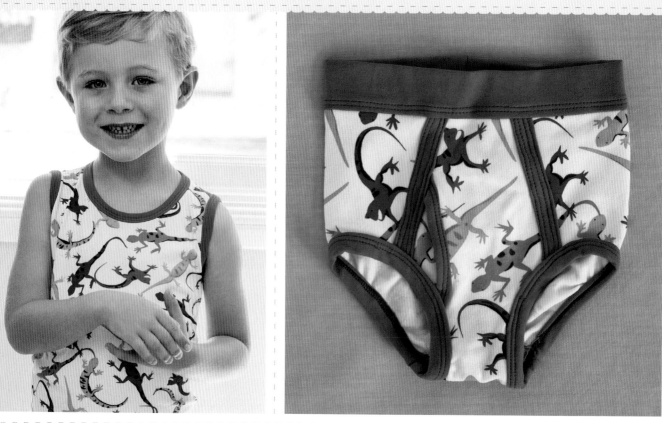

Mister Briefs & Tank Top

Designed by Rebecca Yaker

Can't find briefs that aren't emblazoned with superhero characters? We've definitely noticed this trend. Grab a yard of your favorite knit fabric and get to work creating the perfect brief-and-tank set for the little dude in your life!

MATERIALS

* Pattern pieces (2 for tank), *see* sheet 5; (1 for briefs), *see* sheet 4
* 1 yard of 54/60" cotton/spandex knit fabric (preferably jersey)
* ¼ yard of coordinating 54/60" cotton/spandex knit fabric (preferably jersey) for waistband and trim
* 1 spool of coordinating thread

Sizes – 2T/3T, 4/5, 6/7, 8, 10, 12

Seam allowance – ½" unless otherwise specified

① Determine Your Child's Size

Measure your child's chest and hip to find the right size.

For the Briefs	2T/3T	4/5	6/7	8	10	12
Waist	21"	21½"	22½"	23½"	24½"	25½"

For the Tank	2T/3T	4/5	6/7	8	10	12
Chest	21"	23"	25"	26½"	28"	30"

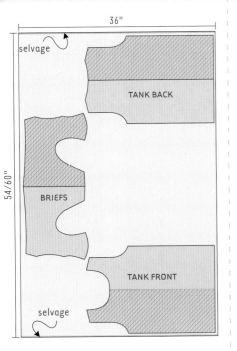

36"

selvage

TANK BACK

BRIEFS

TANK FRONT

selvage

54"/60"

CUTTING LAYOUT

② Measure, Mark, and Cut

Place your fabric in a single layer with the right side facing up. Position the pattern pieces according to the layout and cut them out. Transfer markings from the pattern to the wrong side of the fabric. Separate the pieces by project.

* **Tank front** (cut 1)
* **Tank back** (cut 1)
* **Briefs** (cut 1)

NOTES: *Mirror all pattern pieces along the line indicated on the pattern. Cutting layout is illustrated with size 12. Smaller sizes can be placed more economically.*

Mister Briefs

① Cut the Contrast Fabric Pieces

Cut the following pieces from the ¼ yard of coordinating knit fabric, cutting cross grain to maximize the stretch of the fabric.

	2T/3T	4/5	6/7	8	10	12
Waistband (cut 1)	14½" × 3"	15½" × 3"	16¼" × 3"	17¼" × 3"	18¼" × 3"	19" × 3"
Leg binding (cut 2)	9" × 1½"	10" × 1½"	10¼" × 1½"	10¾" × 1½"	11½" × 1½"	12" × 1½"
Fly binding (cut 2)	3¾" × 1⅛"	4" × 1⅛"	4¼" × 1⅛"	4½" × 1⅛""	4¾" × 1⅛""	5" × 1⅛""
Angled trim (cut 2)	4" × 1"	4¼" × 1"	4¾" × 1"	5" × 1"	5½" × 1"	5¾" × 1"

② Bind the Fly Opening

* With right sides together, pin one fly binding piece along one curved edge of the brief's fly between the marked dots. Stitch in place using a ⅜" seam allowance.
* Press the binding over the edge of the seam allowance to the wrong side of the briefs. Pin the binding to cover the seam allowance on the wrong side (see Binding with Knit Fabric on page 13). From the right side, use a zigzag or coverstitch close to the folded edge, catching the raw binding edge on the wrong side of the brief's in the stitching.
* Repeat with the second fly binding piece and remaining curved edge.

③ Stitch the Crotch Seam

* With wrong sides together, fold over the right front, aligning the raw edges of the right front crotch seam with the back crotch seam. Baste using a ⅜" seam allowance.

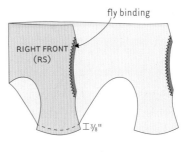

fly binding

RIGHT FRONT (RS)

⅜"

STEPS 2 AND 3

❸ Stitch the Crotch Seam, *continued*

* With right sides together, fold the left front to the back of the briefs, aligning the raw edges of the left-front crotch seam with the back/right-front crotch seam. Stitch through all three layers using a ½" seam allowance. Turn right side out and press seam.

* Align the left and right fronts at center front and baste together through both layers along the top edge. Baste the front leg openings together to secure the fabric layers.

left front folded to the back

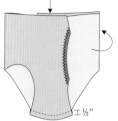
I ½"

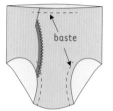
baste

STEP 3

❹ Add the Angled Trim

* Fold and press one angled trim piece to create ½" single-fold bias tape (see page 12). Repeat with the second angled trim piece.

* With both right sides facing up, pin each angled trim piece along the placement lines as indicated on the pattern piece. Topstitch in place along both folded edges through both front layers.

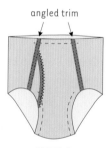
angled trim

STEP 4

❺ Bind the Leg Openings

* With right sides together, stitch the short ends of one leg binding together to create a circle. Press the seam open. Repeat with the second leg binding.

* Mark the binding pieces in half. Pin one binding along the leg opening edge with right sides together, matching the binding seam with the crotch seam and the halfway mark on the binding with the halfway mark as indicated on the pattern piece. Stitch using a ½" seam allowance, gently stretching the binding to fit as you sew, taking care not to stretch the leg opening.

* Press the binding over the edge of the seam allowance to the inside of the briefs to cover the seam allowance inside the briefs (see Binding with Knit Fabric on page 13). From the right side, using a zigzag or coverstitch, stitch close to the folded edge, catching the raw binding edge on the inside of the briefs in the stitching.

* Repeat to bind the second leg opening.

❻ Make and Attach the Waistband

* With right sides together, stitch the short ends of the waistband to create a circle. Press the seam open. Fold the waistband in half lengthwise with wrong sides together and press.

* Mark the waistband in half (the waistband seam is center back, and the point opposite the seam is center front). Pin the waistband along the top raw edge of the briefs with right sides together, matching the waistband seam with center back and the halfway mark with center front.

* Stitch the waistband to the briefs, gently stretching the waistband to fit as you sew.

* Press the seam allowance up, toward the waistband. From the right side, using a zigzag, stretch stitch, or coverstitch, topstitch along the seam on the side of the waistband, catching the seam allowance in the stitching.

Tank

Follow the instructions for the Tank on pages 146–147.

MARY JANE SET

Designed by Sue Kim

Want to look a bit more put-together at home? These indoor shoes will be the footwear of choice for all the ladies of the house, from young to old! They allow you the opportunity to wear shoes that complement your outfit while lounging about or working to keep your house clean. Maintain comfort and style throughout the day! These house shoes are the perfect accessory to give a lift to a casual ensemble. Make coordinating pairs for aunty and niece, mother and daughter, sisters, cousins – the options are endless!

MATERIALS

* Pattern pieces (2 for each of 3 sizes), *see* sheet 5
* 1 yard of 44/45" quilting-weight or home dec-weight fabric
* ¼ yard of nonskid material for use on exterior sole (optional)
* ½ yard of fusible fleece interfacing
* 1 spool of coordinating thread
* 2" piece of ½"-wide Velcro
* 2 decorative buttons, ½"-¾" in diameter (optional)

Sizes – Kids' shoe sizes: 5½-13; Youth shoe sizes: 1-4; Women's shoe sizes: 5-11

Seam allowance – ¼" unless otherwise specified

FABRIC NOTE: *One yard of fabric should be enough for making two pairs of shoes. Instructions and materials list make one pair of shoes. Repeat for additional pairs of Mary Janes in additional sizes.*

❶ Determine Your Shoe Size

Measure foot length, toe to heel, to find the correct size.

Kids (1-5 years)	Size 5½	Size 6	Size 7	Size 8	Size 9	Size 10	Size 11	Size 12	Size 13
Foot length (heel to toe)	5"	5¼"	5½"	5¾"	6¼"	6½"	6¾"	7¼"	7½"

Youth (6-10 years)	Size 1	Size 2	Size 3	Size 4
Foot length (heel to toe)	7¾"	8"	8⅜"	8¾"

Women	Size 5	Size 6	Size 7	Size 8	Size 9	Size 10	Size 11
Foot length (heel to toe)	9"	9¼"	9½"	9¾"	10"	10¼"	10½"

❷ Measure, Mark, and Cut

Fold your fabric in half lengthwise with right sides together, aligning the selvages. Position the pattern pieces according to the layout and measure and mark the strap as shown. Cut out the pieces and transfer the markings from the patterns to the wrong side of the fabric.

* **Mary Jane upper** (cut 4)
* **Mary Jane sole** (cut 6, or cut 4 from fabric and 2 from nonskid material)

Kids	Size 5½–6	Size 7–10	Size 11–13
Strap (cut 2)	4¼" × 1¼"	4¾" × 1½"	5" × 2"

Youth	Size 1–4
Strap (cut 2)	5¼" × 2"

Women	Size 5–6	Size 7–9	Size 10–11
Strap (cut 2)	5" × 2½"	5½" × 2¾"	6" × 3"

From fusible fleece interfacing, cut:

* **Mary Jane upper** (cut 2)
* **Mary Jane sole** (cut 2, one reversed)

❸ Fuse the Interfacing

Following manufacturer's instructions, fuse all the interfacing pieces to the wrong side of their corresponding fabric pieces. The interfaced pieces are the exterior pieces, except the sole.

❹ Make the Straps

* Press under one short end of each strap ¼". Fold and press as you would to make double-fold bias tape (see page 12). Edgestitch along all three finished edges of both straps.

NOTE ABOUT PATTERN PIECES: *When cutting on folded fabric, one set is automatically reversed for a right and left shoe (the uppers are the same; the soles are left and right). To help avoid confusion, separate the right and left pieces of the upper when attaching the sole.*

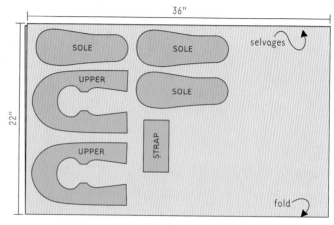

CUTTING LAYOUT

* Cut the Velcro into two 1" pieces. The width should equal the width of the strap, minus ¼". Center a loop piece of Velcro on the end of each strap piece. Stitch it in place. Set straps aside until next step.

❺ Make the Uppers

* With right sides together, stitch the heel of each of the four upper pieces. Press seams open. The interfaced uppers are the exterior pieces.
* Pin each strap with the Velcro facing up on the right side of the upper exterior pieces as indicated on the pattern piece, aligning raw edges. Baste the straps in place with a scant ¼" seam allowance.

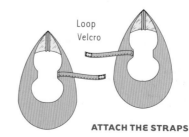

Loop Velcro

ATTACH THE STRAPS

✳ With right sides together align the raw edges of each exterior upper with a lining (non-interfaced) upper. Stitch together along the interior raw edge. Clip seam allowance, turn right side out, and press.

✳ Position the hook piece of Velcro on the right side of the upper, aligning it with the Velcro end of the strap. Stitch the Velcro in place on both the right and left uppers.

⑥ Attach the Bottom Sole

Position a non-interfaced sole piece (or optional nonskid sole, if using) on an upper exterior, with right sides together. Pin the sole in place, taking care to align the toe and heel markings. Stitch the sole and upper together using a ¼" seam. Clip and trim the seam allowance and turn the Mary Jane right side out. Press seam allowance toward the sole. Repeat for the second shoe.

⑦ Make the Insoles

With right sides together, align the raw edges of an interfaced sole piece with a non-interfaced sole piece. Stitch around the sole, leaving a 2" opening along one long edge for turning. Clip and trim the seam allowance and turn the insole right side out. Turn the seam allowance at the opening to the inside and press. Edgestitch all around. Repeat to create the second insole. Insert them into your completed Mary Janes for added comfort.

⑧ Add the Buttons (optional)

For a finishing touch, hand-sew the buttons on the right side of the strap pieces to conceal the stitching lines of the Velcro.

Li'l Tykes Set

Tie and Belt designed by Beth Vermillion

Visor and Moccasins designed by Sue Kim

Looking for some cute, practical, trendy, wearable accessories for your little guy? Enter the Li'l Tykes Set. Whether you are looking for style or functionality, these four pieces will help complete any look! Wear the pieces together, or individually. They are also great accessories for your favorite little lady.

MATERIALS

* Pattern pieces (6*), *see* sheet 4
* 1 yard of 44/45" quilting-weight fabric
* 1 spool of coordinating thread

For the Tie:
* ¼ yard of lightweight, fusible interfacing

For the Belt:
* 2 metal D-rings: 1½" for sizes 12-18 mo and 2T/3T; 2" for sizes 4/5, 6/7, and 8/9

For the Visor:
* ¼ yard of heavyweight fusible interfacing
* ¼ yard of ½"-wide elastic

For the Moccasins:
* ¼ yard of medium-weight fusible interfacing
* Coordinating embroidery floss
* 2 buttons, ½" in diameter

Sizes – the Visor is S, M, L, XL; the Tie is one size (2-8); the Belt is 12-18 months, 2T/3T, 4/5, 6/7, 8/9; and the Moccasins are 0-3 months, 3-6 months, 6-9 months, 9-12 months, and 12-18 months.

Different moccasin top patterns for different sizes.

Seam allowance – ½" for the Visor, Tie, and Belt; ¼" for the Moccasins, unless otherwise specified

❶ Determine Your Child's Size

Measure your child's waist, head circumference, and foot length to find the right size.

For the Belt	12-18 mo	2T/3T	4/5	6/7	8/9
Waist	20½"	21¼"	22"	23"	24"

For the Visor	S	M	L	XL
Head	17"	17½"	18"	19"

For the Moccasins	0-3 mo	3-6 mo	6-9 mo	9-12 mo	12-18 mo
Foot length (heel to toe)	3¾"	4"	4¼"	4½"	4¾"

❷ Measure, Mark, and Cut

Place your fabric in a single layer with the right side facing up. Fold over the top selvage edge 6½". Position the pattern pieces according to the layout and measure and mark the additional pieces. Cut out the pieces, and transfer the markings from the pattern pieces to the wrong side of fabric. Separate the pieces by project.

* **Tie front** (cut 2)
* **Tie back** (cut 2)
* **Visor brim** (cut 2)
* **Moccasin sole** (cut 4)
* **Moccasin upper** (cut 4)
* **Moccasin top** (cut 4)

Belt	12–18 mo	2T/3T	4/5	6/7	8/9
Belt (cut 1)	4" × 26"	4" × 27"	5" × 28"	5" × 29"	5" × 30"

Visor	S	M	L	XL
Front band (cut 2)	2½" × 12½"	2½" × 13"	2½" × 13½"	2½" × 14"
Elastic strap (cut 1)	2½" × 7¾"	2½" × 7¾"	2½ × 8¼"	2½" × 8¾"

NOTE: *Mirror the pattern pieces along the lines indicated.*

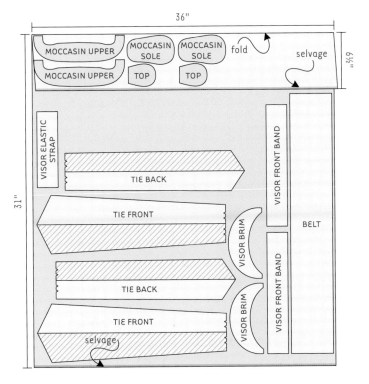

CUTTING LAYOUT

❸ Cut and Fuse the Interfacing

Use the pattern pieces or measurements to cut the following from fusible interfacing. Following manufacturer's instructions, fuse all the interfacing pieces to their corresponding fabric pieces. The interfaced pieces are the exterior pieces.

From lightweight interfacing:

* **Tie front** (cut 2)
* **Tie back** (cut 2)

From heavyweight interfacing:

* **Visor brim** (cut 1)
* **Visor front band** (cut 1)

From medium-weight interfacing:

* **Moccasin sole** (cut 2)
* **Moccasin upper** (cut 2)
* **Moccasin top** (cut 2)

Tie

❶ Make the Exterior and Lining

* With right sides together, align the short, straight edges of one tie front and tie back, matching notches. Stitch together and press seam allowance open. Repeat to make the lining.
* With right sides together, align all raw edges of the tie exterior and lining. Stitch together, leaving a 2" opening along one long edge for turning. Clip corners, turn right side out, and press.

❷ Finish the Tie

Fold the tie in half lengthwise with right sides together (the lining will be on the outside) and stitch together along one long edge creating a tube. Turn right side out and press with the seam centered in the back of the tie.

Belt

❶ Make the Belt

Fold both short ends of the belt piece ½" to the wrong side and press. Fold and press as you would to make double-fold bias tape (see page 12). Edgestitch all four sides of the belt piece.

❷ Attach the D-Rings

Slide the D-rings onto one end of the finished belt piece. Fold the end over 1¼" and topstitch, holding the D-rings in place.

Visor

❶ Make the Elastic Strap

* Fold and press the strap as you would to make double-fold bias tape (see page 12). Edgestitch along both finished edges, leaving the short ends open.

* Thread the appropriate length of elastic (see chart) through one open end of the strap, and out the opposite opening, securing both ends. Edgestitch the elastic in place, gathering the elastic strap piece.

	S	M	L	XL
Elastic length	6"	6¼"	6½"	7"

❷ Make and Attach the Brim

* With right sides together, align the raw edges of the brim pieces. Stitch together around the curved edge. Notch the seam allowance, turn right side out, and press. Topstitch along the finished edge of the brim using a ¼" seam allowance.

* With right sides together, align the raw edge of the brim with the long raw edge of the interfaced front band, aligning centers. Notch the seam allowance of the brim as needed and stitch together.

❸ Attach the Elastic Strap

With right sides together and raw edges even, align one short end of the elastic strap with one short end of the interfaced front band. Center the elastic strap on the front band and stitch using a ¼" seam allowance. Repeat, stitching the remaining short ends of the elastic strap and front band pieces together to complete a circle.

❹ Finish the Visor

* With right sides together, align the raw edges of the front band pieces, sandwiching the visor and elastic strap in between the layers. Note that you have to stretch the elastic strap and roll up the brim piece to keep it out of the way. Pin together and stitch around all four sides, leaving a 3" opening in the top edge (without the visor) for turning. Clip corners, turn right side out, and press the seam allowance at the opening to the inside.

* Neatly edgestitch around all four sides of the front band, closing the opening used for turning.

Moccasins

❶ Make the Uppers

* With right sides together, fold an upper piece in half widthwise so that the toe ends align. Stitch together along the toe edge, and press seam allowance open. Repeat with the remaining upper pieces.

* With right sides together, align the raw edges of one interfaced (exterior) upper with one non-interfaced upper. Stitch together along the inside edge. Clip seam allowance, turn right side out, and gently press.

❷ Attach the Upper to the Sole

Position an upper with the exterior (interfaced) side up on one non-interfaced sole piece with right side up. Match the toe with the marks indicated on the sole pattern piece, and pin in place. Stitch the upper to the sole piece using a ⅛" seam allowance. Repeat for the second moccasin.

toe

❸ Stitch the Bottom Sole

* With right sides together, position an exterior (interfaced) sole on a non-interfaced sole, sandwiching the upper in between the two layers. Pin the sole in place taking care to align the toe and heel.

* Stitch around the perimeter of the sole using a ¼" seam allowance and leaving a 2" opening along one side edge for turning. Clip and trim the seam allowance and turn the moccasin right side out. Turn the seam allowance at the opening to the inside and slipstitch the opening closed.

* Repeat for the second moccasin.

❹ Stitch the Top

* With right sides together, align the raw edges of an interfaced (exterior) top piece with a non-interfaced piece. Stitch together along the curved edge, leaving the straight edge open for turning. Clip the seam allowance, turn right side out, and press the seam allowance at the opening to the inside. Slipstitch the opening closed. Repeat for the second top piece.

* Attach the top to the shoe's upper using a blanket stitch (see glossary, page 339).

* Fold the top along the fold line and hand-sew a button at the placement mark through the folded layers. Repeat for the second moccasin.

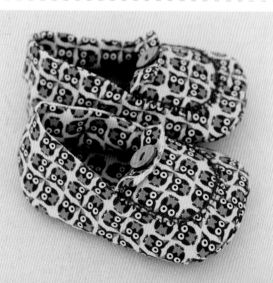

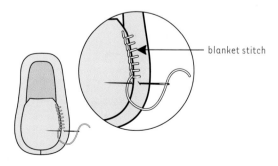

blanket stitch

summer days Hat

Designed by Tanja Ivacic-Ramljak
and Suada Ivacic

*Look no further for a cute, chic,
retro-ish hat for your little one.
This hat fits the bill! As an
added bonus, the Velcro on the
brim allows for some functional
ponytail styling. Go wild — you
can even use two fabrics for this
project to make the hat reversible,
giving you two looks in one for
twice the wearing pleasure.*

MATERIALS

* ✳ Pattern pieces (2), *see* sheet 4
* ✳ 1 yard of 44/45" home dec-weight
  fabric
* ✳ 1 spool of coordinating thread
* ✳ 2" piece of ½"-¾"-wide Velcro

Sizes – S, M, L

Seam allowance – ½" unless
  otherwise specified

① Determine Your Child's Size

Measure your child's head circumference to find the right size.

	S	M	L
Head	19½"	21½"	23"

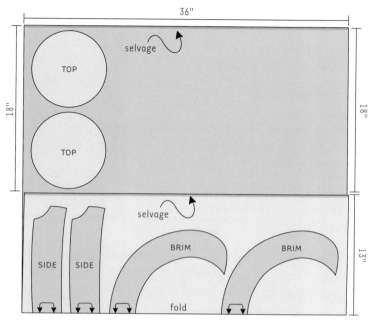

CUTTING LAYOUT

❷ Measure, Mark, and Cut

Lay your fabric in a single layer with the right side facing up. Fold up one selvage edge 13", leaving 18" of a single layer of fabric. Position the pattern pieces according to the layout, and measure and mark the top piece directly onto the fabric. Cut out all pieces and transfer markings from the patterns to the wrong side of the fabric.

* **Side** (cut 2 on fold)
* **Brim** (cut 2 on fold)

	S	M	L
Top	6¾" diameter circle	7½" diameter circle	8¼" diameter circle

❸ Attach the Side and Top

* Fold one side piece with the right sides together, aligning the center-back short raw edges, and stitch the center back seam. Press seam allowance open.
* Fold a top piece in half and gently press a crease to mark the center front and back.
* With the right sides together, match and pin the center front of one top piece with the center front of one stitched side piece. Repeat, matching the center backs of both pieces. Continue pinning the top and side pieces together at regular intervals, easing the top to fit as necessary.
* Stitch the top to the side. Trim the seam allowance to ¼" and press the seam allowance down toward the side piece. Topstitch the side, ⅛" from the seam, catching the seam allowance in your stitching.
* Repeat with remaining top and side pieces to create the lining.

④ Attach the Brim

* With the right sides together, match and pin the center front of one brim with the center front of a side piece. Match the marked dots on the brim with the marked dots on the corners of the side and pin in place. Continue pinning the brim and side pieces together at regular intervals. Stitch together. Trim the seam allowance to ¼" and press it open.
* Repeat with second set of brim and side/top pieces for lining. Turn lining right side out.

⑤ Join the Exterior and the Lining

* Place the sewn hat lining inside the hat exterior with right sides together. Pin together, aligning all raw edges, brim, and center back seams. Stitch around the curved raw edges of the side, at center back, pivoting your needle at the intersection of the side and brim. Continue stitching around the brim, leaving a 3" opening at the marks as indicated on the pattern. Notch the seam allowance, clipping to, but not through, your stitching line.
* Turn the hat right side out through the 3" brim opening. Press the hat, folding in the seam allowance at the opening. Topstitch along the bottom edge of the side piece, around the curved edge at center back, ⅛" from the seam. Topstitch around the edge of the brim, also ⅛" from the edge.

⑥ Finish the Hat

Overlap the brim flap at center back and position the hook and loop sides of the Velcro as needed to align. Edgestitch in place.

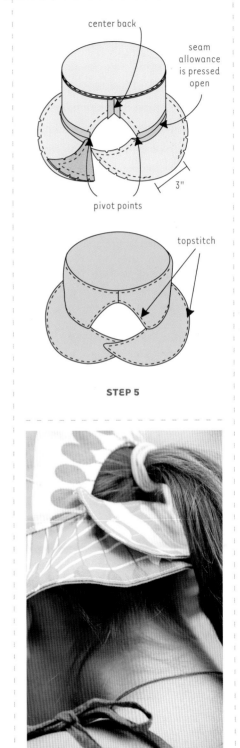

center back

seam allowance is pressed open

pivot points

3"

topstitch

STEP 5

ITTY-BITTY TODDLER BACKPACK

Designed by Sue Kim

This is the perfect backpack for your child's day out. Keep toys, trinkets, snacks, and a favorite beverage at the ready. The elastic band at the top opening of the bag creates easy access to the items inside. Best of all, this backpack means that you no longer need to carry everything yourself!

MATERIALS

* ✳ 1 yard of 44/45" home dec-weight fabric
* ✳ ½ yard of heavyweight fusible interfacing
* ✳ 5" diameter circle template, mug, or bowl
* ✳ 9½" diameter circle template or dinner plate
* ✳ Two 8½" lengths of 1"-wide webbing
* ✳ 1 spool of coordinating thread
* ✳ One 1" parachute buckle
* ✳ ½ yard of ½"-wide elastic

Finished dimensions –
10" wide × 4" deep × 11" tall

Seam allowance – ½" unless otherwise specified

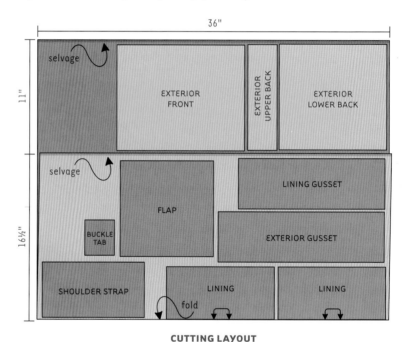

CUTTING LAYOUT

❶ Measure, Mark, and Cut

Lay your fabric in a single layer with the right side facing up. Fold up the bottom selvage edge 16½", leaving 11" of a single layer of fabric at the top. Measure and mark the following pattern pieces onto the fabric and cut them out.

* ✳ **Exterior front** 13" × 10½" (cut 1)
* ✳ **Exterior upper back** 3" × 10½" (cut 1)
* ✳ **Exterior lower back** 11" × 10½" (cut 1)
* ✳ **Lining** 11" × 10½" (cut 2 on fold)

* ✳ **Flap** 9½" × 9½" (cut 2)
* ✳ **Exterior gusset** 17" × 5" (cut 2)
* ✳ **Lining gusset** 15" × 5" (cut 2)
* ✳ **Shoulder strap** 10½" × 5½" (cut 2)
* ✳ **Buckle tab** 3" × 3½" (cut 2)

From the fusible interfacing, cut the following for the lining:

* ✳ **Lining** 11" × 10½" (cut 2)
* ✳ **Flap** 9½" × 9½" (cut 1)
* ✳ **Lining gusset** 15" × 5" (cut 2)

❷ Interface the Lining Pieces

Fuse the interfacing to the wrong side of the corresponding pieces according to the manufacturer's instructions. These will be the lining pieces.

❸ Make Rounded Corners

* On the wrong side of the exterior front, exterior lower back, and lining pieces, trace the 5" circle template on each bottom corner with a fabric pen. Trim away the excess fabric.

* On the wrong side of the flap pieces, trace the 9½" circle template on the lower edge. Trim away the excess fabric.

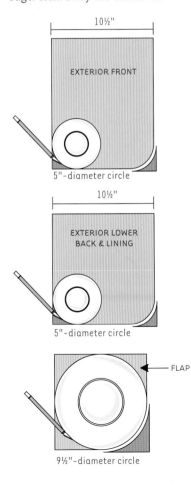

10½"

EXTERIOR FRONT

5"-diameter circle

10½"

EXTERIOR LOWER
BACK & LINING

5"-diameter circle

FLAP

9½"-diameter circle

4 Assemble the Shoulder Straps

* Fold and press one short end of each shoulder strap piece ½" to the wrong side. Fold and press as you would to make double-fold bias tape (see page 12).

* Tuck ½" of one short end of each webbing piece into the folded short end of each strap. Edgestitch around all three finished sides, securing the webbing.

5 Assemble and Attach the Buckle Tabs

* Fold and press a buckle tab as you would to make double-fold bias tape (see page 12). Stitch long edge to close. Slide the female side of the parachute buckle onto the tab and fold the tab in half, aligning the short raw edges, and baste with a ¼" seam allowance. Repeat with the male side of the parachute buckle and the second tab piece.

* Lay the exterior (non-interfaced) front piece on a work surface with right side facing up. Center the female buckle and tab piece along the bottom/rounded edge of the exterior piece, aligning raw edges, and baste in place.

* Lay the exterior (non-interfaced) flap piece on a work surface with right side facing up. Center the male buckle and tab piece along the rounded edge of the flap, aligning raw edges, and baste in place.

6 Make the Flap

Pin the flap pieces with right sides together, sandwiching the male buckle and tab in between the layers, and stitch around the curved edge, leaving the straight edge open. Notch the curved seam allowance and turn the flap right side out. Press and edgestitch around the curved finished edge.

7 Assemble the Exterior Back Pieces

* Lay the exterior (non-interfaced) lower back piece on a work surface with right side facing up. Make a placement mark at the center point along the top edge. Align the raw edges of the shoulder straps with the top raw edge of the lower back piece, abutting them at the center mark. Baste in place at a ¼" seam allowance.

* Center the raw edges of the webbing pieces on the bottom rounded corners of the lower back piece, aligning the raw edges, and baste.

* With right sides together, center the exterior (non-interfaced) flap along the top edge of the exterior lower back piece and pin in place. Again, with right sides together, align the raw edges of the lower and upper back pieces, sandwiching the flap between the layers. Stitch together along the top edge, through all layers.

* Press the flap and upper back pieces up, away from the lower back. Press the seam allowance toward the lower back.

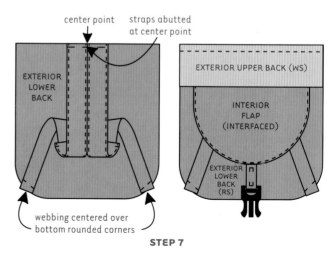

center point   straps abutted at center point

EXTERIOR LOWER BACK

EXTERIOR UPPER BACK (WS)

INTERIOR FLAP (INTERFACED)

EXTERIOR LOWER BACK (RS)

webbing centered over bottom rounded corners

STEP 7

⑧ Attach the Gusset

* Align the short edges of the exterior gusset pieces and stitch together along one short edge. Press seam allowance open. This piece will become the sides and bottom of the backpack.

* With right sides together, align one long edge of the exterior gusset with the side and bottom raw edges of the exterior upper/lower back pieces, matching the gusset seam with the center of the lower back bottom edge. Stitch together and notch the curved seam allowance. Press seam allowance toward the gusset.

* In the same way, attach the other long edge of the exterior gusset with the side and bottom raw edges of the exterior front piece. Turn right side out.

* Repeat to attach the lining gusset to the lining pieces, leaving a 5" opening along one seam for turning.

⑨ Attach the Exterior and Lining

* Place the backpack lining inside the exterior, with right sides together. Pin, aligning the top raw edges, matching fronts, backs, and gusset seams. Stitch together around the top raw edge.

* Turn the backpack right side out through the opening left in the lining seam, and position the lining on the inside of the bag. Note that the lining is shorter than the exterior and that the top edge of the exterior will naturally fold to the inside of the bag by 2". Press a crease along the folded top edge of the bag. Slipstitch the opening in the lining closed.

⑩ Make the Elastic Casing

* Edgestitch a ⅛" seam allowance along the top edge of the bag, through the top edges of the shoulder straps, and taking care to keep the flap out of the stitching line. Stitch again ¾" away from the top edge of the bag. This time, do not stitch through the shoulder straps.

* On the inside of a bag, use a seam ripper or a small pair of sharp scissors to snip a small opening in one gusset seam between the two stitching lines. Thread the elastic through this casing opening. Overlap the ends of the elastic ½", making sure the elastic is not twisted and stitch them together securely. Slide the ends of the elastic back in the casing. Slipstitch the opening closed by hand.

TOT TOTE & WALLET

Designed by Trish Hoskins

What toddler and preschooler wouldn't love his or her own tote for collecting treasures or simply playing pretend? The tote has room for lots of toys and trinkets, sunglasses, and more! Cinch it up with the handle for an easy closure. The slightly oversize wallet is easier for small hands to manipulate, but it makes a great billfold for any age! This is a particularly fun project for those specialty border prints and large-scale striped designs; you can make use of the varying design elements for contrast, as shown here.

MATERIALS

* 1 yard of 44/45" quilting-weight or home dec-weight cotton fabric
* 1 spool of coordinating thread

For Tot Tote:

* ⅛ yard of lightweight fusible interfacing
* 8 grommets with ⅜", ⁷⁄₁₆", or ½" interior diameter
* 1¼ yard of ⅞"-wide ribbon for handles*

For Wallet:

* 4" zipper
* ⅛ yard of ¾"-wide Velcro

*Sample used the selvages of the fabric as the ribbon handles, but this will not be possible in most cases.

Finished dimensions – tote 8" tall × 9" wide × 5" deep; wallet 4" × 5", folded.
Seam allowance – ½" unless otherwise specified

❶ Measure, Mark, and Cut

Fold your fabric in half lengthwise with the right sides together, aligning the selvages. Measure and mark the following pieces directly on the wrong side of your fabric and cut them out.

* **Tote front/back** 9" × 10" (cut 4)
* **Tote side** 9" × 6" (cut 4)
* **Tote bottom** 6" × 10" (cut 2)
* **Tote front/back pocket** 6" × 16" (cut 2)
* **Tote side pocket** 6" × 8" (cut 2)
* **Tote interior pocket** 5" × 10" (cut 2)
* **Wallet exterior/interior** 9" × 6" (cut 2)
* **Wallet large pocket** 9" × 5½" (cut 2)
* **Wallet card pocket A** 5½" × 3¼" (cut 1)*

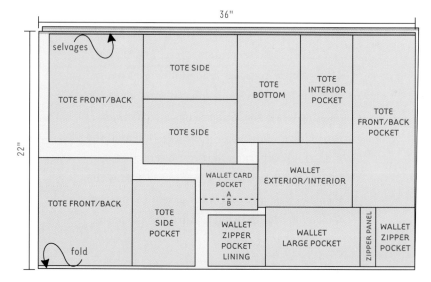

CUTTING LAYOUT

* **Wallet card pocket B** 5½" × 4¼" (cut 1)*
* **Wallet zipper pocket** 3¾" 5½" (cut 2)
* **Wallet zipper panel** 1½" × 5½" (cut 2)
* **Wallet zipper pocket lining** 4¾" × 5½" (cut 2)

NOTE: Cut wallet card pocket B through both layers, then separate the layers and cut one to pocket A size.

Cut from interfacing:

* **Tote front/back facing** 1" × 10" (cut 4)
* **Tote side facing** 1" × 6" (cut 4)

Tot Tote

❶ Prep the Fabric Pieces

* Hem the top raw edge of *all* tote pocket pieces with a ¼" double-fold hem.

* Fuse each facing piece to the wrong side of each corresponding tote piece, ¾" down from and parallel to the top raw edge, following manufacturer's instructions. This will reinforce the grommets.

❷ Pleat and Attach Exterior Front/Back Pockets

* Measure and mark pocket dividers and pleats along the bottom edge of each front/back pocket piece as shown. Fold to align the pleat marks and press to form pleats. Baste along bottom edge to hold pleats in place.

* Place one front/back pocket piece, right side up, on the right side of a front/back tote. Align bottom raw edges. Stitch along the pocket divider lines, taking care not to catch the pleats in your stitching. Baste the pocket to the tote along the side and bottom edges with an edgestitch, securing the pleats.

* Repeat with the remaining front/back pocket and front/back tote.

❸ Pleat and Attach Exterior Side Pockets

* Measure and mark along the bottom edge of each side pocket piece as shown, then fold to align the pleat marks and press to form pleats.

* Place one side pocket piece, right side up, on the right side of one tote side piece. Align the side and bottom raw edges and baste in place along raw edges to secure the pocket and pleats. Repeat with the remaining side pocket piece and tote side piece. Press all seams open.

❹ Make the Tote Exterior

* Pin one exterior front/back to one exterior side piece, right sides facing and one side edge aligned. Stitch along the side edge, taking care not to catch the pleats in your stitching. Stop your stitching ½" from the bottom raw edge.

* Attach the remaining exterior side piece to the opposite side edge of the exterior front/back in the same way. Attach the remaining exterior front/back piece to both sides, again stopping ½" from the bottom raw edge.

* Pin one tote bottom to the bottom edge of one front/back piece, right sides facing and raw edges aligned. Stitch one long side, starting and stopping ½" from each corner, then stitch the opposite long side. Finish by stitching the short sides. Press all seams open.

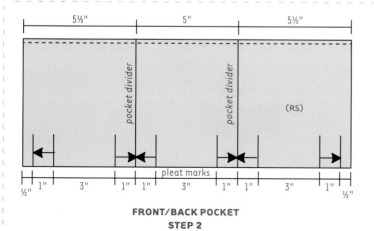

**FRONT/BACK POCKET
STEP 2**

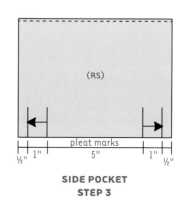

**SIDE POCKET
STEP 3**

⑤ Make the Tote Interior

* Pin each interior pocket piece, right side up, on the right side of a remaining tote front/back piece, aligning side and bottom raw edges. Baste side and bottom edges.

* Fold each piece in half across the width and press to mark a crease down the center of the interior pocket. Unfold and topstitch a vertical line on each pocket, through both layers, along the crease.

* Stitch the interior front/back pieces and remaining side and bottom pieces together as you did for the exterior, to assemble the tote interior. Press seams open as you go.

⑥ Assemble the Tote

Turn the interior right side out and insert it into the exterior. Pin together, right sides facing and top raw edges aligned. Align all side seams and stitch around top edge, leaving a 4"-5" opening in the middle of one front/back for turning. Turn right side out. Turn raw edges of opening ½" to wrong side and press all around. Edgestitch on all sides, closing the opening as you stitch.

⑦ Install Grommets and Ribbon Handle

* On the interior of the tote, measure and mark the following grommet placement points:

    Tote sides: One mark on each side panel, ⅞" down from the top edge and centered between the side seams.

    Tote front and back: Three marks on each front and back panel, ⅞" down from the top edge. One mark should be centered between the side seams, and the others should be placed ⅞" from each side seam.

* Center and install the grommets over each of the marks, following manufacturer's directions.

* Weave the length of ribbon through all the grommets. Making sure the ribbon isn't twisted, align the short raw ends of the ribbon, right sides together, and stitch. Finger-press the seam open. Fold each seam allowance ¼" to the wrong side and stitch to the ribbon to secure and hide raw edges.

Wallet

① Make the Zipper Pocket

* Pin both zipper panel pieces together, right sides facing and raw edges aligned. Sandwich the zipper between the layers, aligning one edge of the zipper tape with one long edge of the zipper panels and centering the zipper between the corners. Using a zipper foot, stitch through all layers close to the zipper coil. Flip right side out, aligning raw edges of the zipper panels, and press. Topstitch along zipper panel close to the seam.

* In the same way, pin both zipper pocket pieces together, right sides facing and raw edges aligned. Sandwich the opposite edge of the zipper tape between the layers, centering the free edge of the zipper tape along one long edge of the pocket. Stitch through all layers close to the zipper coil. Flip right side out, aligning raw edges of both pocket

pieces, and press. Topstitch along the zipper pocket close to the seam.

* Pin the loop half of the Velcro to the right side of the zipper pocket, ¼" from the long raw edge, and centered between the side edges. Stitch all around the Velcro through both zipper pocket layers to attach.

* Pin both zipper pocket lining pieces together, right sides facing and raw edges aligned. Sandwich the zipper assembly between the layers, aligning all raw edges. Stitch through all layers along the zipper *panel's* long edge. Flip so that both zipper pocket linings are together, wrong sides facing, and the zipper assembly is on top. Topstitch close to the seam you just stitched. Baste all layers together with an edgestitch along all three raw edges.

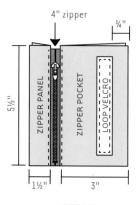

STEP 1

❷ Make the Card Pockets

* Hem the top edge of both card pocket A and B pieces.

* Pin the remaining hook Velcro to the right side of the smaller card pocket A, ¾" in from the long raw edge opposite the hem, and centered between the side edges. Stitch all around the Velcro to attach.

* With both right sides facing up, place the smaller card pocket A on top of card pocket B, aligning side and bottom raw edges. Baste together with an edgestitch along the side and bottom edges.

❸ Assemble the Interior

* Place one large wallet pocket piece on your work surface, right side up, with one 9" edge at the top.

* Place the card pocket assembly on the left half of this large pocket piece, with the hemmed edges of the pockets facing toward the center and raw edges aligned.

* Place the zipper pocket assembly on the right half of this large pocket piece, with the finished edge of the zipper pocket facing toward the center and raw edges aligned. Baste together with an edgestitch all around.

* Pin both large pocket pieces together, right sides facing and raw edges aligned. Stitch along the top raw edge. Flip so that both large pocket pieces are together, wrong sides facing, and the finished edge is on top. Press.

❹ Assemble the Wallet

* Place one wallet exterior/interior piece on your work surface, right side up, with one 9" edge at the top.

* Place the large pocket assembly on top, right side up, aligning bottom and side raw edges. Baste together with an edgestitch all around.

* Pin both wallet exterior/interior pieces together, right sides facing and raw edges aligned. Stitch all around, leaving a 4"-5" opening at the top for turning. Clip corners and turn right side out. Press the seam allowances at the opening to the wrong side. Stitch along the top edge with an edgestitch, closing the opening.

POOR BOY (anD DaD) Cap

Designed by Trish Hoskins

The only thing cuter than a little boy in a poor boy cap is a boy and his dad in matching caps! A riff on the classic topper, this cap is sized so you can make one for all the boys and men in your life, from an infant's head circumference of 16 inches (or smaller), on up to an extra-large adult's of 24/25 inches. The elastic makes it adjustable within a couple of inches, and fully lined means that it's also fully reversible in case you choose to use two fabrics! You may even be able to get a father-son combo out of a single yard of fabric, as long as one cap is a medium or smaller.

MATERIALS

* Pattern pieces (2), *see* sheet 4
* 1 yard of 44/45" home dec-weight fabric, corduroy, or wool
* ⅛ yard of extra-firm stabilizer such as Peltex, or 4½" × 12" piece of sturdy template plastic
* 1 spool of coordinating thread
* ⅛ yard of ¼"-wide elastic

Sizes – determine by measuring head circumference

Seam allowance – ½" unless otherwise specified

	XS	S	M	L	XL
	Infant	Toddler/ child	Youth	Adult	Large adult
Head	16"-17"	18"-19"	20"-21"	22"-23"	24"-25"

❶ Measure, Mark, and Cut

Lay your fabric in a single layer with the right side facing up. Fold down the top selvage edge 11", and the bottom selvage edge up 11" so both selvages meet in the middle. Then fold your fabric on the left side in the cross grain direction so that you have four layers of fabric, large enough to cut out the crown pattern piece (7½"-9½" long).

Position the pattern pieces according to the cutting layout and cut them out. Transfer the markings from the patterns to the wrong side of fabric.

* **Crown** (cut 2 on folds)
* **Brim** (cut 2 on fold)

From extra-firm stabilizer, cut:

* **Brim** (cut 1 on fold)

❷ Shape the Crown

Fold one crown piece, right sides together, so that the adjoining raw edges are aligned as shown below. Stitch the raw edges together, starting at the outer raw edge. Continue stitching all the way to the fold, curving slightly toward the center. Stitch the remaining raw edges together in a similar fashion all around the crown to complete cap shape. Repeat with remaining crown piece for lining.

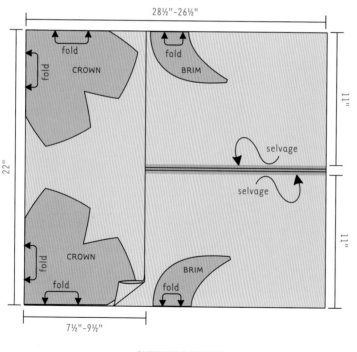

CUTTING LAYOUT

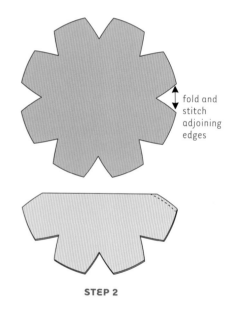

STEP 2

❸ Make the Brim

* Pin the brim pieces together, right sides facing and raw edges aligned. Stitch along the outer curve using a ¼" seam allowance. Trim seam allowance with pinking shears, or notch the curve every ½", taking care not to cut into stitching. Turn right side out and press.

* Trim the brim stabilizer by ¼" on both curved edges so that the stabilizer fits fully between the brim fabric layers. Insert into the brim, taking care to align the stabilizer with the brim's outer seam. Baste the raw edges with an edgestitch. Topstitch the outer curve ⅛" from finished edge, then topstitch again ¼" from finished edge.

❹ Attach the Brim and Elastic

* Find and mark the center of the brim's inner curve as well as the center point between two seams, along the edge of one crown piece. Pin the brim to the crown, right sides together, aligning center marks and raw edges. Baste together. This becomes the front of the cap.

* Find and mark the center of the elastic. Find and mark the center of the back of the cap, opposite the brim. Pin the center of the elastic to the wrong side of the back at the center mark, aligning one long edge of the elastic with the fabric raw edge.

* Stretch the elastic as far as it will go at each end. Pin where the end of the stretched elastic meets the cap on each side. Pin along the length; when the elastic is relaxed, the cap will be gathered. Set your sewing machine to a zigzag stitch, using the widest and longest stitch settings. Stitch the elastic to the cap, stretching the elastic as you go, keeping the elastic close to the raw edge of the fabric.

❺ Complete the Cap

* Pin the cap pieces together, right sides facing and aligning raw edges and seams, sandwiching the brim in between the layers. Stitch all around, leaving a 4" opening at the back for turning. Make sure your seam is at least ⅛" from the edge of the elastic. Turn right side out and press all around.

* Stitch the opening closed with an edge-stitch, stretching the elastic as you go. Take care not to catch the elastic or any fabric gathers in your stitching. If desired, hand-tack the front of the cap to the top of the brim, to keep the hat in a classic poor boy shape.

CHAPTER 9

tactile play

- -

BABIES AND TODDLERS INTERACT WITH THE WORLD
through touch. Encourage their curiosity and exploration
with the wide variety of tactile objects in this chapter.
These sensory objects will stimulate your child and
help create the building blocks for self-awareness.

TODDLER ACTIVITY BOOK

Designed by Erin Currie

This soft activity book for toddlers features snaps, buttons, zippers, buckles, hook-and-eye closures, as well as a marble and lacing maze. Feel free to come up with your own tactile play ideas and activities using the notions you have on hand! Larger notions are best for chubby hands still learning fine motor skills. (Please note that the use of drawstrings and ties can present a safety hazard for very young children. Do not let your infant or toddler play with the laces in this book unsupervised.)

* 1 yard of 44/45" nondirectional flannel or quilting-weight cotton
* 1 spool of coordinating thread
* Fabric scraps for front or back appliqué (optional)
* One ½" or smaller marble
* 25–35 large or extra-large eyelets
* One 9" plastic zipper (preferably heavy duty/larger scale)
* 8" length of extra-large hook-and-eye tape
* 3 buttons, 1" in diameter
* 6 sets of size-24 snaps
* Scraps of medium- or heavyweight interfacing (optional)
* 2 shoelaces, one approximately 60" long for lacing page; one approximately 36" long for hole maze
* Two 1" parachute buckles

Finished dimensions – 7" × 7"

Seam allowance – ½" unless otherwise specified

 Measure, Mark, and Cut

Fold your fabric in half lengthwise with the right sides together, aligning the selvages. Measure and mark the following pieces on the wrong side of your fabric. Cut them out and label each piece in a side seam allowance to help you keep track.

* **Front** 8" square (cut 2 on fold)
* **Back** 8" square (cut 2)
* **Inside pages** 8" square (cut 10; label as follows)
  · Marble base (2)
  · Hook-and-eye base (1)
  · Zipper base (1)
  · Buckle base (1)
  · Lace base (1)
  · Holes base (2)
  · Snap base (1)
  · Button base (1)
* **Lace sides** 5" × 8" (cut 2)
* **Zipper sides** 5" × 8" (cut 2)
* **Hook-and-eye sides** 5" × 8" (cut 2)
* **Buckle straps** 4" × 3" (cut 4)
* **Button flaps** 4" × 3" (cut 6)
* **Snap flaps** 4" × 3" (cut 6)
* **Binding** 4" × 8½" (cut 1 on fold)

CUTTING LAYOUT

36"

22"

BUTTON FLAPS		selvages		
BUTTON FLAPS	BACK	INSIDE PAGES: MARBLE BASE	INSIDE PAGES: HOOK & EYE BASE /ZIPPER BASE	INSIDE PAGES: BUCKLE BASE /LACE BASE
BUTTON FLAPS				
SNAP FLAPS	LACE SIDES	ZIPPER SIDES	HOOK & EYE SIDES	INSIDE PAGES: HOLES BASE
SNAP FLAPS				INSIDE PAGES: SNAP BASE /BUTTON BASE
SNAP FLAPS	BUCKLE STRAPS	BUCKLE STRAPS		
fold	BINDING		FRONT	FRONT

② Make the Front and Back Covers

* If desired, appliqué your child's name or another motif of your choosing on one of the front pieces (see glossary, page 339). Our sample has some topstitching around a few of the fabric motifs for accent.

* Pin the two front pieces together, right sides facing and raw edges aligned. Stitch the top, right (outside), and bottom edges, leaving the left (inside) edge open for turning. Clip corners, turn right side out, and press. Edgestitch around the three finished sides.

* Repeat the process to stitch the two back pieces.

③ Make the Marble Maze Page

Stitch, turn, and edgestitch the two marble base pieces together as done for the front and back covers. Use the illustration as a guide for topstitching the maze pattern. The left edge has an extra ½" left unstitched for assembling the book in a later step. When done stitching, insert the marble into the maze, pushing it to the right edge so that it won't get in the way when you sew the book together.

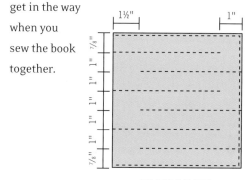

**MARBLE MAZE
STITCHING GUIDE**

④ Make the Hole Maze Page

Stitch, turn, and edgestitch the two holes base pieces together as done for the front and back covers. Mark 10–20 scattered points around the page, at least 1" from each finished edge and at least 1½" from the raw edge. You may wish to create a connect-the-dots type picture, or simply create a random design. Install eyelets at marked points, following manufacturer's directions.

⑤ Make the Zipper Page

Pin a zipper side piece to one side of the zipper tape, right sides together and raw edges aligned. Stitch ¼" away from the zipper coil and press seam allowance away from the zipper. Edgestitch zipper side piece close to the seam. Repeat to attach the opposite side of the zipper to the remaining zipper side piece. Close the zipper, leaving 1" unzipped. Center the completed zipper panel, right side up, on the right side of the zipper base piece, and pin in place. Trim excess from zipper side pieces so that raw edges align. Baste all around with edgestitch, trimming zipper tape as necessary.

ZIPPER PAGE

⑥ Make the Hook-and-Eye Page

Construct as for zipper page, substituting hook-and-eye tape, sides, and base for the respective zipper page pieces.

HOOK-AND-EYE PAGE (L) AND MARBLE MAZE PAGE (R)

MARBLE MAZE PAGE (L) AND HOLE PAGE (R)

ACTIVITY BOOK COVER

HOLE PAGE (L) AND BUCKLE PAGE (R)

INSIDE COVER (L) AND SNAP PAGE (R)

BUTTON PAGE (L) AND ZIPPER PAGE (R)

LACING PAGE (L) AND INSIDE BACK COVER (R)

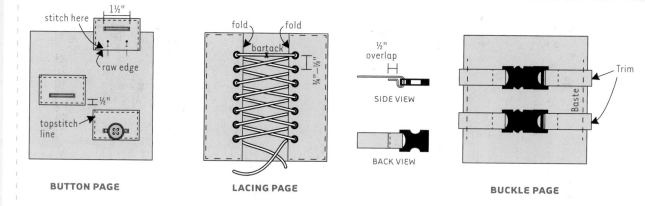

BUTTON PAGE   **LACING PAGE**   **BUCKLE PAGE**

⑦ Make the Button Page

* Pin two button flap pieces together, right sides facing and raw edges aligned. Stitch along one long and both short edges. Clip corners, turn right side out, and press. Edgestitch along finished sides. Stitch a horizontal 1½" buttonhole at least ½" up from the long finished bottom edge.

* Edgestitch the raw edge of each button flap using the illustration as a placement guide, to the right side of the button base, with the long finished edge pointing up. Fold and press each flap down and topstitch each flap, to the button base, concealing the raw edge in your stitching.

* Hand-sew buttons to the button base to line up with each buttonhole.

⑧ Make the Snap Page

Construct as for button page, substituting snap flap pieces for button flap pieces and the snap base for the button base. Do not stitch buttonholes or buttons; instead, install two male snap halves on each flap, and female snap halves on the snap base so that they line up with the male halves. It's a good idea to interface the wrong side of the snap base piece before installing the female snap halves for extra stability.

⑨ Make the Lacing Page

Fold both lace side pieces in half lengthwise, wrong sides facing. Install eyelets along the folded edge spaced approximately ¾"–⅞" apart on both lace side pieces. If your eyelets/grommets are too large to space as illustrated, you can decrease the number of grommets and rearrange them. With right sides up, place both lace side pieces on the right side of the lace base, aligning raw edges. Baste all around with edgestitch. Lace the longer shoelace through the holes as if lacing a shoe. You may wish to tack the center of the shoelace in place between the top two eyelets as a safety precaution.

⑩ Make the Buckle Page

* Fold each buckle strap piece in half lengthwise, right sides together. Stitch the long raw edge and one short end. Turn right side out and press.

* Thread the finished end of each strap through the top of one buckle half, folding the end under so that it overlaps the strap by just ½". Stitch to secure. Repeat with remaining buckle pieces.

* Buckle the buckles and center them on the right side of the buckle base. Baste in place and trim excess from the straps.

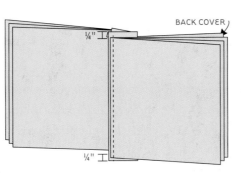
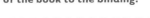

Attaching the front cover and first half of the book to the binding.

Attaching the back cover and second half of the book to the binding.

Topstitching the binding.

⑪ Assemble the Book

Start by attaching the *zipper* page to the *hook-and-eye* page:

* Pin the pages together, right sides facing and raw edges aligned. Stitch the top, right (outside), and bottom edges together. Leave the left (inside) edge open for turning.

* Clip the stitched corners, turn right side out, and press. Edgestitch around the three finished sides.

* Repeat these steps to stitch the *button* page to the *snap* page, and the *lacing* page to the *buckle* page.

* For the *hole maze*, clip the tip off of the remaining shoelace, and baste it to the center of the left raw edge of the hole maze page so that the lace lies horizontally, and is attached to the page. Thread the rest of the shoelace through the holes so that the length isn't stitched when binding the book together.

* Arrange the seven pages in any order you like, starting with the front cover and ending with the back cover.

⑫ Bind the Book

* Fold the binding piece in half lengthwise, right sides together. Starting at the fold, stitch the short edges together for only ½", leaving the remainder of the short edges unstitched. Turn right side out and press the seam allowances to the wrong side.

* Pin and stitch the first three pages to one long edge of the binding, front cover facing the right side of one long binding edge. Raw edges should be aligned, and the pages should be centered ¼" in from the short ends of the binding.

* Stitch the last four pages to the opposite long edge of the binding in a similar fashion, back cover facing the right side of the binding.

* Flip the book so that the raw edges of the pages tuck into the binding, the book is right side out, and all pages are in the correct order.

* Hand-sew the opening closed with an invisible slipstitch or whipstitch along the top folded short ends of the binding. Open to the center of the book and sew together the back of the third page to the front of the fourth page with an invisible slipstitch or whipstitch, as close to the binding as possible. This hand-stitching will close the gap between the center two pages and keep the book from being flipped inside out. Finish by sewing along the rest of the bottom binding seam if any remains open.

* Topstitch several decorative vertical lines down the length of the binding, about ⅛" apart, starting from the fold.

STORY CUSHION

Designed by Jo Ebisujima

This project is designed to inspire storytelling. Once you've made the cushion, find nine little objects and pop them into the pockets. Improvise a story that includes all of the objects. Sit back and see where the tale leads you!

MATERIALS

* 1 yard of 44/45" quilting-weight fabric
* Four felt squares in your choice of colors; sample uses 1 blue (A), 2 yellow (B), and 1 orange (C)
* 18" square pillow form
* 1 spool of coordinating thread
* 2 circle templates, 2¾" and 3½" in diameter
* ⅛ yard of fusible web for appliqués
* 5 small fabric scraps for appliqués, with kid-friendly motifs suitable for appliqué

Finished dimensions – fits an 18" pillow

Seam allowance – ½" unless otherwise specified

① Measure, Mark, and Cut

Lay out your fabric in a single layer with the wrong side facing up. Measure and mark the following pieces on the wrong side of your fabric and cut them out.

* **Cushion front** 19" square (cut 1)
* **Cushion back** 13" × 19" (cut 2)
* **Pockets** 3½" square (cut 9)

From felt, cut the frills:

* **Color A:** 3½" diameter circle (cut 6)
* **Color B:** 3½" diameter circle (cut 12)
* **Color C:** 2¾" diameter circle (cut 4)

② Prepare the Pockets

Press the sides and bottom of each pocket ¼" to wrong side. Press a ¼" double-fold hem on the top edge of each pocket. Edgestitch along the top edge only.

③ Add the Appliqués

* Apply the fusible web to the wrong side of each fabric scrap, following manufacturer's instructions. Fussy cut (see glossary, page 341) each scrap to size. Appliqué four motifs to four pockets using a narrow, tight zigzag or satin stitch (see glossary, page 342). These will be the corner pockets.

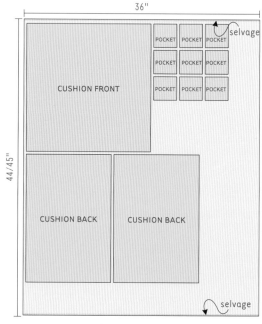

CUTTING LAYOUT

* The fifth appliqué will be peeking out of the middle pocket. Find the center of the cushion front, and center a pocket at this mark. Position the fifth appliqué so that it peeks out of the pocket. Remove the center pocket and appliqué this fifth fussy cut motif to the cushion front.

④ Attach the Pockets

With right sides facing up, pin a pocket at the cushion's center point. Using this pocket as a point of reference, pin all the other pockets on the cushion front, 1¾" apart. The four appliquéd pockets should be placed in each corner. Edgestitch all pockets in place along the side and bottom edges.

⑤ Assemble the Cushion's Envelope Back

∗ Hem one long edge of each cushion back piece with a ½" double-fold hem. If using a directional fabric, hem the top edge of one piece and the bottom edge of the other piece.

∗ With right sides facing up, layer the two hemmed back pieces on top of each other, overlapping the hemmed edges by 5" to create a 19" square. Baste the back pieces together along the overlapping raw side edges.

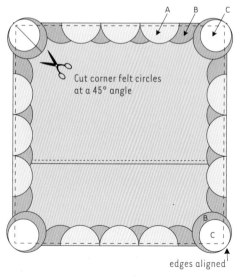

Cut corner felt circles at a 45° angle

edges aligned

STEP 6

⑥ Add the Felt Frills

∗ Position the cushion back right side up on a work surface. Pin a color B felt circle to each corner of the cushion back, overhanging the fabric edge slightly. Pin a smaller color C felt circle on top of each B circle, aligning the far edges as shown.

∗ Cut all remaining felt circles (colors A and B) in half. Pin four B semicircles along each side edge to edge (the two inner semicircles on each side should meet at the center point). Slip the outer semicircles under the corner circles.

∗ Pin three color A semicircles along each cushion side on top of those previously placed, alternating their position with that of the previous felt layer. The middle semicircle A should be centered along the cushion side.

∗ Baste all felt in place with edgestitch.

⑦ Assemble the Cushion

Pin the cushion back and front together, right sides facing. Stitch around all sides. Clip all corners and cut corner felt circles at a 45 degree angle up to the seam line. Remove any excess fabric and felt from the seam allowance to help reduce bulk. Turn right side out. Press all around and insert the pillow form.

⑧ How to Use the Cushion

Find nine small objects to put in the pockets and then get busy creating your own stories.

∗ **Version 1** Put the characters or props from a favorite story in the pockets. As you tell the story, take out the prop to make the story come alive.

∗ **Version 2** Place random small objects in the pockets, then build a story by taking one object out at a time and incorporating it into the story. For a twist, have your child stuff the pockets without your looking, handing you the props as you spin the tale – a "Mad Libs" approach!

∗ **Version 3** Have each person pull out an object in turn, adding to a collaborative story.

∗ **Version 4** Make your own game!

SECRET POCKETS PILLOW

Designed by Katherine Donaldson

Do you have a young friend with treasures to hide? If you have a young friend, then the answer to this question is almost certainly yes! This pillow comes with 12 pockets perfectly sized for small hands; grownups keep out! The pressure of the stuffing around the pockets holds them closed and keeps all the treasures safe, no matter the orientation of the pillow.

MATERIALS

* Pattern pieces (2), *see* sheet 5
* 1 yard of 54" quilting-weight or home dec-weight cotton fabric
* Two 13" squares of cotton batting
* 1 spool of coordinating thread
* 16 ounces of fiberfill
* Kit for 2 fabric-covered buttons, ¾"–1½" in diameter (sample shows ⅞" buttons)

* Scraps of coordinating fabric for covering buttons
* ⅔ yard of tufting twine or other strong cord
* 1 doll or upholstery needle, 5" or longer
* Coordinating embroidery floss if hand quilting, or to substitute for tufting twine (optional)

Finished dimensions – 4½" × 15"

Seam allowance – ½" unless otherwise specified

1 Measure, Mark, and Cut

Fold your fabric in half lengthwise with the right sides together, aligning the selvages. Position the pattern pieces according to the layout, measure and mark the additional pieces, and cut them out. Transfer markings from the pattern to the wrong side of the fabric.

* **Pillow face** (cut 2 on fold)
* **Petal** (cut 12)
* **Pocket** 4¾" × 8¾" (cut 12)

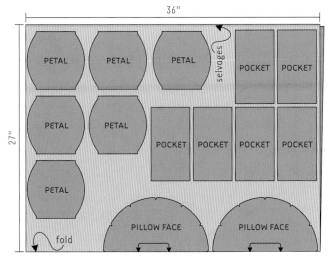

CUTTING LAYOUT

2 Quilt the Pillow Face

Pin one batting square to the wrong side of each pillow face. Machine or hand quilt each along the marked quilting lines. Trim batting to size.

3 Assemble the Side Gusset of the Pillow

Pin a petal piece to a pocket piece, right sides facing and short straight raw edges aligned. Stitch. Pin another petal to the opposite edge of the pocket piece and stitch. Continue joining petals and pocket pieces into one long gusset strip, alternating pocket and petal pieces. Press all seam allowances toward pockets.

④ Join the Side Gusset Strip into a Circle

Reinforce the two short raw ends of the assembled side by staystitching ⅜" from the raw edge and finish the seam allowance with a zigzag stitch. Fold the side strip with right sides facing and align the staystitched ends. Stitch two short ⅜" long seams, starting at each raw edge, leaving a 4" opening in the center for turning and stuffing in a later step. Press seam allowances open, pressing the raw edges of the opening ½" to wrong side.

⑤ Make the Pockets

Fold one pocket piece in half across the width, right sides together, aligning raw edges and seams. Stitch down both side edges from the seam to the fold. Repeat for all remaining pockets.

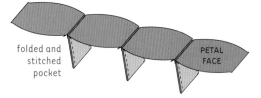

folded and
stitched
pocket

PETAL
FACE

⑥ Gather Petals, Attach Sides to Faces

* Baste a gathering stitch along both curved edges of each petal piece, ¼" from the raw edge (within the seam allowance). Leave a 3" tail at each end for gathering.

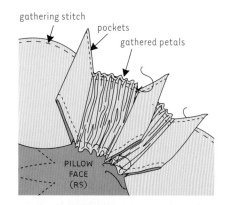

gathering stitch

pockets

gathered petals

PILLOW
FACE
(RS)

* Pin two adjacent pocket openings to two neighboring notches on a pillow face piece, right sides facing. Pull the gathering thread until the petal section fits the edge of the face, and distribute gathers evenly. Align raw edges and pin well. Stitch the gathered petals to the pillow face between the notches, backstitching at each notch to reinforce seams as they will experience a lot of pull and stress as pockets are filled and unfilled.
* Repeat for all remaining petals, then gather and attach the opposite edge of the side piece to the remaining pillow face.

⑦ Complete the Pillow

* Turn the pillow right side out through the side gusset opening. Wash and dry the pillow to shrink the batting and bring out the quilting lines.
* Stuff the pillow, starting at the individual petals, taking care not to trap the pockets. Make sure the pockets are all sandwiched between the fabric layers and point toward the center of the pillow. Periodically stick your hand into the pockets and check to make sure the stuffing is even on both sides. Continue stuffing the pillow to your desired firmness, then close the opening with an invisible slipstitch.

⑧ Make and Attach the Buttons

* Cover the two buttons with coordinating fabric, following manufacturer's directions.
* Find and mark the center of each pillow face. Fold the tufting twine in half and thread the fold through the shank of one button. Slip the button through the loop to secure the button onto the thread with a lark's head knot (see page 251).
* Thread both ends of the twine onto the doll needle. Pull the needle through the pillow at the center marks. Unthread the needle and tie the second button to the twine with a square knot or other strong, secure knot.
* Rethread the needle with both ends of the twine and pull back through the pillow, trimming the twine as needed and burying the ends in the bulk of the pillow.

NO-TOY-LEFT-BEHIND TRAVEL BLANKET

Designed by Kathy Beymer

This blanket is perfect for travel when you don't want dropped toys to land on a floor of questionable cleanliness or to get left behind. The Velcro loops hold toys while offering easy access for play. Two Velcro-closure pockets give you additional places to stash toys and small books on-the-go, and the ribbons add another level of tactile play and cuteness. As an extra bonus, the snag-free Velcro, wrapped through or around each toy, sticks to itself, but not to mommy's or daddy's clothing! Happy travels!

MATERIALS

* 1 yard of 44/45" quilting-weight cotton or flannel
* ¼ yard of Velcro Soft & Flexible Sew-On Tape
* 2 yards of Velcro Snag-Free Sew-On Tape
* Assorted ribbons and rickrack for trim
* 1 spool of coordinating thread

Finished dimensions – 28" × 21"

Seam allowance – ½" unless otherwise specified

Measure, Mark, and Cut

Lay out your fabric in a single layer with the wrong side facing up. Measure and mark the following pieces on the wrong side of the fabric and cut them out.

* **Blanket** 28" × 22" (cut 2)
* **Large divided pocket** 8" × 14" (cut 1)
* **Small pocket** 8" × 10" (cut 1)

From Velcro Soft & Flexible Sew-On Tape, cut:

* **Small closure** 2" (cut 1)
* **Medium closure** 3" (cut 1)
* **Large closure** 4" (cut 1)

From Velcro Snag-Free Sew-On Tape, cut:

* **Toy straps** 9" strips (cut 8)

From ribbon, rickrack, and/or trims, cut:

* **Accents** 4" strips (at least 24)

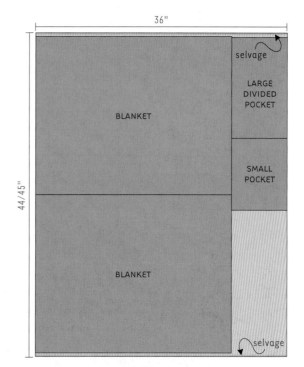

CUTTING LAYOUT

36"

44/45"

selvage

LARGE DIVIDED POCKET

BLANKET

SMALL POCKET

BLANKET

selvage

② Make the Pockets

* Hem the top long edges of both pockets with a ¼" double-fold hem.

Large divided pocket: Press the left and bottom raw edges ½" to the wrong side (the right-hand edge will be in the blanket side seam). On the wrong side, mark a vertical dividing line 5½" from the folded side edge. Center the hook half of the 3" piece of Velcro on the wrong side of the larger pocket segment, ¼" down from the top hemmed edge, and stitch.

Small pocket: Press both side and bottom raw edges of the small pocket ½" to the wrong side and press. Center the hook half of the 4" piece of Velcro on the wrong side of the pocket, ¼" down from top hemmed edge, and stitch.

③ Attach Pockets to the Blanket Front

Large divided pocket: Place the blanket front right side up on your work surface.

* Pin the pocket, right side up, on the blanket front, 6½" up from bottom edge. Align right-hand raw edges.
* Using the Velcro placement as a guide, position the loop halves of the 2" and 3" Velcro pieces on the blanket front. Holding the pocket out of the way, stitch the Velcro in place.
* Edgestitch the pocket to the blanket front along the left-hand and bottom edges. Topstitch a second row of stitching ½" from the pocket edge, for extra security. Stitch the dividing vertical line 5½" from the left edge.

Small pocket: Pin the small pocket on the blanket front, right side up, 3" down from top edge and 4½" from right-hand edge. The pockets should line up on the left side.

* Using the Velcro as a guide, position the loop half of the 4" Velcro piece on the blanket front and stitch in place as before.
* If desired, fold one 4" strip of ribbon or other trim in half, and tuck between the small pocket and the blanket front on one edge of the pocket.
* Edgestitch the small pocket to the blanket front along the side and bottom edges. Topstitch a second row of stitching as before.

④ Add Toy Straps and Trim

Fold all remaining 4" trim pieces in half, matching raw edges, before attaching them to the blanket. Pin the folded ribbon pieces around all four sides of the blanket front every 3" or so, right sides together, aligning raw edges. Place two Velcro strips on each side of the blanket, approximately 4" from the corners as shown in the photo. Please note that the Snag-Free Velcro strips should *not* be folded as the ribbon is. Baste all trims and Velcro in place with edgestitch.

⑤ Assemble the Blanket

* Pin the blanket front and back, right sides together, sandwiching the trims and Velcro in between. Stitch all around, leaving a 6" opening at the bottom for turning. Clip corners and turn right side out, squaring off the corners.
* Press all around, turning the raw edges of the opening ½" to wrong side. Edgestitch on all sides, closing the opening as you go.
* Attach toys to the Velcro loops and commence play!

FaBRIC PHOTO BLOCKS

Designed by Lindsay Conner

These soft, stackable blocks can hold treasured photos of family and friends or even educational flash cards. Better still, the photos can be removed and toys wiped clean with warm, soapy water after playtime.

MATERIALS

* 1 yard of 44/45" home dec-weight fabric
* ¼ yard of 54"-wide 12-gauge clear vinyl
* 8¾ yards of ¼"-wide coordinating ribbon
* 1 spool of coordinating thread
* 10-ounce bag of fiberfill
* Low-tack double-sided tape (optional)
* Teflon presser foot (optional)

Finished dimensions – Small block 5" × 5"; medium block 7" × 7"; large block 9" × 9".

Seam allowance – ½" unless otherwise specified

 **Measure, Mark, and Cut**

Lay your fabric in a single layer with the wrong side facing up. Measure and mark the following pieces on the wrong side of your fabric and cut them out.

* **Small block** 6" × 6" (cut 6)
* **Medium block** 8" × 8" (cut 6)
* **Large block** 10" × 10" (cut 6)

From vinyl, cut:

* **Medium/large window** 4¼" × 4¼" (cut 12)
* **Small window** 3½" × 3½" (cut 6)

From the ¼"-wide ribbon, cut:

* 3½"-long strips (cut 6 for the open ends of the small windows)
* 11½"-long strips (cut 6 for the closed edges of the small windows)
* 4¼"-long strips (cut 12 for the open ends of the medium/large windows)
* 13¾"-long strips (cut 12 for the closed edges of the medium/large windows)

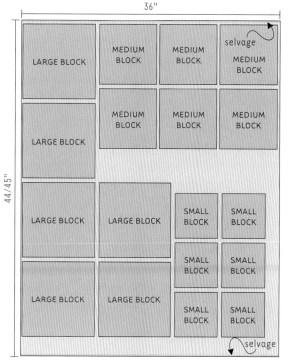

CUTTING LAYOUT

❷ Prep the Vinyl Windows

Place a 4¼" length of ribbon along one edge of a medium/large vinyl window. Zigzag-stitch the ribbon in place. You may find it easiest to use a Teflon foot to help prevent the vinyl from sticking to your machine as you sew. Repeat with the remaining 11 windows of this size. Repeat the process to finish one edge of each small vinyl windows with the 3½" pieces of ribbon. These will be the open/top edges on the finished cubes.

❸ Position and Attach Vinyl Windows

With both right sides facing up, center one medium/large vinyl window on the right side of a large block piece. If desired, you may wish to use low-tack double-sided tape to temporarily hold vinyl in place while stitching. Position a 13¾"-long piece of ¼" ribbon along the three unfinished edges of the vinyl window to create a continuous border, folding the cut end of ribbon ½" on one end over the top edge of the vinyl window and to the wrong side. Use a wide zigzag stitch to secure the ribbon and window to the fabric, mitering the ribbon (see mitering instructions on page 13) at the corners and folding the remaining ½" of ribbon to the wrong side of the opposite top corner of the vinyl window. Repeat using the medium/large vinyl windows and remaining 13¾"-lengths of ribbon for the remaining large and medium blocks. Repeat to attach the small vinyl windows to the small block fabric piecess using the 11½"-lengths of ribbon.

❹ Make the Blocks

* With right sides together, position two large block pieces with all raw edges aligned. Stitch along one side, stopping and starting ½" from each corner; press seam allowance open.

NOTE: *Be very careful to keep your iron away from the vinyl windows as they will melt, damaging your project and your iron.*

* Continue stitching a total of four large block pieces together, end to end, in the same manner, finishing by joining the first large block to the fourth large block to create a frame.

* With right sides together, pin a large block piece to one open end of the frame created above. Pin together, making sure that the corners meet. Stitch together, leaving the sewing machine needle in the down position ½" from each corner; pivot your work 90 degrees and continue stitching the square in place.

* Repeat to stitch the sixth large block piece to the remaining open end of the large block cube. Leave a 4" opening along one edge for turning.

* Turn the block right side out, and use fiberfill to firmly stuff the block. You may find it helpful to use a turning tool (such as a chopstick) to push the fiberfill into the four corners of the block. Slipstitch the opening closed.

* Repeat to create the medium and small photo blocks.

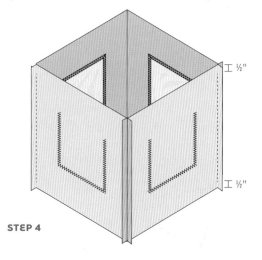

STEP 4

SILLY CIRCLES TUMMY TIME PLAYMAT

Designed by Rachel M. Knoblich

Use up some scraps to create this playmat, which can double as a changing pad, nap mat, or blanket. For extra tactile interest, use flannels, corduroy, faux fur, and other textured fabrics for the appliqués; for visual stimulation, stick with bold designs with high contrast.

MATERIALS

* 1 yard of 44/45" quilting-weight fabric
* Fabric scraps for appliquéd circles, at least 4"-6" in all directions
* 1 yard of double-sided fusible web
* 2 circle templates, 4" and 6" diameter

* 1 spool of coordinating thread
* 22" × 36" piece of lightweight, low-loft batting
* 3½ yards of ½"-¾"-wide double-fold bias tape
* 4" piece of ¾"-1"-wide Velcro

Finished dimensions – 36" × 22"

Seam allowance – ½" unless otherwise specified

① Measure, Mark, and Cut

Fold your fabric in half lengthwise with the right sides together, aligning the selvages. Cut two 36" × 22" pieces by cutting along the fold and trimming off the selvages. If fabric isn't quite 44" wide, simply cut two pieces of equal size.

From the fabric scraps and fusible web, cut:

* **Small circles** 4" in diameter (cut 7)
* **Large circles** 6" in diameter (cut 7)

② Appliqué the Circles

* Fuse the web to the wrong sides of the circle appliqués following the manufacturer's instructions.
* Arrange circles as desired on the right side of one playmat piece. Keep all circles at least 2" from the playmat's raw edges, and overlap some of the circles as shown. Fuse the appliqués to the playmat, following the manufacturer's instructions.
* Zigzag-stitch around all circle edges to secure.

③ Quilt the Playmat

* Place the playmat front and back on a surface with wrong sides together, raw edges aligned, and the batting sandwiched in between. Pin the layers on all sides and baste with an edgestitch.
* Topstitch around the border of each appliquéd circle to quilt the playmat.
* Fold the playmat in half lengthwise and press to crease. Open and topstitch down the crease from one end to the other.

④ Bind the Playmat

Starting at one short end, pin the double-fold bias tape around all edges, mitering corners as you go (see page 13). Zigzag stitch on all sides, stopping 2" from the start of your stitch line; trim the tape to overlap the beginning by 2". Fold under the loose end of bias tape ½" to the wrong side before stitching the rest of the way.

⑤ Attach the Velcro

* Fold the playmat in half lengthwise along the stitched center line. Roll up the playmat, starting at one short end. Pin the loop tape to the outer bound edge, centered between the fold and the corner. The far end of the loop tape should extend at least 2" onto the back of the playmat, leaving 2" exposed. Pin the hook tape to the back of the playmat where the loop half falls when rolled up, centered side to side.

* Unroll the playmat. Stitch the loop tape to the playmat with a box stitch (see glossary, page 340). Stitch the hook tape with an edgestitch.

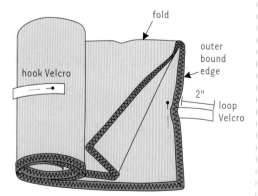

BABY PHOTO ALBUM

Designed by Rebecca Yaker

Babies love faces, so why not make a photo album perfect for your little bean? Choose a bold fabric for your baby's first photo album. The finished book will be brimming with colorful graphics, crinkly sounds, and faces of loved ones! Watch your baby's eyes light up as he or she recognizes a familiar face on every page. You may even choose to customize the front of the book with your baby's name or initials. The finished album holds ten 4-by-6-inch photos.

MATERIALS

* 1 yard of 44/45" quilting-weight cotton
* ¾ yard of fusible fleece
* Cellophane, enough to cut six 3" × 14" pieces
* ¼ yard of 54"-wide 12-gauge clear vinyl
* Ten 24"-long pieces of ¼"-wide double-fold bias tape
* 1 spool of coordinating thread
* Teflon presser foot (optional)
* One coordinating craft felt square for appliqué letters (optional)
* Embroidery floss for appliqué (optional)
* 1½ yards of ½"–1"-wide double-fold bias tape

Finished dimensions – Closed, the album is 7½" wide × 9" tall and holds ten 4" × 6" photos.

Seam allowance – ½" unless otherwise specified

Note about bias tape: *Use purchased double-fold bias tape or make your own (see page 12). To create more visual appeal, bind each photo window with a different color or pattern. This will help keep the book interesting for baby.*

① Measure, Mark, and Cut

Fold your fabric in half lengthwise with the right sides together, aligning the selvages. Measure and mark the following pattern pieces, and cut them out.

* **Album cover** 9" × 16½" (cut 2)
* **Pages 1/4** 8½" × 16" (cut 2)
* **Pages 2/3** 8½" × 15½" (cut 2)
* **Crinkle strips** 3" × 14" (cut 6)

From fusible fleece, cut:

* **Album cover** 9" × 16½" (cut 2)
* **Pages 1/4** 8½" × 16" (cut 2)
* **Pages 2/3** 8½" × 15½" (cut 2)

From cellophane, cut:

* **Crinkle strips** 3" × 14" (cut 6)

From clear vinyl, cut:

* **Photo window** 4¼" × 6¼" (cut 10)

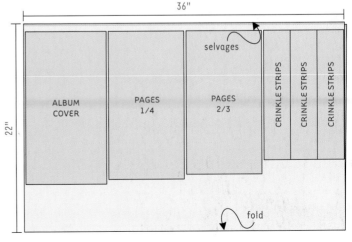

CUTTING LAYOUT

② Apply the Fusible Fleece

Fuse the fleece to the wrong sides of the corresponding pieces according to the manufacturer's instructions.

③ Bind the Photo Windows

Use the ¼"-wide double-fold bias tape strips to bind the edges of each of the vinyl photo windows, mitering corners as you go (see page 13). You may find it easiest to use a Teflon foot to help prevent the vinyl from sticking to your machine as you sew.

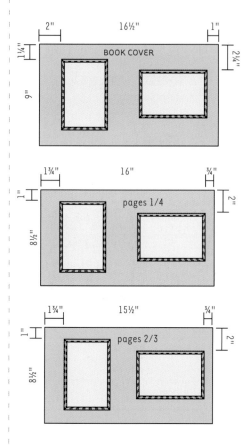

STEP 4

④ Attach the Photo Windows

With both right sides facing up, position the bound photo windows on the right sides of all pages, and one cover piece (this becomes the inside cover). You have the choice to make some photos windows suitable for vertical images, and others for horizontal. Follow the diagram for window placement locations, choosing either the vertical and/or horizontal placement possibilities. Edgestitch the windows along the side and bottom edges, leaving the top edges open for inserting photos.

⑤ Make the Pages

* Position pages 1/4 with right sides together. Stitch around all four sides, leaving a 2" opening along the bottom edge. Clip corners and turn right side out, turning the edges at the opening to the inside. Carefully press the edges of the pages, taking care that your iron does not come in contact with the vinyl photo windows, which will melt. Edgestitch around all four sides, closing the opening as you stitch.
* Repeat with pages 2/3. Set pages aside.

⑥ Make the Crinkle Strips

* Pin two cellophane pieces to the wrong side of a fabric crinkle strip piece. Baste together with a ¼" seam allowance around all four sides. Repeat with the remaining cellophane and two fabric crinkle strips.
* With right sides together, place a cellophane-lined strip on a cellophane-free crinkle strip, aligning raw edges. Stitch together, leaving a 2" opening in the center of one long side for turning. Clip corners, turn right side out, and press with a low heat setting, so as not to damage the cellophane, or your iron. Invisibly slipstitch the opening closed.
* Repeat to make two more crinkle strips from the remaining pieces.

7 Assemble the Pages

On a flat surface, arrange the finished pieces in the order shown, carefully centering the pages. Pin together. Use a disappearing fabric pen to mark a line through the center of the innermost pages, parallel to the side edges. Topstitch through all pieces on both sides of the marked line, ½" away from the marked line.

8 Personalize the Outside Cover

* Use a bold graphic font to print out the letters of your child's name, initials, or some other message to appliqué to the front cover. The finished front cover is 8" tall × 7½" wide, so your design needs to fit within these dimensions.

* Cut the letters from the printer paper, then use them as pattern pieces to cut letters from the felt. Place as desired on the right side of the right-hand side of the remaining cover piece, and stitch in place with a zigzag or straight stitch, or embroider by hand.

9 Finish the Photo Album

* Position the album covers with wrong sides together, aligning raw edges and ensuring that the appliqué is positioned on the front cover. Baste covers together using a ¼" seam allowance.

* Use the ½"-1"-wide double-fold bias tape to encase the four edges of the album cover. Unfold the bias tape and turn one end ½" to the wrong side. Starting with the folded end, with right sides together, attach the bias tape to the inside of the album cover, along the bottom edge. Pin the tape in place, and miter it at each corner (see page 13). Stitch in the crease closest to the raw edge.

* Fold the bias tape over the edge to the front of the album cover and pin in place. From the inside cover, edgestitch close to the folded edge of the bias tape, taking care to catch the front folded edge of bias tape and the mitered corners in the stitching line.

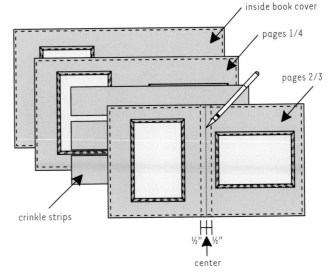

inside book cover

pages 1/4

pages 2/3

crinkle strips

½"   ½"

center

STEP 7

CHAPTER 10

DOLLS & PLUSHiES

LITTLE ONES LOVE THEIR SNUGGLY, STUFFED FRIENDS.

Find projects in this chapter to create a menagerie of new friends: giraffes, whales, and even a zebra marionette, to name a few. As an added bonus, there's a baby-doll carrier and a doll-size bed for when the day is done.

DOLL BED (WITH STORAGE!)

Designed by Brie Jensen

Take a handy storage bin and turn it into a bed for your little one's best-loved dolls or plushies! Great for travel, too; just place the little doll, quilt, and pillow inside, shut the lid, and go.

MATERIALS

* 1 yard of nondirectional 44/45" quilting-weight cotton or flannel
* ½ yard of batting, at least 40" wide
* 1 spool of coordinating thread
* 1"-wide (or wider) painter's tape
* 16-quart plastic storage bin, approximately 12" × 16"
* Drill with small drill bit
* Clothespins (optional)

* Large embroidery needle
* Coordinating embroidery floss
* 30 (2-hole) buttons, ½"–1" in diameter. These can all be the same, or an assortment.
* Hot glue gun and hot glue sticks
* 1⅔ yards of ¼"-wide pompom or other trim (optional)
* Approximately 1 oz. of fiberfill

Finished dimensions – approximately 12" × 16" × 7" (the size of the 16 quart plastic storage bin)

Seam allowance – ½" unless otherwise specified

① **Measure, Mark, and Cut**

Lay out your fabric in a single layer with the wrong side facing up. Measure and mark the following pieces on the fabric and cut them out.

* **Bed skirt** 7" × 44" (cut 3)
* **Pillow** 7" × 10" (cut 1 from the end of one bed skirt piece)
* **Mattress** 15" × 19" (cut 1)
* **Quilted blanket** 15" × 25" (cut 1)

From batting, cut:

* **Mattress** 13" × 17" (cut 2)
* **Blanket** 15 × 12½" (cut 1)

② **Make the Bed Skirt**

* Stitch all three bed-skirt pieces with the short ends together, right sides facing, forming a large ring. Press seams open. Serge or zigzag-stitch both long edges of the bed skirt, then finish both with a ¼" single-fold hem.

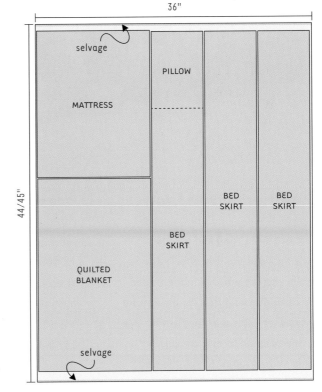

CUTTING LAYOUT

* To form the gathers, baste along the top edge, leaving 4"-5" thread tails at the beginning and end of your stitching; do not backstitch. Gather the bed skirt by pulling on the thread tails until that edge fits snugly around the top of the storage bin. Tie off the thread ends. Distribute gathers evenly and zigzag-stitch all the way around to secure the gathers.

③ Prep the Storage Bin

* Affix painter's tape around the top edge of the bin's interior. Measure and mark a placement line ½" down from the top edge all around. On each long side of the bin interior, make nine evenly spaced button placement marks on the marked line, starting 1" in from each corner. In our sample, marks are 1½" apart. Your distance may vary, depending on the bin's size. On each short side of the bin interior, make six evenly spaced marks in the same way.

* Drill two holes approximately ⅛" apart at each mark. Drilling through the painter's tape will ensure the plastic does not crack while drilling. Do check the placement of the holes with your button(s) before drilling, to see if the drilled holes should be placed vertically or horizontally, depending on how you want your buttons to lay.

④ Attach the Bed Skirt to the Bin

Slip the bed skirt around the bin exterior. Secure temporarily with clothespins or painter's tape all around. Starting from the bin interior, bring embroidery needle and floss through one drilled hole, through the bed skirt, and through a button. Leaving a tail inside for tying, bring the needle back through the opposite buttonhole, bed skirt, and adjoining drilled hole. Tie off to secure the button. Repeat with remaining buttons.

⑤ Make the Mattress

* Glue the two mattress battings together with a small bead of hot glue, then glue the batting to the top outside of the bin lid with another small bead of hot glue.

* Press the raw edge of the mattress fabric ¼" to wrong side all around, then place it wrong side up on your work surface. Center the bin lid, batting side down, on the mattress fabric.

* Apply a 2" bead of hot glue along the side edge of the lid just above the bottom edge of the lip, centered on one long edge. Press the mattress fabric to hot glue to secure. Apply a bead of hot glue to the opposite long edge and secure in a similar fashion, then repeat for both short sides. Continue gluing the fabric to the bin lid all around, working out from the center of each side and leaving the corners for last. Box fold each corner as if you are wrapping a gift, trim the fabric to minimize bulk, then fold in, apply hot glue to the lid, and secure.

* Apply pompom or other desired trim around the base of the mattress (edge of the lid) with hot glue.

⑥ Make the Pillow

Fold the pillow fabric in half, right sides facing, to form a 7" × 5" pillow. Stitch around all three open edges, leaving a 3" opening on the long edge. Clip corners, turn right side out through the opening, and press, turning in the edges of the opening ½" to the wrong side. Stuff to desired firmness, and hand-sew the opening closed with an invisible stitch.

⑦ Make the Quilted Blanket

Fold the remaining fabric in half, right sides facing, to form a 15" × 12½" blanket. Place blanket batting on top and stitch all around, leaving a 4" opening on one edge for turning. Trim the batting close to the stitching, clip corners, and turn right side out. Press and complete as for the pillow. Hand-tie the blanket with embroidery floss, or machine- or hand-quilt.

PHILIPPE THE WHALE PILLOW

Designed by Emily Steffen

A simple pillow-y toy that will dress up any kid's room, Philippe loves being a reading pillow – especially if his favorite friend will read aloud to him sometimes!

MATERIALS

* Template (see page 336)
* 1 yard of 44/45" quilting-weight cotton or flannel
* ⅛ yard of contrast fabric for edging
* 6" square of double-sided fusible webbing
* 6" square of scrap fabric for embellishment
* Coordinating embroidery floss for embellishment appliqué (optional)
* 1 spool of coordinating thread
* 12 ounces of fiberfill

Finished dimensions – 15" × 17" × 3"

Seam allowance – ½" unless otherwise specified

① Measure, Mark, and Cut

Fold your fabric in half lengthwise with the right sides together, aligning the selvages. Using the template on page 336 as a guide, draw the body with a fabric marker or pencil, and cut:

* **Body** cut 2
* **Whale side gussets** 2½" × 42" (cut 2)

Out of contrast edging fabric, cut:

* **Edging strips** 2" × 42" (cut 2)

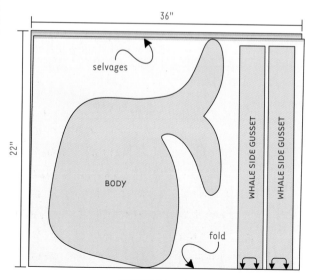

CUTTING LAYOUT

(Layout labels: 36", 22", selvages, BODY, fold, WHALE SIDE GUSSET, WHALE SIDE GUSSET)

② Make the Appliqué

* Draw a heart motif onto the paper backing of the fusible webbing. Apply fusible webbing to the wrong side of the scrap embellishment fabric, following manufacturer's instructions, and cut out the heart.
* Remove the paper backing and fuse the heart appliqué onto the body, using the photo as a guide. With embroidery floss and needle, use your favorite outline stitch to sew around the heart, about ¼" from the edge of the appliqué.

③ Make the Contrast Edging

Pin the two contrast edging strips with right sides together at one short end, and stitch to join. Press seam open. Press one short raw edge ½" to wrong side. Fold the pieced edging in half lengthwise, wrong sides together, and press.

④ Make the Side Gusset

Pin the side gusset pieces with right sides together and stitch along one short edge. Press seam open.

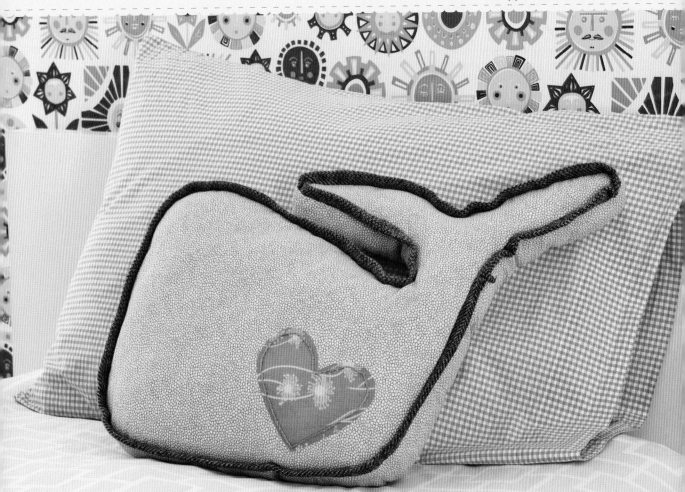

⑤ Assemble the Whale Front

Pin the pieced side gusset strip to the front body with right sides together, sandwiching the edging in between the layers and aligning all raw edges. Stitch all around, starting and stopping 2" from the beginning and end of the side gusset pieces and edging. Trim any excess from the gusset and edging pieces, allowing at least 1" overlap. Stitch the short ends of the side gusset piece together to join. Tuck the short raw edge of the edging into the folded end, and complete the stitching.

⑥ Finish the Whale

Pin the back body to the side piece with right sides together. Stitch all around, leaving a 4" opening for turning and stuffing. Clip and notch the seam allowances along all curved edges and corners, taking care not to clip into the stitching. Turn the whale right side out, pushing all corners out at the tail. Stuff to desired firmness and hand-sew the opening closed.

HEIGH-HO HORSEY MARIONETTE

Designed by Jessica Puckett Fishman and Trish Hoskins

Here's a project that isn't as ambitious as it looks. Make a zebra or a horse, depending on your child's interests. Don't fancy yourself a puppeteer? Use the instructions to make a cute plush, omitting the strings and slats, that is the perfect size for giving rides to your child's dolls or action figures.

MATERIALS

* Pattern pieces (9), *see* sheet 3
* 1 yard of 44/45"quilting-weight or home dec-weight flannel, light wool, or lightweight pile fabric
* 1 felt square in coordinating color for hooves
* 1 spool of coordinating thread
* 6 yards each of black and white worsted-weight yarn for a zebra (24 yards of any coordinating color, if making a horse with longer mane)
* 2 safety eyes or buttons, approximately ½" in diameter
* 12 ounces of fiberfill
* 6" diameter circle template

For marionette version only:
* 6½ yards of strong yarn, kite string, or similar for marionette strings
* Large crewel or embroidery needle
* 3 jumbo craft sticks or wood slats, 6"-9" long and ¾"-1½" wide
* Drill and small drill bit, ⁷⁄₁₆"-⅛" in diameter
* Fine-grit sandpaper
* Wood glue
* ¼ yard of twill tape or ribbon, no wider than the craft sticks
* Staple gun and staples
* Pliers or masking/duct tape (optional)

Finished dimensions – Stuffed horse is approximately 15" long and 15" tall, including head.

Seam allowance – ¼" unless otherwise specified

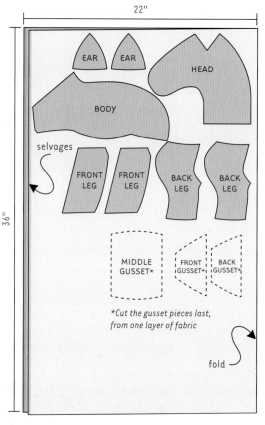

CUTTING LAYOUT

Make the Horsey

❶ **Measure, Mark, and Cut**

Fold your fabric in half lengthwise with the right sides together, aligning the selvages. Position the pattern pieces according to the layout and cut them out. Transfer markings from the patterns to the wrong side of fabric.

* **Head** (cut 2)
* **Front leg** (cut 4)
* **Ears** (cut 4)
* **Back leg** (cut 4)
* **Body** (cut 2)

Unfold your fabric and cut:

* **Front gusset** (cut 1)*
* **Middle gusset** (cut 1)*
* **Back gusset** (cut 1)*

From the felt, cut:

* **Hoof bottom** (cut 4)
* **Front hoof** (cut 4, traced from the front leg)
* **Back hoof** (cut 4, traced from the back leg)

② Make and Attach the Ears

* Pin two ear pieces right sides together. Stitch along both curved edges, leaving the bottom edge open. Clip stitched corners, turn right side out and press. Fold the bottom corners of each ear to meet in the middle of the ear, and baste in place. Repeat for the other ear.

* Pin each ear on the right side of a head piece, centered on one side of the dart as shown, with the folded side facing down. Fold each head, with right sides facing, to match up the other side of the dart, sandwiching the ear in between the layers. Stitch the seams and ears together.

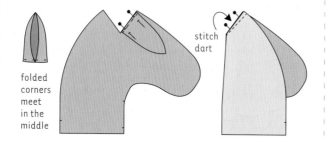

folded corners meet in the middle

stitch dart

③ Make and Attach the Mane

For the zebra: Cut yarn into 80 pieces measuring 3". For the sample, we cut 40 black strands and 40 white strands for a striped mane.

For a horse: Cut yarn into about 80 pieces measuring 7"-9".

* Fold each yarn segment in half; place them on the right side of one head piece, from the ears down the length of the neck, to about 1" from the bottom raw edge. Align the folded ends of the yarn with the fabric's raw edge and baste. It may work best to add the yarn lengths as you stitch, in a density that gives you the fullness you want.

④ Complete the Head

* Install safety eyes at placement marks, following manufacturer's instructions. (For children over three years of age, it's okay to substitute buttons.)

* Pin the two head pieces together, right sides facing and raw edges aligned. Stitch to attach, leaving the neck and marked opening unstitched for turning and stuffing. Turn right side out and press.

* Flatten the open neck edge of the horse so that the front and back seams align. Baste the neck closed and set aside.

⑤ Make the Legs

* Pin a front hoof felt piece on the right side of a front leg, aligning side and bottom raw edges. Stitch all around with edgestitch. Repeat for remaining front hoof and front leg pieces, and back hoof and back leg pieces.

* Pin two front leg pieces right sides together and raw edges aligned. Stitch along both sides, stopping ¼" from the bottom edge. Leave the top and bottom ends open. Repeat for all remaining front and back legs.

* Pin one hoof bottom piece to the bottom edge of one leg, right sides facing and raw edges aligned. Stitch all around, clipping the bottom edge of each leg as needed to ease curves. Repeat for remaining legs, then turn all legs right side out.

* Stuff the bottom half of each leg lightly. Be sure to push fiberfill into the hock (pointed part) of the back leg. Flatten each leg so that the front and back seams align. Stitch across the leg 3½" up from the bottom seam to form a knee joint. Stuff the top half of each leg lightly, and baste opening closed.

⑥ Attach the Legs to the Gusset

* Place the front legs on the right side of the middle gusset at the placement marks, aligning raw edges. Make sure the front seam of each leg faces *away* from the middle gusset. Baste in place.

* Place the back legs on the right side of the middle gusset at the placement marks, aligning raw edges. Make sure the front seam of each leg faces *toward* the middle gusset. Baste in place.

* Pin the front gusset to the middle gusset, aligning raw edges and sandwiching the front legs between the fabric layers. Stitch. Attach the back gusset in the same way.

⑦ Make and Attach the Tail

Cut yarn into ten 13" lengths, and gather them together. Tie in the center with a short length of yarn. Fold the bunch in half at the tie and place on the right side of one body piece at placement marks, aligning the fold with the raw edge. Baste in place.

⑧ Attach the Head to the Body

Pin the body pieces together, right sides facing and raw edges aligned. Stitch together at the chest and along the back, leaving the neck and bottom edge unstitched.

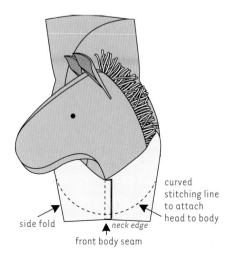

side fold   *neck edge*
front body seam

curved stitching line to attach head to body

* With the body still wrong side out, insert the neck end of the head into the body through the bottom; align the raw neck edges of both pieces. Flatten the body at the neck opening so that the chest and back seams of the body are aligned with each other, and with the front and back seams of the head.

* Use the circle template to trace a stitching line that curves inward toward the body at the side folds. Stitch along this curve to attach the head to the body.

⑨ Attach the Gusset to the Body

Pin the pieced gusset to the body, right sides together. Align the gusset front raw edge with the body front raw edge, and likewise align the back gusset and body back raw edges. Stitch all around, clipping and pivoting the raw edge of the body at the gusset corners, and leaving an opening between the front and back legs on one side for turning and stuffing. Take it slowly, adjusting the legs as you go. You may find that a zipper foot helps with this step, as it will be a bit tight with all the bulk of the legs between your fabric layers.

⑩ Complete the Horse

Turn the horse right side out. Stuff the body to desired fullness and hand-sew the opening closed. Stuff the head to desired fullness through the front neck opening, taking care to fully stuff the nose and all curves. Hand-sew the opening closed.

Make the Marionette

① Prepare the Strings

From the yarn or kite string, cut four 36" lengths, two 30" lengths, and one 24" length. Knot one end of each length with a double knot, about 2" from the end.

② String the Legs

* Thread the large crewel/embroidery needle with one 36" length. String through one front knee joint, back to front, so the knot is at the back of the knee. Repeat for the other front leg. Bury the 2" tails, using the needle.

* Thread the needle with another 36" length. String it through the pointed hock in a back leg, from bottom to top, so the knot is below the hock. Repeat for the last 36" length of string and the other back leg. Bury each of the 2" tails in between the fabric layers, using the needle.

❸ String the Head and Body

Thread the needle with one 30" length and string it through a few stitches in the back seam at the base of the neck. String the remaining 30" length through a few stitches at the back seam an inch or so above the tail. String the 24" length through a few stitches in the seam between the ears. Bury the tails as before.

❹ Make and String the Controls

On each of the three control sticks (craft sticks or wood slats), drill a small hole ½" from each end and centered side to side. On one of the control sticks only, also drill a hole through the center of the stick (this becomes the front control). Sand around all holes to smooth.

Form a T with the two-hole sticks as shown, with the top control centered and overhanging the other by 1". Glue together with wood glue according to manufacturer's directions.

Cut two 4½" lengths of twill tape or ribbon. Fold each end under ¼" to the wrong side twice and stitch to finish the ends. Use these to form a strap loop on each set of control sticks:

* *Front control:* Center one strap on control stick with the ends about 2"-2½" apart. Staple both ends to secure.
* *Back control:* Position the remaining strap on the crossbar of the control, straddling the top control with the ends about 2"-2½" apart. Staple both strap ends.

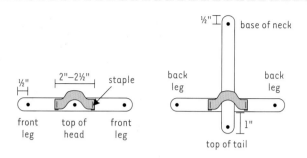

FRONT CONTROL   **BACK CONTROL**

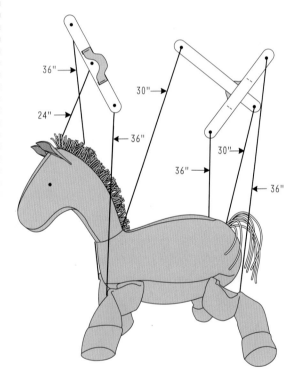

If the ends of the staples poke through the underside, use pliers to crimp the ends, or cover them with a small piece of masking or duct tape.

String each of the controls with the corresponding strings, as shown in the diagrams, from bottom to top, tying a square knot at the top to secure.

OCT-TOY-PUS ANIMAL ORGANIZER

Designed by Katherine Donaldson

This eight-legged friend will hang around your bed and hold onto eight of your toys, only nibbling a little bit when you aren't looking. And it won't ever come after you, honest! This octopus was designed to feel at home under a bunk bed, but you can also hang it from the wall with a bracket.

MATERIALS

* Pattern pieces (2), *see* sheet 6
* 1 yard of nondirectional 44/45" wide quilting-weight cotton
* 2 felt squares in coordinating colors for eyes, one light and one dark (pink and black shown)
* Circle templates: 1⅜", 1½", 1¾", and 2" in diameter
* 1 spool of coordinating thread
* Coordinating embroidery floss (optional)
* 20 ounces of fiberfill
* ⅔ yard of ⅛"-¼"-wide ribbon

Finished dimensions – 9" tall × 27" diameter

Seam allowance – ¼" unless otherwise specified

① Measure, Mark, and Cut

Fold your fabric in half lengthwise with the right sides together, aligning the selvages. Position the pattern pieces according to the layout and cut them out. Transfer markings from the pattern to the wrong side of fabric.

* **Body** (cut 2)
* **Head** (cut 6)

From lighter felt, cut:

* **Eye** 2" circle (cut 2)
* **Siphon** 1½" circle (cut 1)

From darker felt, cut:

* **Eye interior** 1¾" circle (cut 2)
* **Siphon interior** 1⅜" circle (cut 1)

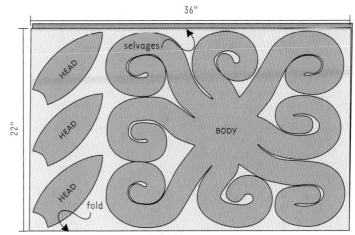

CUTTING LAYOUT

❷ Assemble the Body

* Cut out the inner marked neck opening from just one body piece. Staystitch around the opening, ¼" from the finished edge. This keeps the fabric from stretching out, and provides a guide for attaching the head in a later step.
* Pin the octopus body pieces together, right sides facing and raw edges aligned. Stitch all around, taking care to keep your stitch line fluid and curvy. Clip and notch curves and set aside.

❸ Appliqué the Head

Refer to head pattern and center and mark the cutout shapes onto the lighter-colored eye and siphon pieces, and carefully cut them out. Refer to the head pattern to place the eyes and siphon pieces, layering the darker pieces under the lighter pieces. (The darker interior pieces will be visible through the cutouts.) Zigzag-stitch or hand-sew the eyes and siphon in place and around the cutouts with a blanket stitch (see glossary, page 339), using embroidery floss.

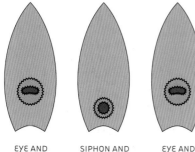

| EYE AND INTERIOR CUTOUT | SIPHON AND INTERIOR CUTOUT | EYE AND INTERIOR CUTOUT |

STEP 3

❹ Assemble the Head

* Pin a head piece with eye appliqué to the head piece with siphon appliqué, right sides facing and raw edges aligned. Stitch along one curved side edge, stopping ¼" from the top raw edge and leaving the bottom edge open.
* Stitch the remaining head piece with eye appliqué to the opposite side of the siphon head piece, making sure that all seams meet at the top. Press seam allowances toward the eye pieces. Topstitch close to both seams.
* Assemble the remaining three non-appliquéd head pieces in the same way to create the back of the head.
* Form a loop at the center of the ribbon and tack to hold. Pin the loop to the top of the head (where the seams meet), and stitch the ribbon along the raw edge with a zigzag stitch, keeping within the seam allowance.

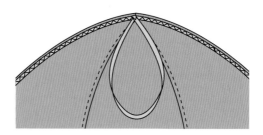

* Staystitch the head front and back pieces ¼" from all raw edges. This keeps the bias-cut fabric from stretching out in the following steps.
* Pin the head front and back pieces together, right sides facing and raw edges aligned. Align the top center seams and make sure the ribbon loop is sandwiched between the fabric layers.
* Stitch up one side, across the center point, and down the other side, leaving a 2"-3" break in the stitching on one side for turning and stuffing. This keeps the circle of the neck together.
* Press the seam allowance toward head back and topstitch up and over the head along the back half, close to the seam. Do not topstitch along opening.

⑤ Assemble the Octopus

* Insert the head into the neck opening of the body, right sides facing and raw edges aligned. Stitch all around, clip the seam allowance, and turn right side out through the opening in the head. Take care to turn out all tentacles fully. Press all seam allowances down toward the body. Topstitch around the neck close to the seam.

* Stuff, starting with small pieces in the tips of the tentacles. Take it slowly, making sure each part is stuffed fully before moving upward along the tentacle. Stuff densely so the tentacles are stiff, able to keep their shape for holding toys.

* Finish by stuffing the head. To determine if the head is stuffed to optimum fullness, pick the octopus up by the ribbon loop. You don't want the head to distend too much when it's hanging. Hand-sew the opening closed, using the staystitching as a guide.

DOLL CARRIER

Designed by Kristie Thompson

This mini-size version of a popular baby carrier fits most kids, and almost any doll or stuffed animal. Suitable for wearing on either the front or the back, it even features a functional headrest, which can be unsnapped and folded back as needed! A front patch pocket can hold smaller dolls and necessities, and there are instructions for both a tie and a buckle closure.

MATERIALS

* 1 yard of 44/45" home dec-weight cotton, twill, corduroy, or denim
* ⅓ yard of 44"-wide fusible fleece
* ¼ yard or fat eighth of contrast fabric
* 1 spool of coordinating thread
* 2 size 16 or size 20 snaps for headrest closure
* One 1" side parachute buckle for waist closure (optional)

Finished dimensions – 13" tall × 10" wide, with adjustable waist

Seam allowance – ½" unless otherwise specified

1 Measure, Mark, and Cut

Fold your fabric in half lengthwise with the right sides together, aligning the selvages. Measure and mark the following pieces directly on the wrong side of your fabric, as shown in the cutting layout.

* **Carrier body** 11" × 11" (cut 2)
* **Headrest** 4½" × 10" (cut 2)
* **Waistband** 8" × 19" (cut 1)*
* **Waist ties** 21" × 4" (cut 2)
* **Shoulder straps** 25" × 6" (cut 2)

*Open up your fabric and cut the waistband last, as it only needs to be cut from a single layer of fabric.

From fusible fleece, cut:

* **Carrier body** 11" square (cut 1)
* **Headrest** 4½" × 10" (cut 1)
* **Waistband** 4" × 19" (cut 1)
* **Shoulder straps** 25" × 3" (cut 2)

From contrast fabric, cut:

* **Pocket** 7" × 7" (cut 2)

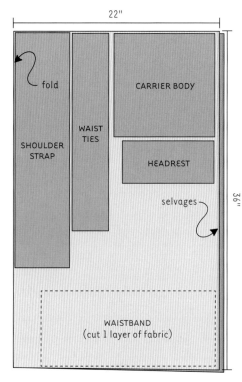

CUTTING LAYOUT

② Make and Attach the Pocket

* Pin the pocket pieces right sides together, aligning all raw edges. Stitch all sides, leaving a 2" opening along the bottom for turning. Clip the corners and turn the pocket right side out. Push out the corners and press, turning and pressing the raw edge of the opening ½" to the wrong side. Edgestitch the top edge, and topstitch ⅛" below the edgestitching.

* Place the pocket on the right side of one carrier body piece, with the stitching at the top. Position the pocket 2" down from the top raw edge of the carrier and centered side to side. Edgestitch along sides and bottom of pocket, and topstitch a second line as before.

③ Make the Headrest

* Fuse the fleece to the wrong side of one headrest piece, following manufacturer's instructions. Pin the headrest pieces with right sides together, aligning all raw edges. Mark 2" from both top corners, as shown, then mark diagonal lines between the marks. Cut off both triangles, through all three layers.

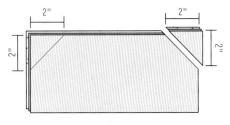

STEP 3

* Stitch around the top and side edges, leaving the bottom edge open. Clip the corners and trim the seam allowances. Turn right side out and press, pushing out the corners. Edgestitch along the finished edges, then stitch two or more lines, ¼" apart, inside the edgestitching.

④ Make the Waist Ties

Press under one short raw edge of each waist tie ¼". Fold each tie and press as you would to make double-fold bias tape (see page 12). Edgestitch along the three finished edges.

⑤ Make the Waistband

* Place the waistband piece on a work surface, right side up. Position the waist ties 1½" down from the top raw edge of the waistband as shown, aligning raw edges, and baste in place. Fold and pin the ties to the center of the right side of the waistband to keep them out of the way as you continue.

* Fold the waistband in half lengthwise, right sides together. Fuse the fleece following manufacturer's instructions to a wrong side of the folded waistband. Stitch around the sides and top raw edges, leaving an 11" opening centered in the long edge for turning and inserting the carrier body in a later step. Take care not to catch the long waist straps in your stitching. Stitch a reinforcement seam within the seam allowance where the waist straps are attached at the sides of the waistband.

* Clip the corners and trim the seam allowance. Turn right side out through the opening, push out the corners, and press, turning under raw edges of the opening ½" to the wrong side. Press and edgestitch around, leaving the 11" opening unstitched.

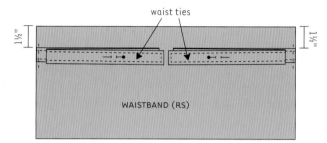

waist ties

1½" 1½"

WAISTBAND (RS)

⑥ Make the Shoulder Straps

Fold the shoulder straps in half lengthwise, right sides together, and fuse the fleece following manufacturer's instructions to a wrong side of the folded straps. Stitch along the long raw edge and the short bottom edge, leaving the top short edge open for turning. Clip the corners and trim the seam allowance. Turn right side out. Push out the corners, press, and edgestitch all finished sides.

⑦ Attach the Headrest and Top of Straps

* Fuse fleece to the carrier body piece without a pocket, following manufacturer's instructions. This becomes the interior.

* Place the carrier interior right side up on work surface. Position the raw edges of the shoulder straps along the top edge, 1" from each side of the carrier interior, aligning top raw edges, and baste.

* Center the headrest along the top of the carrier interior on top of the shoulder straps, aligning raw edges, and baste. Pin the shoulder straps to the center of the right side of the carrier interior to keep them out of the way as you continue.

* Pin the carrier exterior and carrier interior, right sides facing and raw edges aligned. Stitch around the top and side edges, leaving the bottom open for turning. Clip the corners and trim the seam allowance. Turn right side out, press, and baste the bottom opening closed.

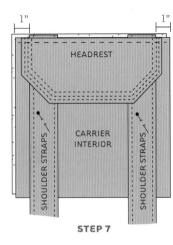

STEP 7

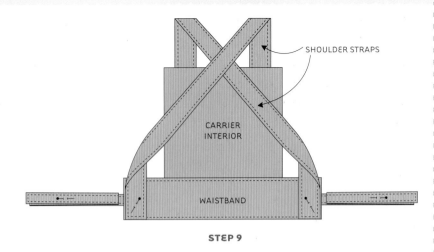

SHOULDER STRAPS

STEP 9

⑧ Attach the Waistband

* Place the carrier, exterior side up, on work surface. Make a placement mark on each side, 1" up from the bottom raw edge.
* Insert the bottom raw edge of carrier into the waistband opening, taking care to center the carrier along the length of the waistband. Align the top edge of the waistband with the placement marks on the carrier. Stitch in place with an edgestitch, taking care to catch all layers in the stitching.

⑨ Secure the Shoulder Straps

* Place the carrier, interior side up, on work surface. Cross the shoulder straps, taking care not to twist them.
* Position each strap end on the inside of the waistband, aligned with the opposite side edge as shown. Align the bottom edge of the strap with the bottom edge of the waistband.

* Pin and check the fit. Shorten the shoulder straps if necessary, by folding the strap end up, and hiding it between the strap and waistband when stitching. Stitch the straps to the waistband with an edgestitch at the sides and bottom. Finish by stitching over the existing edgestitch on the outside top edge of the waistband, where it overlaps the straps.

⑩ Install the Snaps and Buckle

* Place the carrier exterior side up and flip the headrest up. Measure and mark 2" up from the bottom of the headrest, and ½" in from the outside edge.
* Attach the female half of the snap with the decorative side facing the headrest exterior. Mark where the snap meets the shoulder straps while the headrest is flipped up. Attach the male half of the snap at this spot on each shoulder strap.
* If you choose the tie closure, you are done. If you want to use a buckle, thread the female half of the buckle through one waist strap, fold it over, and stitch the tail of the strap to secure. Thread the male half of the buckle to the opposite strap, and adjust length as desired.

ALBERTO THE WOOLIE BEAR

Designed by Marlene Gaige

*Here's a modern Japanese chibi-style take on the classic teddy bear.
Washing the wool felt before you cut and sew with it gives the material a
lovely nubby texture. Quirky Alberto would love to give you a hug!*

MATERIALS

* Pattern pieces (7), *see* sheet 2
* 1 yard of 60" wool or wool-blend felt or 100% wool fabric (to be felted)
* Card stock or template plastic for pattern pieces (optional)
* 1 spool of coordinating thread
* Two 24mm safety eyes or black buttons
* Sewing awl
* 24 ounces of fiberfill
* Three 55mm plastic doll joints for head and legs
* Two 45mm plastic doll joints for arms
* Long doll needle (optional)
* Waxed linen thread, upholstery thread, or unwaxed dental floss
* Perle cotton or embroidery floss (for the nose and mouth)
* ¾ yard ⅜" wide ribbon (for neck)
* 1 yard of 1"–1½"-wide silk or satin ribbon (optional)
* Poly pellets (optional)

Finished dimensions – 18" × 9", not including legs and ears

Seam allowance – ¼" unless otherwise specified

❶ Prepare the Fabric

Wash the wool felt or fabric in hot water, and dry in a very hot dryer. This will cause it to shrink and develop a unique bumpy texture; the edges will be wavy and uneven. Because this fabric becomes so nubby and warped, you will have the best results if you trace the pattern pieces onto template plastic or card stock before using them to cut the fabric.

❷ Measure, Mark, and Cut

Fold your fabric in half lengthwise with the right sides together, aligning the selvages. Position the pattern pieces according to the layout and cut them out. Transfer markings from the pattern to the wrong side of fabric.

* **Head side** (cut 2)
* **Body front** (cut 2)
* **Body back** (cut 2)
* **Arm** (cut 4)
* **Leg** (cut 4)
* **Ear** (cut 4)

Unfold your fabric and cut:

* **Head gusset** (cut 1)*

NOTE: *By cutting the pieces from folded fabric, one of each piece will be reversed, so you will have right and left arms and legs. Grainline is not important in this project.*

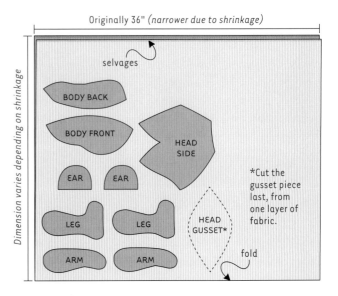

Originally 36" (*narrower due to shrinkage*)

selvages

Dimension varies depending on shrinkage

BODY BACK

BODY FRONT

HEAD SIDE

EAR EAR

LEG LEG

ARM ARM

HEAD GUSSET*

*Cut the gusset piece last, from one layer of fabric.

fold

CUTTING LAYOUT

❸ Make the Body

* Pin body front pieces together, right sides facing and raw edges aligned. Match A and B markings and stitch along the wavy front seam. Leave side seam open.

* Pin back pieces together, right sides facing and raw edges aligned. Match C and D markings and stitch along the wavy back seam, leaving an opening as marked on the pattern. Do not stitch the side seam.

* Pin the body front to body back at the side seams, right sides facing. Match front A to back C, and front B to back D, and stitch all the way around the side seams.

❹ Make the Head

* Pin two ear pieces, right sides facing, aligning raw edges. Stitch along curve, leaving straight edge open. Repeat for second ear. Notch curve and turn right side out.

* Pin each ear on the right side of a head side piece, centered on one side of each dart. Fold each head, with right sides facing, matching and pinning the dart openings on each head side piece. Stitch the dart seams and ears together.

* Pin the head gusset to one head side, right sides facing and raw edges aligned. Match A and B markings and stitch from A to B. Repeat for the remaining head side piece on the opposite side of the gusset.

* Pin the head sides together, right sides facing and raw edges aligned. Match A and D markings, pinching gusset down as needed to close seam. Stitch from A to D to form front seam. Match the B and C markings and stitch to form the back seam.
* If using plastic safety eyes, install them now, following manufacturer's instructions. Use the photograph for guidance on eye placement. (If using buttons, wait until step 7.)

⑤ Make the Arms and Legs

* Pin two arm pieces, right sides facing and raw edges aligned. Stitch all around, leaving an opening as marked. Repeat for remaining arm and leg pieces.
* Check to make sure the marked joint placement marks are symmetrical on each pair of arms and legs, and that limbs are in right and left pairs. Using the sewing awl, carefully poke joint placement dots one at a time where marked on the inner half of each limb, taking care not to poke through the outer fabric layer. Turn all pieces right side out.

⑥ Install the Joints

* Stuff the head firmly. Insert the male end of one 55mm doll joint into the neck. Gather and tie off the bottom of the head as tightly as possible, leaving the end of the joint sticking out.
* Poke a hole at the top of the body, just slightly off center from the seams. Insert the head joint into this hole. Place the joint washer and locking washer inside the body and press firmly. Twist head and press the joint firmly again to lock.
* Insert the male end of one 45mm joint into each arm, pushing the end of the joint out through the hole you made with the awl. Place the matching joint washer and locking washer inside the body at each arm joint placement mark. Press each arm joint into its respective joint washer, pressing just as hard as you can through the fabric. Twist each limb back and forth and press firmly again. Repeat for leg joints, using the leg joint placement marks.

⑦ Complete the Bear

* Stuff all pieces firmly, and then close all openings with an invisible slipstitch. For extra heft, use a combination of poly pellets and fiberfill, particularly in the limbs.

Eyes: If using buttons for eyes, sew them now, using the photograph for guidance on placement. To indent eyes, thread a doll needle with the waxed linen thread, upholstery thread, or unwaxed dental floss and loop the thread around the shaft of the eye. Slip the needle in through the head and out at the other eye. Pull the thread tightly and loop around the other eye. Continue pulling and looping until eyes are indented evenly and to your liking.

Nose and mouth: Embroider with satin stitch and embroidery floss, using the illustration as a guide.

Neck: If desired, tie silk ribbon in a bow around Alberto's neck. It makes him feel fancy!

nose and mouth embroidery

Mac the Magnificent Monster

Designed by Rachel M. Knoblich

Mac is a very large, happy, snuggly plush monster. He makes a great pillow or cuddle buddy for any child. Choose your kid's favorite color for the body, and accent it with some contrast felt for a monster as unique as your little one! While corduroy gives great texture, denim or home dec-weight cottons will also do nicely.

MATERIALS

* Pattern pieces (3), *see* sheet 6
* 1 yard of 56" corduroy, velveteen, or home dec-weight fabric
* 3 craft felt squares in contrasting colors for face, belly, and paws
* 2 felt squares in white for eyes, teeth, and claws

* Scrap of black felt for pupils
* 1 yard of red yarn, perle cotton, or embroidery floss for mouth embroidery
* 1 spool of coordinating thread
* 24-40 ounces of fiberfill

Finished dimensions –
  26½" × 16", not including arms

Seam allowance – ½" unless otherwise specified

① Measure, Mark, and Cut

Fold your fabric in half lengthwise with the right sides together, aligning the selvages. Position the pattern pieces according to the layout and cut them out. Transfer appliqué placement markings from the pattern to the right side of the fabric using chalk or white fabric pencil. Trace the face, eyes, belly, claws, and other embellishments onto the felt and cut them out.

* **Body** (cut 2)
* **Arms** (cut 4)
* **Legs** (cut 4)

From contrast felt, cut:
* **Face** (cut 1)
* **Belly** (cut 1)
* **Foot pad** (cut 2)
* **Paw pad** (cut 2)

From white felt, cut:
* **Claws** (cut 28)
* **Eyes** (cut 2)
* **Teeth** (cut 4 total)

From black felt, cut:
* **Pupils** (cut 2)

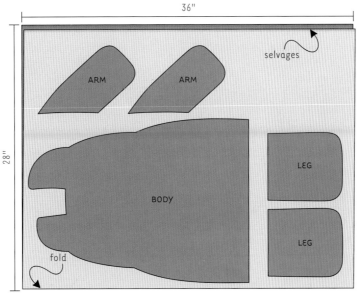

CUTTING LAYOUT

❷ Appliqué the Monster Front

With a fabric pencil or washable marker, draw a smile on the face, following the pattern template. Hand-embroider with a running stitch. Appliqué the following with an edgestitch as indicated on the pattern:

* black pupils onto white eyes
* eyes and teeth onto face
* face onto one body piece
* belly onto this same body piece

❸ Appliqué Arms and Legs

* Appliqué one paw pad to an arm piece. Appliqué the remaining paw pad to a reversed arm piece. Repeat to appliqué each foot pad to a leg piece. These become the front limb pieces.
* Pin two claw pieces together and edgestitch on all sides. Repeat with remaining claw pieces to form 14 claws in all. Position three claws on each arm, and four claws on each foot, all pointing inward with raw edges aligned. Baste in place.

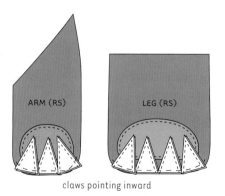

claws pointing inward

STEP 3

❹ Make Two Legs and Two Arms

* Pin a front leg piece (with paw or foot pad) to a back leg piece, right sides facing and raw edges aligned. Stitch together, leaving the short straight edge open for turning. Clip curves and turn right side out. Repeat with remaining leg and arm pieces.
* Stuff arms and legs, leaving the upper 2"–3" unstuffed near the opening.
* Baste arms and legs closed with an edgestitch.

❺ Assemble the Monster

* Pin the arms and legs to the front body at placement marks, appliquéd sides together and raw edges aligned. Pin both body pieces together, right sides facing and raw edges aligned. Arms and legs will be sandwiched between the fabric layers.
* Stitch all around, leaving one side open underneath the arm, as indicated on the pattern. Clip and notch curves and corners and turn right side out. Start by gently pulling the limbs out of the opening before turning the bulk of the body out.
* Stuff the body firmly, starting with the head. Hand-sew the opening closed with an invisible slipstitch.

JuJu Giraffe

Designed by Sarah Faix

Giraffes are one of the world's tallest mammals — who knew it would be possible to make such an impressive animal with just a single yard of fabric? Use a cute patterned print reminiscent of giraffe spots for JuJu, or use up some scraps to create your own spots! She's so quick and easy for sewists with just a little sewing experience, before you know it, you'll have a giraffe of your own. And as an added bonus, you can even make a pair of giraffes out of a single yard of fabric!

MATERIALS

* Pattern pieces (5), *see* sheet 6
* 1 yard of 44/45" cotton flannel
* Scrap of wool felt or flannel for the face patch
* Scraps of quilting weight cotton, flannel, or fleece for spots (optional)
* 1 spool of coordinating thread
* 12 ounces of fiberfill
* Two 12mm safety eyes (optional)
* Embroidery floss for face

Finished dimensions – 15" × 5", not including arms and legs

Seam allowance – ¼" unless otherwise specified

① Measure, Mark, and Cut

Fold your fabric in half lengthwise with the right sides together, aligning the selvages. Position the pattern pieces according to the layout, measure and mark the additional pieces listed, and cut them out. Transfer markings from the pattern pieces to the wrong side of the fabric.

* **Head** (cut 2)
* **Body** (cut 2)
* **Ear** (cut 4)
* **Arm** (cut 4)
* **Leg** (cut 4)
* **Tail** 6" × 1½" (cut 2)
* **Horn** 4¼" × 1¼" (cut 4)

Trace the following from the pattern pieces and cut them from scraps (the spots are optional):

* **Face patch** (cut 1)
* **Large spots** (cut 6)
* **Medium spots** (cut 6)
* **Small spots** (cut 6)

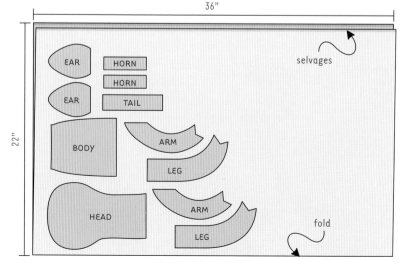

CUTTING LAYOUT

❷ Add the Spots (optional)

Arrange the spots on the head and body pieces as desired (see page 224). Have fun with this! Stitch with a tight zigzag stitch all around. Trim any spots that hang off the edges. (Project illustrations are shown with optional spots appliquéd in place.)

❸ Attach the Head and Body

Pin one head to one body piece, right sides together, aligning the bottom edge of the head with the top edge of the body. Stitch and press seam allowance open. Repeat for remaining head and body.

❹ Make the Limbs

* Pin two arm pieces together, right sides facing, aligning all raw edges. Stitch all around with scant ¼" seam allowance, leaving the straight edge open for turning and stuffing. Stitch a reinforcement seam within the seam allowance just inside the original stitch line. Repeat for remaining arms, legs, and ears.

* Repeat for horn and tail pieces, leaving one short end open. Omit the reinforcement seam. You may find it necessary to trim the seam allowance.

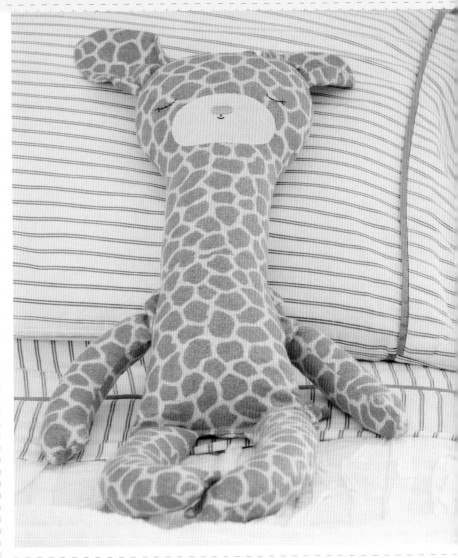

* Turn all limbs right side out. Stuff arms and legs with fiberfill, leaving the last 1½" near the opening unstuffed.
* Tie a knot in each of the horns and in the tail, close to the finished edge. Turn the raw edge of the tail ¼" to wrong side and stitch the opening closed.
* Fold both sides of each ear ¼" to the front, and baste across the raw edge.

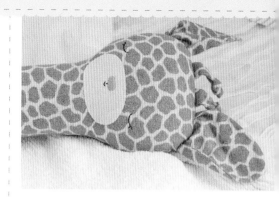

⑤ Assemble the Giraffe

Finish the face:

* Pin the face patch to one head piece and stitch it in place with a tight zigzag stitch.
* Pin the horns to the right side of the face, raw edges aligned, and baste.
* Pin the folded ears to the face, right sides together and raw edges aligned, just outside of each horn. Baste in place.
* If using safety eyes, install them following manufacturer's instructions.

Attach the arms and tail:

* Pin the arms to the right side of the front body, raw edges aligned, and baste in place with edgestitch.
* Pin the tail to the back body, approximately 1½" from the bottom raw edge and centered side to side. Stitch to secure.

Attach front to back:

* Pin the body front to the body back and stitch all around, leaving the bottom edge open for turning and stuffing. Arms should be sandwiched between the fabric layers.
* Turn the giraffe right side out. Turn the raw edges of the opening ¼" to wrong side and press.
* Stuff head and body firmly, paying special attention to the neck to keep it from flopping.

Attach the legs:

* Insert the legs into the bottom of the body where indicated on pattern piece. JuJu Giraffe is pigeon-toed, so her little toes point in.
* Stitch the bottom opening closed, taking care to stitch through all fabric layers. You may wish to add a second reinforcement seam close to the first stitch line.

⑥ Embroider the Face

Mark the nose, mouth, and eye placement as shown on the pattern piece, using a fabric pencil or disappearing marker. Embroider features with three strands of embroidery floss.

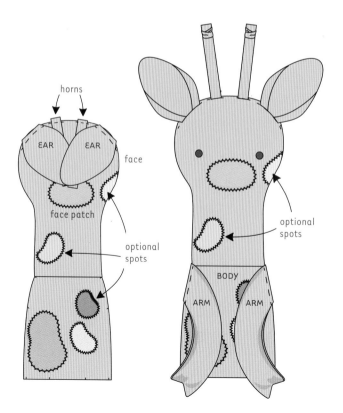

horns

EAR   EAR

face

face patch

optional spots

optional spots

BODY

ARM   ARM

Baby Doll Layette

Designed by Stephanie Sterling

Let your little one outfit his or her favorite pretend friend with this layette set. Complete with bib, diaper, bonnet, and diaper bag, it's the perfect start to a childhood full of pretend parenthood. Clothing fits most 13- to 16-inch dolls or stuffed animals.

MATERIALS

* Pattern pieces (4), *see* sheet 5
* 1 yard of 44/45" quilting-weight cotton or flannel
* 1 spool of coordinating thread
* 2½ yards of ¼"-wide double-fold bias tape
* One ½"-wide Velcro square or circle (for the bib)
* Two ½"-wide Velcro squares or circles (for the diaper)

* ⅓ yard of lace, between ½" and 1" wide (for the hat)

For the Diaper Bag
* Serger (optional)
* 8 grommets, ⅜"-½" in diameter
* Two 1¼"-1½" D-rings
* Pliers

Finished dimensions – bib 3½" high, 6½" neck circumference; diaper 3¼" high closed, with 10" waist; diaper bag 8½" × 10"; hat 6½" neck circumference.

Seam allowance – ¼" unless otherwise specified

① Measure, Mark, and Cut

Fold your fabric in half lengthwise with the right sides together, aligning the selvages. Position the pattern pieces according to the layout, measure and mark the additional pieces as listed, and cut them out. Transfer markings from the pattern pieces to the wrong side of the fabric.

* **Bib** (cut 2)
* **Diaper** (cut 2)
* **Diaper bag body** (cut 2)
* **Diaper bag pocket** (cut 2)
* **Diaper bag gusset** 4" × 26" (cut 1 on fold)
* **Diaper bag strap** 4" × 40" (cut 1 on fold)
* **Hat** (cut 2)

NOTE: *Mirror the pattern pieces along the lines indicated.*

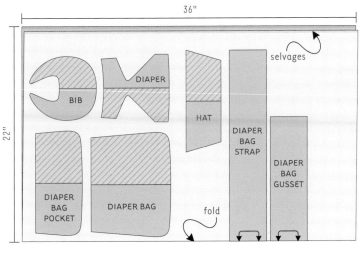

CUTTING LAYOUT

Bib, Diaper, and Hat

❶ Make the Bib

* Pin the bib pieces, right sides facing and raw edges aligned. Stitch all around, leaving a 3" opening at the bottom of the bib. Clip and notch curves or trim seam allowance with pinking shears.

* Turn right side out and press all around, turning in the raw edges of the opening ¼" to wrong side. Edgestitch all around, closing opening as you go.

* Stitch each Velcro half to opposing ends of the bib neck, as marked on the pattern.

❷ Make the Diaper

* Pin the diaper pieces, right sides facing and raw edges aligned. Stitch all around, leaving a 3" opening at the back of the diaper. Clip and notch curves or trim seam allowance with pinking shears.

* Turn right side out and press all around, turning in raw edges as before, and edgestitch. Stitch the Velcro as indicated on the pattern.

❸ Make the Hat

* Pin the hat pieces, right sides facing and raw edges aligned. Sandwich the lace between the fabric layers along the longest edge, aligning raw edges. Trim excess lace.

* Cut two 9" lengths of bias tape. Make each into a tie by turning one short end ¼" to the wrong side and stitching both long sides. Sandwich the ties between the fabric layers, just below the lace on opposite sides, aligning raw edges at the placement mark.

* Stitch both short sides and the longest (lace) edge of the hat. Turn right side out and press, aligning raw edges. Baste the bottom raw edge of the hat and gather slightly, until the bottom edge measures 6". Evenly distribute gathers and edgestitch to secure.

* Cut an 18" length of bias tape and turn and press both short ends ¼" to the wrong side. Center the bottom edge of the hat along the length. Encase the bottom raw edge of the hat within the bias tape (see page 13), taking care that 6" of bias tape extends beyond the hat at each end. Stitch along the entire length of bias tape, binding the bottom edge of the hat as you go. Tie these ends together in a bow to close back of hat. Use the bias tape ties at the lace front to tie under doll's chin.

Diaper Bag

❶ Make Pockets

* Bind the top raw edge of each pocket piece with bias tape (see page 13). With both right sides facing up, pin one pocket onto one diaper bag body, aligning side and bottom raw edges. Stitch a vertical line down the center of the pocket to form two identical divided pockets.

* Repeat for remaining pocket and body piece, but stitch two vertical lines every 3¼" to form three identical divided pockets.

❷ Make the Bag Body

* Pin the gusset to one bag body, right sides facing, aligning one long raw edge of the gusset with the side and bottom edges of the bag body. Stitch. Pin the other long edge of the gusset to the remaining bag body, right sides facing. Stitch.

* Finish seam allowances with serger or zigzag stitch. Clip curves and turn right side out. Bind the top raw edge of the bag with bias tape.

❸ Install Grommets and D-Ring

* On each side of the bag and on each gusset, measure and make a mark 1" down from the top edge and 1" in from each side seam. Install a grommet at each mark following manufacturer's instructions for a total of 8 grommets.

* Using pliers, open one D-ring slightly and pass it through all four grommets on one side of the bag, folding gusset inward as you thread the D-ring through. Repeat on the other side of the bag. Close both D-rings by hand or with pliers.

❹ Make and Attach the Strap

* Press both short ends of the strap ½" to wrong side. Fold and press as you would to make double-fold bias tape (see page 12). Edge-stitch along both long edges.

* Thread one end of the strap through one D-ring, from outside to inside. Fold the strap 1" from the end, and stitch to secure. Repeat for the opposite end of the strap and remaining D-ring.

imaginative PLAY

WE'LL IMMODESTLY GO OUT ON A LIMB AND SAY that we think the projects here are just about the most imaginative play accessories you'll find in any sewing book — fluttery butterfly wings, a hallway house that doubles as a fantastic puppet theater, a tea party set, and more! Watch as your child's imagination soars with these unique, creativity-inspiring toys.

FLUTTER-BY, BUTTERFLY WINGS

Designed by Felicia Balezentes

Colorful, kaleidoscopic butterflies captivate children of all ages! Your little one can slip these on and flutter away, flit from flower to flower, or even transform into a fairy princess. What a fab way to celebrate (or anticipate!) spring and summer after (or during!) a long winter cooped up indoors.

MATERIALS

* Template (1), *see* page 337
* 1 yard of 44/45" quilting-weight cotton
* 1¼ yards of ½"-wide elastic
* 1 spool of coordinating thread
* ½ yard of ⅞"-wide (or wider) ribbon or other trim
* 3 yards of ¼"–½"-wide double-fold bias tape

Finished dimensions – 18" × 32"

Seam allowance – ½" unless otherwise specified

① Measure, Mark, and Cut

Fold your fabric in half in the cross-grain direction, wrong sides together, aligning the cut edges, then fold your fabric the other direction, so that one selvage is positioned approximately 8" from the other selvage. You should have a portion of fabric that is four layers thick and approximately 18" square. Using the template on page 336 as a guide, draw the butterfly wings front/back with a fabric marker or pencil, and cut:

* **Butterfly wings front/back** (cut 1 on both folds)
* **Shoulder straps** 2½" × 30" (cut 2 on fold)
* **Wrist straps** 2½" × 10" (cut 2)

From elastic, cut:

* **Shoulder straps** 17" (cut 2)
* **Wrist straps** 7" (cut 2)

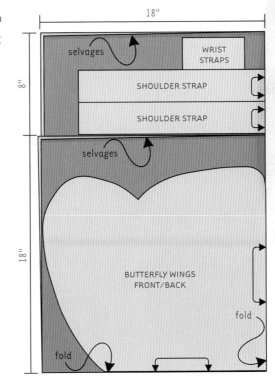

CUTTING LAYOUT

❷ Gather the Wings

* Unfold the wings once; you will have a double-layer set of wings with the right side of fabric on both the front and back, and a fold along the top edge. Run a basting stitch down the center crease through both layers to form the "spine" of the wings. Gather the center spine until it measures 8"-9". Distribute gathers evenly. Stitch the gathers to secure.
* Starting at the bottom edge of the spine, on one side of the wings, center the ribbon over the gathers. Fold it over the top edge to the other side of the wings, and center it over the gathers on the back side. Edgestitch along both edges of the ribbon to attach, taking care to catch both ribbon layers in your stitching.

❸ Bind the Wings

Baste the front and back wing layers together with edgestitch. Fold short ends of bias tape ½" to the wrong side. Starting on the right wing where it meets the top of the spine, bind the raw edges of the wings with double-fold bias tape (see page 13).

❹ Make the Straps

* Fold each strap in half lengthwise, right sides together. Stitch the long raw edge using a ¼" seam allowance. Turn right side out and press.
* Thread one piece of shoulder strap elastic through each fabric shoulder strap, gathering the strap as you go. Secure the elastic to each end with an edgestitch. Fold each end ¼" to one side and edgestitch to create a finished edge.
* Repeat for the wrist straps.

❺ Attach the Straps

* Overlap the ends of one shoulder strap by 1" to form a ring, making sure a finished end is visible on the inside of the ring. Pin the joined ends to one wing, 2" from the top edge and ½" from the edge of the center ribbon. Stitch in place with a box stitch (see glossary, page 340). Repeat for remaining shoulder strap on the opposite wing.
* Overlap the ends of one wrist strap by ½" to form a ring. Pin to one wing, 1" from the top edge and 1" from the outside edge. Stitch in place with a box stitch. Repeat for remaining wrist strap on the opposite wing.

House in a Hallway

Designed by Lorraine Teigland

This house is inspired by a traditional tension-rod doorway puppet theater. Although the overall shape is simple (and very compact when stored), the strategically placed tension rods allow you and your child to change the shape and size of the house. You may set up this shape-shifting tent as a traditional puppet theater with an angled roof or with a flat roof, depending on your child's mood. As an added bonus, almost all the parts are functional. You may leave the gate up, or fold it down to reveal a cute floral welcome mat. The mailbox opens and closes, as do the curtains. Let your child's imagination soar!

MATERIALS

* Pattern pieces (14), *see* sheet 6

Fabrics:

* 1 yard of 54" home dec-weight fabric
* Quilting-weight or home dec-weight cotton as follows:
  · 18" × 16" piece for the doormat (gray)
  · 7" × 10" piece for mailbox (dark blue)
  · ⅛ yard for curtains (yellow gingham)
  · 18" × 12" piece for the gate background (medium blue)
  · Scraps for sconce lights (yellow)
* ¼ yard of flannel for window frames, bricks, and mailbox post (light brown)
* ⅓ yard of flannel for doorway and top of light sconces (dark brown)
* Assorted felt squares/scraps for tulips, leaves, doormat flowers, and mailbox flag
* 1 yard of medium-weight fusible interfacing

Notions/Trims:

* Multiple spools of coordinating threads
* Serger (optional)
* 8½ yards of ¼"-wide single-fold bias tape for roof shingles (red)
* ⅔ yard of ¼"-wide ribbon for outline of light sconces (brown)
* 3 coordinating buttons, ½"–¾" in diameter, for light sconces and mailbox
* ½ yard of ¾"-wide twill tape or ribbon for curtain tiebacks and mailbox tab (gray)
* 6" piece of ¾"-wide Velcro (white to match house, you may also choose to find in additional colors to coordinate with the house details)
* ⅔ yard of ⅜"-wide green ribbon for flower stems
* Three curtain tension rods in a length to fit your hallway

Finished dimensions – 36" wide × 48" tall

Seam allowance – ½" unless otherwise specified

❶ Measure, Mark, and Cut

From the 18" × 16" piece of cotton (gray), cut:

* **Doormat** 18" × 12" (cut 1)
* **Doormat tension rod channel** 15" × 4" (cut 1)

From the 7" × 10" piece of cotton (dark blue), cut:

* **Mailbox** (cut 1)
* **Mailbox door** (cut 2)

From the ⅛ yard of cotton (yellow gingham), cut:

* **Curtains** 11" × 4½" (cut 4)

From the ¼ yard of flannel (light brown), cut:

* **Window frame** (cut 2; do NOT cut out the center hole until instructed)
* **Brick A** (cut 7)
* **Brick B** (cut 8)
* **Mailbox post** 2" × 10½" (cut 1)
* **Horizontal window divider** 6" × 3" (cut 2)
* **Vertical window divider** 7½" × 3" (cut 2)

From the ⅓ yard of flannel
(dark brown), cut:

* **Doorway** (cut 2; do NOT cut out
  the center hole until instructed)
* **Sconce top** (cut 2)

From the cotton scraps (yellow), cut:

* **Light sconce** (cut 2)

From the assorted felt, cut:

* **Tulip** (cut 3)
* **Leaf** (cut 6)
* **Daisy** (cut 3)
* **Daisy centers** (cut 3)
* **Mailbox flag** (cut 1)

From fusible interfacing, cut:

* **Doorway** (cut 2; DO cut
  out the center hole)
* **Window frame** (cut 2; DO
  cut out the center hole)
* **Doormat** (cut 1)
* **Mailbox** (cut 1)
* **Mailbox door** (cut 2)

2 Prep Your Main Fabric and Make the Tension Rod Channels

* Finish the 54" raw edges of your
  fabric using either a zigzag stitch
  or a serger overcast stitch. There
  is no need to trim your selvages.
* Orient the fabric so that the
  selvages are at the top and bottom
  and the wrong side is facing up.
  Measuring down from the top
  selvage edge, make four marks at
  the following measurements across
  the entire width of the fabric: 4",
  7", 21", and 24" (see page 234).

* Fold the fabric with the right sides together, matching up the 4" and 7" marks. Stitch along these lines to form a tension rod channel (this should be left open on both ends). Stitch a second channel, matching up the 21" and 24" marks.

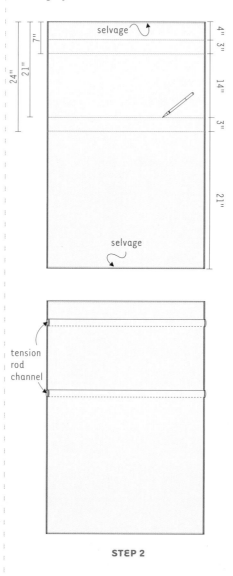

STEP 2

❸ Stitch the Shingles

Using a removable or disappearing fabric marking method, use the roof shingle template to mark the placement lines for the shingles on the right side of the fabric as shown, offsetting the shingles every other row. Carefully curve the ¼" single-fold bias tape along these placement lines and stitch in place along both edges of the bias tape, keeping the tension rod channels free of the stitching.

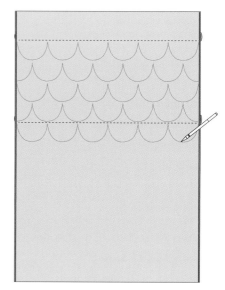

STEP 3

❹ Make the Windows

* Fuse interfacing to the wrong side of the window frame pieces following manufacturer's instructions. Press all outside edges of the windows ½" to the wrong side.

* Lay the main house fabric wrong side up on a work surface. Position the interfaced window frames wrong side up on the house fabric 2½" in from the side edges and 4" below the lower tension rod channel. Stitch together along *inner* stitching line of window, leaving four 1" openings for the window dividers, as indicated on the pattern.

* Cut out the centers of the window frames, through all layers, along the indicated cutting line. Clip into your seam allowance along the curved edge, and notch the corners. Save the main fabric from your window cutout, as this will be used in a later step. Turn the window frames to the right side of the house through the cut opening and press.

* Prepare each window divider as you would double-fold bias tape (see page 12), and edgestitch along both folded edges. Insert them into the openings in the window frame, and pin in place. Edgestitch around both the inside and outside edge of the window.

⑤ Make the Doorway

* Fuse interfacing to the wrong sides of both doorway pieces, following manufacturer's instructions. With right sides together, align the raw edges of the doorway pieces and stitch along the center seam. Press seam open.

* Press the side edges of all brick A and brick B pieces ½" to the wrong side as indicated on the pattern pieces. The brick B pieces make up the straight side edges of the doorway (four on each side), while brick A pieces form the top curved arch of the doorway. Using the photograph as a guide, position and stitch the bricks in place. Use a ¼" seam allowance along the inside and outside raw edges to secure the bricks, then press the outside curved edge of the doorway ½" to the wrong side.

* Lay the main house fabric wrong side up on a work surface. Position the interfaced and bricked doorway wrong side up on the wrong side of the main house fabric, centered along the bottom edge, aligning the bottom raw edges. Stitch together along inner stitching line of the doorway, as you did for the window. Cut out the center through all layers as before, and clip the seam allowance, saving the main fabric for a later step.

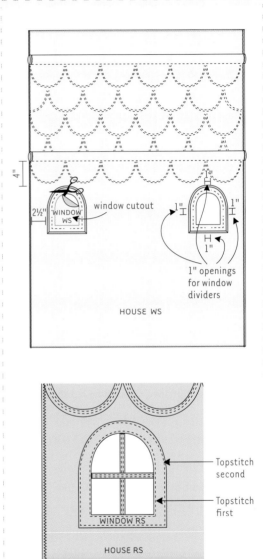

HOUSE WS

STEP 4

* Turn the doorway to the right side of the house through the cut opening and press. Edgestitch around the inner and outer edge of the doorway to secure. Baste across the bottom edges of the doorway.

6 Make and Attach the Light Sconces

* With both right sides facing up, sew the light sconces on either side of the doorway, below the windows. Edgestitch in place. Position the ¼"-wide ribbon down the two center lines on the sconce, as indicated on the pattern. Topstitch in place. Likewise, cover the side and bottom raw edges of the sconce with ribbon and topstitch.

* Press under all raw edges of the sconce top pieces ½". Position them above the light sconce, overlapping the top edge. Edgestitch in place and hand-sew decorative buttons to the top of both sconces.

7 Make and Attach the Mailbox

* Fuse interfacing to the wrong side of the mailbox and mailbox door pieces. Press all outside edges of the mailbox ½" to the wrong side. Lay the main house fabric wrong side up on a work surface.

Mailbox: Position the interfaced mailbox wrong side up on the wrong side of the main house fabric to the left of the door, approximately 9½" up from the bottom edge and centered between the doorway and fabric edge (when viewed from the right side, the mailbox will be to the right of the door). Stitch together along the inner stitching line of mailbox, as indicated on the pattern. As you did with the windows, cut out the center of the mailbox through all layers, clip into the seam allowance, and turn the mailbox to the right side and press.

Mailbox post: Press under both long edges of the post ½". With both right sides facing up, position the post underneath the mailbox so that the mailbox overlaps the top raw edge of the post. Edgestitch the post only.

Mailbox door: Position the door pieces with right sides together. Cut a 1½" piece of twill tape and fold it, aligning the cut ends. Sandwich the folded twill tape between the mailbox door layers as indicated on the pattern piece, aligning the raw edges. Stitch around the curved edge of the door, leaving the short straight edge unstitched. Notch seam allowance, turn right side out, and press.

With the wrong side facing up, pin the door underneath the front edge of the mailbox, so that the mailbox overlaps the door's raw edge. Edgestitch around the outside edge of the mailbox, securing the mailbox door in the stitching line. Cut a small piece of Velcro, and sew the hook piece to the wrong side of the mailbox door and the loop piece on the right side of the top mailbox opening. This allows your mailbox to be functional!

Mailbox flag: Appliqué the flag to the mailbox using your desired technique. Sew a button to the base of the flag as in the project photo.

8 Appliqué the Tulips

Cut the ribbon for the flower stems into three 8" pieces. Position them next to the door, opposite the mailbox, evenly spaced. Pin tulip flowers and leaves on the stems, and edgestitch all pieces in place.

9 Make and Attach the Curtains

* Hem both long sides of the curtains with a ¼" double-fold hem. Repeat for the short, bottom edges only. Trim the top raw edges of the curtains to match the shape of the top of the windows. Zigzag or overcast stitch to finish this raw edge.

* With both wrong sides facing up, pin two curtains in place on each window on either side of the vertical dividers, with the

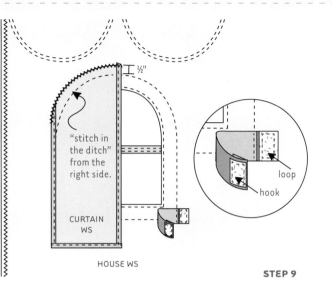

STEP 9

overcast edge ½" above the top edge of the window frame. From the right side of the house, stitch the curtains using a "stitch in the ditch" technique along the edge of the window frames to invisibly secure the curtains (see glossary, page 343).

* Cut four 4" pieces of twill tape and fold all ends ½" to one side. Cut four ½" pieces of Velcro and stitch them on the ends of the twill tape (hook on one end, loop on the opposite end), covering the folded ends. On the wrong side of the house, stitch these twill tape pieces in place at the bottom corners of the window (two on each window) so that they fold into a loop to create curtain tiebacks.

⑩ Cut and Make the Picket Fence/Gate

From your reserved piece of doorway fabric, cut out the following pieces and press all raw edges ½" to the wrong side:

* **Horizontal fence beam** 2" × 17" (cut 2)
* **Vertical fence post** (cut 4)

With right sides facing up, pin the horizontal fence beams on the 18" × 12" gate background, 1" from the side edges and 3" from the top and bottom edges. Edgestitch in place. In the same way, pin two vertical fence posts 2" from each side edge, overlapping the horizontal beams. Evenly space the remaining posts between the outer posts, pin, and edgestitch.

⑪ Make the Floral Doormat

Center the three felt daisies and their centers onto the doormat. Edgestitch in place. Cut two ¾" pieces of Velcro and stitch the hook sides in two corners of the doormat, ¾" from the edges.

⑫ Finish the Gate/Doormat

From your reserved piece of window fabric, cut out the following pieces:

* **Doormat tabs** 3½" × 2" (cut 2)
* Fold the tabs with right sides together, aligning the 2" edges. Stitch along one 2" edge, turn right side out, and press.
* Hem both short ends of the doormat channel with a ¼" double-fold hem. With wrong sides together, fold the channel and baste the long raw edges together using a ¼" seam allowance.

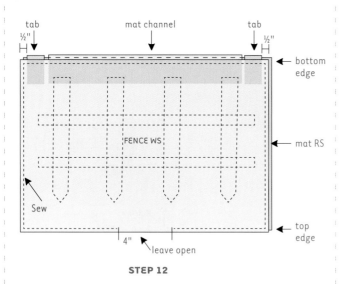

STEP 12

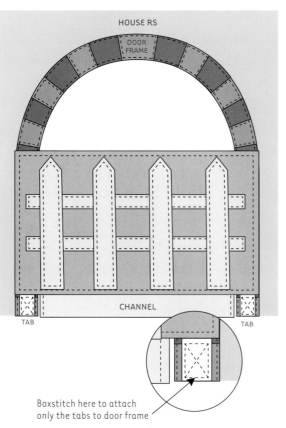

Boxstitch here to attach
only the tabs to door frame

STEP 13

* Position the gate and floral doormat with right sides together. The top of the picket fence and the Velcro halves on the doormat should be at the same end. Insert the doormat tabs between the layers on the side opposite the Velcro, ½" from the side edges with edges aligned. Insert the mat channel between the layers, centered between the tabs, raw edges aligned. Stitch around the gate/doormat, leaving a 4" opening for turning as shown.

* Clip corners, turn right side out, and press. Edge-stitch around all four sides of the gate/doormat, closing the opening in your stitching.

⑬ Attach the Gate/Doormat

* Lay the house right side up on a work surface. Position the gate/doormat over the doorway opening, with the picket fence facing up. Align the ends of the doormat tabs with the bottom raw edge of the doorway. Stitch tabs to the main house fabric using a box stitch (see glossary, page 340). Leave the mat channel free/unstitched.

* Turn and press the bottom raw edge of the house on both sides of the door opening ¼" to the wrong side, and then another 1". Topstitch in place close to the folded edge. The bottom hem, along with the mat channel, creates a third tension rod channel.

* Fold the gate up and stitch the remaining ¾" loop pieces of Velcro to the doorway where they align with the hook Velcro on the corners of the floral doormat.

* Insert three tension rods through the channels and watch your child's creativity unfold!

MUSHROOM TEA PARTY

Designed by Rachel Le Grand

Teatime for two! Place this tablecloth and tea set on a small table for a formal tea party, or lay it out on the floor picnic-style for a more casual affair. Appliquéd saucers provide a little extra je ne sais quoi to the table setting. With the red and white polka dots, your little one can feel a bit like Alice in Wonderland. The fleece lets the teacups and teapot stand up on their own; felt would also work, or you could use flannel in a pinch, with interfacing to stiffen the play pieces.

MATERIALS

* 1 yard of 44/45" fleece
* Approximately 25" of string to draft the tablecloth
* ¼ yard of white or light-colored contrast fleece
* Circle templates: 2½", 3", 3½", and 5" in diameter
* 1 spool of coordinating thread
* 3¼ yards of 1"-wide pompom trim
* Coordinating embroidery floss

Finished dimensions –
Tablecloth is 36" across.

Seam allowance – ½" unless otherwise specified

1 Measure, Mark, and Cut

Lay out your fabric in a single layer with the wrong side facing up. Measure and mark the following pieces on the wrong side of the fabric. (For the tablecloth circle, cut a length of string long enough so you can tie one end to a straight pin and the other to a washable fabric marker and still have 18" between them. Hold the pin firmly in the center of the fabric, and trace a circle all the way around with the marker.) Cut out the pieces.

* **Tablecloth** 36" diameter circle (cut 1)
* **Teacup** 3" × 8" (cut 2)
* **Teacup handle** 1" × 3" (cut 2)
* **Teapot lid** 5" diameter circle (cut 1)

From contrast fleece, cut:

* **Saucer** 3½" diameter circle (cut 2)
* **Teapot** 4" × 9½" (cut 1)
* **Teapot handle** 1" × 3" (cut 1)
* **Teapot bottom** 3" diameter circle (cut 1)
* **Teapot spout** 1" × 1½" (cut 1)
* **Teacup bottom** 2½" diameter circle (cut 2)

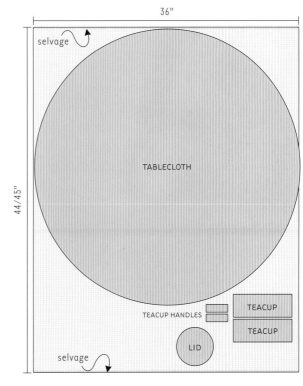

CUTTING LAYOUT

2 Make the Tablecloth

* Stitch the pompom trim to the right side of the tablecloth, concealing the raw edge under the pompom tape while allowing the pompoms to dangle off the edge.
* Fold the tablecloth in half, then in half again to find the center. Pin to mark the center and unfold. Place the saucers 16" apart on the right side of the tablecloth, on opposite sides of the center point. Appliqué each saucer onto the table-cloth with a zigzag stitch (see glossary, page 343).

3 Make the Teacups

* Fold each teacup piece across the width, wrong sides together, slightly overlap-ping the short raw edges to make a ring. Hand-sew the edges together using the embroidery floss and a blanket stitch (see glossary, page 339).
* Center a teacup handle on a teacup seam, right side facing out, and curl both short edges under to form a handle shape. Hand-sew using the embroidery floss and a blanket stitch. Repeat for the other handle.
* Hand-sew a teacup bottom to each teacup with a blanket stitch.

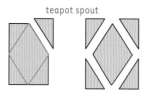

teapot spout

STEP 4

4 Make the Teapot

* Assemble the teapot as you did the teacups, forming a ring and adding handle and bottom. Clip the corners of the teapot spout, starting and stopping at the middle of each side. This will create a diamond shape.
* Cup the diamond shape slightly, referring to the project photo and hand-sew the spout to the teapot opposite the handle, lining up the top of the spout with the top of the handle. The tip of the spout should jut out from the teapot.
* Fold the teapot lid in half, then in half again to find the center and the quarter-circle points. Press gently on low heat to mark crease. Unfold and cut a quarter-circle wedge from the lid, using creases as a guide.
* Overlap the edges of the cutout to form a cone, and hand-sew the seam with a blanket stitch starting from the out-side edge. Before closing up the center, clip a pompom from the leftover trim and tuck it up through the center of the lid. Hand-sew pompom in place.

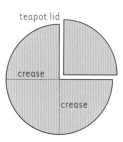

teapot lid

crease

crease

STEP 4

casey apron

Designed by Sue Kim

Easy as 1-2-3, this delightful apron is perfect for your child to throw on for an impromptu afternoon baking session. Velcro closures at the waist and the neck allow your little kitchen helper to put this apron on all by him- or herself. The Casey Apron promises all the fun with half the mess!

MATERIALS

* Pattern pieces (3), *see sheet 5*
* 1 yard of 44/45" quilting-weight cotton (not suitable for one-way prints)
* 1 spool of coordinating thread
* 6" piece of 1"-wide Velcro
* 8" piece of ⅜"-wide elastic

Sizes – S, M

Seam allowance – ½" unless otherwise specified

① Determine Your Child's Size

Determine the correct size of apron based on your child's age. Small typically fits ages 2-4, and medium typically fits ages 5-7.

② Measure, Mark, and Cut

Lay your fabric in a single layer with the wrong side facing up. Position the pattern pieces according to the layout, measure and mark the additional pieces, and cut them out. Transfer markings from the patterns to the wrong side of the fabric.

* **Apron** (cut 2)
* **Pocket** (cut 2)
* **Neck strap** (cut 4, 2 of which must be reversed)

	S	M
Waist Straps (cut 4)	7½" × 2¾"	8" × 2¾"

NOTE: *Mirror the pattern piece along the line indicated on the pattern.*

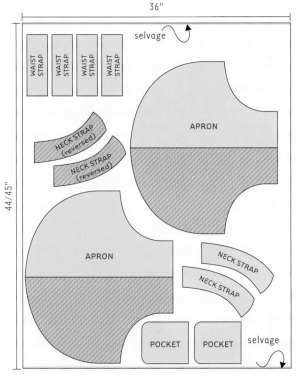

CUTTING LAYOUT

3 Make the Waist Straps

* Place two waist strap pieces with right sides together. Stitch around three sides, leaving one short end unstitched. Clip corners, turn right side out, and press. Edgestitch along the three finished edges. Repeat for second waist strap.
* Cut a 4" piece of Velcro. Center the loop piece of Velcro on the inside finished end of one of the straps and stitch in place. Center the hook piece of Velcro on the exterior side of the second strap and stitch in place.

4 Make the Neck Straps

* Place two neck strap pieces with right sides together. Stitch around three sides, leaving the notched edge unstitched. Clip corners, turn right side out, and press. Edgestitch along the three finished edges. Repeat for second neck strap.
* As you did for the waist straps, center and stitch the remaining loop Velcro on the inside finished end of one strap and the hook Velcro on the exterior end of the second strap.

5 Attach the Neck and Waist Straps

On a work surface, lay one apron piece with the right side facing up. Place the neck straps at the top edge of the apron as marked, aligning notches and raw edges. Do the same with the waist straps. All straps should be ½" from the corners. Baste all straps in place.

6 Assemble the Apron

Pin the apron pieces with right sides together, sandwiching the straps in between the two layers. Stitch around all edges of the apron, leaving a 4" opening along the top edge, between the neck straps, for turning. Clip corners, notch and clip seam allowance along the curves, turn right side

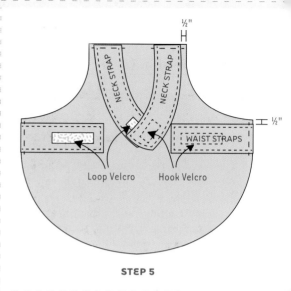

STEP 5

out, and press. Edgestitch around the finished edge of the apron, closing the opening used for turning.

7 Make and Attach the Pockets

* Press the top, straight raw edge of the pockets ½" to the wrong side, then press under an additional ¾". Stitch close to the folded edge to create a casing.
* Cut the elastic into two 4" pieces. Thread the elastic through the pocket casing. Stitch both ends of the elastic in place using a ¼" seam allowance. Press the side and bottom raw edges ½" to the wrong side.
* With both right sides facing up, position the pockets on the right side of the apron along the placement lines as indicated on the pattern piece. Edgestitch in place along the side and bottom edges.

car cozy playmat

Designed by Tara Kolesnikowicz

Here is a great playmat and travel/storage roll all in one! Toy cars tuck into the parking-space pockets when play is all done; decorate the remainder of the playmat to feature roads, buildings — anything you want!

* 1 yard of 44/45" black or charcoal color quilting-weight cotton
* ⅔ yard of light- or medium-weight fusible interfacing
* 1 spool of coordinating thread

* Yellow embroidery floss
* Fabric scraps for appliqué
* Scraps of double-sided fusible webbing for appliqué (optional)
* 4" of ⅛"-wide elastic
* One 1" button

Finished dimensions – 17" × 21"

Seam allowance – ¼" unless otherwise specified

➊ Measure, Mark, and Cut

Lay out your fabric in a single layer with the wrong side facing up. Measure and mark the following pieces on the wrong side of your fabric and cut them out.

* **Car cozy** 18" × 22" (cut 2)
* **Pocket** 10" × 22" (cut 1)

From interfacing, cut:

* **Car cozy** 18" × 22" (cut 1)
* **Pocket** 5" × 22" (cut 1)

➋ Attach the Interfacings

* Fold the fabric pocket piece lengthwise aligning the long edges, wrong sides together, and press. Sandwich the pocket interfacing between the fabric layers and press to adhere, following manufacturer's instructions.
* Fuse the remaining interfacing to the wrong side of one fabric car cozy piece.

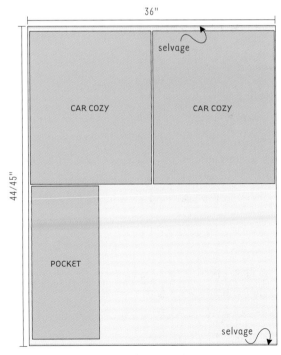

CUTTING LAYOUT

❸ Attach the Pocket

Pin the pocket to the right side of the interfaced car cozy, aligning bottom and side raw edges. Starting ½" from each corner, create seven parking spaces by marking vertical lines 3" apart along the pocket's long raw edge. Stitch along marked lines to form the individual parking pockets. Embroider using your favorite outline stitch on top of the stitching lines to make the parking lines more prominent.

❹ Appliqué the Scenery

Embroider a roadway on the remainder of the interfaced car cozy piece. Add appliqués for buildings, trees, street signs, and any other design elements you may wish to use. Use double-sided fusible webbing to fuse the appliqués in place and to minimize fraying, if desired. Stitch with straight or zigzag stitch to attach.

❺ Assemble the Car Cozy

* Pin the two car cozy pieces right sides together and raw edges aligned. Fold the elastic in half to form a loop and sandwich it between the layers on one short end, 10" above the top edge of the pocket.
* Stitch all around the playmat with a ¼" seam allowance, leaving a 5" opening on the side opposite the pocket for turning. Clip corners and turn right side out, press. Edgestitch all around the playmat, closing the opening as you go.
* Fill the pockets with cars and fold the playmat in thirds, keeping the cars secure and cozy in the folds. Roll up the playmat, keeping the elastic loop on the last free end. Determine the button placement once you see where the elastic loop falls. Hand-sew the button to the back of the cozy so that you can fasten the elastic loop over the button to secure.

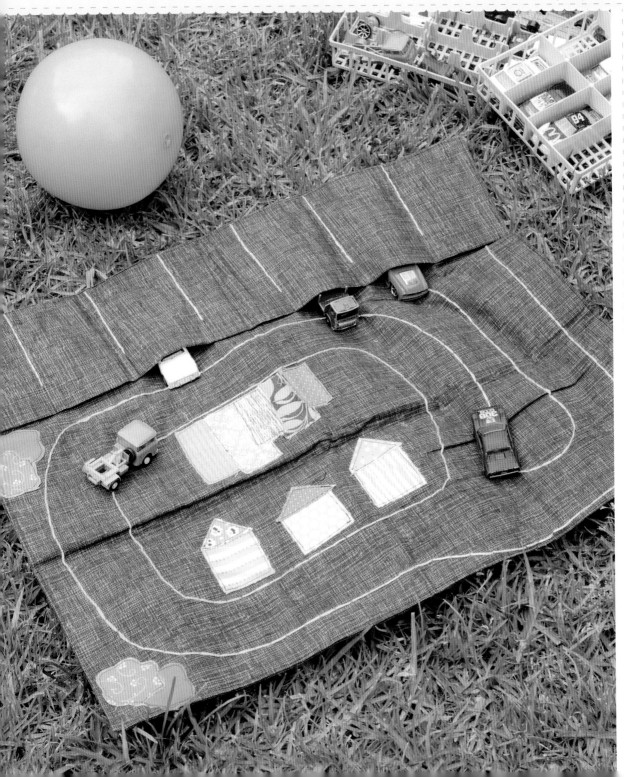

CHAPTER 12

Games & Hobbies

THERE'S SOMETHING IN THIS CHAPTER FOR EVERYONE.

Take the whole family out to fly a kite, or stave off cabin fever with a selection of board games. For the gamer or the artist in your life, make the perfect carryall to transport his or her gear. You can even get the body moving with an indoor version of a playground classic — hopscotch!

POCKET SLED KITE

Designed by Don Morin

Every child thrills at flying a kite on a breezy summer day. When it comes to easy kites to fly, they don't get much easier than this single-line pocket sled! This is a light-to-moderate wind kite. Just hook the line on and let it soar. It's easy to transport, too. Cram it into your pocket, ever ready for an unexpected gust of wind!

MATERIALS

* Pattern pieces (2), *see* sheet 5
* 1 yard of 54/55" ripstop nylon
* 1 spool of coordinating thread
* 1"-wide sticky tape, such as electrical
* 2 small metal grommets, no more than ¼" inner diameter
* Kite string

Finished dimensions – 19" × 30", not including tails

Seam allowance – ¼" unless otherwise specified

① Measure, Mark, and Cut

Fold your fabric in half lengthwise with the right sides together, aligning the selvages. Position the pattern pieces according to the layout, measure and mark the additional pieces, and cut them out. Transfer markings from the pattern to the wrong side of the fabric.

* **Main sail** (cut 1 on fold)
* **Air pocket** (cut 2)
* **Tail** 3" × 48" (cut 2 on fold)

② Hem and Reinforce the Main Sail

Stitch a ¼" double-fold hem around the entire main sail piece. Reinforce each top outer corner of the main sail with two strips of the tape as shown. Center a grommet on the tape at each corner, and install according to manufacturer's directions.

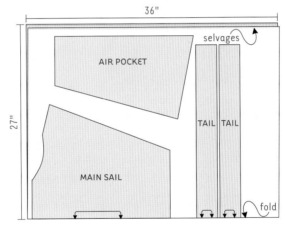

CUTTING LAYOUT

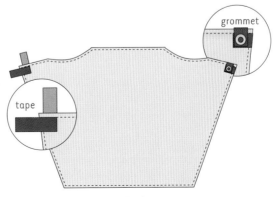

STEP 2

3 Hem and Attach the Air Pockets

* Hem the short edges of each air pocket (top and bottom) with a ¼" double-fold hem. Place one air pocket on the main sail, right sides together, aligning the "X" placement marks as shown. Stitch two parallel stitch lines, ⅛" apart, to attach.

* Flip the air pocket over to align the "O" placement marks. Fold under the raw edge of the air pocket ¼" to the wrong side and stitch to the main sail as you did for the other edge. The short top and bottom edges will remain free.

* Repeat for the second air pocket.

4 Hem and Attach the Tails

Hem both long edges and one short edge of both tails with a ¼" double-fold hem. Fold the top raw edge of each tail ¼" to the wrong side and tuck that end into the narrow end of an air pocket, just meeting the hemmed bottom edge of the main sail (not the pocket). Edgestitch to attach.

5 Attach the Lines

* Cut one 100"-length of kite string. Tie each end to a grommet with a small nonslip loop knot (see box). Fold the string in half, letting the kite dangle. Make sure the two sides line up exactly, and tie a small loop knot at the center fold of the string. Take care that the two sides still line up after the center knot is tied. This becomes the bridle.

* Tie your flying string to the center of the bridle with a lark's head knot (see box), which is easy to attach and remove.

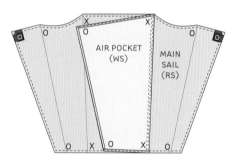

STEP 3: Align "X" placement marks

STEP 3: Align "O" placement marks

ON KITE STRING AND KNOTS

For single-line kite flying, there are three main types of line:

Cotton. Often sold with cheaper kites for kids. It's inexpensive and reasonably strong for its weight, but it tangles easily.

Twisted Nylon. A common choice for flying a wide range of single-line kites, particularly in the smaller sizes. Use it on kites that have a 24" wingspan or less. It tends to unwind and will tangle unless you are careful.

Twisted Polyester. This is a bit more expensive, but stronger than the other types. You do still need to be careful with tangles.

The Nonslip Loop Knot

This knot is simple to tie, and it won't slip. The loop allows the bridle free movement on the kite.

1 Make a simple overhand knot, leaving about 6" free toward one end, now called the tag end.

2 Pass the tag end through the eye of the grommet and then into the loop and out again. Note that the tag end, the far end (now called the standing end) and the loop pass through the overhand knot in the same over and under direction.

3 Make four wraps with the tag end around the standing line. Then put the tag end back through the overhand knot.

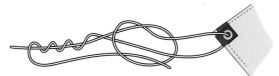

4 Pull the standing end to tighten. As the knot tightens, snug up on the tag end.

The Lark's Head Knot

Use this type of knot to connect your flying line to the kite's bridle. This knot is the easiest way to quickly attach and remove a flying line.

1 Fold the end of the kite string in half to create a loop.

2 Take the loop and slide it over the bridle line and pull it down a bit so that you can see the loop below the bridle line.

3 Take the bulk of your kite string and pass it through the loop made by the fold of the string.

4 Pull tight to remove the slack and draw up on the string to tighten the loop around the bridle string.

INDOOR HOPSCOTCH

Designed by Fiona Tully

Now kids can have the all the fun of playing hopscotch even on cold and rainy days – indoors! Use our diagram to draw the board, then use your favorite block font to make the number and letter templates. Do you have very active kids or slippery floors? Add the optional backing to ensure a non-slip project.

MATERIALS

* Template, *see* page 338
* 1 yard of 44/45" nondirectional quilting-weight cotton
* 1 yard of 44/45" cotton batting
* 1 spool of coordinating thread
* 5½ yards of coordinating ¼"-wide grosgrain ribbon (red)
* Double-sided fusible web
* 4-6 assorted felt squares in coordinating colors (for letters and numbers)
* 1" or larger button or coin as a marker
* 15" × 42" piece of non-skid rubberized shelf liner or similar material (optional)

Finished dimensions – 42" × 15"

Seam allowance – ¼" unless otherwise specified

① Measure, Mark, and Cut

Fold your fabric in half across the width with the right sides together, aligning the cut edges. Using the template on page 338 as a guide (following the dimensions given), draw the game board with fabric marker or pencil, and cut:

* **Game board** (cut 2)

Using the fabric game boards as a template cut from batting:

* **Game board** (cut 2)

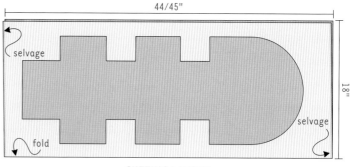

CUTTING LAYOUT

② Assemble the Hopscotch Course

* Place the two batting layers together, then place the two fabric layers with right sides facing, aligning all raw edges. Pin in place, then stitch all around, leaving an opening at the bottom as indicated on the template.

* Clip outside and inside corners and turn right side out. Use a turning tool to square off all corners. Press. Edgestitch all around, closing opening as you go.

③ Add the Ribbon

Fold the hopscotch course in half lengthwise and press to mark a crease down the center. This marks the border between 2/3, 5/6, and 8/9 blocks. Measure around each square and cut lengths of ribbon as needed. Topstitch to the hopscotch course to outline all squares, folding or mitering the ribbon at the corners. Use the photograph as your guide.

④ **Make and Attach the Appliqués**

Using a bold graphic font, print out the numbers 1-9 and the letters for "home," each approximately 3-4" tall. Cut the numbers and letters from the printer paper to use as pattern pieces. Press the fusible web onto the wrong side of the felt, following manufacturer's instructions. Cut the pattern pieces out of the interfaced felt. Peel off the paper backing and press each felt appliqué to the center of its respective square. Edgestitch around each appliqué to secure.

⑤ **Make and Attach the Non-Skid Backing (optional)**

Trace the completed hopscotch course onto the nonskid backing and cut out. Pin the backing to the bottom side of the hopscotch course, aligning all edges. A walking foot may help with this step. From the top side of the hopscotch course, stitch the backing to the fabric using a "stitch in the ditch" technique (see glossary, page 343) along the edgestitching.

I-SPY Game

Cards designed by June McCrary Jacobs

Bag designed by Rebecca Yaker

This I-Spy game is a spin on the classic game bingo. Each player has a game card with 16 words embroidered on it. Accompanying the cards is an I-Spy Bag filled with an assortment of trinkets that correspond to the words embroidered on the cards. The children (and adults) playing the game take turns shaking the bag until an item appears in the window, then the item is quickly called out (only one item is called out per turn). Each player then marks his or her corresponding square on his or her game card. Pass the bag to the next player, shake, and repeat. The first player to make a horizontal, vertical, or diagonal row wins the game, much like bingo. This game is suitable for two to four players. With some practice, you'll likely find ways to put your own spin on the game.

MATERIALS

* 1 yard of 44"/45" quilting-weight fabric
* 1 spool of coordinating thread

For the I-Spy Cards

* ⅔ yard of medium-weight sew-in interfacing
* ⅔ yard of cotton batting
* 7⅓ yards of rickrack (one color or an assortment)
* Embroidery floss in assorted colors

For the I-Spy Bag

* 3" diameter circle template
* 4" × 4" piece of clear vinyl
* 1½ cups of poly pellets
* Assorted trinkets, approximately 20 unique pieces (such as a penny, marble, screw, button, etc.)

Finished dimensions –
4 game cards, 10" × 10" each; bag 6" × 7"

Seam allowance – ½" unless otherwise specified

① Measure, Mark, and Cut

Fold your fabric in half lengthwise with right sides together, aligning the selvages. Measure and mark the pattern pieces directly onto the fabric, and cut them out. Separate the pieces by project.

For the Game Cards:

* **Cards** 11" × 11" (cut 8)

From medium-weight interfacing, cut:

* **Cards** 11" × 11" (cut 4)

From cotton batting, cut:

* **Cards** 11" × 11" (cut 4)

For the I-Spy Bag:

* **Bag front/back** 7" × 8" (cut 4)

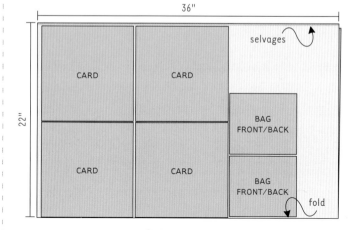

CUTTING LAYOUT

Game Cards

1 Stitch the Rickrack

* Baste a piece of medium-weight interfacing to the wrong side of four card pieces. Press all edges of these squares ½" to the wrong side.

* To mark four equal 2½"-wide columns, fold the squares in half and press. Fold in half again and press. Unfold the square (leaving edges folded ½" to the wrong side) and fold the square in half in the opposite direction twice, and press. Unfold the cards, including the ½" edges. Your cards should resemble the illustration.

* Cut the rickrack into 24 pieces that are 11" long. Position three pieces of rickrack vertically, then horizontally, on each of the four cards along the pressed lines. Topstitch all in place and press cards flat. These are the card fronts.

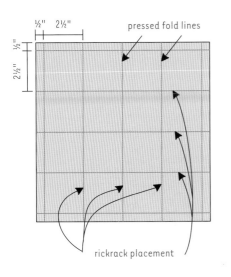

½" 2½" pressed fold lines

rickrack placement

❷ Embroider the Cards

Make a list of 20 unique trinkets. Include 16 trinket names on each card, omitting four different items per card to help make the game interesting. Once you have decided on 16 items per card, use embroidery floss to hand-embroider (or machine-embroider, if this is an option) the item names, each in its own square on the card fronts. Make the placement of each item different on each of the four cards.

❸ Finish the Cards

Position an embroidered card and a plain card with right sides together, aligning all raw edges, and place a batting piece on top. Stitch around all four sides, leaving a 2" opening along the bottom edge. Clip corners, turn right side out, and press. Edgestitch around the card, closing the opening. Repeat to finish the remaining cards.

Game Bag

❶ Make the Window

* Draw a 3"-diameter circle on the wrong side of one of the bag pieces, at least 1" from all edges. Position two bag pieces with right sides together, aligning raw edges. Stitch around the marked circle through both layers.
* Cut out the center of the circle, leaving ½" seam allowance. Clip into the seam allowance around the circle. Turn the pieces right sides out through the circle opening and press.
* Center the 4" square of clear vinyl underneath the circle and pin in place. Carefully edgestitch around the circle opening, stitching the vinyl to both fabric layers. This is the bag front. Baste a ¼" seam allowance on the outside raw edges of the bag front.

❷ Finish the Game Bag

* Place the two remaining bag pieces with wrong sides together and baste the pieces together. Place the two sets of bag pieces with right sides together, aligning raw edges. Stitch together around all four sides, leaving a 2" opening for turning. Clip corners and turn bag right side out.
* Place all 20 trinkets inside the bag through the 2" opening, then fill the bag with the poly pellets. Carefully and securely stitch the opening used for turning. Give the bag a healthy shake and let the game begin!

ARTIST PORTFOLIO

Designed by Rebecca Yaker

Perfect for the beginning or seasoned artist, this sturdy, portable portfolio has it all! It features a cover for a drawing pad (or coloring book, if you prefer) plus flip-out pockets for crayons, colored pencils, and markers. Everything you need for art making is at the ready! Convenient carrying handles mean that your artist can easily transport art supplies and be ready to create wherever and whenever inspiration strikes!

MATERIALS

* 1 yard of 54" home dec-weight fabric
* ¾ yard iron-on vinyl (typically 17" wide) (optional)
* ⅜ yard of ultra-firm fusible stabilizer
* 1 spool of coordinating thread
* 1½ yards of 1"-wide webbing
* 3 magnetic snaps, ½" in diameter
* Supplies: 8½" × 11" drawing pad, 8-pack of markers, 12-pack of colored pencils, 24-pack of crayons

Finished dimensions – 9½" × 13" when closed; 19" × 13" when open

Seam allowance – ½" unless otherwise specified

① Measure, Mark, and Cut

Place your fabric in a single layer with the wrong side up. Measure and mark the pieces directly onto the fabric, with the straight edges parallel to the grainline, and cut them out.

* **Interior/exterior** 14" × 20½" (cut 2)
* **Notebook pocket** 14" × 13" (cut 1)
* **Pencil pocket** 13" × 11" (cut 1)
* **Marker pocket** 13" × 7" (cut 1)
* **Crayon/pencil backing** 13" × 9½" (cut 2)
* **Marker backing** 13" × 7" (cut 2)
* **Crayon pocket** 7" × 13" (cut 2)
* **Tabs** 3" × 6" (cut 6)

From iron-on vinyl (optional), cut:

* **Crayon/pencil backing** 13" × 9½" (cut 2)
* **Marker backing** 13" × 7" (cut 1)

From ultra-firm fusible stabilizer, cut:

* **Interior/exterior** 12¾" × 19¼" (cut 1)

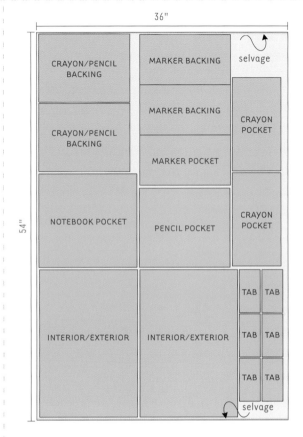

CUTTING LAYOUT

② Apply the Iron-On Vinyl (optional)

Apply the iron-on vinyl to the right sides of both crayon/pencil backings and one marker backing, following manufacturer's instructions. Set the pieces aside. Laminating these pieces helps keep your portfolio clean from stray crayon, marker, and pencil marks. Simply wipe the vinyl clean when necessary.

③ Make the Crayon Pockets

* Fold one crayon pocket in half with wrong sides together, aligning the long edges and press. Edgestitch along the folded edge. Position this folded crayon pocket on the right side of one laminated crayon/pencil backing piece, aligning the side and bottom edges, and baste in place.

* Fold the second crayon pocket in half with right sides together, aligning the long edges. Stitch the long raw edges, creating a tube. Turn right side out and press. Edgestitch one long finished edge to create the top edge of the pocket. Position this pocket on the right side of the laminated backing piece, 1¼" above the top edge of the other crayon pocket, aligning the side raw edges. Stitch in place along the bottom edge, and baste the sides.

* Using a washable fabric pen or tailor's chalk and, starting 1½" from each side edge, draw vertical lines on the crayon pockets every 1", for a total of 22 lines (11 on each pocket). Topstitch along the lines through all layers, backstitching securely at each top edge.

* Cut three 2" pieces of webbing and position them along the bottom raw edge of the crayon pocket, aligning raw edges. Center one piece and place the others 1½" from the sides. Baste in place and set aside.

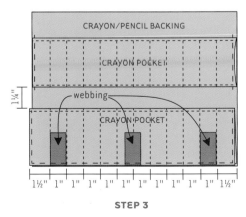

STEP 3

④ **Make the Pencil Pockets**

* Fold the pencil pocket in half with wrong sides together, aligning the long edges, and press. Edgestitch along the folded edge. Position this pocket on the right side of the remaining laminated pencil/crayon backing, aligning side and bottom edges, and baste in place.

* As you did for the crayon packet, start 1½" from each side edge and draw vertical lines every 1", for a total of 11 lines. Topstitch along the lines as before.

⑤ **Join the Crayon and Pencil Pockets**

With right sides together, align the raw edges of the two backing pieces, sandwiching the pockets and webbing in between the layers. Make sure that the top edges of the pockets are facing in the same direction. Stitch around all four sides, leaving a 4" opening for turning along the top edge. Clip corners, turn right side out, and carefully press from the backside (taking care that the iron does not touch the laminated piece). Edgestitch around all four sides, closing the opening in your stitching line.

6 Make the Marker Pocket

* Fold the marker pocket in half with wrong sides together, aligning the long edges, and press. Edgestitch along the folded edge. Position this folded marker pocket on the right side of the laminated marker backing piece, aligning side and bottom edges, and baste in place.

* As before, draw vertical lines, this time starting 2" from each side edge and every 1½", for a total of seven lines. Topstitch along the lines through all layers, as before.

* Cut two 2" pieces of webbing and position them along the bottom edge of the pocket, 3½" from the side edges, aligning the raw edges. Baste in place as before.

* With right sides together, align the raw edges of the two marker backing pieces, sandwiching the pocket and webbing in between the layers. Stitch around all four sides, leaving a 4" opening for turning along the top edge. Clip corners, turn right side out, and carefully press from the backside (taking care that the iron does not touch the laminated piece). Edgestitch around all four sides, stitching the opening closed.

7 Attach the Notebook Pocket to the Interior

Fold the notebook pocket piece in half with wrong sides together, aligning the 14" edges, and press. Edgestitch along the folded edge. Position this folded pocket on the right side of one interior/exterior piece, aligning the right-hand side, bottom, and top edges, and baste in place. This piece is the now the interior.

8 Attach the Handles to the Exterior

* Cut two 21" lengths of webbing for the handles. Turn and press the raw ends of the webbing ½" to the wrong side. With right sides facing up, position the folded ends of the handles on the short ends of the remaining exterior piece, 4½" from the sides and 3½" down from the top. Stitch handles in place, stopping 1½" from the side of the exterior.

* With right side facing up, position the three male halves of the magnetic snaps on the right-hand side of the exterior at the locations as indicated on the diagram. Attach the snaps following manufacturer's instructions.

9 Make the Tabs

* Attach the female half of a magnetic snap on the right side of one tab piece, 1¼" from an end. Repeat to attach the remaining two female snap halves to two additional tab pieces.

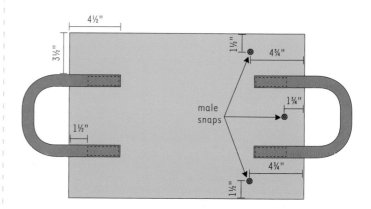

PORTFOLIO EXTERIOR
STEPS 8 AND 9

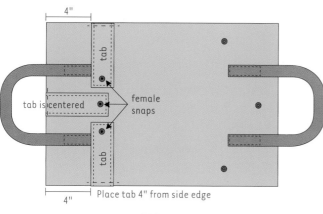

STEP 9

* With right sides together, align the raw edges of two tab pieces (one with a snap, one without). Stitch around three sides, leaving the short end without the snap unstitched. Clip corners, turn right side out, and press. Edgestitch around the three finished sides. Repeat to make two more tabs.
* With right side facing up, position the tab pieces on the left-hand side of the exterior with the snaps facing up at the locations indicated on the diagram. Baste tabs in place.

⑩ Assemble the Portfolio

* Place the exterior on a work surface with the right side facing up, and the tabs positioned on the left-hand side. Fold the handles in toward the center of the piece and pin in place. Also pin the tabs toward the center, to keep them out of the stitching line.
* Center the crayon/pencil piece along the *right-hand* side edge of the exterior piece, with the crayon pocket side facing up. Align the loose edges of the webbing with the side raw edge of the exterior. Baste webbing in place.
* Center the marker piece along the *right-hand* side edge, on top of the crayon/pencil piece, with the marker pocket down. Align the webbing with raw edges and baste in place as before.
* Place the interior on top of the other pieces, right side down, with the notebook pocket positioned along the *left-hand* edge (the side opposite the crayon, pencil, and marker pockets).

* Stitch around all four sides, leaving a 6" opening in the center of one long edge for turning. Clip corners, turn right side out, and press.
* Insert fusible stabilizer through the opening, with the fusible side toward the exterior. Carefully smooth in place and press from the exterior to adhere. Edgestitch around all four sides of the exterior, closing the opening as you stitch.
* Load up the portfolio with crayons, colored pencils, markers, and paper, and let the art making begin!

ULTiMaTe GaMeR's TOTe

Designed by Stacy Schlyer

Looking to take your gaming on the go? Here's the perfect solution! The sturdy bag is padded to protect your system, the individual pockets hold up to 16 games, and the zippered back pocket holds cords and batteries securely. The Velcro closure ensures you don't have to worry about a magnetic snap erasing any games. The removable wrist strap helps the gamer hold onto his or her treasures extra tight.

MATERIALS

* 1 yard of 44/45" quilting-weight cotton
* ⅜ yard of fusible fleece
* ½ yard of single-sided fusible stabilizer
* 10" diameter dinner plate or circle template
* 1 spool of coordinating thread
* 1" Velcro square
* 14" zipper
* 1" D-ring
* 1" swivel clasp

Finished dimensions – 4½" × 8"

Seam allowance – ½" unless otherwise specified

① Measure, Mark, and Cut

Lay out your fabric in a single layer with the wrong side facing up. Measure and mark the following pieces on the wrong side of the fabric and cut them out.

* **Body** 5½" × 9" (cut 4)
* **Flap** 8" × 9" (cut 2)
* **Side** 5½" × 4" (cut 4)
* **Bottom** 4" × 9" (cut 2)
* **Large interior pocket** 8" × 9" (cut 2)
* **Small interior pocket** 3½" × 9" (cut 2)
* **Zipper pocket** 9" × 9" (cut 1)
* **Zipper panel** 2" × 9" (cut 1)
* **Wrist strap** 3" × 10" (cut 1)
* **D-ring tab** 3" × 4" (cut 1)

From fusible fleece, cut:

* **Body** 5½" × 9" (cut 2)
* **Flap** 8" × 9" (cut 1)
* **Side** 5½" × 4" (cut 2)
* **Bottom** 4" × 9" (cut 1)

From fusible stabilizer, cut:

* **Body** 4½" × 8" (cut 2)
* **Flap** 7" × 8" (cut 1)
* **Side** 4½" × 3" (cut 2)
* **Bottom** 3" × 8" (cut 1)

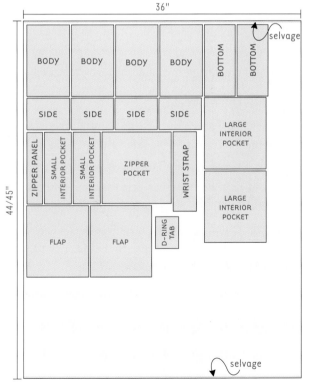

CUTTING LAYOUT

❷ Round off the Flap

Round one 9" edge of both flap fabric pieces, using the dinner plate or circle template (see illustration and text on page 163, step 3). Do the same with the corresponding fusible fleece and stabilizer pieces. Note that the stabilizer piece is 1" smaller, so the curve should also be a bit smaller.

❸ Fuse the Interfacing and Fleece

* Center each stabilizer piece on the wrong side of a corresponding fabric piece with ½" of fabric overhanging the stabilizer on all sides. Fuse according to manufacturer's directions.

* Fuse each fleece piece directly to the stabilizer on the corresponding fabric piece. The fleece will help keep the stabilizer in place and reduce bulk while sewing. These pieces become the tote exterior.

❹ Make the Flap

On the right side of the non-interfaced flap piece, stitch the loop half of the Velcro square 1" in from the curved raw edge, centered side to side. Pin both flap pieces together, right sides facing, and stitch along the curve, leaving the long straight edge open. Trim seam allowance, notch curves, and turn right side out. Press. Baste the open raw edges together and edgestitch all finished edges.

❺ Make the Zippered Pocket

* Fold the zipper pocket in half, wrong sides together. Pin the folded edge to the right side of the zipper tape, close to the zipper coil. Edgestitch to attach.

* Fold the zipper panel in half lengthwise, wrong sides together. Pin the folded edge to the right side of the zipper tape to the left and close to the zipper coil, opposite the pocket. Edgestitch to attach.

* Pin the pieced zippered pocket, right side up, on the right side of an exterior body piece with the zipper panel at the top edge. Trim excess fabric or zipper tape if needed, and baste all around with edgestitch. This becomes the tote exterior back.

❻ Complete the Exterior

* On the remaining interfaced body piece (now the exterior front), make a mark 3" down from the long top raw edge and centered from side to side. Stitch the hook half of the Velcro at this mark.

* Pin the bottom edge of the tote exterior back to the exterior bottom, right sides together. Stitch, starting and stopping ½" from each corner. Repeat to attach the tote exterior front and both tote exterior sides to the exterior bottom.

* Pin each exterior side to the tote exterior front and back pieces, right sides together. Stitch, stopping ½" from the bottom corner only. Turn exterior right side out.

* Pin the flap to the exterior back, right sides together, aligning raw edge (Velcro should face away from zippered pocket). Baste with edgestitch.

❼ Make and Attach D-ring Tab

* Press under both 4" ends of the D-ring tab ¼", then fold and press as you would to make double-fold bias tape (see page 12). Edgestitch both long edges.

* Make a mark 1" down from the top raw edge of the right-hand exterior side and centered between the seams. Center the top short end of the D-ring tab on this measurement and stitch in place with edgestitch. Thread the D-ring onto the tab and stitch the bottom folded end of the tab to the exterior side, 2½" below the first stitching to secure.

⑧ Make the Game Pockets

* Fold one large interior pocket in half lengthwise, aligning the 9" edges, wrong sides together. Topstitch along the folded edge. Place it on the right side of an interior body, matching side and bottom raw edges, and baste along sides and bottom.

* Topstitch a horizontal line across the pocket, 1¼" below the top folded edge. This creates a shallow pocket for the game cartridges.

* Fold one small interior pocket piece in half lengthwise, aligning the 9" edges, wrong sides together. Topstitch along the folded edge, and place it on top of the large interior pocket, aligning side and bottom raw edges. The top folded edge should lie approximately 1" below the topstitching on the larger pocket. Baste with edgestitch along sides and bottom.

* Fold interior body and pockets in half across the width to crease the center halfway point. Measure 2" to the right and left of the center crease and mark vertical dividing lines.

* Stitch down the center crease and both marked lines to form the game pockets.

* Repeat for the remaining large interior pocket, small interior pocket, and interior body piece.

⑨ Make the Interior

* Assemble the interior body, side, and bottom pieces as you did the exterior pieces. Place the exterior inside the interior, right sides facing and top raw edges aligned. Stitch all around the top edge, leaving a 4" opening at the front for turning. Trim seam, turn right side out, and press.

* Press raw edges of the opening ½" to the wrong side. Topstitch all around, closing the opening as you go while keeping the flap out of the way.

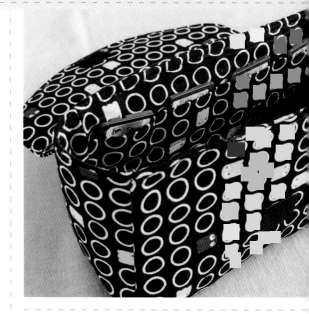

⑩ Make the Wrist Strap

* Fold, press, and stitch the wrist strap as you did the tab, as if to make double fold bias tape. Slide the swivel clasp onto the strap, fold the strap in half aligning the short raw edges, and stitch along the raw edge at a ¼" seam allowance to form a loop.

* Press the seam allowance open and flip the wrist strap loop so the raw edges are inside the loop.

* Slide the clasp so it is directly over the seam. Stitch across the loop, below the clasp, catching the seam allowance in the seam. Clip clasp to D-ring.

bunnies vs. chicks four-in-a-row

Designed by Adrienne Lodico

Are the kids a little bored with tic-tac-toe? Four-in-a-Row is a great next step! The game board and pieces of this project are completely self-contained for easy cleanup, fast packing for the beach, and keeping everything together. A perfect rainy-day or outside play-day game, this quick project also makes a fab gift.

MATERIALS

* Pattern pieces (2), *see* sheet 1
* 1 yard of 44/45" nondirectional quilting-weight cotton
* 4 white and 1 pink felt squares for bunnies
* 4 yellow and 1 orange felt squares for chicks
* 7½ yards of ¼"-wide grosgrain ribbon
* ⅝ yard of cotton batting
* 1 spool of coordinating thread

* ½ yard of 1"-wide elastic
* 2½ yards of ½"-wide double-fold bias binding (coordinating with ribbon)
* Black embroidery floss
* Filler for game pieces, such as poly pellets, rice, dry beans, or buckwheat hulls
* Fabric glue
* 21 pink ¼" pompoms for bunny noses

Finished dimensions – Game board 22" × 19"; bags 12" × 9"; game pieces 3" × 2½" (21 individual bunnies and 21 chicks).

Seam allowance – ½" unless otherwise specified

① Measure, Mark, and Cut

Fold your fabric in half lengthwise with right sides together, aligning the selvages. Measure and mark the following pieces on the wrong side of the fabric and cut them out.

* **Game board** 22" × 19" (cut 2)
* **Drawstring bag** 14" × 11" (cut 4)
* **Elastic casing** 22" × 2" (cut 2)

Trace the bunny inner ears and chick beaks from the patterns to make separate templates, and cut from felt:

* **Bunnies** (cut 42) from white
* **Bunny inner ears** (cut 42) from pink
* **Chicks** (cut 42) from yellow
* **Chick beaks** (cut 21) from orange

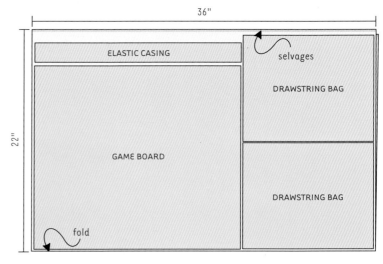

CUTTING LAYOUT

(Layout labels: 36"; 22"; ELASTIC CASING; selvages; DRAWSTRING BAG; GAME BOARD; DRAWSTRING BAG; fold)

Game Board

❶ Mark the Ribbon Grid

* Cut ribbon into six 19" lengths for vertical lines, and five 22" lengths for horizontal lines. Place one game board on your work surface, right side up, with one 22" edge on top.

* Starting from the left-hand side, measure and mark a vertical line 3½" from the edge, then continue marking lines as shown in diagram. Mark horizontal lines in the same way.

❷ Assemble the Board and Stitch the Ribbons

Place the remaining (unmarked) game board piece on a work surface, wrong side up. Place quilt batting on top, aligning raw edges. Pin the marked game board to these two layers, right side up, aligning raw edges. Pin all layers together between the grid markings. Stitch lengths of ribbon onto the game board grid markings with a wide zigzag stitch, beginning at the center, and through all layers.

❸ Attach the Casing and Binding

* Pin elastic casing pieces together, right sides facing and raw edges aligned. Stitch both long edges, leaving the short ends open. Turn right side out and press. Thread the 18" piece of elastic through the casing, edgestitching at both short ends to secure.

* Fold the elastic casing in half across the width, aligning short raw edges. Pin in place, centered along the 22" edge of the game board back, aligning raw edges. Baste with edgestitch.

* Use the ½"-wide double-fold bias tape to bind the raw edges of the game board, mitering corners as you go (see page 13).

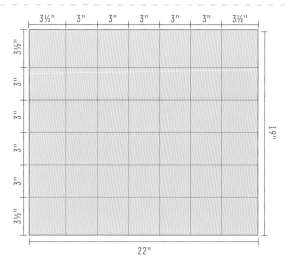

STEP 1: Grosgrain ribbon grid game board

Drawstring Bags

➊ Prepare the Opening

* Place two drawstring bag pieces on a work surface, side-by-side, with wrong sides facing up, with one 11" edge on top. Fold the top right-hand corner of each by 1" to the wrong side to create an angled folded edge. Press and stitch to secure with a ¼" seam allowance.

* Repeat with remaining two drawstring bag pieces, but folding and stitching the top *left-hand* corner instead.

➋ Stitch the Bags with a French Seam

Pin two drawstring bag pieces together, wrong sides facing and raw and folded corners aligned. Stitch the side and bottom edges with a French seam (see glossary, page 341), leaving the short top edge and folded corners unstitched.

➌ Complete the Casing

* Press under the top edge of the bag ¼", then another ¾". Stitch along the bottom fold to create a casing. Stitch the second drawstring bag in a similar fashion.

* Cut two 18" lengths of ribbon for drawstrings. Insert each drawstring into a casing. Knot the ribbon ends together to secure.

FOUR-IN-A-ROW GAME RULES

Two players take turns setting game pieces on the grid, trying to get four pieces in a row. Players may block their opponent's runs. The first player to get four consecutive pieces, either horizontally, vertically, or diagonally, wins the game.

Game Pieces

➊ Make the Bunnies

* Appliqué two inner ear pieces in place on 21 bunny pieces using a straight stitch. Embroider two eyes on each of these bunnies with French knots (see glossary, page 341).

* Pin one appliquéd bunny piece to a plain bunny piece, wrong sides facing and raw edges aligned. Edgestitch all around, leaving a ½" opening for stuffing. Fill the game piece about ¾" full. Stitch the opening closed and glue a pompom in place for the nose. Repeat for remaining bunny pieces.

➋ Make the Chicks

* Appliqué a beak in place on 21 chick pieces in the same way. Stitch a line down the center of the beak to create a top and bottom beak. Embroider two eyes on each of these chicks with French knots.

* Pin one appliquéd chick piece with a plain chick piece, wrong sides facing and raw edges aligned. Edgestitch, fill, stitch, and close the opening as before. Repeat for remaining chick pieces.

CHAPTER 13

on the go

TRY THESE ON-THE-GO PROJECTS for keeping everything

just where you need it when you're out and about.

In the car, at a sleepover, at the library, or even on

the beach, these are the perfect items that you

didn't even know you needed — until now.

NIGHT OWL SLUMBER PARTY BAG

Designed by Calli Taylor

Is your little night owl ready to party? For all-night adventures featuring popcorn, scary stories, and games, this slumber party bag is just the ticket! It's perfect for holding a small sleeping roll or bag, pillow, and PJs. The owl pocket can stash toothpaste and toothbrush, and the smaller pocket is handy for little necessities such as nail polish.

MATERIALS

* Pattern piece (1), *see* sheet 1
* 1 yard of 44/45" nondirectional home dec-weight cotton fabric
* ¼ yard of coordinating quilting-weight cotton for straps
* ⅛ yard of light-colored solid flannel for strap reinforcement (optional)
* 9" square scrap of corduroy for owl pocket
* Assorted cotton and felt scraps for tummy pocket and appliqués
* 1 spool of coordinating thread
* Two 10" lengths of 1"-wide non-roll elastic

Finished dimensions – about 12" wide drawn up (33" wide expanded) × 19" tall, excluding handles

Seam allowance – ½" unless otherwise specified

❶ Measure, Mark, and Cut

Lay out your fabric in a single layer with the wrong side facing up. Trim the selvage of the main fabric, leaving a piece that is approximately 36" × 44". If you are using wider (54" or 56") home dec-weight fabric, keep the full width of the fabric for a roomier bag. Measure and mark the straps as follows.

From coordinating fabric, cut:

* **Straps** 4½" × 44" (cut 2)

If using flannel reinforcement, cut:

* **Strap reinforcement** 2" × 44" (cut 2)

Trace the individual parts of the owl (eyes, beak, etc) from the pocket pattern and use them to cut out the following.

From corduroy, cut: *From cotton, cut:*

* **Owl pocket** (cut 2)   * **Tummy pocket** (cut 2)

From assorted felt scraps, cut:

* **Eyes** (cut 2)   * **Beak** (cut 1)
* **Pupils** (cut 2)

❷ Make the Owl Pocket

* Pin the tummy pocket pieces together, right sides facing and raw edges aligned. Stitch along top curved edge only. Clip the curve, turn right side out, press, and edgestitch the top finished edge.
* Pin tummy pocket to the right side of one owl pocket piece, aligning side and bottom raw edges. Baste in place. On this same piece, appliqué felt eyes and beak with edgestitch or satin stitch.
* Pin owl pocket pieces together, right sides facing, and stitch with a ¼" seam allowance, leaving a 2" opening at the bottom. Clip corners and curves and turn right side out. Turn in the edges of the opening and press all around, using a pressing cloth to protect the corduroy.

❸ Attach the Owl Pocket to the Bag

Lay the bag fabric on a work surface, right side up, with one selvage edge at the top. Position the owl pocket 6½" below the top selvage edge, centered side

to side. Edgestitch the owl in place, closing the opening as you go, while leaving the top of his head (between the ears) open. For added strength, topstitch a second stitch line ⅛" from the first.

❹ Make the Sides

* Lay the bag fabric on a work surface with the owl pocket facing up. Press under the right- and left-hand raw edges ¼", then another 1¼" to the wrong side. On the wrong side of the bag, measure and mark the hem 7" from the top and bottom selvage edges, on both sides of the bag. Now stitch the casings between the 7" marks.
* Thread a 10" length of elastic through each side casing. Center and box-stitch (see glossary, page 340) each end of the elastic at the 7" marks. Stitch the remainder of each side hem to complete the sides of the bag.

❺ Make and Attach the Straps

* Press under the top and bottom selvage edges of the bag ¼", then another 2". Stitch the casings.
* Press all raw edges of the straps ¼" to the wrong side, then press in half lengthwise, wrong sides facing. Sandwich the flannel reinforcement between the strap layers, if using, and edgestitch all around.
* Thread each strap through a casing. Tie the ends of each strap into a knot to finish.

TODDLER NaPTime MaT

Designed by Caroline Critchfield

Little guys and gals will love to take a break on this puffy little mat, complete with a pillow. It's also perfect to take to preschool if they stay for naptime. When it's time to put away, the mat rolls up compactly, making it a cinch to transport.

MATERIALS

* 1 yard of 44/45" quilting-weight cotton
* 1 spool of coordinating thread
* 32 ounces of fiberfill

Finished dimensions – 21" wide × 35" long

Seam allowance – ½" unless otherwise specified

① Measure, Mark, and Cut

* Lay out your fabric in a single layer with the right side facing up. Cut and square off your fabric as neatly and evenly as possible, trimming ½" off both selvage edges to make one piece that is 36" × 43/44".

* Fold your fabric in half with right sides together, aligning the long edges. Stitch along the bottom and side raw edges of the folded rectangle. Turn right side out, and press the top edges ½" to the inside.

② Measure the Padded Channels

With the open end at the top of the mat, use a removable or disappearing fabric marker to draw the vertical and horizontal lines as shown.

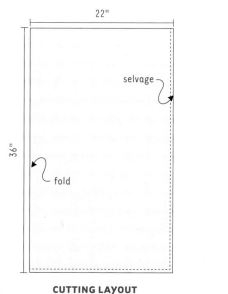

22"

selvage

36"

fold

CUTTING LAYOUT

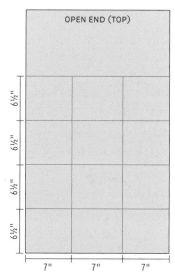

OPEN END (TOP)

6½"

6½"

6½"

6½"

7"   7"   7"

❸ Stitch and Stuff the Channels

* Topstitch along the two vertical lines. Take care to backstitch at the beginning and end of the stitching lines to lock the stitches.

* Stuff a few handfuls of fiberfill into each channel and push it all the way down to the bottom, keeping the stuffing below the first horizontal marked line. Lay the mat on a work surface and pin along the first marked horizontal line to help hold the channels closed while you sew. Stitch across this line to create three soft little pillows, backstitching as before. Repeat this step three more times until all 12 square channels have been stuffed and sewn closed (the top rectangular pocket should still be empty).

NOTE: *Don't worry if a little fiberfill gets stuck in your seams. You'll stitch right over it and won't notice it when the project is complete.*

❹ Finish the Naptime Mat

Edgestitch along the folded edges of the open top, leaving a 5" opening in the center for stuffing the top pillow. Stuff this final section, then pin and edgestitch the opening closed.

car seat HOT/COLD pack

Designed by Georgia Solorzano

This project is designed to warm up your child's car seat during those bitter winter months, or cool it off during the sweltering heat of summer. The hot/cold pack drapes over the seat and fits right in, conforming to most every seat on the market. It is filled with flaxseeds, which retain both heat and cold very well.

SAFETY NOTE: *The Car Seat Hot/Cold Pack is only to be used prior to the kids getting in their seats. It cannot be used while the kids are in their seats, as it would jeopardize the safety of your child and integrity of the car seat.*

MATERIALS

* 1 yard of 44/45" quilting-weight cotton fabric
* 1¼ yards of ¾"-wide grosgrain ribbon
* 1 spool of coordinating thread
* Funnel (for distributing the flaxseeds)
* 8 pounds of flaxseeds (approximately 12-16 cups)

Finished dimensions –
21" wide × 34" long

Seam allowance – ½" unless otherwise specified

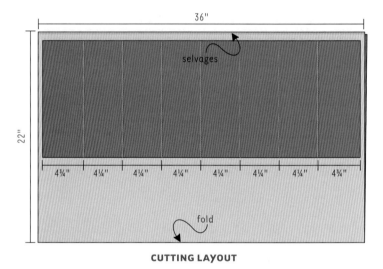

CUTTING LAYOUT

① Measure, Mark, and Cut

Fold fabric in half lengthwise with right sides together, aligning the selvages. Measure and mark the hot/cold pack onto the fabric, and cut it out.

* **Hot/cold pack** 35" × 12½" (cut 2)

Use a removable or disappearing fabric marker to mark the lines shown on the *right* side of one of the pieces.

② Assemble the Hot/Cold Pack

* Fold the piece of grosgrain ribbon in half and center the folded end along the top short edge and right side of the marked piece. Stitch in place using a ¼" seam allowance. If desired, seal the unfinished ends of the ribbon by slowing passing them through a flame, such as a lighter.
* Pin the two pack pieces together with right sides facing and raw edges aligned. Stitch around all four sides, leaving a 4" opening along the bottom edge for turning, as well as a 1" opening in the center of each marked section along one edge (eight openings total). Clip corners, turn right side out, and press. Press the seam allowances of all openings ½" to inside.
* Edgestitch across the bottom edge, closing the 4" opening in your stitching. Topstitch across each marked line through both layers of fabric, backstitching at both ends of each seam.

❸ Fill with Flaxseeds

Using a funnel, pour 1½–2 cups of flaxseeds in each section through the 1" openings. Pin the openings closed. Edgestitch around sides and top edges of the pack, making sure each opening is securely closed.

❹ Use the Hot/Cold Pack

To heat the pack: Place in a microwave for about 1 minute on high, depending on your microwave.

NOTE: *Never leave your microwave unattended while heating. If necessary, heat further at 30-second intervals, checking for overheating or scorching. For added safety, sprinkle with water, or place a microwave-safe container full of water next to the pack while heating. After heating, flaxseeds retain some heat up to 1 hour.*

To cool the pack: Place it in the freezer for at least 1 hour.

When the pack has achieved the desired temperature (hot or cold), place in your child's car seat. Once the car seat has reached the desired temperature, remove the pack before buckling your child into the seat.

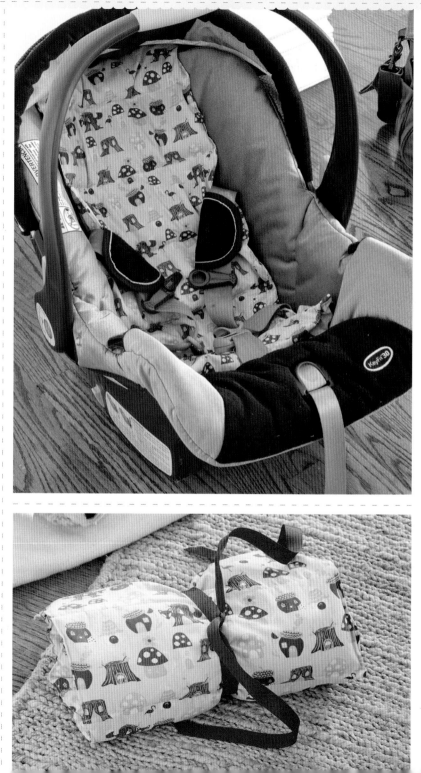

snail face suitcase

Designed by June McCrary Jacobs

Snails take their homes along with them as they travel, and now your little ones can take bits and pieces of home with them as well! Children love to have their own luggage to pack clothes, PJs, and special treasures, whether it's for nights at Grandma's, sleepovers, or a longer journey. Surprise your child with this kid-size suitcase, adding whatever special embellishment will delight him or her!

MATERIALS

* 1 yard of 54/55" home dec-weight fabric
* ⅔ yard of 44/45" fusible fleece
* 1 spool of coordinating thread
* 3" diameter circle template, cup, or saucer
* 24" polyester zipper
* ⅝ yard of ½"-wide rickrack or other trim for handles, cut in half

For the snail appliqué
* 12" of ½"-wide braid, ribbon, or other trim (body)
* 1 yard of ½"-wide rickrack
* Embroidery floss (for antennae)
* 1 button, 1½" in diameter (for the head)
* 1 button, 1" in diameter (for the shell center)

* 2 buttons, ⅜" in diameter (for antennae)
* 2 beads or ³⁄₁₆"-wide buttons (for eyes)

Finished dimensions –
    12" tall × 14" wide × 5" deep

Seam allowance – ½" unless otherwise specified

1 Measure, Mark, and Cut

Fold your fabric in half lengthwise with the right sides together, aligning the selvages. Measure and mark the following pieces on the wrong side of your fabric.

* **Suitcase exterior/lining** 13" × 15" (cut 4)
* **Zipper panels exterior/lining** 3" × 23" (cut 4)
* **Gusset exterior/lining** 29" × 5¾ (cut 2)
* **Handles** 8" × 5" (cut 2)

From fusible fleece, cut:

* **Suitcase exterior** 13" × 15" (cut 2)
* **Zipper panels** 3" × 23" (cut 2)
* **Gusset exterior/lining** 29" × 5¾ (cut 1)
* **Handles** 6½" × 1" (cut 2)

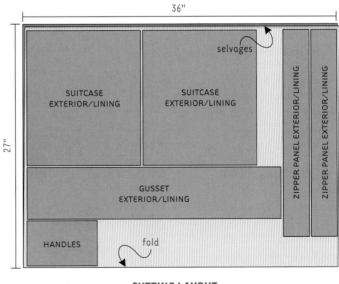

CUTTING LAYOUT

❷ Appliqué the Suitcase Front

* Select a suitcase piece for the front exterior and lay it out horizontally, right side facing up. Pin the 12" length of trim in an angled L-shape for the body of the snail, using the photograph as a guide.

* Starting about 2½" from the snail L-shaped body, spiral the yard of rickrack outward to form the shell. You should be able to make about five spirals before running out of rickrack; tuck the end under the body trim. Stitch trim and rickrack in place with straight stitch.

* Embroider two 2" antennae in a V-shape with embroidery floss, using a chain stitch (see glossary, page 340). Hand-sew the buttons for the head, eyes, antennae, and shell center, as shown in the photograph.

❸ Apply Fusible Fleece

Fuse fleece, following manufacturer's directions, to the wrong side of the following (which all become exterior pieces):

* Two suitcase exterior/lining pieces
* one gusset piece
* two zipper panels

❹ Round the Corners

Use a circle template to round all four corners of the suitcase front (see page 163). Then use the trimmed suitcase front as a template to round all four corners of the suitcase back and lining pieces.

❺ Install the Zipper

Press one long edge of both exterior zipper panels ½" to the wrong side. Pin the folded edge of one exterior zipper panel along one edge of the zipper tape, ⅛" from the zipper teeth. Topstitch, using a zipper foot. Repeat to install the second exterior zipper panel on the opposite side of the zipper. If the length of the zipper tape overhangs the panel by more than ½", center the zipper panel along the length and trim the zipper to fit, bartacking along both ends of the cut zipper (see glossary, page 339). Make sure to open zipper so you don't cut off the pull tab.

❻ Attach the Gusset Exterior to Zipper Panel

With the right sides together, pin one short end of the completed zipper panel to one short end of the exterior gusset, aligning raw edges. Stitch and press the seam allowances toward the gusset. Repeat with the other end of the zipper panel and gusset. Press seam allowance towards gusset. Topstitch both ends of the gusset ¼" from each seam.

❼ Construct the Exterior

* Fold the zipper and gusset panel in half across the width, aligning the side seams, and press gently to mark the center creases. Unfold. Do the same with the exterior suitcase body pieces to mark the center of the top and bottom edges. Pin the zipper and gusset panel to the suitcase front, right sides together, aligning center points at the top and bottom edges. Notch the zipper panel seam allowances to ease the curves. Stitch to attach.

* Open the zipper a few inches and attach the other side of the zipper panel and gusset to the suitcase back in the same way. Press seam allowances away from gusset. Topstitch the suitcase front and back ¼" from the seams.

⑧ Stitch the Zipper Panel Lining

Press one long edge of each zipper panel lining ½" to the wrong side. Lay out the panels side by side, with the folded edges to the inside, about ½" apart. Pin and stitch the panels, with right sides together to the remaining gusset, maintaining the ½" spacing of the zipper panel pieces, as in step 6.

⑨ Assemble the Lining

Attach the zipper gusset panel lining to the suitcase body lining pieces in the same manner as the exterior of the bag, in step 7.

⑩ Complete the Suitcase

※ Turn the suitcase exterior right side out through the zipper opening. Insert the lining into the exterior with wrong sides together, aligning all seams and corners. Hand-tack the lining to the exterior at each of the corners so the lining lies smoothly inside the suitcase.

※ Turn the top of the suitcase inside out slightly, just so you can see the folded edge of one zipper panel lining and the wrong side of the zipper tape. Hand-sew each zipper panel lining to the wrong side of the zipper tape with a slipstitch or whipstitch, taking care that your stitches don't come through the bag exterior, or get too close to the zipper teeth.

⑪ Make and Attach Handles

※ Press the short raw edges of the handle pieces ½" to the wrong side. Fold and press each handle as you would to make double-fold bias tape (see page 12). Sandwich and center the fusible fleece between the folded layers. Press.

※ Pin a piece of rickrack trim down the center of each handle, tucking raw edges in between the fabric layers at each end. Topstitch the trim and edgestitch the handles all around.

※ Center the handle ends 6" apart, one on each zipper side panel, and stitch the ends with a box stitch (see glossary, page 340).

INSULATED LUNCH BOX

Designed by Rebecca Yaker

This insulated, soft-sided lunch box is the perfect solution to enjoying the food you love on the go. The coated fabric makes cleanup a cinch, while the insulated lining helps retain the appropriate food temperature. There's even a pocket on the inside for an ice pack. The zipper closure adds extra convenience, helping to contain messes. It's time to say goodbye to brown-bag lunches once and for all!

MATERIALS

* 1 yard of 44/45" coated cotton
* ⅓ yard of 45"-wide or ¾ yard of 22"-wide insulated batting, such as Insul-Bright
* 1 spool of coordinating thread
* Large spool of thread or 1½" diameter circle template
* 1½ yards of ½"-wide decorative ribbon
* 1½ yards of 1"-wide nylon webbing
* Fray Check (optional)
* 1" piece of ¾"-wide Velcro
* 28" (or longer) coordinating zipper

Finished dimensions – 9½" wide × 7½" tall × 3¾" deep

Seam allowance – ½" unless otherwise specified

① Measure, Mark, and Cut

Fold your fabric in half lengthwise with right sides together, aligning the selvages. Measure and mark the following pieces on the fabric, and cut them out.

* **Front/back** 8½" × 10½" (cut 4)
* **Exterior pocket** 6¾" × 10½" (cut 2)
* **Interior pocket** 7½" × 10½" (cut 2)
* **Bottom gusset** 4¾" × 9" (cut 2)
* **Wide zipper gusset** 3¼" × 26½" (cut 2)
* **Narrow zipper gusset** 2" × 26½" (cut 2)

From insulated batting, cut:

* **Front/back** 8½" × 10½" (cut 2)
* **Bottom gusset** 4¾" × 9" (cut 1)
* **Wide zipper gusset** 3¼" × 26½" (cut 1)
* **Narrow zipper gusset** 2" × 26½" (cut 1)

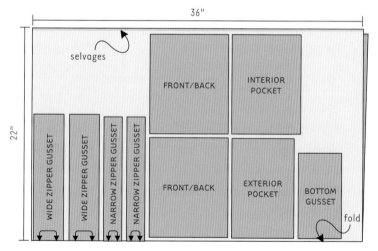

CUTTING LAYOUT

② Attach the Insulated Batting

Use a ¼" seam allowance to baste the insulated batting to the corresponding pieces. The insulated pieces will be the exterior pieces.

③ Make Rounded Corners

On the front/back pieces, place a large spool of thread in all four corners, lining it up with the raw edges and trace the portion that falls within the seam allowance, using a fabric pen (see page 163). Trim away the excess fabric. Repeat in the bottom two corners of the exterior and interior pocket pieces (or use one of the cut pieces as a template).

④ Prepare the Webbing

With both right sides facing up, center the decorative ribbon on the webbing. Stitch in place along both edges of the ribbon. Cut the webbing/ribbon into the following lengths:

* **Pocket trim** 10½" (cut 2)
* **Handles** 14" (cut 2)

To prevent the webbing's cut ends from fraying, use either Fray Check or carefully melt them with a lighter flame.

Fold the handle pieces in half lengthwise with wrong sides together. Edgestitch together along the center 4" of each handle to make them easier to hold when carrying.

⑤ Attach the Handles

* Position the cut ends of the handles on the right sides of the two insulated front/back pieces (the exterior pieces) as shown, 2½" from the side edges and 3" down from the top edge. Box-stitch the handles (see glossary, page 340) 1" below the top raw edge of the front/back pieces.

* On one piece (now the exterior back), position one pocket trim webbing piece across the width of the piece 2¼" down from the raw edge, covering the cut ends of the handles. Edgestitch both long edges.

* On the remaining (front) exterior, center half of the 1" Velcro piece 2⅜" from the top edges and edgestitch.

* Find and mark the center points on all four sides of the exterior and lining front/back pieces.

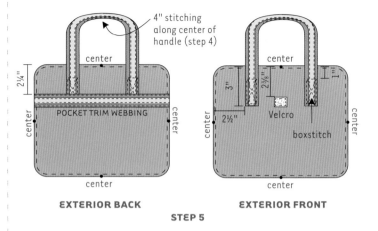

EXTERIOR BACK　　　**EXTERIOR FRONT**

STEP 5

⑥ Make the Exterior Pocket

* With right sides together, align the top raw edges of the exterior pocket pieces. Stitch together along the top straight edge. Turn exterior pocket pieces right side out and finger-press seam. Edgestitch along the finished edge.

* On the wrong side of the exterior pocket, center the remaining half of the 1" piece of Velcro along the top edge of the pocket, ¼" from the top edge. Stitch in place. On the right side of this pocket (the side without Velcro), position the remaining webbing pocket trim along the top edge and edgestitch along both long edges. This will cover the Velcro stitching lines.

* With both right sides facing up, position the exterior pocket on the exterior front piece and align the bottom rounded corners. Baste in place along the three unfinished sides. The Velcro halves will align and the top edge of the pocket will conceal the cut ends of the handles.

⑦ Install the Zipper

* Finger-press one long edge of one exterior wide and one narrow zipper gusset piece ½" to the wrong side.

* Center and pin the folded edge of the wide gusset to one side of the zipper tape ⅛" from the zipper teeth (zipper should be ¾" longer than the gusset at each end). Topstitch, using a

zipper foot. Repeat to install the narrow gusset piece on the opposite side of the zipper. Open zipper and bartack (see glossary, page 339) along both short ends of the zipper and trim the zipper teeth/tape that extend beyond the gusset, taking care not to cut off the zipper pull.

✻ Set the two remaining lining zipper gusset pieces aside.

⑧ Assemble the Exterior Gussets

✻ Staystitch both long raw edges of the zipper gusset using a ½" seam allowance.

✻ With right sides together, align the short ends of the exterior bottom gusset with the zippered gusset and stitch, forming a circle. Finger-press the seam allowances toward the bottom gusset and edgestitch the seams on the bottom gusset piece.

✻ Fold the gusset in half, aligning the bottom gusset seams. Place four marks along both raw edges at the folds to mark the top and bottom points of the gusset. Refold in the other direction and repeat. These marks will serve as center placement marks when attaching the gusset to the front and back pieces.

⑨ Assemble the Lunch-Box Exterior

✻ With right sides together, pin the exterior front to the narrow zipper gusset and bottom gusset, aligning the raw edges. Match up the marks along the edge of the gusset with the center marks on the front piece. Stitch together. You may need to clip into the seam allowance of the gusset to help stitch around the curved corners.

✻ Unzip the zipper and attach the exterior back to the wide zipper gusset and bottom gusset in the same way. Turn right side out.

⑩ Make the Interior Pocket

✻ With right sides together, align the top raw edges of the interior pocket pieces. Stitch together along the top straight edge. Turn interior pocket pieces right side out and finger-press the seam. Edgestitch along the finished edge.

✻ With both right sides facing up, position the interior pocket on one lining front/back piece and align the bottom rounded corners. Baste along the three unfinished sides.

⑪ Make the Lining

✻ Finger-press one long edge of the remaining wide and narrow zipper gusset pieces ⅝" to the wrong side. With right sides together, align the short ends of the remaining bottom gusset piece and the wide and narrow zipper gusset pieces, leaving a ½" gap between the folded edges of the wide and narrow gusset pieces to allow for the zipper.

✻ Stitch and finger-press the seam allowances toward the bottom gusset and edgestitch on the bottom gusset piece.

✻ Using the remaining front/back pieces, assemble the lining in the same manner as the exterior. Leave the lining wrong side out.

⑫ Finish the Lunch Box

With wrong sides together, place the lining inside the exterior. Slipstitch the folded edges of the wide and narrow zipper gusset lining to the zipper tape to finish.

STROLLER LINER

Designed by Sarah Pilling

Babies are messy, and it's a pain to wash or wipe down a stroller. So make a comfortable and warm liner for baby's stroller that's easy to take out and wash! As an added bonus, it can jazz up even the most drab stroller. This basic liner can be easily adapted for different strollers by simply adjusting the placement of the strap slots.

MATERIALS

* Pattern piece (1), *see* sheet 6
* 1 yard of 44/45" quilting-weight cotton
* 1 yard of 44/45" cotton batting
* 1 spool of coordinating thread
* Walking foot (optional)
* 3 yards of ½"-wide double-fold bias tape

Finished dimensions – 33" long × 13" wide

Seam allowance – ½" unless otherwise specified

1 Quilt the Fabric

* With wrong sides together, fold the fabric in half lengthwise, matching up the selvages. Fold the batting in half similarly, and sandwich the batting between the layers. Pin through all four layers.
* Mark your choice of quilting lines using a disappearing marker, washable fabric pen, or tailor's chalk. Machine-quilt the layers together, following your lines. You may want to use a walking foot, if you have one.

2 Measure, Mark, and Cut

* Before cutting out your fabric, it's a good idea to compare the pattern piece to your actual stroller to ensure that the stroller strap openings are correctly placed. If not, adjust as necessary.
* Position the pattern piece along the length of the quilted fabric and cut it out. Transfer the markings for the strap openings before removing the pattern.

NOTE: *Mirror the pattern piece along the line indicated.*

3 Mark and Create Stroller Strap Openings

Using a tight zigzag or buttonhole stitch, stitch all around each of the marked strap openings as if stitching a very large buttonhole, using wide bartack stitching (see glossary, page 339) at the top and bottom of each opening. Carefully cut through all layers along both of the marked lines, taking care not to cut into the buttonhole stitches.

4 Bind the Stroller Liner

Pin double-fold bias tape around the liner, enclosing all fabric raw edges in bias tape (see page 13). Stitch the tape in place, making sure to catch the back side of bias tape in the stitching.

KID CAR SET

Designed by Stacey Whittington

This lap desk and seat-back caddy are a great combo for keeping kids entertained on those dreaded long road trips! Sized just right for a child's lap, the lip of the desk tray keeps pencils, crayons, and other little bits from rolling out of reach. What's more, the magnetic chalkboard surface is a great art and play surface on its own! Keep art supplies, toys, and snacks close at hand with the accompanying seat-back caddy.

MATERIALS

* 1 yard of 44/45" nondirectional quilting-weight or home dec-weight cotton fabric
* 1 spool of coordinating thread

Lap Desk
* 9" × 13" metal tray or cookie sheet
* Fine-grit sandpaper
* Spray latex primer made specifically for metal, such as automobile primer
* Chalkboard spray paint

* Hot glue gun and glue sticks
* 7" × 11" template plastic, corrugated plastic, or other durable, stiff material
* 2 pounds of poly pellets or dried beans
* Industrial-strength glue

Seat-Back Caddy
* 2 yards of medium-weight fusible interfacing (if using quilting-weight cotton)

* 3 yards of ½"-wide double-fold bias tape
* 1⅜ yards of ¼"-wide elastic
* ½ yard of 1"-wide webbing
* One 1"-wide parachute buckle

Finished dimensions – desk 13" × 9"× 2"; caddy 13" × 23"

Seam allowance – ½" unless otherwise specified

① Measure, Mark, and Cut

Lay out your fabric in a single layer with the wrong side facing up. Measure and mark the following pieces on the fabric and cut them out.

* **Lap desk pillow** 13" × 17" (cut 1)
* **Caddy front and back** 23" × 13" (cut 2)
* **Caddy pocket #1** 8" × 13" (cut 1)
* **Caddy pocket #2** 10" × 17" (cut 1)
* **Caddy pocket #3** 16" × 13" (cut 1)

If using quilting-weight cotton, also cut all caddy pieces from interfacing and apply them to the wrong side of the corresponding fabric pieces, following manufacturer's instructions.

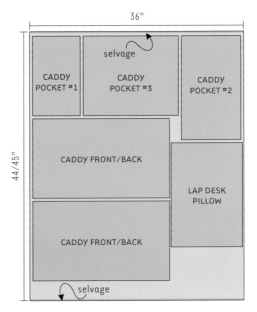

CUTTING LAYOUT

Lap Desk

1 Prepare the Cookie Sheet

* Prewash the cookie sheet with hot soapy water. Sand the entire surface — front, back, and sides — with sandpaper. Wash once more and dry completely.

* Spray the top, sides, and bottom edges with the metal primer. Let dry completely.

* Lightly sand the entire surface once more before washing and applying another coat of primer. Let the sheet dry completely.

* Spray the top, sides, and the bottom edges with the chalkboard paint. Dry completely, then spray the top once more and let dry.

2 Make the Lap Desk Pillow

Cut a 2½" square out of each corner of the lap desk pillow. Fold and pin the edges of each cutout together, right sides facing, and stitch (see Box Corners, on page 339). Turn the fabric "box" right side out and press; press the top raw edge ½" to the wrong side all around.

3 Assemble the Lap Desk

Hot glue the template plastic to the folded raw edge of the lap desk pillow, all around, leaving at least a 3" opening on one long side for stuffing. Stuff the pillow with beans or poly pellets, then glue the opening closed. Center the template plastic on the bottom of the cookie sheet and adhere with industrial-strength glue.

Seat-Back Caddy

1 Make Pockets

Fold each of the pocket pieces in half lengthwise to form pockets with the following dimensions:

* **Caddy pocket #1** 4" × 13"
* **Caddy pocket #2** 5" × 17"
* **Caddy pocket #3** 8" × 13"

Each folded edge becomes the pocket bottom. Bind each top raw edge with bias tape, encasing both fabric layers as you stitch (see page 13).

② Gather and Pleat Pocket #2

* Press or mark the center of the pocket's bottom edge. On the wrong side of the pocket, measure and make pleat marks 2" from each side of the center. Fold the pocket so the pleat marks meet in the center. Baste along the bottom edge with an edgestitch to secure the pleat.

* Cut a 13" length of elastic and feed it through the bias binding at the top edge of caddy pocket #2, stitching at both ends to secure. This will slightly gather the top edge of the pocket.

POCKET #2 (WS)

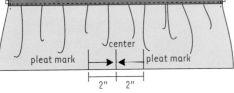

pleat mark — center — pleat mark

2" 2"

③ Attach Pockets to the Caddy Front

Place the caddy front on your work surface, right side up. Pin the pockets as follows, starting at the bottom:

* pocket #3 at the bottom, aligning bottom and side edges

* pleated pocket #2 with the bottom edge 2" above the top edge of pocket #3

* pocket #1 with the bottom edge 2" above the top edge of pocket #2

Topstitch the pockets to the caddy front along each pocket's bottom edge. Create divided pockets as desired by stitching vertical lines through all layers. The sample pictured has three 4" divided pockets at the top, and the bottom pocket is divided into two (4" and 9" wide).

④ Create and Attach the Strap

* Cut the strap webbing into one 5" and one 13" piece. Thread the female half of one buckle onto the 5" webbing. Fold the webbing in half and stitch to secure.

* Thread the remaining male buckle half onto the 13" webbing to create an adjustable strap. Finish one end of the strap by folding it over ½" twice, and stitching in place.

* Place each strap piece on opposite side edges of the caddy front, 2" down from the top edge on the right side. Align raw edges and baste in place.

⑤ Finish the Caddy

* Place the remaining length of elastic on the right side of the car caddy front, ⅝" above the bottom edge, aligning the ends of the elastic with side raw edges, making sure the elastic is not twisted. Baste in place.

* Pin the caddy front and caddy back together, right sides facing and raw edges aligned. Stitch all around, leaving a 5" opening at the bottom for turning. Take care not to catch the loose lengths of elastic or strap in your stitching.

* Clip corners and turn right side out. Press all around, turning raw edges of opening in ½". Edgestitch all around, closing the opening as you go.

⑥ Install the Caddy

Slide the elastic down over and around the front car seat, positioning the caddy on the back of the front seat. Buckle the top strap around the base of the headrest and pull tight. Fill with road-trip goodies, and you can be on your way!

BOO-BOO BUDDY

Designed by Tammie Schaffer

Bring this fun and functional first-aid kit along to soccer games and campouts, or simply store it in your bathroom vanity drawer, always at the ready. Wherever you need it, your first-aid supplies are guaranteed to be neat and tidy, with everything to care for those scraped knees and insect bites. Well, almost everything – kisses aren't included.

MATERIALS

* 1 yard of 44/45" quilting-weight cotton
* ½ yard of heavyweight sew-in interfacing
* ½ yard of cotton batting
* One 8" zipper
* 1 spool of coordinating thread
* 1 yard of ½"-wide rickrack

* Walking foot (optional)
* Additional fabric scraps, patches, and notions (for appliqué embellishment)
* 1 ponytail elastic
* 1 button, 1" in diameter
* 1½ cups of flaxseeds
* 8" piece of ¾"-wide Velcro

Finished dimensions – kit folded 12" × 6"; kit unfolded 12" × 18"; hot pack 4" × 8"; ice pouch 8" × 6½"

Seam allowance – ½" unless otherwise specified

1 Measure, Mark, and Cut

Place your fabric in a single layer with the wrong side facing up. Measure and mark the following pieces on the fabric, with straight edges parallel to the grainline, and cut them out.

* **Main exterior/interior** 19" × 13" (cut 2)
* **Divided pocket** 10" × 13" (cut 1)
* **Zipper top panel** 3" × 13" (cut 1)
* **Zipper pocket** 10" × 13" (cut 1)
* **Zipper end tab** 1½" × 3" (cut 2)
* **Center pocket** 5" × 11" (cut 2)
* **Hot pack** 10" × 9" (cut 1)
* **Ice pouch** 14" × 9" (cut 1)

From heavyweight interfacing, cut:

* **Main exterior/interior** 19" × 13" (cut 1)

From cotton batting, cut:

* **Main exterior/interior** 19" × 13" (cut 1)
* **Hot pack** 10" × 9" (cut 1)

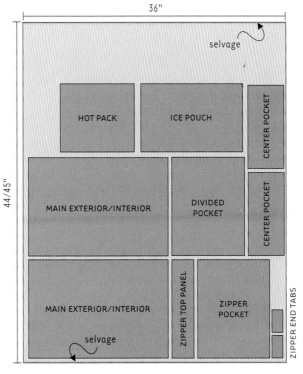

CUTTING LAYOUT

First-Aid Kit

① Make and Attach the Zippered Pocket

* Press under one short end of both zipper end tabs ½". With both right sides facing up, center one end of the zipper under the folded end of a tab and edgestitch close to the fold. Repeat on the opposite end of the zipper with the remaining tab. Once stitched together, the zipper and tabs combined should be 13" wide.

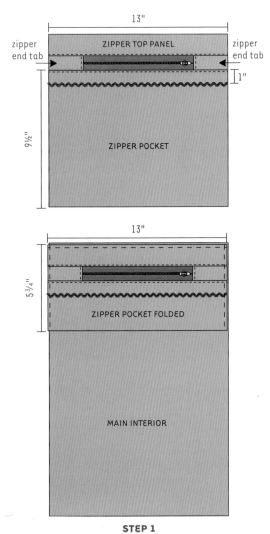

STEP 1

* With wrong sides together, fold the zipper top panel in half lengthwise. With right sides facing up, position the folded edge of the top panel along the top edge of the zipper teeth and extend to include end tabs. Using a zipper foot, edgestitch the folded edge of the zipper top panel to the zipper tape, close to the teeth and end tabs.

* Press one 13" edge of the zipper pocket under ½". With right sides facing up, position the folded edge of the zipper pocket along the bottom edge of the zipper teeth and end tabs and edgestitch as you did on the opposite side of the zipper.

* If desired, topstitch a 13" length of decorative rickrack 1" below the top folded edge of the zipper pocket.

* Fold the zipper pocket with wrong sides together, aligning the 13" raw edge of the zipper pocket with the 13" raw edge of the zipper top panel. Press. With right sides facing up, position the folded zipper pocket on the top edge of the main interior piece, aligning raw edges, and baste in place along raw edges.

② Make and Attach the Divided Pocket

* Fold the divided pocket in half lengthwise with wrong sides together. Topstitch a 13" length of rickrack 1" below the folded edge. With right sides facing up, position the divided pocket along the bottom edge of the main interior piece and baste in place (see illustration, page 292).

* Using a washable fabric pen or tailor's chalk, measure 3½" from both short ends of the divided pocket, and draw five vertical lines on the pocket every 1½". Topstitch along the lines through all layers of fabric, making sure to backstitch securely at the top edge. Alternatively, you can make customized pockets: measure the tools or supplies you want to store, add a little wiggle room, and stitch pockets in the widths that fit your needs.

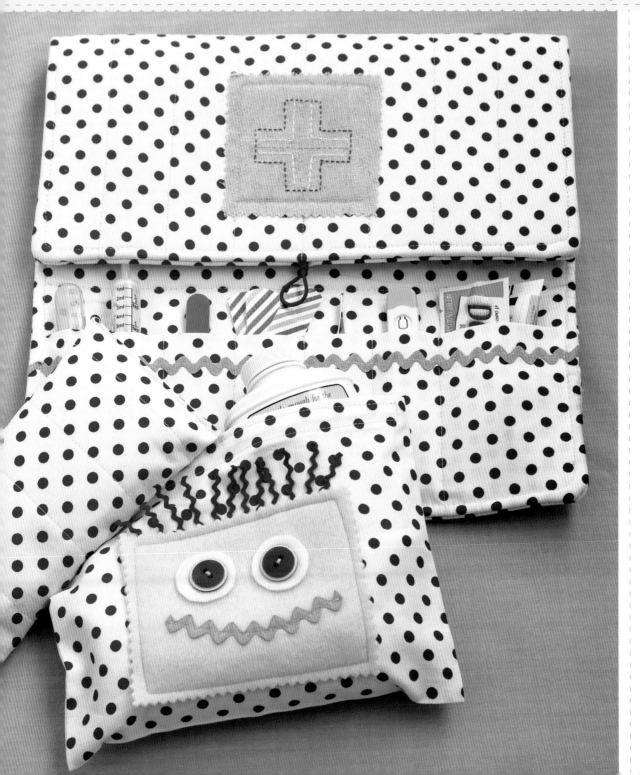

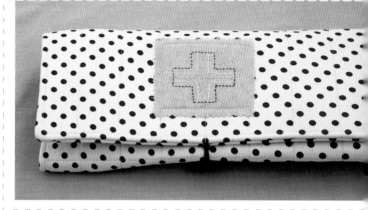

③ Make and Attach the Center Pockets on Interior

* Topstitch a 5" piece of rickrack along the narrow width of one pocket, 6" from one end. Repeat with second pocket. With right sides together, fold the center pockets in half widthwise. Stitch along the 5½" edges, leaving the 5" edge open for turning. Clip corners, turn right side out, and press.
* With right sides facing up, center the center pockets along the side edges of the main interior piece, aligning the raw edges. Edgestitch the pockets in place on the sides, leaving the top edge open. Baste together along the raw edges.

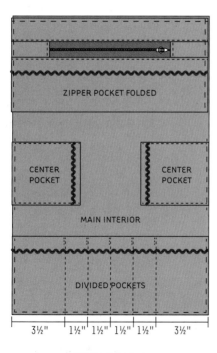

STEPS 2 AND 3

④ Make the Main Exterior

* On a work surface, lay your main exterior piece with the wrong side facing up. Position the batting piece on the wrong side of the exterior, and the heavyweight interfacing on top of the batting. Pin together through all three layers.
* Use a disappearing fabric marker or tailor's chalk to mark the right side of the main exterior panel with your choice of quilting lines. For the sample pictured here, we quilted straight lines, parallel to the 19" edge, spaced about 2¼" apart. Machine-quilt the layers along your marked lines, using a walking foot if you have one.
* Add patches or appliqué as desired. For the sample, we used a 3½" square of linen with pinked edges, and stitched a first-aid cross with embroidery floss. Center your appliqué on one short end of the exterior panel, mindful that the kit will be folded in thirds.

⑤ Stitch the Exterior and Interior Together

* Position the main exterior and interior with right sides together, aligning all raw edges. Note that the appliquéd exterior end should correspond to the end with the zippered pocket.
* Center the ponytail elastic along the short zippered pocket end of the kit, sandwiched between the layers. This will be used (with a button) to close the first-aid kit.

* Stitch the pieces together, backstitching over the ponytail elastic for strength and leaving a 5" opening for turning along the divided pocket edge. Clip corners, turn right side out, and press. Topstitch around all four edges of the piece using a ¼" seam allowance, closing the opening.
* Use a disappearing fabric marker or tailor's chalk to mark the caddy into thirds. Take care that the lines fall between the pocketed areas. Topstitch along these lines through all layers. Fold the kit and mark the button placement, opposite the elastic. Hand-sew the button in place.

Hot Pack

* Pin the batting to the wrong side of the hot/cold pack. Quilt lines parallel to the 10" side, about 1½" apart. Quilting this piece gives the pack a nice heft and helps disperse the heat more evenly.
* With right sides together, fold the pack in half along the 10" edge, aligning the 9" edges. Stitch together around two sides, leaving one short end open for turning. Clip corners, turn pack right side out, and turn the raw edges at the open end ½" to the inside. Fill the pack with flaxseeds, pin the open end closed, and edgestitch.
* Heat the pack in a microwave for 1 minute on high, depending on your microwave.

NOTE: *Never leave your microwave unattended while heating. If necessary, heat further at 30-second intervals, checking for overheating or scorching. For added safety, sprinkle with water, or place a microwave-safe container full of water next to the pack while heating. After heating, flaxseeds retain some heat up to 1 hour.*

Ice Pouch

* Fold and press the short edges ½" to the wrong side. Trim Velcro to 7¾" long. Center and edgestitch hook and loop halves of Velcro on the wrong sides of each of the short folded ends of the ice pack.
* Using scrap materials and notions of your choice, appliqué a face (or other design) on the right side of one half of the ice pouch, parallel to the Velcro. For the sample, we used fleece, felt, buttons, and rickrack.
* With right sides together, fold the ice pouch in half, aligning the Velcro edges. Stitch along both side edges. Clip corners, turn right side out, and gently press. Your ice pouch is now ready to hold a frozen gel pack or ice-filled plastic bag. You could also certainly use the pouch to carry other non-frozen necessities.

road trip wrangler

Designed by Trish Hoskins

Keep your kids happy on long car trips by bringing all of their essentials, and keep yourself happy by corralling those same basics. Since the Wrangler slips over a collapsible fabric bin, the whole thing can be dismantled, washed, and stored as needed. A wide elastic band in front can be used as a drink holder, while plenty of pockets (in any configuration you choose) offer lots of storage for all those little odds and ends, such as art supplies, little toys, books, and more.

MATERIALS

* 1 yard of 44/45" home dec or quilting-weight fabric, nondirectional or bidirectional prints
* 2 yards of ½"-wide double-fold bias tape (optional)
* 1 spool of coordinating thread

* ⅓ yard of 2"-wide elastic
* One collapsible 10½"-11" fabric storage bin cube
* ⅞ yard of 1"-wide home dec Velcro tape (optional; with this type of fastener, one half has an adhesive back and the other half is sew-in)

Finished dimensions – fits a standard collapsible 10½"-11" storage cube

Seam allowance – ¼" unless otherwise specified

① Measure, Mark, and Cut

Lay out your fabric in a single layer with the wrong side facing up. Measure and mark the following pieces and cut them out.

* **Bottom** 11" × 11" (cut 1)
* **Panels** 23" × 11" (cut 4)
* **Pockets** 6½" × 11" (cut 6)

② Hem and Attach the Pockets

* Finish the top long edge of each pocket with bias tape or a narrow ¼" hem.
* With all fabrics right side up, place two pocket pieces on the opposite ends of a panel as shown, aligning raw edges. (One pocket will be outside the box, the other inside the box.) Baste each pocket along the side and bottom edges. Repeat with two more pockets and a panel. These become side panels.

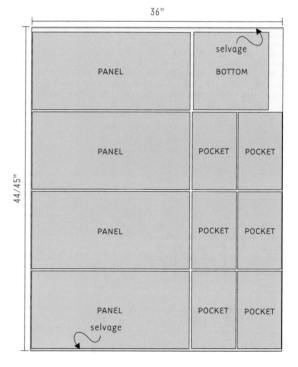

CUTTING LAYOUT

* Place a pocket piece on one end of a remaining panel, aligning raw edges. Baste this in place as before. This becomes the back panel.

* Repeat for the remaining pocket piece and panel. Opposite the pocket, pin the elastic 3" from the raw edge (as shown in step 3 diagram, page 296) and baste in place along the raw ends. Find and mark the center of the elastic and stitch along the center to divide it into two drink holders. This becomes the front panel.

* Divide the pockets on each panel into smaller compartments as desired with topstitching. In our sample, two of the pockets have three equal sections; two have two equal sections; one has four equal sections; and one is left undivided.

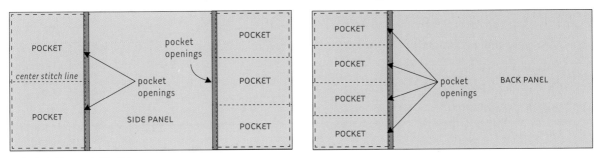

make two side panels like this

STEP 2

③ Attach the Panels to the Bottom

If using the Velcro tape, cut the sew-in half into four 7" segments. Pin each segment to the wrong side of the bottom piece, 1" from a raw edge and centered between the corners. Stitch in place. Stitch the panels to the bottom, as shown, starting and stopping ¼" from each corner.

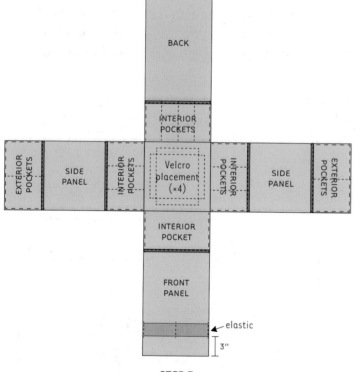

STEP 3

④ Complete the Assembly

* Pin one long edge of a side panel to the adjacent long edge of the back panel, right sides facing. Stitch together, taking care to start your stitching at the bottom seam ¼" from the raw edge. Repeat for the remaining side seams. Finish the open raw top edge with a ¼" narrow double-fold hem.

* If using the Velcro tape, cut the adhesive half into four 7" segments. Install each segment on the inside bottom of the fabric bin, positioned to line up with the Wrangler bottom. (If the bin has a removable insert, install the Velcro on the insert.)

* Insert the Wrangler into the bin, pushing the bottom piece completely down into the bin and aligning the corners. Push the Velcro halves firmly together. Fold the Wrangler down and over the fabric bin, making sure the seams align with the corners of the bin and the hemmed edge meets the bottom edge of the bin exterior.

SELF-STORING PLAYMAT

Designed by Trish Hoskins

The possibilities are practically endless with this playmat that folds into a storage box! Whether your little one is into animals, trains, cars, superheroes, outer space, or something else entirely, you're sure to find a great fabric to suit – be it a zoo or farm scene, train tracks or roads, a space scene, or even a comic-panel print! Flatten the entire piece for a large play surface then, when done, snap it up to make a totally self-contained storage cube for those same toys. The handle makes for easier carrying of the folded storage box.

MATERIALS

* 1 yard of 44/45" quilting-weight or home dec-weight fabric
* 1 yard of extra-firm stabilizer (preferably double-sided fusible)
* 1 spool of coordinating thread

* 9" piece of 1"-2"-wide webbing for handle
* 6 sets of snaps (sew-in, prong, or plastic; size 16 or 20)
* 3¼ yards of ½"-wide double-fold bias binding

Finished dimensions – 35" × 21" playmat folds up into a 7" cubic box.

Seam allowance – ½" unless otherwise specified

❶ Measure, Mark, and Cut

Fold your fabric in half lengthwise with the right sides together, aligning the selvages. Measure and mark one big rectangle that is 35" × 21". When you cut it out, you will have two pieces.

From stabilizer, cut:

* **Box and lid sides** 7" square (cut 9)

❷ Mark the Stitching Lines

With a disappearing marker or tailor's chalk, mark stitching lines on the right side of one playmat piece, every 7" down the length and across the width. On the wrong side only, you may want to label the individual marked squares as indicated in the illustration.

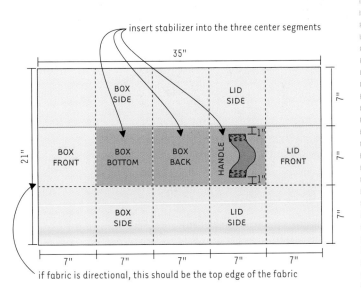

insert stabilizer into the three center segments

if fabric is directional, this should be the top edge of the fabric

STEP 2: Marking the stitching lines
STEP 3: Attaching the handle
STEP 4: Installing the stabilizer

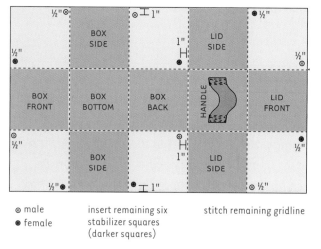

⊚ male
● female

insert remaining six
stabilizer squares
(darker squares)

stitch remaining gridline

STEP 5: Installing the snaps
STEP 6: Installing the stabilizer

③ Attach the Handle

Finish both ends of the handle with a ½" double-fold hem. Position each end 1" from a gridline on the right side of the marked playmat piece as indicated in the illustration (the handle will be slightly bowed). Stitch each end in place with a box stitch (see glossary, page 340).

④ Install the Center Stabilizer

* Pin both playmat pieces together, wrong sides facing and raw edges aligned. Stitch along all four marked 21" gridlines running across the width of the fabric. Stitch along just one of the marked 35" gridlines running down the length of the fabric, as shown on previous page.

* Insert three stabilizer squares into the three center segments of the playmat, as shown, between the fabric layers. Stabilizer should fit very snugly but without warping; if needed, trim squares slightly to fit. If using fusible stabilizer, press all around to adhere, following manufacturer's instructions.

⑤ Install the Snaps

Stitch along the remaining marked 35" gridline. Install snaps as indicated in the illustration, with the corresponding male/female sides facing up on the outside of the box (the side with the handle). The snaps on the four corner segments should be installed as close to the raw edge as possible, while leaving at least ½" free for the binding. The snaps in the center segments should allow at least 1" clearance where indicated.

⑥ Finish Installing Stabilizer

Insert the six remaining stabilizer squares into the outer segments, between the fabric layers as indicated in the illustration. If using fusible stabilizer, press all around to adhere, following manufacturer's instructions.

⑦ Bind the Raw Edges

* Starting at one of the non-interfaced segments, encase raw edges with double-fold bias tape around the entire perimeter, mitering the corners (see page 13).

* To close the box, fasten the snaps on each of the corner (non-interfaced) segments, folding the excess fabric inward as you go. Fill the box bottom with toys before slipping the lid section over the box.

LIBRARY PORTFOLIO

Designed by Trish Hoskins

It can be challenging to keep up with your bookworm's many library materials, due dates, and cards! If you have more than one bookworm in the family, that only adds to the challenge. This portfolio has two separate book pockets, which can help you group and track books by due date, child, or library (school versus public, for instance). Small outer pockets can hold library cards, too! An inner pocket holds DVDs, CDs, or smaller books. As a bonus, the straps support the weight of the books from underneath for extra strength and durability.

MATERIALS

* 1 yard of nondirectional 54/55" home dec-weight cotton fabric
* ¾ yard of fusible fleece
* 2½ yards of 1"-1½"-wide webbing
* 1 spool of coordinating thread

Finished dimensions – 13" square when closed, not including handles

Seam allowance – ½" unless otherwise specified

① Measure, Mark, and Cut

Fold your fabric in half length-wise with the right sides together, aligning the selvages. Measure and mark the following pieces on the wrong side of your fabric and cut them out.

* **Portfolio** 27" × 27" (cut 2)
* **Pocket** 8" × 27" (cut 2)

From fusible fleece, cut:

* **Portfolio** 27" × 27" (cut 1)

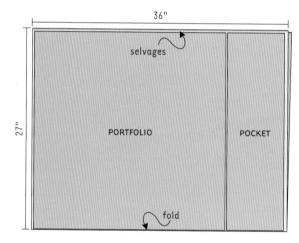

CUTTING LAYOUT

② Position the Handles

* Fold the webbing in half across the width, right sides together, aligning raw ends. Stitch short ends together. Mark the opposite fold with a pin. Finger-press the seam open.

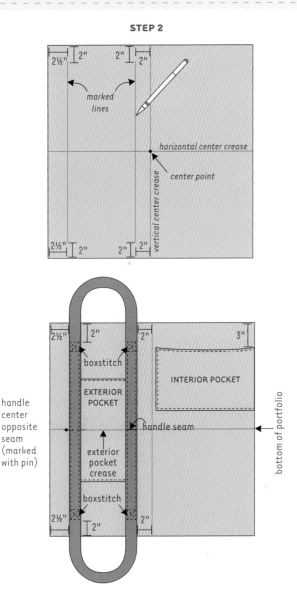

STEP 2

STEP 2: Positioning the handles
STEP 3: Attaching the exterior pocket
STEP 4: Attaching the interior pocket

* Fold one portfolio piece in half lengthwise, then in half across the width, and press to crease the folds. This will mark the quadrants and center point. Unfold the portfolio piece and lay it on your work surface, right side up.

* Measure and mark a vertical line 2½" from the left raw edge, starting and stopping 2" from the top and bottom edges. Measure and mark another vertical line 2" to the left of the vertical center crease, starting and stopping 2" from the top and bottom edges.

* With both right sides facing up, place the webbing on top of the portfolio piece, positioning both the webbing seam and the pin (that marks the fold) along the horizontal center crease. The handle loops should overhang the top and bottom raw edges of the portfolio. Align the outer edge of each strap with the vertical marked lines and pin in place, but do not stitch yet.

③ Attach the Exterior Pocket

* Fold one pocket piece in half across the width, right sides facing and aligning the short raw ends. Stitch along the short edge, leaving the longer side edges open. Turn right side out and press flat with the seam at one side. Edgestitch along both short, finished ends.

* Fold the pocket in half across the width and press to mark a center crease.

* Unfold and with right side facing up, place the pocket on the right side of the portfolio, aligning the center crease with the center horizontal crease on the portfolio. Tuck the unfinished sides of the pocket under the straps, trimming the raw edges of the pocket as needed to be completely hidden under the straps.

✳ Starting at the strap seam, stitch the strap to the portfolio with an edgestitch along both the outer and inner edges catching sides of pocket in stitching. Be sure to stop 2" from the raw edge of the portfolio. Add a boxstitch (see glossary, page 340) 2" from the top raw edge of the portfolio to more securely attach the handle.

❹ Attach the Interior Pocket

✳ Fold the remaining pocket piece in half across the width, right sides facing and aligning the short raw ends. Unlike how you stitched the exterior pocket, leave the short edge opposite the fold open; instead, stitch along both 13½" sides. Turn right side out and press flat. Edgestitch along one long finished edge to create the top edge of the pocket.

✳ Place the pocket on the right hand side of the portfolio, 3" from the top raw edge, aligning the pocket's raw edge with the right hand raw edge of the portfolio. Edgestitch around the inside only and bottom of the pocket.

❺ Complete the Portfolio Exterior

✳ Fold the portfolio piece in half from left to right with right sides facing. The handle loops should be visible at the top and the bottom of the folded portfolio.

✳ Stitch the long side edge to form a tube, being sure to catch the interior pocket's raw edge in your stitching. Leave the top and bottom edges open. Turn right side out and press side seam open.

❻ Complete the Portfolio and Attach Lining

✳ Interface the remaining portfolio piece with fusible fleece following manufacturer's instructions. Fold the interfaced piece in half and stitch down the long raw side edge to form a tube. Press seam open.

✳ Insert the portfolio exterior into the portfolio lining, right sides facing, and raw edges aligned. Tuck the straps into the center of the bag, to keep them out of the stitching line. Stitch around one end of the tube. Turn right side out and press. Edgestitch this finished edge.

✳ Fold and press both remaining raw edges of each portfolio "tube" ½" to the wrong side. Align the folded edges and edgestitch lining to exterior.

✳ Fold the tube in half across the width aligning handles and press to mark a crease across the bottom. Topstitch along the crease to form the bottom of the portfolio and to divide the exterior pocket.

✳ Fill up with library materials, fold along the bottom seam, and get going!

winter warmer infant bucket-seat cover

Designed by Trish Hoskins

Remember the old adage, "Never wake a sleeping baby"? With this winter warmer, you'll never have to! Keep your little one cozy in the harshest of winter climates with this slip-on cover that fits any infant bucket seat. There's a convenient opening and snap flap for attending to your baby's needs.

MATERIALS

* Pattern pieces (2), *see* sheet 6
* 1 yard of 56/58/60" fleece
* 1 spool of coordinating thread
* 2 yards of 1"-wide fold-over elastic or ½"-wide double-fold stretch binding
* Saucer or other 5"-6" diameter circle template for rounding corners
* 1⅔ yards of ⅛"-thick elastic cord or ¼"-wide elastic
* 4 sets of size-24 snaps (metal prong snaps preferred)

Finished dimensions – fits most infant bucket seats

Seam allowance – ½" unless otherwise specified

1 Measure, Mark, and Cut

Fold your fabric in half across the width with the right sides together, aligning the cut ends. Position the pattern pieces according to the layout, measure and mark the additional piece, and cut them out. Transfer markings from the pattern to the wrong side of the fabric.

* **Main cover** (cut 1 on fold)
* **Top snap flap** (cut 1 on fold)

Open up fabric and cut:
* **Bottom flap** 16" × 13" (cut 1)*

2 Assemble the Main Cover

* Fold the main cover piece in half lengthwise at the fold line, right sides together, aligning raw edges. Stitch along the short straight bottom seam to form a ring.

Make the outer edge casing: Fold under the outer raw edge ½" to the wrong side, pin, and press. Stitch along the raw edge all around to form the elastic cord casing, leaving 1" open at the bottom seam for inserting elastic. Don't feed the elastic cord through yet – the following steps will be easier without it.

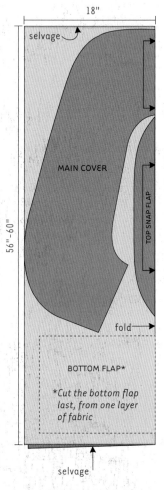

18"

selvage

MAIN COVER

TOP SNAP FLAP

56" - 60"

fold

BOTTOM FLAP*

*Cut the bottom flap last, from one layer of fabric

selvage

CUTTING LAYOUT

Bind the inner edge: Cut ⅔ yard of fold-over elastic or binding. Fold elastic in half across the width to find and mark the center. Unfold and pin this center point to the inside raw edge of the main cover, at the bottom seam. Fold the elastic in half, wrong sides together, and encase the raw inside edge of the main cover, pinning each end of the elastic at the placement marks as indicated on the pattern piece. Stitch, stretching the elastic slightly as you go.

❸ Make and Attach the Top Snap Flap

* Fold the top snap flap in half lengthwise at the fold line, wrong sides together, aligning raw edges. Serge or zigzag stitch along the curved raw edge.

* Pin the main cover and top flap with right sides facing and center marks aligned. Stitch from the center and work your way out toward the ends of the snap flap. The ends of the top snap flap should slightly overlap the ends of the elastic binding applied in the previous step.

❹ Bind and Attach the Bottom Flap

* Round all four corners of the bottom flap with a saucer or small plate, trimming off excess fabric (see illustration on page 163). Bind the entire raw edge of the flap with fold-over elastic (or binding), stretching it slightly as you go.

* Fold the bottom flap in half lengthwise to find and mark the center of the bottom edge. Unfold and pin this center point to the bottom seam of the main cover 2½" down from the bound edge. Keeping the flap's bottom edge perpendicular to the seam, continue pinning along the bottom edge of the flap.

* Topstitch the flap to the main cover with a zigzag stitch just above the flap's bottom binding, starting and stopping just inside each bottom corner.

❺ Add Elastic and Snaps

* Thread the elastic cord through the casing. Check fit by slipping over your infant's bucket seat; trim elastic if needed, allowing for at least a 1" overlap. Knot the cord ends, or overlap and stitch together. Tuck into casing and stitch the casing closed.

* Slip the cover over the bucket seat. This will help you position the snaps. Install the female halves of two snaps to the wrong side of the bottom flap following manufacturer's directions, 1" below the top bound edge and at least 7" apart, checking where the bottom flap meets the top flap as a guide.

* Place the male halves of four snaps on the right side of the top flap, two on each side following the placement marks on the pattern piece. You may also wish to verify where the bottom flap meets the top flap as a guide. Install snaps following manufacturer's instructions. The extra pair of male snaps is for adjustability — in particularly cold or windy weather, you may want more protection for your precious cargo.

Beach Tent

Designed by Rachael Theis

This tent has been designed to keep sun off of your kids while they lie out in the warm sun at the beach, at a park, or even in your own backyard. Openings allow the air to circulate so that the summer breeze can keep your little ones cool. The frame is constructed out of PVC piping — don't be intimidated! PVC is really quite simple to work with, and it's available at a very reasonable price from your local hardware store. Now go grab a towel and enjoy the summer sun and air!

MATERIALS

- 1 yard of 58/60" home dec-weight fabric, preferably an outdoor upholstery fabric for durability and extra UV protection
- 1 spool of coordinating thread
- 3⅓ yards of ½"-wide double-fold bias tape (purchased or make your own, see page 12)
- PVC pipe cutter or hacksaw
- Permanent marker
- Four 10' lengths of ½" PVC piping
- Ten ½" PVC schedule-40 tee fittings
- Four ½" PVC schedule-40 elbows
- Two ½" PVC schedule-40 side outlet elbows
- 6" piece of 1"-wide home dec Velcro with one side sew-in, the other side with self-adhesive
- PVC cement or polyurethane glue (optional)

Finished dimensions –
26" high × 36" deep × 57" wide

Seam allowance – ½" unless otherwise specified

① Prepare the Tent Awning

- Lay out your fabric in a single layer with the right side facing up. Cut and square off your fabric as neatly and evenly as possible. There is no need to trim the selvage edges. Bind both raw edges with the ½"-wide double-fold bias tape (see page 13).
- Fold the selvage edges ½" to the wrong side and stitch in place. Turn under an additional 2" and press. Stitch close to the folded edge, leaving 2½" unstitched at each end. You will slide the PVC through these channels in a later step to attach the tent to the frame.

② Cut the PVC Piping

Using a hacksaw or PVC pipe cutter, cut the PVC piping into the following lengths. Using a permanent marker, label both ends of each cut piece according to the designated letter. This will help you keep the pieces straight when it comes time for assembly.

- 11¾" – cut 8 pieces Ⓐ
- 35" – cut 5 pieces Ⓑ
- 9½" – cut 4 pieces Ⓒ
- 32¾" – cut 2 pieces Ⓓ
- 55" – cut 1 piece Ⓔ
- 1" – cut 2 pieces Ⓕ

SCHEDULE-40
TEE FITTINGS

SCHEDULE-40
ELBOWS

SCHEDULE-40 SIDE
OUTLET ELBOWS

PVC FITTING PIECES

❸ Assemble the Tent Frame

✳ a) Following the diagram, assemble the back corner pieces, pushing them together.

✳ b) Assemble the top halves of the tent frame and push the pieces together as shown.

✳ c) Finish the frame assembly, incorporating the remaining B, E, and side outlet elbow pieces. Push all pieces together.

❹ Attach the Shade

Carefully remove the two lowermost B pieces on both sides of the frame. Slide these PVC pieces through the tent channels created in step 1, and reattach the PVC pieces to the frame. Your tent awning should fit very snugly over the top of the frame.

❺ Add the Velcro

✳ Cut the Velcro into twelve ½"-wide pieces. Apply the adhesive sides of the Velcro to the eight tee fittings and both side outlet elbows located at the top of the awning.

✳ Pin the sew-in side of the Velcro to the wrong side of the awning as it corresponds to the adhesive Velcro locations. Remove the awning and stitch Velcro in place.

❻ Glue the Frame (optional)

Now that you have fully assembled your tent frame and awning, you may choose to glue some of the pieces together to ease assembly in the future. We found it simplest to glue the tee fittings and side outlet elbows to the ends of the B pieces, as well as the back corner pieces and elbow pieces to the D pieces.

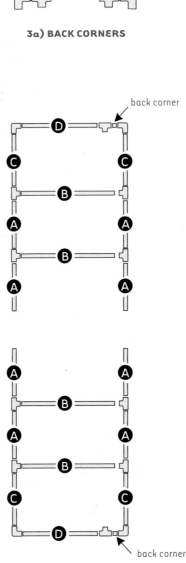

3a) BACK CORNERS

3b) TOP HALVES OF FRAME

STEP 3

A A B

A
A
A B

C
A B
C A
A B
C
B
A B
D
A
C
B D
A
C
D E
C

side
outlet
elbow

3c) FINAL FRAME ASSEMBLY

CHAPTER 14

MOMS & DADS

KEEP PARENTING NECESSITIES AT YOUR FINGERTIPS! These useful projects will get you through pregnancy and beyond. Think diaper bags and wet bags for caregivers of all stripes, perfect projects to wrangle the messier sides of parenting. There's even a photo collage and memory board for displaying school pictures and daily schedules!

WET BAG SET

Designed by Candace Davis

A set of three wet bags helps you solve the messiest of all parenting dilemmas. Sized from small to large, they hold anything from one dirty diaper and wipes up to a complete wet and dirty outfit. Once you're past the diapering and potty training years, you can use them to hold cosmetics, swimwear, and gym items for yourself. The optional seam-sealing tape can be used for extra protection against wicking and leakage.

MATERIALS

* 1 yard of nondirectional 44/45" PUL (polyurethane laminated knit fabric), with the laminate on the wrong side of the fabric
* 1 spool of coordinating 100% polyester thread*
* 3 sets of size-16 or size-20 snaps
* Two 9" polyester zippers
* One 14" polyester zipper
* 3 yards of seam-sealing tape (optional)

It is best to use 100% polyester thread when working with PUL. Do not use 100% cotton or cotton coated polyester thread, as these thread types can lead to moisture wicking along the seam lines. When it is necessary to press the seam allowance of PUL projects, it is often best to finger-press the seams. If the seams do not lie flat enough, you may also use an iron and steam-press PUL on the fabric side, but never use an iron on the laminate side of PUL, as it will damage both the fabric and your iron.

Finished dimensions – large bag 16" × 13"; medium bag 12" × 8"; small bag 8" × 8"

Seam allowance – ½" unless otherwise specified

① Measure, Mark, and Cut

Lay out your fabric in a single layer with the wrong side facing up. Measure and mark the following pieces on the fabric and cut them out.

* **Small bag** 17" × 9" (cut 1)
* **Medium bag** 25" × 9" (cut 1)
* **Large bag** 33" × 14" (cut 1)
* **Strap** 13" × 3" (cut 3)

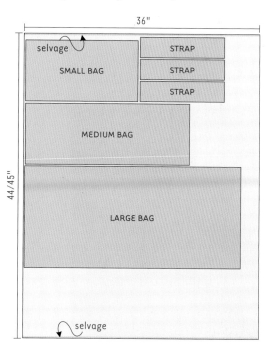

CUTTING LAYOUT

❷ Make the Straps

* Fold each strap piece in half lengthwise, right sides together. Stitch the long and one short edge of each strap. Turn right side out and finger press.
* Install the female half of each snap 1½" from the short raw, open end of each strap. On the same side of the strap, install the male half ¾" from the short finished end of each strap. Snap the ends together and set the straps aside.

❸ Install the Zippers

* Pin one 9" zipper to one short raw edge of the small bag, right sides together and raw edges aligned. Stitch. Finger-press seam allowance toward fabric and topstitch close to the seam. Repeat with the other side of the zipper tape and the opposite short end of the bag. You will have formed a fabric tube.
* Repeat for remaining 9" zipper and the medium bag piece, and for the 14" zipper and the large bag piece.

❹ Complete the Bags

* Turn the small bag wrong side out. Flatten the tube so that the zipper coil lies 2" below the top folded edge; finger-press.
* Sandwich one strap between the layers of fabric, just under the top fold, on the side adjacent to the zipper pull, aligning raw edges. Stitch down this side, catching the strap as you go.
* Unzip the zipper halfway and stitch down the opposite side, taking care not to catch the strap in your stitching. Clip corners and turn right side out through zipper opening.
* Repeat for medium and large bags.

❺ Seal the Seams

* Moisten the finished wet bags and throw in the clothes dryer on high heat. This will close up the pin holes created during stitching. If you lack access to a clothes dryer, you can use a hair dryer or a hot iron, using a thin pressing cloth between the PUL and the iron.
* Alternatively, seal the seams more thoroughly using seam-sealing tape, following manufacturer's directions, before turning the bag right side out.

make any bag a diaper bag

Designed by Michelle Fante

This practical organizer is actually an insert designed to fit neatly into your favorite (non-diaper) bag, thereby transforming it into a functional diaper bag. It is perfect for organizing baby bottles, sippy cups, diapers, wipes, smartphone, snacks, pacifiers, keys, and more! You may choose to leave it rolled and tied for easy transfer, or unroll so that it stands up inside your bag around the perimeter. Simply grab and go, making any bag a diaper bag!

MATERIALS

* 1 yard of 54" home dec-weight cotton (not suitable for one-way designs)
* 1 spool of coordinating thread
* 5¾ yards of ½"-wide double-fold bias tape (store bought or make your own, see page 12)
* Two 1" swivel clasps

Finished dimensions – 10" tall × 35" long

Seam allowance – ½" unless otherwise specified

❶ Measure, Mark, and Cut

Lay your fabric in a single layer with the wrong side facing up. Measure and mark the following pieces according to the layout. Cut out the pieces.

* **Main panel**
  35" × 10" (cut 2)
* **Large pocket**
  35" × 7" (cut 2)
* **Snack pocket** 4" × 5" (cut 2)
* **Smartphone pocket**
  5" × 5" (cut 2)
* **Tie sleeve** 2½" × 5" (cut 2)
* **Swivel clasp tab**
  7" × 3½" (cut 2)

❷ Make the Snack and Smartphone Pockets

* Pin the snack pocket pieces with the right sides together and stitch on three sides, leaving the top, shorter edge open. Clip the corners, turn the pockets right side out, and press. Cut a 5" piece of bias tape. Center the bias tape along the top raw edges of the pocket and fully encase the raw edge; ½" of bias tape should extend beyond the both edges of the pocket (see page 13). Press the ½" ends of bias tape to the wrong side of the pocket.
* Repeat for smartphone pocket, cutting a 6" piece of bias tape. Set both pockets aside.

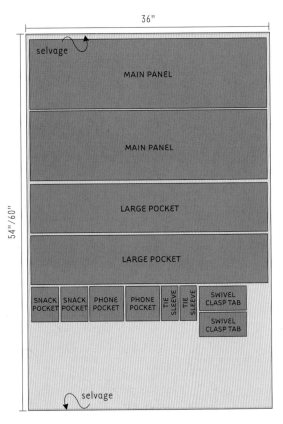

CUTTING LAYOUT

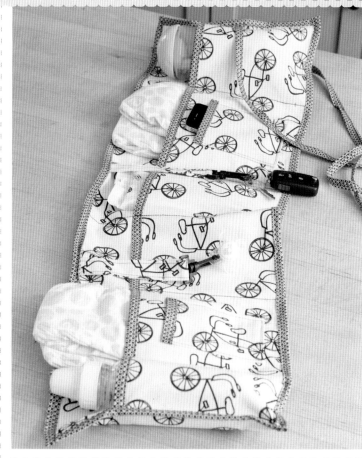

③ Assemble the Large Pocket

* Pin the large pocket pieces with wrong sides together, aligning all raw edges. Baste along four sides with a ¼" seam allowance. Cut a 35" length of bias tape and fully encase the top raw edge of the large pocket (see page 13).

* Place the large pocket on a work surface with the right side facing up. Measure 5½" from the left side edge and 1" up from the bottom edge. Position the snack pocket at this location and edgestitch in place along the bottom and side edges, leaving the top edge of the pocket open.

* Measure in 8¼" from the right-hand edge and 1" up from the bottom edge. Position the smartphone pocket at this location and edgestitch the bottom and side edges in place.

④ Make the Swivel Clasp Tabs

Fold and press the swivel clasp tabs as you would to make 1" double-fold bias tape (see page 12). Edgestitch along both long edges. Fold under one short end ½" and press. Slide the pressed end of the tab through the swivel clasp, folding another 1" on this end to hold the clasp in place; stitch close to fold. Repeat for second swivel clasp. Set pieces aside.

⑤ Make the Tie Sleeve

Pin the tie sleeve pieces with the right sides together, and stitch on all four sides, leaving a 2" opening along one long edge for turning. Clip the corners, turn the sleeve right side out, and press. Edgestitch along the two 4" side edges.

Place one main panel on a work surface with the right side facing up. Position the tie sleeve on the main panel centered from top to bottom and 3½" in from the right-hand edge. Edgestitch the tie sleeve along the short top and bottom edges. This sleeve will hold the ties in place when they are not in use. This piece is now the exterior of the organizer.

❻ Assemble the Organizer

* Place the main panel pieces with wrong sides together, aligning all edges. Baste along four sides with a ¼" seam allowance.

* With right sides facing up, place the large pocket on top of the interior main panel, aligning bottom and side raw edges (make sure the tie sleeve on the exterior panel is on the right-hand side). Baste the large pocket in place along the outside edges with a ¼" seam allowance.

* Use a removable or disappearing fabric marker to measure and mark the vertical divider lines as shown. Topstitch along these guidelines through all layers.

* With right sides facing up, position the short raw ends of the swivel clasp tabs along the top edge of the main panel 11" from the left edge and 14½" from the right edge. Baste in place.

❼ Finish the Organizer

* To make the ties, cut a 2-yard length of bias tape. Turn the ends ½" to the inside and edgestitch the bias tape closed along the long folded edge and both short ends. Fold the tape in half and center the folded edge along the left edge of the main panel piece on the interior (pocket) side. Baste in place.

* Use the remainder of the bias tape to encase the four edges of the organizer, mitering the corners as you go (see page 13). As you approach the end, cut the bias tape, turn the end to the wrong side, overlap the ends by ½", and complete the stitch line.

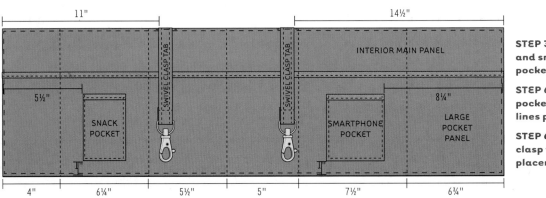

STEP 3: Snack and smartphone pocket placement

STEP 6: Vertical pocket divider lines placement

STEP 6: Swivel clasp tab placement

small and secret diaper bag & changing pad

Designed by Molly Deschenes

This discreet bag is perfect for both moms and dads on the go. It can fit easily inside a backpack or purse, or be left in the car. The folded changing pad fits inside the bag with room for a couple of diapers. Best of all, it makes a great toiletry kit for men or women once the little ones are out of diapers.

MATERIALS

* 1 yard of 54/55" nondirectional home dec–weight cotton
* ⅜ yard of 44/45"-wide (or ¾ yard of narrower) medium-weight fusible interfacing
* ⅝ yard of fusible fleece or batting
* 14" zipper
* 1 spool of coordinating thread
* 6"–8" diameter plate for circle template

Finished dimensions – bag 3" tall × 9" long × 5" wide; pad 18" × 20"

Seam allowance – ½" unless otherwise specified

① Measure, Mark, and Cut

Lay out your fabric in a single layer with the wrong side facing up. Measure and mark the following pieces directly on the wrong side of your fabric.

* **Changing pad front and back** 19" × 21" (cut 2)
* **Diaper bag interior and exterior** 13¼" × 17½" (cut 2)
* **Tab** 3" × 4" (cut 2)

From remaining fabric, cut enough 2"-wide bias strips to make at least 2½ yards of bias tape. (You will need to piece the lengths together to achieve necessary yardage).

From fusible interfacing, cut:

* **Diaper bag interior and exterior**
  13¼" × 17½" (cut 2)

From fusible fleece or batting, cut:

* **Changing pad**
  19" × 21" (cut 1)

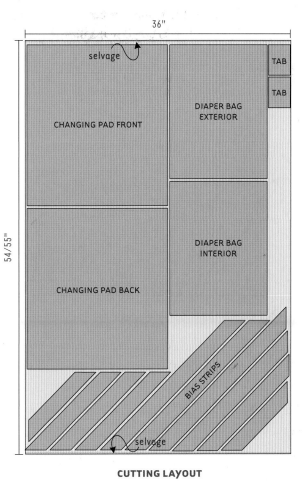

CUTTING LAYOUT

(Labels within diagram: 36"; selvage; CHANGING PAD FRONT; DIAPER BAG EXTERIOR; TAB; TAB; 54/55"; DIAPER BAG INTERIOR; CHANGING PAD BACK; BIAS STRIPS; selvage)

Diaper Bag

❶ Attach the Interfacing

Fuse the interfacing to the wrong side of the bag interior and exterior, following manufacturer's instructions.

❷ Attach the Zipper

* Center and pin the closed zipper to the exterior with right sides together, aligning one zipper tape edge with one 13¼" raw edge. Stitch together, with the zipper foot close to the zipper coil.

* Open the zipper and press the seam allowance toward the exterior piece. Edgestitch the exterior close to the seam. Stitch the other side of the zipper to the opposite short raw edge of the exterior in the same way, forming a tube.

❸ Make and Attach the Tabs

* Fold and press the tabs as you would to make 1" double-fold bias tape (see page 12), aligning the 4" edges. Edgestitch both long edges.

* Close the zipper halfway and turn tube wrong side out. Flatten the tube with the zipper centered along the top. Press. Mark the center point of each open raw edge on the bottom fabric layer, directly under the zipper.

* Fold the finished tabs in half across the width and pin each one on a center mark, sandwiched between the layers and aligning raw edges. Stitch along each side of the tube.

❹ Box the Corners

Cut a 1" square from each corner of the tube. Open up the sides at each cutout and pin and stitch the raw edges to make four boxed corners (see glossary, page 339). Turn the bag right side out.

❺ Make and Attach the Lining

* Press each short edge of the bag interior ½" to the wrong side. Fold and pin the interior as you did for the exterior, with the folded edges centered on top; leave a ½" gap between the folded edges to allow for the exterior zipper. Stitch along both short raw ends and box the corners as before.

* Insert the lining into the bag exterior, with wrong sides facing. Hand-tack the pieces together at each of the corners. Hand-sew each folded edge of the interior to the wrong side of the zipper tape, taking care that your stitches don't show on the exterior.

Changing Pad

❶ Make the Bias Binding

Stitch all bias binding strips together to make a continuous strip. Press under both short ends ½". Press under one long edge ½" to the wrong side.

② Assemble the Changing Pad

Pin the changing pad front and back with wrong sides facing and raw edges aligned. Sandwich the fleece or batting between the layers. Use the circle template to round all four corners (see page 163), then baste the layers together with an edgestitch.

③ Bind the Changing Pad

* Pin the unpressed raw edge of the bias tape around the entire front of the changing pad with a slight overlap at the ends. Trim bias tape as needed. Stitch through all layers around the entire perimeter of the changing pad.
* Turn the folded edge of the bias tape to the back and carefully press. Stitch or hand-sew in place.

pregnancy survival kit

Designed by Paula Storm

Here are a few necessities to make those tough days of pregnancy a little more bearable: a wedge belly pillow, a heat pack for the lower back (or for postpartum pain), an eye mask to help you sleep in a busy hospital, and a notebook cover. Use a notebook for your pregnancy journal or for taking notes during your hospital stay. We've provided a cute footprint template for embroidering each piece, or use your own embroidery motif for a custom look.

MATERIALS

* ⁕ Pattern pieces (2), *see* sheet 5 for mask; sheet 6 for belly pillow
* ⁕ 1 yard of 44/45" quilting-weight cotton
* ⁕ ⅓ yard of cotton batting or fusible fleece
* ⁕ 1 spool of coordinating thread
* ⁕ Embroidery floss
* ⁕ 12 ounces of fiberfill
* ⁕ ⅜ yard of 1"-wide elastic
* ⁕ 6 cups of flaxseeds
* ⁕ 6" × 4¼" blank notebook

Finished dimensions –
Belly Pillow 7½" × 12½";
Eye Mask 4" × 8½"; Heat Pack 5½" × 19½"; Notebook Cover fits a 6" × 4¼" notebook.

Seam allowance – ½" unless otherwise specified

① Measure, Mark, and Cut

Fold your fabric in half lengthwise with the right sides together, aligning the selvages. Position the pattern pieces according to the layout, measure and mark the additional pieces, and cut them out.

* ⁕ **Belly pillow** (cut 2)
* ⁕ **Eye mask** (cut 2)
* ⁕ **Eye mask strap** 2" × 20" (cut 2)
* ⁕ **Heat pack** 6½" × 20" (cut 2)
* ⁕ **Notebook cover** 7" × 10" (cut 2)
* ⁕ **Notebook pockets** 7" × 5½" (cut 2)

From batting or fusible fleece, cut:

* ⁕ **Belly pillow** (cut 1)
* ⁕ **Eye mask** (cut 1)
* ⁕ **Notebook cover** 7" × 10" (cut 1)

NOTE: *Mirror the pattern piece along the line indicated on the pattern.*

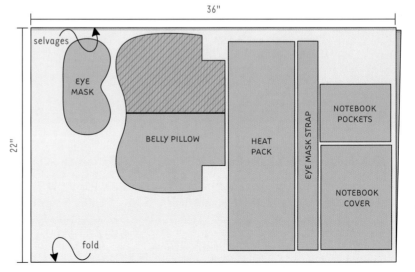

CUTTING LAYOUT

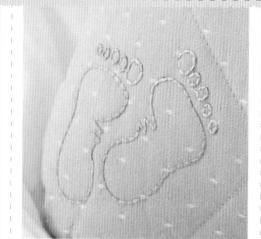

Belly Pillow

❶ Prepare the Pillow Front

∗ Fuse the fleece or baste the batting to the wrong side of one belly pillow piece. Machine-quilt as desired (sample is quilted with straight lines, 3" apart, in a diamond pattern). This becomes the pillow front.

∗ Trace the embroidery design (shown on the mask pattern) on the right side at one corner, at least 2" from the raw edge. Hand-embroider with floss using a backstitch or your favorite outline stitch.

❷ Assemble the Pillow

∗ Pin belly pillow pieces together, right sides facing and raw edges aligned. Stitch the curved side and top edges, leaving the cutouts at the bottom corner open. Stitch the straight bottom edge, leaving a 3" opening in the center for turning and stuffing.

∗ Open up the sides of the pillow at each cutout, pin with right sides together and stitch the raw edges to make two box corners (see glossary, page 339). Clip and notch the curved seam allowance and turn the belly pillow right side out. Fold the raw edges of the opening ½" to the wrong side and press all around. Stuff the pillow firmly with fiberfill and hand-sew the opening closed.

Eye Mask

❶ Prepare the Eye Mask Front

∗ Fuse fleece or baste batting to wrong side of one eye mask piece. This becomes the eye mask front.

∗ Trace the embroidery design on the right side of the eye mask front, at one corner, at least 1" from the raw edge. Hand-embroider as before.

❷ Make the Straps

Pin the eye mask strap pieces together, right sides facing and raw edges aligned. Stitch the long edges with a scant ½" seam. Turn right side out and press. Thread elastic through the casing, basting both ends with an edgestitch to secure.

❸ Assemble the Eye Mask

Pin the front and back pieces together, right sides facing and raw edges aligned. Sandwich the strap between the layers, centering the ends of the strap on each side of the mask. Stitch all around, leaving a 3" opening at the top for turning. Clip and notch the curved seam allowance and turn right side out. Fold the raw edges of the opening ½" to the wrong side and press all around. Edgestitch all around the mask, closing the opening as you go.

Heat Pack

❶ Embroider the Heat Pack

Trace the embroidery design on the right side of one heat pack piece, least 1" from the raw edge. Hand-embroider as before.

❷ Assemble the Heat Pack

* Pin both heat pack pieces together, right sides facing and raw edges aligned. Stitch all around, leaving 2" open at one short end. Clip corners and turn right side out. Fold the raw edges of the opening ½" to the wrong side and press all around.

* Fill heat pack with flaxseeds to desired fullness. You may wish to sew three channels, 4¾" apart, to keep the filling distributed evenly. Edgestitch to close the opening.

To heat the pack: place in a microwave for about 1 minute on high, depending on your microwave.

NOTE: *Never leave your microwave unattended while heating. If necessary, heat further at 30-second intervals, checking for overheating or scorching. For added safety, sprinkle with water, or place a microwave-safe container full of water next to the pack while heating. After heating, flaxseeds retain some heat up to 1 hour.*

Notebook Cover

❶ Prepare the Front Cover

Fuse the fleece or baste the batting to the wrong side of one cover piece. This becomes the cover exterior. Trace the embroidery design on the right side of the fabric, near the bottom right-hand corner, at least 2" from the raw edge. Hand-embroider as before.

❷ Make and Attach Pockets

Fold each pocket piece in half lengthwise aligning the 7" edges, wrong sides together, and press. Pin each pocket on the right side of the remaining cover piece, on opposite short ends, with the folded edges pointing inward and raw edges aligned with the cover. Baste with an edgestitch.

❸ Complete the Cover

Pin the cover pieces together, right sides facing and raw edges aligned and pockets sandwiched between. Stitch all around, leaving a 3" opening along the bottom edge for turning. Clip corners and turn right side out. Fold the raw edges of the opening ½" to the wrong side and press all around. Hand-sew the opening closed. Tuck the front and back covers of the notebook into the pockets.

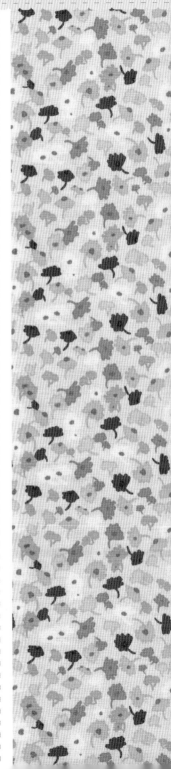

NURSING COVER

Designed by Sarah Pilling

This simple nursing cover sits away from your neck so you can see your baby while nursing. For a step above your run-of-the-mill commercial cover, a standard washcloth is used to provide an easy way to mop up leaks and spills.

Remember, this is your fashion statement, not your baby's, so go wild with the print when choosing your fabrics. You'll surely want to make more than one, to coordinate with all of your outfits! Although quilting-weight cottons will provide more privacy, lightweight cottons such as lawns will be cooler in the summer for you and for babe.

MATERIALS

* 1 yard of 44/45" lightweight or quilting-weight cotton
* 1 coordinating cotton terry washcloth or 9"-10" square of cotton terry cloth
* 1 spool of coordinating thread
* Two 1" D-rings
* ½ yard of ½"-wide boning

Finished dimensions – 24" long × 34" wide

Seam allowance – ½" unless otherwise specified

❶ Measure, Mark, and Cut

Lay out your fabric in a single layer with the wrong side facing up. Measure and mark the following pieces on the fabric and cut them out.

* **Nursing cover** 26" × 36" (cut 1)
* **Facing** 35" × 2" (cut 1)
* **Neck strap** 30" × 4" (cut 1)
* **D-ring loop** 6" × 4" (cut 1)

❷ Prep the Washcloth

If using a washcloth rather than terry-cloth yardage, trim the binding off all sides. Then, for either washcloth or terry cloth, mark a diagonal line from corner to corner. Serge or stitch a tight zigzag on both sides of the marked line, then cut the cloth in half along the marked line.

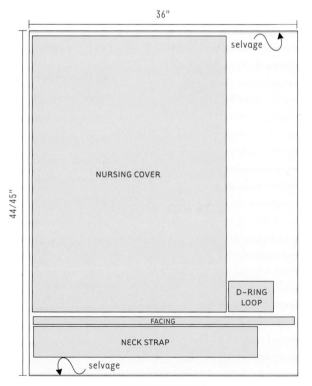

CUTTING LAYOUT

❸ Attach the Terry Cloth and Hem the Nursing Cover

* Press, but do not stitch, a ½" double-fold hem on the long bottom and short side edges of the nursing cover. Tuck each washcloth or terry-cloth triangle into the pressed hems at each bottom corner, with the long finished edge exposed. Stitch the side and bottom hemmed edges in place, securing the terry-cloth triangles in your stitching line.

* Press under the top raw edge of the nursing cover ½" and leave this edge unstitched for now.

❹ Make the Neck Strap

* Fold one short raw end of neck strap ½" to wrong side and press. Fold and press as you would to make double-fold bias tape (see page 12). Edgestitch both long edges. Repeat for the D-ring loop, but leaving both short ends unfinished.

* Thread both D-rings onto the loop, and fold the loop in half across the width. Topstitch across loop as close to the D-rings as possible to secure.

❺ Mark the Boning Placement

* Find the center of the nursing cover's top edge, and mark 8" on either side of the center. Pin the raw edge of the neck strap just outside of one mark, and the raw edges of the D-ring loop to the outside of the opposite mark. The raw edges of the strap and the loop should align with the folded raw edge of the nursing cover.

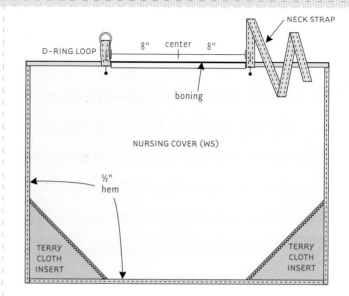

* Trim boning to snugly fit between the strap and the loop, about 16". It's important that this is a tight fit so that the nursing cover curves outward when worn, allowing you to see you baby while nursing.

❻ Install the Facing and Boning

* Press all raw edges of the facing ½" to wrong side, then pin it to the top edge of the nursing cover, wrong sides facing. Tuck the raw edges of the neck strap and D-ring loop into the bottom folded edge of the facing. This will conceal all raw edges.

* Stitch the facing to the nursing cover with an edgestitch, leaving a 1" opening along the bottom edge, just inside where the neck strap meets the nursing cover. Box-stitch (see glossary, page 340) the neck strap and D-ring loop to safely secure strap and to finish the casing.

* Insert the boning into the casing through the opening. Edgestitch opening closed.

* Try on the nursing cover. If you need additional curve in the boning, topstitch an additional line at one end of the casing to reduce its length. This will cause the boning to bow out further.

BOSTON DIAPER BAG

Designed by Sue Kim

Inspired by the timeless Boston bag, this stellar diaper bag is the perfect size. Neither too big nor too small, it features very functional interior pockets, so you can sort your necessities by size and importance. The slight dip at the center top of the bag adds a fun twist to this modern classic. Use the two top handles or attach the removable/adjustable shoulder strap for your on-the-go experience!

MATERIALS

* Pattern pieces (2), *see* sheet 6
* 1 yard of 54" home dec-weight cotton
* ⅓ yard of fusible fleece
* 1 spool of coordinating thread
* Two 1½"-wide D-rings or rectangles
* 24" medium- to heavyweight zipper

* 3 yards of ½"-wide double-fold bias tape (store-bought or make your own, page 12)
* 16" length of ¼"-wide elastic
* 1 yard of 1"-wide webbing (for handles)

* 1½ yards of 1½"-wide webbing (for shoulder strap)
* One 1½"-wide slide buckle (for shoulder strap)
* Two 1½"-wide swivel clasps (for shoulder strap)
* 1 split key ring

Finished dimensions – 16½" wide × 10" high × 4" deep

Seam allowance – ½" unless otherwise specified

❶ Measure, Mark, and Cut

Lay your fabric in a single layer with the wrong side facing up. Position the pattern pieces according to the layout, draw the additional pieces, and cut them out. Transfer markings from the pattern to the wrong side of the fabric.

* **Front/back** (cut 4)
* **Elasticized interior pocket** (cut 1)
* **Zipper gusset panel** 2¾" × 21" (cut 4)

* **Bottom gusset** 5" × 29" (cut 2)
* **Interior pocket** 6½" × 9½" (cut 2)
* **Shoulder strap loops** 3½" × 4" (cut 2)

From fusible fleece, cut:

* **Front/back** (cut 2)
* **Zipper gusset panel** 21" × 2¾" (cut 2)
* **Bottom gusset** 29" × 5" (cut 1)

NOTE: *Mirror the pattern pieces along the line indicated on the patterns.*

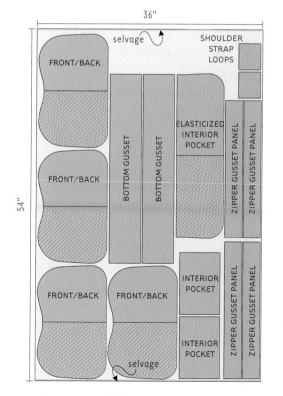

CUTTING LAYOUT

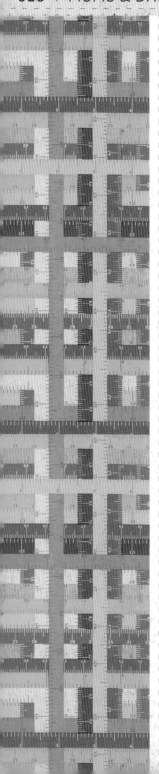

❷ Apply the Fusible Fleece

Fuse the fleece to the wrong sides of the corresponding pieces, following manufacturer's instructions. These pieces will become exterior pieces.

❸ Make and Attach Shoulder Strap Loops

* Fold shoulder strap loop pieces in half with right sides together, aligning the 4" edges. Stitch along the 4" edge, turn right side out, and press.

* Fold the loops in half, aligning the raw edges. Slide a D-ring (or rectangle) onto each loop. Center the folded loops on the right side of the short ends of the exterior bottom gusset piece, aligning the raw edges. Stitch in place with a ¼" seam allowance.

* Pin the exterior and lining bottom gusset pieces with *wrong* sides together and baste a ¼" seam allowance around all sides. Mark the center of the bottom gusset along both raw edges.

❹ Install the Zipper

* Close the zipper, center, and pin it to an exterior zipper gusset panel with right sides together, aligning the zipper tape edge with one panel raw edge. The zipper will extend off both ends of the panel by approximately 1½". You will trim the zipper in a later step.

* Position a lining zipper gusset panel on top of the exterior panel, right sides facing, aligning raw edges and sandwiching the zipper in between the layers.

* Stitch the zipper and zipper gusset panels together, with the zipper foot close to the zipper teeth. Fold the exterior and lining zipper gusset panels away from the zipper and edgestitch along the zipper panel seam. Repeat to attach the remaining exterior and lining zipper gusset panels to the opposite side of the zipper teeth. Mark the center of the zipper gusset panels along both raw edges.

* Baste the raw edges of exterior and lining pieces together. With the zipper pull located between the gusset pieces (not on the extended end of the zipper), stitch a bartack (see glossary, page 339) across the ends of the zipper teeth ¼" from the ends of the panels. Cut off excess zipper tape. Take care that you do not cut off the zipper pull in this step!

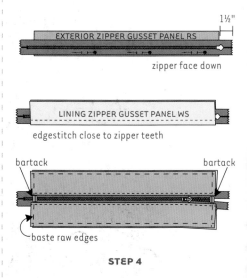

1½"

EXTERIOR ZIPPER GUSSET PANEL RS

zipper face down

LINING ZIPPER GUSSET PANEL WS

edgestitch close to zipper teeth

bartack   bartack

baste raw edges

STEP 4

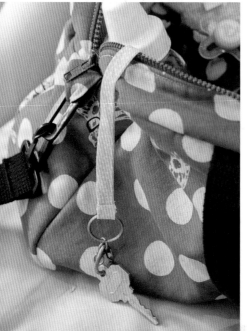

❺ Assemble the Gussets

With right (exterior) sides together, pin the bottom gusset to the assembled zipper gusset panel, aligning short ends. Stitch together across short ends. Encase both seam allowances, each with a 5" piece of bias tape, and press toward the bottom gusset.

❻ Make and Attach Interior Pockets

Rectangular Pocket

* Pin the two smaller interior pocket pieces with right sides together and stitch on three sides, leaving the top, longer edge open. Clip the corners and turn right side out, pushing out the corners, and press. Turn the top raw edge ½" to the inside and edgestitch closed.
* Pin the pocket on the right side of one front/back lining piece as indicated on the pattern piece. Edgestitch along the side and bottom edges, leaving the top edge open. Topstitch down the center of the pocket to create two compartments, if desired.

Elasticized Pocket

* Make a casing by pressing under the top edge ¼", then another 1". Topstitch close to the folded edge. Insert elastic into the top edge of this pocket. Be sure to secure the other end of the elastic before you pull the elastic all the way through. Stitch the ends securely in place.
* Use a basting stitch to gather the bottom edge of the elasticized pocket between the gather marks as indicated on the pattern. Adjust gathers until the bottom edge of the pocket is the same size as the front/back. With both right sides facing up, align the elasticized pocket on the remaining front/back lining piece. Baste in place along side and bottom edges. Topstitch two vertical lines as indicated on the pattern.

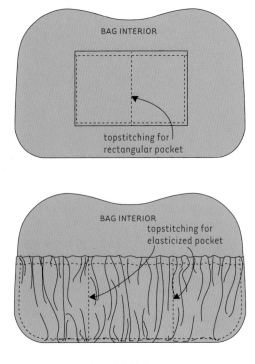

BAG INTERIOR

topstitching for rectangular pocket

BAG INTERIOR

topstitching for elasticized pocket

STEP 6

❼ Assemble the Handles and Shoulder Strap

Handles

* Pin one set of exterior and lining front/back pieces with wrong sides together and baste a ¼" seam allowance around all raw edges. Repeat with the second set of exterior and lining front/back pieces.
* Cut the 1" wide webbing into two 18" pieces for handles. Pin the ends on the exterior front/back pieces as indicated on the pattern, with raw edges aligned. Make sure that the handles are not twisted. Baste in place close to the raw edge.

Shoulder Strap

* For the remaining webbing, press under one raw end ½", and thread it through the slide buckle over the center bar. Fold under another 1" and stitch close to the fold to secure the buckle.

* Thread a swivel clasp onto the free end of the webbing, and thread the webbing back through the slide buckle. Press under the raw end ½" and slide it through the second swivel clasp. Fold under another 1" and stitch the second swivel clasp in place.

❽ Attach the Gusset

With exterior sides facing, pin one front/back piece to the assembled gusset, aligning the gusset seams with placement marks indicated on the pattern. Stitch together using a scant ½" seam allowance. Note that you may need to clip the gusset seam allowance around the curved corners of the front/back piece. Unzip the zipper and repeat to attach the remaining front/back piece to the gusset.

❾ Make the Key Ring Tab

Cut a 7" length of bias tape and edgestitch closed along the open, folded edge. Fold under one end of the bias tape ½". Thread the key ring onto the folded end of bias tape, and fold the end over the ring, edgestitching close to the fold to secure the ring.

❿ Bind the Interior Seam Allowance

* Press one short end of the bias tape ½" to the wrong side. Unfold one edge of the bias tape and pin it in place along the seam allowance with right sides together, aligning raw edges. Overlap the ends by 1", and cut off excess bias tape. Stitch together using a ½" seam allowance.

* Refold the bias tape along the original fold line, turning it over the edge of the seam allowance to fully encase it. Tuck the raw end of the key ring strap under the folded edge of the bias tape close to one of the top rounded corners of the bag. Pin and stitch in place close to the bias tape. Reinforce your stitching at the key ring strap for additional security.

* Repeat to bind the second seam allowance edge, but without the key ring strap. Turn the bag right side out and clip swivel clasps to the shoulder strap loop D-rings (or rectangles) on either side of the zipper to attach the adjustable shoulder strap.

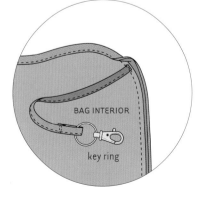

BAG INTERIOR

key ring

STEP 10

ARGYLE MEMORY BOARD & PHOTO COLLAGE

Designed by Trish Hoskins

A great gift to extended family or yourself, this matched set pairs an upholstered ribbon memory board with a fabric-covered photo collage. The photo collage offers places for 12 smaller photos and one larger photo, making it the perfect way to display a series of school portraits, or a month-by-month timeline of baby's first year. Use the center to highlight a newborn, first birthday, or graduation photo!

MATERIALS

* 1 yard of 44/45" quilting-weight cotton
* 8 yards of coordinating ⅜"–½"-wide ribbon
* 9 yards of contrasting ⅜"–½"-wide ribbon
* 1 spool of coordinating thread
* Two 18" square low-profile (¾" or ⅞" deep) stretched artist canvases
* Craft glue or spray adhesive
* Staple gun and staples

* 24 buttons, about ¾" in diameter
* 13 photos, at least 4" square
* Binder clips (optional)

For memory board:

* 18" square of cork sheeting (optional, if you want to use the memory board as a corkboard)
* Two to six 18" squares of batting

Finished dimensions – Each board is 18" × 18".

Seam allowance – ½" unless otherwise specified

1 Measure, Mark, and Cut

Fold your fabric in half lengthwise with the right sides together, aligning the selvages. Measure and mark the following on the wrong side of your fabric and cut them out.

* **Board cover** 22" × 22" (cut 2)

For photo collage, open up fabric and cut:

* **Facing** 14" × 14" (cut 1)*

Memory Board

1 Apply the Coordinating Ribbon

Cut two 30" lengths and four 20" lengths of coordinating ribbon. Pin the longest two in an X formation on the right side of one board cover piece, corner to corner. Edgestitch along both sides of each ribbon to attach. Pin the shorter four ribbons 6" apart as illustrated. Edgestitch as before.

2 Upholster the Canvas

* Place one stretched canvas on a work surface, right side up. If using cork sheeting, place it on the right side of the stretched canvas, aligning all edges. Affix in place with spray adhesive or craft glue.

* Place batting squares on top of canvas or cork, aligning all edges, adding layers until you have your desired thickness. If you want this to be used as a corkboard as well, fewer batting layers are advised. Affix batting layers in place with spray adhesive or craft glue.

* Center the ribbon-stitched board cover piece on top of all layers, right side

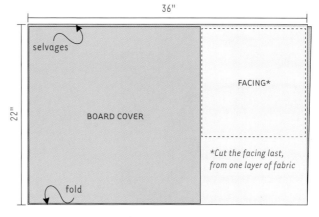

CUTTING LAYOUT

facing up, with the ribbon center directly over the center of the canvas. Carefully flip over your work so the fabric is on the bottom and the wrong side of the canvas is facing up.

* At the center of each side edge, pull the fabric raw edges to the back of the canvas frame and staple to secure, pulling taut as you go. At each corner, fold the fabric over the frame at a 45-degree angle to the corner, and staple.

* Continue pulling the fabric over the frame and stapling on the wrong side, working from the center of each side and from the corners. Smooth the fabric as you go, taking care that the ribbon design is not skewed on the right side.

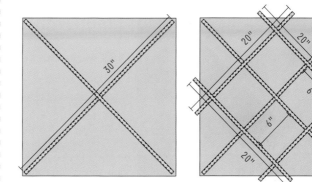

STEP 1

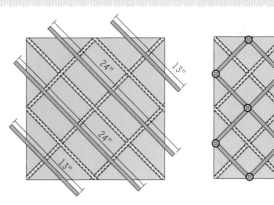

STEP 3

3 Apply the Contrasting Ribbon

* Cut four 24" lengths and four 13" lengths of contrasting ribbon. Center and pin each length of contrasting ribbon between the stitched ribbons to form an argyle pattern as shown. Hand-sew a button anywhere two contrasting ribbons meet, going through all batting and canvas layers and pulling tight to tuft the board slightly. If an intersection is located on top of the wooden canvas frame, just sew the button through the fabric and batting layers. Staple the ends of each ribbon to the wrong side of the canvas frame.
* The canvas frame can hang self-supported on a hook or tack, but you can also staple a small loop of excess ribbon to the top edge of the board to create a decorative hanger.

Photo Collage

1 Apply the Coordinating Ribbon

Apply two 30" lengths and four 20" lengths of coordinating ribbon to the remaining board cover as for the memory board.

2 Apply the Contrasting Ribbon

Cut four 24" lengths and four 13" lengths of contrasting ribbon. Center and pin each length between the stitched ribbons as for the memory board. Edgestitch along both sides of each contrasting ribbon to attach.

❸ Make the Photo Cutouts

* Place the photo collage fabric on a work surface, right side up. Place the facing on top at a 45-degree angle, right side down, so that right sides are together and the facing is centered on the main piece. Pin in place at the corners.

* Flip the work over so that the wrong side of the main photo collage piece is facing up. Mark the diamond cutouts between the ribbon stitching as shown. For the larger center cutout, measure 1" from the stitching for the contrast ribbon surrounding the center diamond, and draw a 4½" diamond that is centered where the coordinating ribbons cross.

* Stitch a diamond shape to outline each of the outer cutouts, ¼" from the ribbon stitching. Repeat for all 12 outer cutouts. Stitch the center cutout at the markings. Cut an X in each of the cutouts all the way to the corners, without cutting into the stitching.

❹ Finish the Facing

Flip the work over so the right side is facing up. Carefully cut the facing between each cutout, taking care not to cut into the main fabric. Push the facing through each cutout to the wrong side, folding it all the way back so the seams form the outlines of each cutout. Press, then edgestitch all around each cutout. On the wrong side of the fabric, trim fabric seam allowance on the facing piece as needed.

❺ Finish the Photo Collage

* Hand-sew buttons at each intersection of the contrasting ribbon.

* Drape the stitched fabric right side up over canvas square, making sure that the longest coordinating ribbons meet the canvas corners and the middle cutout is centered on the canvas. Pin or clip in place temporarily. Taking care not to shift the fabric, use a pencil or disappearing marker to mark the position of the cutouts on the canvas.

* Remove the fabric from the canvas and position your photos as desired at the markings. Trim the photos into diamond shapes at least ½" larger than each cutout. Adhere the photos to the canvas at each marking with craft glue or spray adhesive.

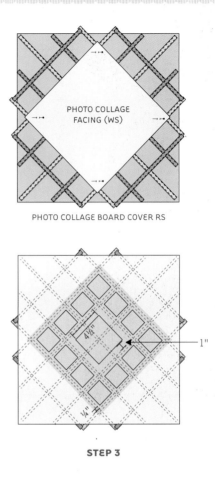

PHOTO COLLAGE FACING (WS)

PHOTO COLLAGE BOARD COVER RS

4½"

1"

¼"

STEP 3

* Place the fabric on the canvas once more, right side up, and pin or clip in place. Carefully flip over your work and staple the fabric in place as for the memory board. Occasionally check the right side to make sure the cutouts stay positioned over your photos. If desired, hand-tack the fabric to the canvas near the corners of each cutout to help flatten the fabric against the photos, and attach a small loop of ribbon for hanging.

PATTERN TEMPLATES

PHILIPPE THE WHALE PILLOW, PAGE 202

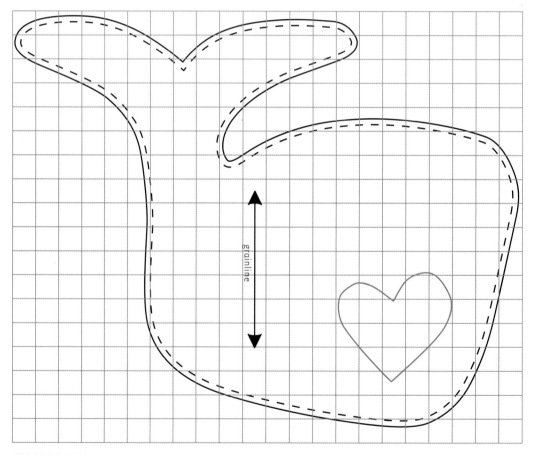

grainline

ENLARGE 400%
1 SQUARE = 1"

FLUTTER-BY, BUTTERFLY WINGS, PAGE 229

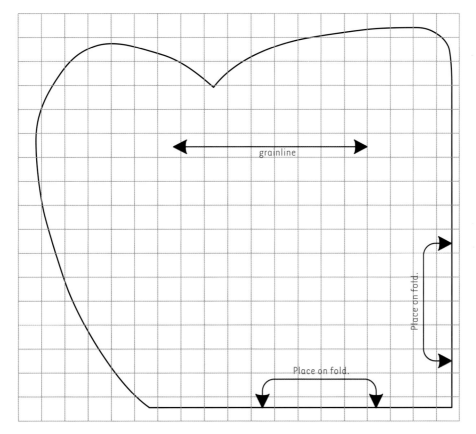

grainline

Place on fold.

Place on fold.

ENLARGE 400%
1 SQUARE = 1"

INDOOR HOPSCOTCH, PAGE 252

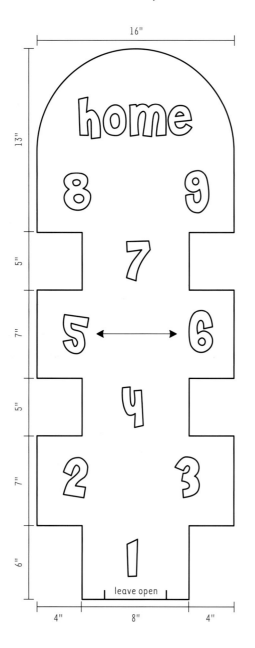

GLOSSaRY

Appliqué. Any technique that adheres one fabric piece to another in a decorative fashion. An appliqué may be applied with double-sided fusible interfacing, a zigzag/satin topstitch along the edges of the top fabric, or a slipstitch with the top fabric's raw edges turned under, among other techniques. Hand embroidery is also often incorporated.

Backstitch. Two or three straight, reverse stitches used to secure and reinforce your stitching at the beginning and end of a seam to keep it from coming apart.

Bartack. Several straight stitches made very close together, by hand or machine; on a machine, you could use a dense buttonhole stitch. Often used to create a new zipper stop when you need to shorten a zipper.

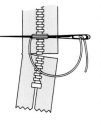

Basting. Long stitches, done by hand or by machine, to temporarily hold fabric sections together. The stitches can be removed once the final seaming is complete, so do not backstitch at the beginning or end of the seam. Basting is also used to gather an area of fabric. Leave the beginning and ending thread tails long and carefully pull the tails to draw up the fabric and create gathers.

Bias. The diagonal grain of the fabric, it accents the natural stretch of the fabric. True bias is found at an exact 45-degree angle from both the straight and cross grain of the fabric.

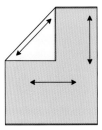

Bias tape (or bias binding). Made from a strip of fabric that has been cut along the bias grain of the fabric. You can buy it packaged with a single or double-fold, or make it yourself. It is often used to finish or encase garment edges. See pages 12–14.

Blanket stitch. A decorative stitch, used for edge finishing, appliqué, and buttonholes. The blanket stitch is worked the same as the button-hole stitch, only with space between the stitches. Working from left to right, insert the needle the desired stitch length from the edge and bring it out below the fabric edge, and over the thread as shown. Carry the thread to the right of the previous stitch to form a loop for the next stitch.

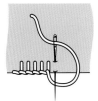

Box corners. To make box corners in a bag, fitted sheet, or other project, cut a square out of the corners as instructed (the size of the square will vary depending on the project). Fold the corner diagonally, with right sides together, so the outer corners meet. (If the corner has been cut from two joined fabrics, the side seam and the bottom seam will meet in the center of the folded edge.) Stitch the seam.

Box stitch. Often used to secure handles and straps to bags. Using a short, straight stitch, stitch a square or rectangle, typically 1" or 1½" in size, close to three finished edges. Then, stitch an X between the stitched corners.

Buttonhole elastic. Elastic with a series of buttonhole slots which allow for adjustability, most commonly used in the waistbands of children's clothing. Typically, a button is stitched on the inside of the garment at each side seam; you cinch the elastic as necessary, using a different buttonhole as needed to secure it.

Casing. A channel created by sewing a line of stitching parallel to a finished edge, or by sewing two lines of stitching parallel to each other, through two layers of fabric to allow elastic, cording, ribbon, or other material to pass through. Casings are a popular finishing technique for elastic and drawstring waistbands.

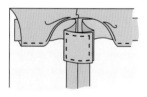

Chain stitch. Looped embroidery stitches that, when combined, look like links in a chain.

Clipping corners. Cut corner seam allowances at a 45-degree angle close to where the two stitching lines meet. This will ensure a sharp corner once the fabric is turned right side out.

Clipping curves. Used to reduce tension on concave seams (inward curves). Clip within the seam allowance to, but not through, the stitching line. Sharper curves require more clipping, and corners are typically clipped at a 45-degree angle. For outer curves, *see* Notching.

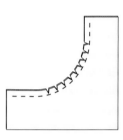

Coverstitch. Executed with either a serger, overlock, or coverstitch machine, this stitch is great when working with knit fabrics, as it looks like a regular straight stitch on the right side, but has excellent stretch. You would use either two or three needles to create a coverstitch. On the right side of the fabric, you see parallel rows of straight stitching, while the wrong side has the appearance of "serger loops" which actually cover the turned, raw edge of the hem.

Crossgrain, or crosswise grainline. The direction of the fabric threads which are perpendicular to the selvage and parallel to the cut end of the fabric. It is the opposite of lengthwise grain, and there is a little bit of natural stretch when the fabric is pulled in this direction. *See* Bias.

Darts. Small seams that take in fullness and add shaping to a project. They are wide at the seam edge and taper to a point.

Doll needle. A very long, thin needle that can completely pierce a three-dimensional stuffed sewn object such as a doll or plush animal.

Double-fold hem. Fold or press the raw edge to the wrong side of the fabric (typically ¼"), then fold or press it to the wrong side again (anywhere from ¼" up to 1" or more). Topstitch close to the first fold. A narrow ¼" double-fold hem is folded twice at ¼".

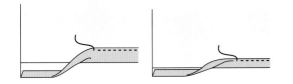

Edgestitch. A style of topstitching that is typically stitched ⅛" away from an edge, with a slightly longer stitch length than what is used for structural seams. Edgestitching may be used to close an open seam after turning, or may simply be a decorative touch.

Facing. A pattern piece that is often used to finish shaped garment edges, such as the neckline, armhole, or button placket. Facings are typically 2" to 3" wide, but the width can depend on the application, placement, and size of the garment.

Finger-press. To manually crease a seam allowance, fold, or other part of a fabric piece with your fingers. Frequently used to press fabric out of the way during stitching, when it would be impractical or inconvenient to remove the fabric from the sewing machine to press with an iron.

French knot. A decorative embroidery stitch, made by wrapping the floss around the needle one or more times, before pulling the needle back through the fabric at the same point the stitch began.

French seam. Often used for durability and tidiness to hide raw edges of seams in unlined and sheer fabric projects. Stitch a scant ¼" seam with the wrong sides together. Then, turn the fabrics wrong side out (right sides together) at the seam and stitch another ¼"-⅜" seam to enclose the raw edges.

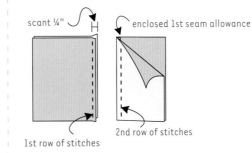

scant ¼"

enclosed 1st seam allowance

1st row of stitches

2nd row of stitches

Fussy cut. Cutting a specific motif from a printed fabric in order to isolate the design, as opposed to randomly cutting pattern pieces from fabric yardage. Often used for appliqué, either cut a specific motif from printed fabric or carefully place the motif where you would like it in your cut fabric. The motifs are often positioned for the most dramatic results.

Gathering. Used to draw up a larger piece of fabric by pulling basting stitches (*see* Basting) so it can be sewn to a smaller piece. To adjust gathers evenly, mark the halfway, quarter-length, and even eighth-length distances on both the main fabric and the piece that is to be gathered before beginning the gathering process. Match the marks as you pull the gathering threads to ensure that you join the pieces evenly. The piece to be gathered is typically about twice as long as the main fabric, so these marks will be farther apart on the gathering piece.

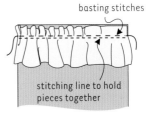

basting stitches

stitching line to hold pieces together

Grainline. The direction of the fabric threads that runs parallel to the selvage edges. The sewing patterns in this book have a double-ended arrow printed on the individual pattern pieces indicating grainline. When laying out your pattern pieces, make sure that the arrow lines up with the straight grainline. *See* Crossgrain *and* Bias.

Interfacing. Used to provide shape, stiffness, and support; it is typically found in collars, cuffs, lapels, waistbands, and bags. It is available in either iron-on/fusible or sew-in versions, and in many weights.

Lengthwise grainline. This is the edge parallel to the selvage. *See* Grainline, Crossgrain, *and* Bias.

Notching. Used to make convex seams (outward curves) lie flat, notches are cut at regular intervals within the seam allowance to, but not through, the stitching line. Sharper curves require more notches.

Pintucks. Often decorative and sometimes used for shaping, pintucks are formed by matching two lines (typically ⅛" apart), wrong sides together, stitching close to the fold, thereby creating a folded tuck. Most commonly, tucks are stitched along the grainline and are equal distances apart.

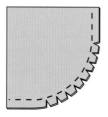

Pivot. A great way to stitch a corner. Stop stitching short of the fabric raw edge, the same width as the seam allowance. Leaving the needle down in the fabric, lift the presser foot up and rotate the fabric 90 degrees to continue stitching the seam.

PUL (Polyurethane laminate) knit fabric. A lightweight polyester knit fabric that has been bonded with a clear, thin layer of plastic film. The benefit of this fabric is that it creates a waterproof barrier, yet remains breathable. This fabric is commonly used for diaper covers, wet bags, and anywhere else you may need a waterproof, breathable moisture barrier. PUL may have laminate applied on either the right or wrong side of the fabric.

Running stitch. An embroidery stitch creating a dashed line on the background fabric, with alternate stitches and blank spaces of equal length.

Satin stitch. Executed by hand or machine, a satin stitch is a tight, narrow, flat stitch used to cover fabric(s). It is often used when stitching appliquéd pieces in place. It is possible to execute this stitch on your sewing machine using the zigzag stitch function. Simply widen the zigzag width as desired, and decrease the stitch distance so that the stitches do not angle (as would a zigzag), but are tight and parallel with one another. In hand embroidery, sew a series of adjacent straight stitches to cover an area of the background fabric.

Scant seam. A seam with slightly narrow seam allowances. For example, to sew a scant ¼" seam, move your fabric over a bit to sew a slightly smaller than ¼" seam (somewhere between ⅛" and ¼").

Seam allowance. The distance between the seamline (stitching line) that joins two or more pieces of fabric together and the cut edge of the fabric. In traditional sewing patterns, seam allowances are often ⅝" wide. That said, it is becoming increasingly common for seam allowances to be ½" wide. You will find ¼" and ½" wide seam allowances used on the bulk of the projects in this book.

Selvage. The selvage is a finished fabric edge that does not fray. The selvages are parallel to the straight grainline and perpendicular to the cut fabric edges. Most pattern pieces are positioned on the fabric parallel to the selvages.

Slipstitch. An invisible hand stitch that joins two fabrics together, also called a blindstitch. Bring the needle out of one fabric, and pierce the other fabric directly opposite, then run the needle under the fabric (or between the fold if you are sewing a folded edge) about ¼". Bring the needle out and repeat for the other fabric layer. Continue so that you are forming straight stitches between the two fabrics, with the thread running under or between the fabric layers between the straight stitches. After a few stitches, pull the thread gently to tighten and hide the stitches.

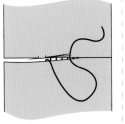

Staystitch. A straight, longer-than-usual stitch, used to stabilize a bias or curved fabric edge to prevent it from stretching or becoming distorted. It is typically done through a single fabric layer, just within the seam allowance.

Stitch in the ditch. A stitch through multiple layers of fabric, used when you don't want topstitching to show. On the right side of the fabric, stitch through all the layers directly over an existing seam, or in the "ditch" of an existing seamline.

Topstitch. Visible stitching on the right side of a project, which can be purely decorative or can provide reinforcement. It can be a single straight stitch, a double stitch created with a twin needle, a shell stitch, or a zigzag. A straight stitch looks best with a slightly longer stitch length than the one used for seams. If your topstitching is slightly irregular, use it on printed fabrics and the print will conceal the irregularities.

Whipstitch. Unlike a slipstitch, a whipstitch is not invisible but is used similarly to stitch two pieces of fabric together. In a whipstitch you always come out of the same piece of fabric and stitch in the same direction into the second piece of fabric. If the whipstitch is done at a raw edge, it will overcast that edge.

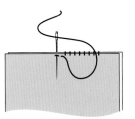

Zigzag. A basic sewing-machine stitch that looks like a zigzag. Typically, it can vary in length and width. A very close zigzag stitch may be called a satin stitch and can be used for buttonholes. Zigzag stitches within a seam allowance can also be used to finish seams when no serger is on hand, and are also frequently used to provide a bit of reinforcement at a stressed seam.

RESOURCES

Fabric

Crafty Planet
612-788-1180
www.craftyplanet.com

Diaper Sewing Supplies
314-255-5118
www.diapersewingsupplies.com

The Fabric Fairy
608-577-3280
www.thefabricfairy.com

Funky Fabrix
sales@funkyfabrix.com.au
www.funkyfabrix.com.au

Monaluna
925-476-5068
www.monaluna.com

Pink Chalk Fabrics
888-894-0658
www.pinkchalkfabrics.com

Spoonflower
919-886-7885
www.spoonflower.com

superbuzzy
805-643-4143
www.superbuzzy.com

Buttons

AccessoriesOfOld.com
202-744-4804
www.accessoriesofold.com

As Cute As a Button
619-223-2555
www.ascuteasabutton.com

Hushco Buttons
877-487-4262
www.hushcobuttons.com

Trims and Other Details

BeadWarehouse
802-775-3082
www.beadwarehouse.com

Cheeptrims.com
877-289-8746
www.cheeptrims.com

Home Sew, Inc.
800-344-4739
www.homesew.com

JKM Ribbon & Trims
800-767-3635
www.jkmribbon.com

Les' Bon Ribbon
225-262-1921
www.lesbonribbon.com

M&J Trimming
800-965-8746
www.mjtrim.com

Nancy's Notions
800-833-0690
www.nancysnotions.com

Rochford Supply
866-681-7401
www.rochfordsupply.com

ZipperStop
888-947-7872
www.zipperstop.com

Kidspiration

Apartment Therapy
www.apartmenttherapy.com

BurdaStyle
www.burdastyle.com

Craftster
www.craftster.org

MADE
www.danamadeit.com

Make: Craft
http://makezine.com/craftzine

***Ottobre Design* Magazine**
www.ottobredesign.com

Pinterest
http://pinterest.com

Pretty Prudent
http://prudentbaby.com

Sew, Mama, Sew
www.sewmamasew.com

***Small* Magazine**
www.smallmagazine.net

This Mama Makes Stuff
http://thismamamakesstuff.com

***Young Image* Magazine**
www.imagewearpatterns.com

And — of course! — the blogs and sites of our amazing contributors, listed on the next pages!

CONTRIBUTOR BIOS

Adrienne Lodico

* *Hexie Pouf, page 49*
* *Bunnies vs. Chicks Four-in-a-Row, page 266*

By day Adrienne is a mild-mannered elementary school teacher. By night she can be found stitching away in her sewing room, playing with her pets, or tooling about her urban farm. www.hermionejschwartz.blogspot.com

Andrea Jones

* *Bohemian's Daughter, page 84*

Andrea has been sewing since she was eight years old. She made her own prom dresses, worked her way through college as a tailor, and currently has an Etsy shop. She considers the best part of her sewing history is teaching her 10-year-old daughter how to sew (and she loves it — yeah!). www.etsy.com/shop/precocious

Angie Lusco

* *Easy Dolman Top or Tunic, page 69*

Angie is a Believer, Daughter, Wife, Mother, Sister, Aunt, Registered Nurse, Seamstress, Crafter, Housekeeper, Cook, Baker, Gardener, Reader, Keeper of the Chickens and usually sane Mom of 3. She is known online as Mama Lusco. www.mamalusco.blogspot.com

Bella van Doorn

* *Shirred Sunsuit, page 111*

Bella is the mum of three little cherubs. She has always sewn, but it has become more important since having someone other than herself to sew for. She loves that, on most days, at least one of her children is dressed in clothes that she has made. www.nisabell-necessary.blogspot.com.au

Beth Vermillion

* *Tie and Belt, page 154*

Beth has two adorable, crazy children (who are learning to sew!). She loves photography, reading in a hammock, family trips to Disneyland, and Target clearance. She and her family currently live in Houston, Texas. www.etsy.com/shop/loveseptember

Bethany Berndt Shackelford

* *Spoonflower Fabric Design Winner for the Riviera Tee, page 88*

Bethany doodled her way through grade school to ultimately enjoy a life of success through her artwork. She has won three Emmys for art direction for NBC News as well as for a Star Trek series. Her experience in computer compositing led to commercials and movies, and she was even on the Oscar-winning special-effects team for the film *Independence Day*. Still in search of a way to use her doodling, Bethany and her business partners started their own company called Pingorama and manufactured colorful kids clothes featuring Bethany's original fabric prints. Now she works from home as a surface designer under the name BZBdesigner, allowing her to spend time with her two kids, Tatum and Teaghan, which she says "is the best job yet." www.spoonflower.com/profiles/bzbdesigner

Brie Jensen

* *Doll Bed (with Storage!), page 199*

Brie is a wife and mother of two living in Hudson, Wisconsin. Growing up with very talented and artistic parents, Brie was surrounded by creativity from a very young age. Her hobbies include sewing, crafting, woodworking, home DIY projects, cooking, and baking. www.iammamab.blogspot.com

Calli Taylor

* *Night Owl Slumber Party Bag, page 270*

Calli keeps a popular blog called *Make It Do*, where she shares quilting and sewing patterns and projects, real-life cleaning advice, and delicious recipes. She writes about being resourceful and finding happiness in simple, everyday activities. www.make-it-do.com

Candace Davis

* *Wet Bag Set, page 311*

Candace taught herself to sew at the age of 12 when she became frustrated with everything in her closet. She still loves to sew her own clothing but spends much more time creating new bags for her business, Wonder Stitching. Candace also teaches sewing classes at her favorite local independent craft shop, Crafty Planet. She spends her spare time, on the rare occasion she finds it, knitting and embroidering.
www.etsy.com/shop/wonderstitching

Caroline Critchfield

* *Simple Pants, page 92*
* *Cargo Board Shorts, page 96*
* *Merry-Go-Round Dress, page 114*
* *Ruffled Romper, page 117*
* *Toddler Naptime Mat, page 272*

Caroline is an avid sewist and blogger. She started her blog to help connect people who sew with the people who write amazing tutorials. She loves making new sewing friends online and being able to feature awesome sewing tutorials that otherwise might go unnoticed. She lives in Florida with her husband and four darling children.
www.sewcanshe.com

Don Morin

* *Pocket Sled Kite, page 249*

Don is a clothing designer, patternmaker, and educator living and working in Toronto, Canada. He writes a design-it-yourself blog called *Bag'n-telle* for the would-be fashionista, demonstrating expert techniques in pattern drafting and handbag construction.
www.bagntell.wordpress.com

Emily Steffen

* *Philippe the Whale Pillow, page 202*

A wedding photographer by day and fabric artist by night, Emily tries to infuse joy in everything she does, complete with a smile on her face, because she is living her dream! She's a midwestern girl who loves people, her sewing machine, her two pugs, Edward and Gweneth, and every flavor of ice cream!
www.emilysteffen.com

Erin Currie

* *Toddler Activity Book, page 175*

Seamstress Erin is an (almost) PhD biochemist who would rather be sewing. By day, she's a mad scientist, finishing her doctorate at the University of California, San Francisco; by night, she's a seamstress. She writes a blog on DIY sewing, home decor, and fashion, and designs sewing and knitting patterns that can be found on her website, on Craftsy, or on Ravelry (as SeamstressErin). Her goal is to make people smile.
http://seamstresserin.com

Felicia Balezentes

* *Flutter-By, Butterfly Wings, page 229*

Felicia is a married mom who works full-time outside the home and sews as much as possible as therapy. Her mother dragged her kicking and screaming to sewing classes the summer after eighth grade, and while Felicia truly did not want to like it or enjoy herself, she finished up with a wraparound skirt and a new passion — and begged to sign up for more lessons. Sometimes Mom knows best.
www.therealeversewsweet.blogspot.com

Fiona Tully

* *Indoor Hopscotch, page 252*

For as long as Fiona can remember, she has been knitting, quilting, embroidering, making softies, or enjoying some other kind of craft. For her, crafting is a way of bringing the ideas that she dreams up to life. It is also a wonderful way for her to relax. Many of her designs have a childlike quality that comes from a combination of playing with her own little girls, memories from her childhood, and her experience as a kindergarten teacher; other times she's inspired by the beautiful forms and colors of flowers, which feature heavily in other projects. When she's not crafting, you'll find Fiona spending time with her awesome husband and beautiful daughters, or baking, gardening, or daydreaming.
www.twobrownbirds.typepad.com

Georgia Solorzano

* *Swing Dress, page 120*
* *Car Seat Hot/Cold Pack, page 274*

Georgia is an experienced pattern designer who has been sell-ing PDF sewing patterns on Etsy since 2011. She has six children under the age of 10, and she loves to sew for each and every one of them! Georgia's mother taught her to sew when she was just eight years old, and she hopes to continue the tradition with her kids. She is a board member at Sew, Mama, Sew! and has completed numerous projects for them. Other interests include geography and playing violin in the local symphony.
www.georgialeigh.com

Halee Schlangen

* *Simple Sunbonnet, page 141*

Halee has been sewing since she was a young child and now loves to sew for her two young children. She has drafted her own original sewing patterns for many years.
www.etsy.com/shop/270degrees

Jamie Halleckson and Carmen Marti (City Chic Country Mouse)

* *Safari Sleep Sack, page 18*
* *Diaper Stacker, page 20*

Jamie (City Chic) lives in Saint Paul, Minnesota, with her hus-band, two fur-babies, and new daughter, Lucy. She recently quit her day job to devote her time to creating new designs for City Chic Country Mouse and, of course, new things for Lucy! Proud new Grandma Carmen (Country Mouse) lives in Cloquet, Minnesota, with her husband and four fur-babies. She was taught to sew by her grandmother and mother at a very early age and can't wait to get started with Lucy!
www.etsy.com/shop/citychiccountrymouse

Jennifer Rodriguez

* *Pajama Monster & Little Stuffie, page 32*

Jennifer lives in Utah with her amazing husband and two ador-able daughters. In the wee hours of the night when her fam-ily is sleeping, she can be found in her studio creating. She designs quilt and crochet patterns for various companies. From art quilts to crocheted dolls, Jennifer will readily admit that a lot of her work is inspired by her children.
http://allthingsbelle.com
www.etsy.com/shop/allthingsbelle

Jessica Puckett Fishman

* *Heigh-Ho Horsey Marionette (with Trish Hoskins), page 204*

Jessica is the self-taught creature creator behind Stardust Stitches and Plushroom Soup. She loves fairy tales, mythology, nature, and the moon. She likes to twist fairy and folktales and infuse them with pop culture references and her own strange sense of humor. Jessica likes things that are just a little off-kilter and wants more people to embrace the quirky. When not sewing, knitting, needle-felting, spinning, or play-ing the fiddle, she enjoys spending time with her husband and their three dogs, and daydreaming about the fiber farm she will soon have.
www.plushroomsoup.com
www.etsy.com/shop/starduststitches

Jessica Roberts

* *Set-the-Table Placemat Set, page 52*

Jessica lives in Columbus, Ohio, where she sews, crochets, embroiders, gardens, and does whatever else occurs to her in addition to her "regular" job. Jessica's husband, dogs, parrot, and chickens tolerate the benign neglect this causes.
http://kusine.com/blog

Jo Ebisujima

* *Seat Cushion and Pocket, page 54*
* *Story Cushion, page 180*

Jo, who goes by the nickname Jojoebi, has an educational background in electronic imaging and media communications. After graduation she decided to travel the world and teach English to pay her way. After a two-year stint in the wilderness of northern Japan, a local boy stole her heart, so they decided to settle down just outside of Tokyo. After baby Ebi-kun was born, Jo gave up teaching and returned to her passion — design. Much of Jo's work is influenced by Montessori, her pas-sion for travel, and all things *kawaii* that make Japan such a wonderful place to live.
www.jojoebi-designs.com

June McCrary Jacobs

* *I-Spy Game Cards, page 254*
* *Snail Face Suitcase, page 276*

June considers herself fortunate to have had many of her original sewing, quilt, and stitchery designs and sewing-related articles published in nationwide magazines, including *Sew News* and *Crafts 'n things*. June openly admits that she enjoys hand-sewing and embroidery even more than she enjoys sewing on her sewing machines! When she's not sewing, June enjoys spending time with her family, reading, and visiting museums and historic homes.
www.junemccraryjacobs.com

Katherine Donaldson

* *Secret Pockets Pillow, page 183*
* *Oct-toy-pus Animal Organizer, page 209*

Katherine loves to make things — anythings! Robots, princess hats, quilts, felt barrettes, an articulated metal hand, her wedding dress, chain mail, dinner, a Lego-powered animatronic birthday cake . . . These days it's mostly toys and clothes (and meal after meal) for her young daughters, but she's really looking forward to the day when her girls are old enough to join her in wild robotic-textile mashups, and is dreaming of getting a family booth at Maker Faire with her awesome "maker" husband.
www.oneinchworld.com

Kathy Beymer

* *Secret Pocket Pillowcase, page 35*
* *Nonslip Messy Mat, page 58*
* *No-Toy-Left-Behind Travel Blanket, page 186*

Kathy loves all things useful and clever, playful and special. She shares her simple and ingenious crafts on her website (see below), named #8 Best Overall of the 2012 Babble Top 50 Mom Craft Blogs. Kathy's designs have been featured on websites such as Daily Candy Kids, Huffington Post Stylelist Home, The Knot, ApartmentTherapy.com, Design*Sponge.com, and Lifehacker, as well as in *Parents, Time Out,* and other magazines. She also dreams up original how-tos for Velcro Corporation (and their national partnership with Jo-Ann retail stores). Kathy has a weakness for sweets, the Chicago skyline, vintage linen calendars, and her two munchkins.
www.merrimentdesign.com

Katy Dill

* *Fun in the Sun(dress), page 134*

Katy loves to sew and sew and sew some more! She has five daughters whom she's had so much fun creating for, and at last a little boy, who has opened up a whole new world of sewing.
www.nobigdill.com

Kristie Thompson

* *Doll Carrier, page 212*

Kristie is a self-taught sewist with an appreciation for all things handmade. She got her first sewing machine a few years ago and quickly became obsessed. She loves making clothing and accessories from upcycled materials and thrifted fabrics. Her two young children are the primary recipients of her creations, and she hopes that they continue to wear what she makes as they get older. Kristie is teaching them both to sew, and her daughter even received a grown-up sewing machine for her fourth birthday and completed several projects independently. In her free time, Kristie also enjoys running, biking, and spending quality time with her husband and children. They live in Seattle, Washington.
www.etsy.com/shop/nixohandmade

Kymy Johnson

* *Playard Sheet, page 22*

Kymy is a wife and stay-at-home mom to five children ages newborn to seven. Growing up, she was inspired by her late grandmother Irene to try anything and everything crafting- and cooking-related. In what free time she has, she enjoys sewing and cooking, and sharing both with the world, and helping others do the same on her blog!
www.everythingyourmamamade.com

Laura Bednash

* *Ruthie Border Print Dress & Tote, page 129*

A simple jacket pattern and broken sewing machine turned a bit of dabbling into an outright obsession. She has two young daughters, and their constantly evolving styles inspire her to keep creating. Laura has found that sewing as a thirty-something, she has more patience to focus on the details of a project. Indeed, practice does make perfect. She's a big believer that sewing from your stash is overrated. Learn more about Laura on her website, where she posts tutorials, pattern reviews, and other sewing mishaps.
www.charmstitch.com

Lindsay Conner

* *Fabric Photo Blocks, page 189*

Lindsay is a writer, editor, and crafter who lives in Nashville, Tennessee. She is the author of the book *Modern Bee: 13 Quilts to Make with Friends* (Stash Books). Her work has also been published in *Fabric-by-Fabric One-Yard Wonders* (Storey), plus *Stitch* and *Stitch Craft Create* magazines.
www.craftbuds.com
www.lindsaysews.com

Lindsey Cooke

* *Frannie Fox Hot & Cold Pack, page 38*

Lindsey is a mom of two living in Winnipeg, Manitoba, who enjoys any and all kinds of crafts and creativity. She makes up one part of *The Bolt and Bobbin*, a family adventure into blogland with a wealth of sewing and crafting tips and tutorials.
www.theboltandbobbin.com

Lisa Powers

* *Prince(ss) Charming Changing Station Cover, page 26*

Lisa is a fiber artist and designer with 30 years of sewing and knitting experience. Sewing and teaching are two of the things that make her happy, in addition to her husband and two awesome little girls. The staff at Crafty Planet sweetly allow her to teach and hang out at their store in Minneapolis, Minnesota.

Lorraine Teigland

* *Racerback Sundress, page 137*
* *House in a Hallway, page 232*

Lorraine is a retired high school physics teacher and stay-at-home mother. She enjoys making things out of cardboard and sewing clothes, toys, and other random items. Many of the things she creates are inspired by watching her girls at play.
www.ikatbag.com

Maggie Bunch

* *Lucy-Cate Smocked Bishop Dress, page 123*

Maggie hails from the smocking and heirloom world. Her designs have been published in *Sew Beautiful* and *Creative Needle* magazines. Teaching smocking through the Smocking Arts Guild of America, Maggie keeps the art of smocking in practice. Mom to two young adults and wife to Lew, a retired USAF pilot, she has used smocking as a means to meet new friends.
www.maggiebsmocks.typepad.com

Marlene Gaige

* *Alberto the Woolie Bear, page 216*

Marlene learned to sew as a small child at her grandmother's feet, and she has sewn, crafted, taught, and sold things within the sewing/crafting community since she was 10. Marlene's passion for all things textile has taken her around the world both for business and pleasure. She finds her sewing life to be in constant flux, and the changes over the years have suited the different aspects of her life and personality. She lives in Maple Grove, Minnesota, with her husband, a college-bound son, and a noisy sheltie.
www.allmyown.etsy.com

Michelle Fante

* *Make Any Bag a Diaper Bag, page 314*

Michelle, born and raised in Michigan, attended the Center for Creative Studies College of Art and Design in Detroit. With a degree in fiber design and seven years of corporate life in her back pocket, she decided that it was time to begin working for herself. Guided by her passion for fashion, Michelle is now an independent consultant and freelancer for the apparel industry. Michelle lives with her husband in Royal Oak and is always working on a new project whenever she gets a chance.

Misty Somers

✳ *Girlie Undies, page 145*

Misty is a part-time waitress and full-time mom. She has been sewing and designing as a hobby since her daughter was born.

Molly Deschenes

✳ *Small and Secret Diaper Bag & Changing Pad, page 317*

After living abroad in places like Budapest and Berlin, Molly settled down in small-town New England with the love of her life and her sewing machine. At her blog, she chronicles her sewing adventures and provides a window into the handmade life she shares with her husband and two young children. www.applecyder.com

Natalie Stone and Naomi Regan

✳ *Long Beach Tee, page 71*

Naomi and Natalie both live in Devon in England, Naomi by the seaside and Natalie in a leafy little suburb. They have been good friends ever since their children were born, little Vince to Naomi and Olive to Natalie. Shortly after meeting, Naomi and Natalie started Olive and Vince, making and selling practical, comfortable, and "fuss-free" clothing for toddlers. They strongly believe that beauty should never compromise comfort, nor overlook practical issues such as how to quickly dress and undress a toddler. In their designs, you'll see hints of retro styles, symmetry, and simplicity, but most of all fun. www.etsy.com/shop/oliveandvince

Pam McFerrin

✳ *Secret Monster Overalls, page 100*

Pam was embroidering pillowcases and sewing on her mom's sea-foam green Sears Kenmore by the age of nine. A graphic designer by trade, with a love of color, patterns, textiles, and fashion, Pam has an overwhelming need to create, and sewing has provided the solution. Pam resides in Southwest Minneapolis with her husband and two funny-looking bulldogs. www.pammcferrin.com

Paula Storm

✳ *Pregnancy Survival Kit, page 320*

Mother of four, Paula is a designer of patchwork and quilting patterns. When she was bored silly after a fall that kept her in a wheelchair for nearly four years, her mum taught her to sew. Paula always had been crafty and had tried almost everything, but sewing has since become her obsession. While she's finally out of the chair, the sewing obsession isn't going anywhere. Her Sit Me Up Donut has been hugely successful in Australia and is starting to trickle into other countries.

Rachael Theis

✳ *Go Away Big Monster Towel, page 41*

✳ *Beach Tent, page 307*

Rachael's grandmother gave her a bag of fabric scraps when she was five years old, and she has been a fabric junkie ever since. In addition to sewing, Rachael likes to crochet, work in her garden, embroider, paint, and spin her own yarn. She is also a junk enthusiast and loves to reuse and recycle neat objects. http://rachaelmade.blogspot.com

Rachel Le Grand

✳ *Mushroom Tea Party, page 239*

Rachel is a married, stay-at-home mother of three living in Minnesota. She enjoys sewing, knitting, paper crafting, photography, and gluten-free baking. She is a project designer in *Craft Challenge: Dozens of Ways to Repurpose Scarves* (Lark Crafts, 2011). She has also contributed a few sewing projects to *Altered Couture* magazine. http://nestfullofeggs.blogspot.com

Rachel M. Knoblich

✳ *Silly Circles Tummy Time Playmat, page 192*

✳ *Mac the Magnificent Monster, page 219*

Rachel loves sewing, creating, and designing. She's a mother of four and grandmother of seven. Whenever she's not sewing or crafting, Rachel is gardening. She's been selling her creations online for over 10 years, first under the name of Googoo a Gogo and more recently, Little Bird Lane. She's very excited about this new beginning. www.etsy.com/shop/littlebirdlanellc

Rebecca Yaker

* *Poufy Ball Mobile, page 24*
* *Storage Bin Redux, page 61*
* *Western Shirt, page 73*
* *Riviera Tee, page 88*
* *Tank Top, page 145 and 148*
* *Mister Briefs, page 148*
* *Baby Photo Album, page 194*
* *I-Spy Game Bag, page 254*
* *Artist Portfolio, page 257*
* *Insulated Lunch Box, page 280*

Rebecca began sewing at the tender age of five. She is known for creating unexpected luxuries using all-American elements and icons in unpredictable ways. Until the birth of her son, Rebecca operated Hazel and Melvin's Room, an online boutique through which she hand-made and sold custom baby bedding and apparel for clients worldwide. Today Rebecca is exploring new, creative opportunities to incorporate many of her honed craft skills. She is a seamstress, hand- and machine-knitter, crocheter, weaver, fabric printer, cordwainer, and design consultant. More than all those crafts combined, she enjoys spending time with her husband and cute-as-a-barrel-full-of-kittens son.
www.rebeccayaker.com

Sarah Faix

* *JuJu Giraffe, page 222*

Sarah is a stay-at-home mom who loves sewing and dolls. She started making cloth dolls originally because of the frustration she experienced while looking for her daughter's first doll. Disappointed when she could not find the "right" doll, Sarah finally designed her own pattern in 2007. Five years later, her kitchen-table idea has moved into a real studio, and she has almost 90 original pattern designs. She is still inspired by her daughter and loves to share her passion with her!
www.bitofwhimsydolls.com.

Sarah Pilling

* *Stroller Liner, page 284*
* *Nursing Cover, page 324*

Sarah is a slightly obsessed seamstress, with a reputation as an "enabler" for fellow addicts at her blog and online store. Selling independent sewing patterns in Australia gives Sarah an excuse to be sewing constantly and stay involved in both the online and Melbourne crafting communities. Her family members patiently model clothes, photograph things, and, most importantly, pretend they don't see the ever-growing fabric stash. Sarah one day hopes to have her own sewing studio, which, if she ever wins millions, will be located in a converted pool house.
www.sewsquirrel.com.au
http://sewsquirrel.wordpress.com

Sharon Madsen

* *Retro-Inspired Bathing Cover-Up, page 45*

Sharon taught herself to sew at a young age. By her teen years she was running a successful small business selling doll clothing. She also began creating original designs for herself using techniques that were more "by the seat of her pants" than by the book, resulting in some hysterical fashion moments. Her designs have been published in multiple sewing magazines. She's as passionate about fitness as she is about sewing and teaches Zumba fitness classes in her spare time. She loves dogs, shoes, and a luscious dark chocolate treat — but not as much as sewing. She lives in Minnesota with her husband and their two dogs.
www.etsy.com/shop/abbyandsophia
http://sharonsews.blogspot.com

Stacey Whittington

* *Pouch Bib, page 58*
* *Kid Car Set, page 286*

Stacey is a business analyst by day and blogger/seamster/crafter/party planner/aspiring Super Mom by night and on weekends. When she's not solving Fortune 500 companies' system and process problems, she's making whatever inspires her at the moment. Her uber-supportive husband, Doug, and adorable daughters, Elle and Liv, are her motivation, inspiration, and sense of accomplishment.
www.ellebellecreative.com

Stacy Schlyer

✳ *Ultimate Gamer's Tote, page 262*

Stacy is a Kansas-based sewing/craft blogger and self-pro-claimed fabric junkie. She taught herself to sew shortly after her oldest child was born and hasn't stopped since. When Stacy isn't attending to her stay-at-home-mom "duties," you can find her in her sewing room, whipping up a tutorial, writing an article, embroidering a design, or testing out a new technique. You can follow Stacy's adventures in crafting on her daily blog. http://stacysewsblog.wordpress.com

Stephanie Sterling

✳ *Baby Doll Layette, page 225*

Stephanie is mom to three terrific little girls in Baltimore. She's a teacher and a lawyer by trade, and now that she's grown up, she's trying to figure out ways to merge what she loves about those two professions. Stephanie likes making stuff, too. You can see some of her work in the two previous iterations of the One-Yard Wonders series and, of course, on her blog. Most of all, she likes having fun. http://neurosesgalore.com

Sue Kim

✳ *Sierra Tiered Skirt, page 105*
✳ *Anabelle Baby Sandals, page 141*
✳ *Mary Jane Set, page 151*
✳ *Visor and Moccasins, page 154*
✳ *Itty-Bitty Toddler Backpack, page 162*
✳ *Casey Apron, page 242*
✳ *Boston Diaper Bag, page 327*

Sue lives in Toronto, Canada, with her three lovely children and husband. Sue has always had a passion for crafts and started sewing when she was 10 years old. She is the author of *Bags: The Modern Classics* (C & T Publishing), a book that includes over 20 of her bags and clutch patterns. Sue has also created patterns for Simplicity and sells her own patterns through her website. www.ithinksew.com

Susan Lirakis and Megan Nicolay

✳ *Yia-Yia's Snuggle Hoodie, page 78*

Susan is a professional photographer and fleece-wear designer living in northern New Hampshire. She exhibits her photographic work nationally, and it has also been included in *The Elements of Photography* and *Photo 1: An Introduction to the Art of Photography*. Susan's sewing work is represented in the League of NH Craftsmen shop in Sandwich, New Hampshire. She's thankful to have a new person to sew for — her first grandchild.

Megan is a book editor by day and author of the bestselling T-shirt refashioning books *Generation T* and *Generation T: Beyond Fashion*. She has developed crafting tools and embellishments with Prym-Dritz, designed patterns for the McCall Pattern Company, and blogs regularly at Generation-T.com. She recently welcomed her first child and is looking forward to continuing to design for her new muse. She lives with her family in Brooklyn, New York. www.generation-t.com www.susanlirakis.com

Tamera Gagne

✳ *Woodland Fun Crib Rail Guard, page 28*

Tamera is a Chicago-based crafter, teacher, and mother of three. She is a self-taught seamstress who creates plush dolls, bags, and more as PeanutEnvy on Etsy. She also sells vintage items, fabrics, and other pretty things as CrankHeartPony on Etsy. She teaches sewing, ceramics, screen printing, and more in the Chicago area. When she's not sewing, crafting, or caring tirelessly for her children, she is helping her husband with their vintage/antique furniture business, ManlyVintage.com. www.crankheartpony1.blogspot.com www.etsy.com/shop/peanutenvy

Tammie Schaffer

✳ *Boo-Boo Buddy, page 289*

Tammie tries to make something every day. She spends time sewing in between ball games and bedtimes. Visit her blog and see what she's making today! www.craftytammie.com

Tanja Ivacic-Ramljak and Suada Ivacic

* *Springtime Top, page 81*
* *Summer Days Hat, page 159*

Tanja and Suada are a mum-and-daughter team from Melbourne, Australia, who together form the Poppy and Lola design team. They design patterns for little ones that are feminine, funky, and, most importantly, comfortable. Daughter Tanja is a passionate designer and crafter with experience in the graphic design industry. Mum Suada is an expert in apparel construction. They are very passionate about creating beautiful things for little ones, and the process of making nice clothing brings them great joy!
www.etsy.com/shop/poppylola

Tara Kolesnikowicz

* *Car Cozy Playmat, page 245*

Tara is a mom, teacher, crafter, and blogger. After the birth of her second son she realized she needed to be something other than a diaper-changing machine and yearned for all those creative things she used to do. Tara's blog started as her personal online journal to document the things she was creating. Her crafting adventures have continued to grow from there.
www.sewtara.com

Trish Hoskins

* *Booster Chair, page 64*
* *Tot Tote & Wallet, page 166*
* *Poor Boy (and Dad) Cap, page 171*
* *Heigh-Ho Horsey Marionette (with Jessica Puckett Fishman), page 204*
* *Road Trip Wrangler, page 294*
* *Self-Storing Playmat, page 297*
* *Library Portfolio, page 300*
* *Winter Warmer Infant Bucket-Seat Cover, page 304*
* *Argyle Memory Board & Photo Collage, page 332*

Patricia (Trish) and her husband, Matt, are co-owners of Crafty Planet, a retail fabric and needlework store, plus craft workshop, located in Minneapolis, Minnesota. Trish dabbles in all manner of things crafty, including knitting, crocheting, spinning, sewing, quilting, embroidery, and cross-stitching. Unsurprisingly, her wildly inventive and enthusiastic son has proven to be a great design inspiration, and has provided wonderful motivation to use up her precious stash!
www.craftyplanet.com

Yasuko Solbes

* *Balloon Skirt, page 107*

Yasuko has designed sewing patterns and made clothes since 2008. Passionate for drawing, making, and wearing clothes, she likes to mix Japanese and Western themes. Her concept is simple and cute. As a mother of three boys, she also came to realize how hard it is to find great designs for them, and she now strives to answer this challenge. Yasuko's atelier moves at the pace of her family's relocations; she started from a flat in Central London and is now based in Hong Kong.
www.lavie-danslalune.blogspot.com

index

Page numbers in **bold** indicate charts, page numbers in *italic* indicate illustrations.

Delight in the Possibilities!

Have you been wondering what to do with that stash of fabric? With the 202 projects in the first two One-Yard Wonders books, you'll have lots of playful, simple, and stylish choices!

304 pages. Hardcover with concealed wire-o and patterns.
ISBN 978-1-60342-449-3.

416 pages. Hardcover with concealed wire-o and patterns.
ISBN 978-1-60342-586-5.

*"**Talk about quality and quantity.** One-Yard Wonders is an impressive volume of super-creative projects all utilizing our favorite scraps and a simple yard of fabric. This book is a keeper!"*

— Amy Butler, AMY BUTLER DESIGN